A Probable State

A PROBABLE STATE

The Novel, the Contract, and the Jews

Irene Tucker

The University of Chicago Press
Chicago and London

IRENE TUCKER is assistant professor of English at Johns Hopkins University.

The University of Chicago Press, Chicago 60637
The University of Chicago Press, Ltd., London
© 2000 by The University of Chicago
All rights reserved. Published 2000
Printed in the United States of America

09 08 07 06 05 04 03 02 01 00   1 2 3 4 5

ISBN: 0-226-81533-1 (cloth)
ISBN: 0-226-81535-8 (paper)

Library of Congress Cataloging-in-Publication Data

Tucker, Irene.
    A probable state : the novel, the contract, and the Jews / Irene Tucker.
        p. cm.
    Includes bibliographical references and index.
        ISBN 0-226-81533-1 (alk. paper)—ISBN 0-226-81535-8 (pbk. : alk. paper)
        1. Eliot, George, 1819–1880. Daniel Deronda. 2. James, Henry, 1843–1916. What Maisie
knew. 3. Mendele Mokher Sefarim, 1835–1917. kitsur mas'ot Binyamin ha-Shelishi. 4. Liberalism in literature. 5. Realism in literature. 6. Jews in literature. 7. Social contract in literature.
I. Title.

PR4658.A7 T83 2000
823'.80911—dc21

                                                                                00-024251

In honor of my mother
Marcia Rabinowitz Tucker
and my sisters
Diane Tucker and Meredith Tucker

and in memory of my father
Leonard Tucker

The great danger arising from the existence of people forced to live outside the common world is that they are thrown back, in the midst of civilization, on their natural givenness, on their mere differentiation. They lack that tremendous equalizing of differences which comes from being citizens of some commonwealth and yet, since they are no longer allowed to partake in the human artifice, they begin to belong to the human race in much the same way as animals belong to a specific animal species. The paradox involved in the loss of human rights is that such loss coincides with the instant when a person becomes a human being in general—without a profession, without a citizenship, without an opinion, without a deed by which to identify and specify himself—*and* different in general, representing nothing but his own absolutely unique individuality which, deprived of expression within and action upon a common world, loses all significance.

HANNAH ARENDT, *The Origins of Totalitarianism* (1950)

Contents

Acknowledgments

A Probable State, which concerns itself in part with the ways texts ranging from the Talmud to the Victorian novel came at the end of the nineteenth century to function as alternatives to territory in organizing communal identity, has gained an oddly grounding solidity as I have moved from city to city in pursuit of the institutional and intellectual resources to bring it to completion. If I were to allow myself the indulgence of a fantasy of self-determination, I would suggest that it was the desire to be right no matter what that fueled the transmutation of my thesis from description to performance; less indulgently, that my sojourn from Berkeley to Tel Aviv to Ithaca to Durham to Baltimore took place in the company, if not as a consequence, of this book, has offered abundant compensation for the strains of displacement in the communities of friends and readers it has enabled.

This project began as a dissertation at the University of California at Berkeley and still bears manifold marks of this origin. The longer my time away, the more I have come to appreciate the ways Berkeley's pervasive spirit of intellectual freedom and free-wheelingness, as well as the sheer brilliance and variety of its thinkers, helped make this book, especially in its less conventional juxtapositions, seem both possible and important. Catherine Gallagher taught me in many significant ways how to read novels, and her unmatched intellectual flexibility and generosity enabled her to figure out what I meant and to convince me it was worth saying while at the same time insisting that I say it ever more clearly and responsibly. Elizabeth Abel's contributions to my development as a thinker began with my earliest days at Berkeley and continued throughout; I benefited from her belief in this project and from her skepticism. Michael Rogin read these chapters promptly and with interest and insight and offered valuable bibliographical suggestions. Frances Ferguson and Jonathan Freedman read the manuscript for the Press and, in their generous and nuanced apprehendings of my project, helped me better to understand it and, I hope, to make it more understandable and persuasive.

Friends in a variety of combinations served as colleagues in the best sense of the term and helped make graduate school a place where the sense of community and mutual support was inextricable from the experience of learning. It is impossible for me to imagine this book in its current form without the members of my nationalism reading group—Kate Brown, Alyson Bardsley, and Curtis Marez—since it was over the course of our many conversations that I developed my fundamental intellectual passions and investments and the project acquired its shape. My Victorian dissertation group—Alyson Bardsley, Danny Hack, Cheri Larsen-Hoeckley, Catherine Robson, and Rebecca Steinitz—helped in many important ways to turn me into a Victorianist and bore with me in the ways I was not. My modernism dissertation group—Kate Brown, Cynthia Franklin, Teresa Fulker, Jane Garrity, Christina Hauck, and Leila May—welcomed me with friendship and insightful criticism. Cindy has been an unflinchingly steadfast friend, even at the moments when I made that a challenge and the geographical distance between us stretched to an ocean and a continent; her ability to offer so many different kinds of support made me understand the relationship between scholarship and ethics in new ways. With her timely phone calls, tasty snacks, and long-distance emollients, both physical and spiritual, Jane helped me believe there would be a place for me in this profession even when the profession seemed to be saying otherwise. Francesca Pish Royster has been a stalwart inhabitant of our joint landscape of jokes, nicknames, and allusions that make friendship its own sort of topography, while Jacqueline Shea Murphy has been there across nearly all the real landscapes of my adulthood, offering a friendship that has now lasted half a lifetime. Simon Stern's intellectual voraciousness and catholicity continue to be a source of inspiration to me, and Kim Drake was a delightful cotraveler on our southern odyssey. Finally, I want to thank Celeste Langan, who has been this project's most intimate and probing interlocutor for the length of its existence. If it was the joyful play of her astonishing intellect that first moved me to read in ways I had not previously thought possible, I have since come equally to learn, take inspiration, and benefit from her generosity of spirit, complexity of emotion, and professional integrity.

Many thanks are also due to those friends who have read selected chapters of the book, or whose support in its production has been less tangible but nonetheless crucial: Tina Brooks, John Fox, Sharon Friedman, Howard Horwitz Meredith Miller, Michael Ragussis, Dan Rosenberg, Ken Saragosa, Tobin Siebers, Elisabeth Sperling, and Denise Wolf.

The difficulties of writing about literature in a foreign language were more than counterbalanced by the new community and intellectual context such research offered. I am especially grateful to Hannan Hever for sharing with me his extensive knowledge of the early Hebrew novel and for his illuminating readings of my work, as well as for his professional support. Various other Tel Aviv friends offered intellectual and emotional succor and lots of practical help: Sinai Alexandrevich, Ziva Ben-Porat, Reut Gruber, Erga Heller, Sharon Himmelfarb, Efrat Levi and Joyce Robbins. Thanks also to Israel Bartal of the Department of Jewish History at Hebrew University and Iris Porush of Ben-Gurion University. Finally, I want to thank the members of my first home in Israel, Kibbutz Mishmar Hasharon, especially Leah Berg, who made it a home to which I could return, and Ronit Sinder, who wielded her magical alchemy to bring a community of Hebrew speakers into being and inspired me to parse the magic.

Timely Mellon postdocs in 1995 and 1996 in Cornell's Near Eastern Studies and English Departments allowed me to stay in the profession, and Cornell remains for me a model of matter-of-fact and sensible humanity. Many people welcomed me in large ways and small: Laura Brown, Walter Cohen, Jonathan Culler, Molly Hite, Dominick LaCapra, Barry Maxwell, Dorothy Mermin, Tim Murray, Reeve Parker, David Powers, Edgar Rosenberg, Steve Rubenstein, Neil Saccamano, Shirley Samuels, Dan Schwarz, Harry Shaw, Sandra Siegel, Sara Wolper, and Shelley Wong. Cynthia Chase and Mary Jacobus were unstintingly generous, interested, and loyal; they made their institution an instrument of, rather than an alternative to, their sense of personal integrity and responsibility. Tamar Katz and Ed Hardy provided—and continue to provide—stimulating conversation on all sorts of subjects and the easy comfort of good friendship. John, Charlotte, Sophie, and Elizabeth Maddock Dillon shared the Ithaca adventure from start to finish, welcoming me into their family and joining me in praying for the sun.

A tenure-track job in the English Department at Duke University gave me the time and resources to complete this book's most extensive round of revisions, plus the eventfulness of ten jobs. Friends and colleagues helped make Duke and Durham an exciting, enriching experience: Wendy Baucom, Ron Butters, Cathy Davidson, Stanley Fish, Karla Holloway, Lisa Laverty, Jan Radway, Eve and Scott Schulman, Eve Kosofsky Sedgwick, Jim Siedow, Barbara Herrnstein Smith, Julie Tetel, Jennifer Thorne, Marianna Torgovnick, Maurice Wallace, Eric Zakim, and Yael Meroz. Laurie Shannon shared Indian food and lots of jokes, while Tyler Curtain's discernment, loyalty, and sympathy mattered to an incalculable degree. Ian Baucom, conavigator of shared shoals, helped me think better and with more integrity about all manner of issues. I value his brilliance and his solidity as well as his capacity to possess both at once.

Although most of the work on this book was finished before I arrived, my new colleagues at Johns Hopkins have made me eager to get on with the next project by making a place for me in their intensely stimulating intellectual environment and for making that intensity a lot of fun: Amanda Anderson, Sharon Cameron, Frances Ferguson, Allen Grossman, Neil Hertz, Walter Benn Michaels, John Plotz, and Sasha Torres. I am grateful to Susie Herrmann and Peggy MacKenzie for their hard work at making my settling in not the least bit hard. In both Durham and Baltimore, Michael Moon and Jonathan Goldberg have been kind and good friends and have made me laugh and think a lot.

Many people helped in the process of giving this book material form. My editors at University of Chicago Press—Alan Thomas, Randy Petilos, and Alice Bennett—provided expert shepherding, and a terrific cohort of proofreaders—Arthur Evenchik, Dana Hollander, and Theo Davis—continued to care about perfecting the details long after my eyes had glazed over. Amit Yahav-Brown has been nothing short of ideal as a research assistant, gamely setting about the necessary mundanities of bibliographical checking and indexing while offering invaluable help and advice in sorting through the more compelling intricacies of Hebrew translation.

Finally, my deepest and most long-standing gratitude is to my family. I am sad that my father, Leonard Tucker, did not live to see the completion of this book, which would have made him proud; he schooled me early in the love of learning. I am grateful to my aunt, Corinne Stone, whose enthusiasm and support have been unwavering; to my sisters, Diane and Meredith, to whose magical necklaces and brainwaves I no doubt owe my career and who have become, more and more in our adulthood, the kind of friends I would have chosen yet am lucky enough not to need to; and last to my mother, Marcia Tucker, without whose strength and unconditional love neither this project nor so much else would have even been imaginable.

Introduction

On 15 April 1881, in a small Russian town north of Odessa called Elisavet-grad, a group of Russian peasants attacked the town's Jewish residents after a quarrel at a Jewish tavern. The three days of rioting—aided and abetted, in the view of most historians, by the studied indifference of the Russian po-lice—set off a series of similar attacks throughout the countryside that con-tinued sporadically over the next four decades.[1] From the point of view of the Russians, the pogroms,[2] which began just six weeks after the assassination of Czar Alexander II had thrown the government into tumult, marked the abandonment of a century-long government effort to solve the country's "Jewish problem" through social engineering, by the use of a patchwork and often incoherent web of laws regulating residency, employment, and army conscription.[3] From the perspective of the Russian Jewish populace at large, the persistent attacks launched a wave of migration to western Europe and the United States and, to a lesser extent, to Palestine. For Jewish intellectuals and political and religious reformers the 1881 pogroms marked finally and unambiguously the untenability of the Haskalah, or Jewish Enlightenment, the movement begun exactly one hundred years earlier in pursuit of the dual goals of political integration and Jewish cultural regeneration.[4] Responding

1. John D. Klier and Shlomo Lambroza, eds., *Pogroms: Anti-Jewish Violence in Modern Russian History* (Cambridge: Cambridge University Press, 1992).

2. Literally "to break or smash." According to Klier, "The events in Odessa during Holy Week in 1871 were the first to be widely called a 'pogrom,' and the events of 1881–2 introduced it into common usage throughout the world." See Klier, "The Pogrom Paradigm in Russian History," in Klier and Lam-broza, *Pogroms,* 34–35.

3. See I. Michael Aronson, "The Anti-Jewish Pogroms in Russia in 1881," in Klier and Lambroza, *Pogroms,* 44–61, and Michael Stanislawski, *Tsar Nicholas I and the Jews: The Transformation of Jewish Society in Russia, 1825–1855* (Philadelphia: Jewish Publication Society of America, 1983).

4. See David Sorkin, *The Transformation of German Jewry, 1780–1840* (New York: Oxford Univer-sity Press, 1987), and Eli Lederhendler, *The Road to Modern Jewish Politics: Political Tradition and Political Reconstruction in the Jewish Community of Tsarist Russia* (New York: Oxford University Press, 1989).

to this new violence, one writer after another announced his abandonment of the Haskalah's moderation for the more revolutionary platforms of Zionism and socialist Bundism, the Enlightenment promise of political emancipation seeming less a viable philosophy of politics and culture than the assimilationist pipe dreams of a people made modest by powerlessness.

❧

In that same year of 1881, halfway across the globe in Boston, a young and relatively obscure Harvard law professor named Oliver Wendell Holmes Jr. published, under the title *The Common Law,* a series of lectures he had delivered several months earlier. Wandering, repetitive, self-contradictory, and occasionally even inaccurate, *The Common Law* nevertheless marked the most ambitious attempt to date to develop a theory of American law. Drawing together precedents from English and American legal history, Holmes concurred, dissented, and reinterpreted at will in an effort to transform the catch-as-catch-can empiricism of a mass of Anglo-American case law barely a century old into a coherent system of thought. Central to Holmes's systemization was the notion that legal authority ought not to be understood as a secular descendant of an originally religious moral authority but should be seen as the institutionalization of a culture's norms. Consequently, externally perceptible behaviors, as opposed to internal intentions or states of mind, should stand as evidence of an individual's adherence to the law. The kinds of behavior the law enjoined were authoritative not because they were transcendently good behaviors, but merely because they were enjoined by the law, a law derived from current and local conventions of behavior. With Holmes's formulation, the rule of law became indistinguishable from the behavior of citizens and their representatives, the realm of politics dispersed within the everyday category of the social.

❧

The year is 1896. Fifteen years after the pogroms dashed the hopes of the Haskalah intellectuals for the ascendancy of a political order whose commitment to the Enlightenment category of humanity would bring about Jewish political emancipation, fifteen years after Oliver Wendell Holmes Jr. fashioned his antifoundationalist theory of juridical authority, Hebrew novelist and former *maskil* Shalom Yaakov Abramovitch publishes his מסעות בנימין השלישי (*The Travels of Benjamin the Third*). That same year, Holmes's friend Henry James began writing *What Maisie Knew,* a novel that, in its synthesis of English and American social and hermeneutical discourses, can be seen to take up the logic of Holmes's own *Common Law*. Moreover, both texts can be seen not only as attempts to represent and respond to the juridical crises posed by the most immediate circumstances of their writing, but as alternative efforts to solve a crisis of generic authority evoked by a third, slightly earlier text: George Eliot's 1876 novel *Daniel Deronda*. As I will argue in the chapters that follow, the nineteenth-century history of Russian-Jewish relations that culminated in the pogroms of 1881 and the often manifestly paradoxical project of institutionalizing norms that characterizes Holmes's legal redactions—particularly his writing on contracts—provide historical contexts within which the two literary texts might productively be read. But I also hope to show that to read these particular works "in context" is to engage in a practice not wholly familiar, since each of these intersections of "text" and "context" can be seen, at least in part, as engaging the question of what it means to read a literary text in historical context in the late nineteenth century, at the moment of the decline of the realist novel. Moreover, in reexamining not just the relation between a particular text and a particular context but the normally tacit presumptions underlying historical reading, literariness, and fictionality more generally, these knots of text and context at once register and bring about fundamental transformations in the form of historical and literary narratives and the nature of historical authority.

What has yet gone unsaid—what remains the tacit, though not quite comfortably so, presumption of my argument—is that my description of these literary-historical moments as meditations on the ways late nineteenth-century novels and their historical settings can be seen to produce one another depends on wrenching both the literary texts and the historical "space" picked out by those texts from their familiar contexts. My argument, in other words, turns on the possibility of seeing as something other than a turning away from history the juxtaposition of Russian pogroms and Anglo-American contract reform, the comparison of a novel about a pair of hapless Russian Jewish pilgrims making their way toward the Holy Land (patched together from the remote written Hebrew of religious texts) and the novel written by an American living in England about a child with too many parents. In part I mean to contend that we can discern common discursive residues—primarily those of late eighteenth-century German idealism—beneath these apparently far-flung clusters of ideas and representational modes. But to summarily write away the unconventionality of such a juxtaposition simply by replacing a discursive or materialist historiography with an equally familiar intellectual historiography is to risk overlooking precisely those unarticulated aspects of the discursive-materialist historiographical practices that would render the juxtaposition startling in the first place.

I want to begin negatively, then, by considering just what it is about the juxtapositions I am proposing that makes them appear to violate conventional historiographical and literary historical categories of analysis. Then I will go on to examine how these analytical terms might be altered if we continue to insist on the *historical* illumination offered by these connections. In my thumbnail accounts of the two sets of "event" and text, I stressed the coincidence: both the pogroms and the publication of *The Common Law* occurred in 1881, and the two literary texts that I am arguing can be understood as readings of these events took place in 1896. So in the most neutral sense, we can say that the two sets of event and text are connected by the fact of their historical simultaneity. But what exactly is the analytical force of this notion of historical simultaneity? What makes it, in other words, not quite so self-evident as it might initially appear? And what might we learn from our impulse—in the "instance" of *The Common Law* and the pogroms, of James and Abramovitch—to qualify this description by appending to it the condition of being "mere," as though scaling back simultaneity to its essence means giving up any interest we might have in it, as though "mere simultaneity" implies acknowledging that, within the frame of historical causality, we can learn nothing from the unadorned fact that two events occur at the same time?

In his 1983 *Imagined Communities*, Benedict Anderson identifies the emergence of secular simultaneity, a "temporal coincidence . . . measured by clock and calendar,"[5] as opposed to the premodern religious temporality of prophecy and fulfillment, as the fundamental shift "in modes of apprehending the world" that "more than anything else, made it possible to 'think' the nation" (28). Whereas once all occurrences were understood to be meaningful in their vertical links to divine providence—they can be conceived of as simultaneous insofar as they become meaningful only in relation to the always future moment of their fulfillment in the coming of the Messiah— they are now seen to occur within a grid of "empty, homogeneous time" (28), time meaningful only as it becomes filled up with events that cross and follow one another in a wholly contingent chain of historical causality. According to Anderson, the novel and the newspaper function both as the privileged formal representations of this new temporal consciousness and as instruments for instilling this consciousness in their readers. In this account, the multiplot novel produces in its readers a sense of the connectedness of characters who may never meet one another yet who, thanks to the authority of the narrative "meanwhile," exist within a single world, a temporal and spatial

---

5. Benedict Anderson, *Imagined Communities: Reflections on the Origin and Spread of Nationalism* (London: Verso, 1983), 30. Subsequent page references will be given in parentheses within the text.

orbit. The "empty, homogeneous time" of novelistic simultaneity allows characters to be absent from readers' immediate consciousness yet understood as persisting somewhere offstage, and it is this peripheral persistence that produces, even as it represents, the consciousness of being part of a nation, part of an "imagined community."

For Anderson, the newspaper functions analogously to produce an imagined community of nations. When readers peruse the front page of a daily newspaper to learn the latest news "about Soviet dissidents, famine in Mali, a gruesome murder, a coup in Iraq, the discovery of a rare fossil in Zimbabwe, a speech by Mitterrand," these events are understood to be in some way related to one another. Anderson concludes: "If Mali disappears from the pages of *The New York Times* after two days of famine reportage, for months on end, readers do not for a moment imagine that Mali has disappeared or that famine has wiped out all its citizens. The novelistic format of the newspaper assures them that somewhere out there the 'character Mali' moves along quietly, awaiting its next reappearance in the plot" (37).

Yet the odd ontological status of Anderson's "character Mali" bespeaks the strains that tug at the terms of his analogy of historical and novelistic consciousnesses. While it is certainly true that the existence of both a national and an international sphere depends on their inhabitants' sense that the relevant entities—novelistic characters, states—continue to exist when they are not immediately present, the sense of causal interconnectedness and communal obligation implied by this persistence is quite different in the two cases. Although the newspaper readers who are the citizens of a particular nation may well be wholly convinced of the continued existence of other countries even when they do not read about them on a given day, their sense that their own fates are somehow caused by or at least imbricated with the fates of those absent yet persistent others is central to what it means to be a member of a nation yet is felt only in an indirect, attenuated, or even negative way in the case of international relations. The fictional authority that draws together the different plots of the multiplot novel—that narrative "meanwhile"—connotes a far greater connectedness among its characters and in their relationship to readers than does the juxtaposition on the front page of a variety of nonfictional events taking place throughout the world on a single day. In contrast, to assume, as Anderson does, a continuity between the national and the international by figuring the communities of both spheres' inhabitants to be grounded entirely on their experiences of "empty, homogeneous time" is to take the novel too much on its own terms. The nineteenth-century realist novel's particular representational force lies in its capacity to make relatively limited sets of detail appear at once constitutive of an entire, wholly seamless world and of a particular nation. The novel's details gain substantiality inasmuch as they bear local, not universal, legibility and weight.

Simultaneity, it thus seems, is not nearly so neutral a description as it might first appear. Insofar as the juxtaposition of the two sets of simultaneous events—1881 as the occasion of the pogroms and of *The Common Law;* the 1896–97 publication of *What Maisie Knew* and *The Travels of Benjamin the Third*—seems willful, justified (or not) by the force of "mere" simultaneity, simultaneity is revealed to be essentially a relation always already framed by, as well as productive of, the existence of a national consciousness and of particular national institutions. Historical causality turns out to begin and end with the crossing of national boundaries: if the fact that Holmes writes *The Common Law* in the same year that a group of Russian peasants attack their Jewish neighbors at a tavern in Elisavetgrad seems to fall into the realm of historical trivia of the slightest order, this sense of triviality, I want to argue, is evidence that much of even the most sophisticated historical thought continues to accept as a matter of habit the categories "mapped out" by national cartographers. The same discursive and materialist historiography that would do away with the positivism of top-down political and military histories remains allied to habits of thought according to which the outer frontiers of the state mark—while leaving largely unmarked—the outer frontiers of relevant happening.

As my account of Anderson should have begun to suggest, this problem of the unexamined adherence to national limits becomes particularly acute and complex when the history in mind is the history of the novel, since the genre's characteristic use of simultaneity acts as an instrument for producing the very consciousness that would dismiss as historically trivial the temporal coincidence of certain events: those happening within and beyond national boundaries. Moreover, as Foucauldian historicist conceptions of cultural production challenge the explanatory privilege granted the aesthetic object, the limits of the newly multifarious "contexts" that can be invoked to illuminate the now decentered text turn out to be the boundaries of the nation-state. The demand for strict demonstrations of causality disappears, only to be replaced by weak claims of relevance whose primary, if largely unarticulated, requirement is that events take place within a certain geographical space. Anything goes, it seems, within limits.[6]

6. I plan to explore in a separate project the specific intersections of the form of the realist novel and the techniques of contemporary historicist literary criticism. For an interesting account of critical "detailism" in relation not to the novel but to the romantic sublime, see Alan Liu, "Local Transcendence: Cultural Criticism, Postmodernism, and the Romanticism of Detail," *Representations* 32 (fall 1990): 75–113.

I mean to show that the Foucauldian notion of discourse presents a version of culture that is not just accidentally national but necessarily so. Moreover, this necessary—and necessarily unacknowledged—nationalism of the culture mapped out by Foucauldian historicism largely determines the ways new historicist critics of the novel define some of the central terms of their analyses of nineteenth-century culture: what they mean by "liberalism," what sorts of social and political work they understand the realist novel to be accomplishing. And if "discourse analysis" has been used as a tool for reading cultures that are decidedly not liberal (whether understood as a term of approbation or denigration), this analytical promiscuity results from the failure of contemporary historicist critics to recognize both how much their own work can be seen as liberalism's legacy and how much the logic of nationalism— and the logic of historicism as well—underwrites the theory and practice of liberalism. But by marking the pressure exerted by the category of the national on both Foucauldian discourse and Anglo-American liberalism, we can begin to generate a new understanding of historicism in which the force of history is registered on subjects and within the writing that they produce and that "produces" them in the variety—the nonnecessity—of its markings.

The historiographical revolution wrought by the notion of discourse lies in the generative power this sort of analysis attributes to writing: the power to generate objects, concepts, and taxonomies before they actually order the world, and the power to generate these taxonomies independent of the interests or agency of any particular writing subject. As Nancy Armstrong and Leonard Tennenhouse put it, "History establishes an unbreachable distinction between the subject and object of writing. To overturn history, one simply has to demonstrate that words come chronologically as well as ontologically before the things they are presumed to represent and the differences that already exist among those things. . . . In Foucault's account of modernity," Armstrong and Tennenhouse go on, "writing ceases to operate as an effect of other causes, located mainly in the church and the nobility, and becomes a cause in its own right."[7] In the instance Armstrong herself has made famous in her important study *Desire and Domestic Fiction,* not only did writings like novels and conduct manuals have the power to bring the figures they described into existence, but the imperative to create such categories came from the taxonomic logic of previous writings.

But if the generative force of writing lies in its absolute independence from

7. Nancy Armstrong and Leonard Tennenhouse, *The Imaginary Puritan* (Berkeley: University of California Press, 1992), 4–5.

the objects of the material world—that "unbreachable distinction between the subject and object of writing"—such autonomy means that writing itself must of necessity be without a history. Or more accurately, while it would certainly be possible to trace not only the subject matter of writing in the narrow, thematic sense but also the patterns of imagery, the systems of logic and opacity, the one aspect of writing that cannot be assigned a history is the fact of the writing itself, both as a particular medium in relation to other linguistic media and, even more fundamentally, as a medium that exists in relation to other languages or in relation to the possibility of its own nonexistence. The power of the concept of discourse to "overturn history," the writing that produces writers who will carry out its logic, thus at once depends on the preexistence of a national cultural infrastructure of schools, dictionaries, and marketplaces in which the very language of the discourse is brought into being and made useful and, at the same time, turns that national culture into something that goes without saying, an unlocatable spirit replacing— unplacing—a set of institutions. Insofar as this complex of institutional and social relations might be called "national culture," and insofar as the descriptive claim of the autonomy of writing renders such institutions of national culture self-evident, the constitutive power of Foucauldian discourse depends on the prior existence of a national culture. In lifting that culture outside history into the realm of the necessary, the noncontingent, discourse analysis turns out to be not merely national but nationalist.

And if the constitutive force of discourse depends on the presence of a system of national culture sufficiently far-reaching to make the medium of writing seem a point of origin, a condition about which the question Why? cannot be asked, such dependence must itself be hidden. In this regard, Foucauldian discourse seems merely to incorporate the national culture's modes of self-effacement as its own. The metaphors by which the analysis of discourse marks writing's triumph are inevitably spatial; for D. A. Miller, it is the "cultural hegemony and diffusion" that "qualifies [the Victorian novel] to become the primary spiritual exercise of an entire age."[8] In the space of a single sentence, the syntax enacting the narrative that has happened too soon to be represented, "cultural hegemony," still indeterminate in its abstraction, becomes "diffuse" and, by virtue of its diffusion through space, is transmuted into a condition of pure temporality—"the primary spiritual exercise of *an entire age*," the momentary detour through spatiality adequate to produce that infinitude of simultaneity, "the age." The spectacle of the scaffold having long since moved inaccessibly behind prison walls, the town square retains

---

8. D. A. Miller, *The Novel and the Police* (Berkeley: University of California Press, 1988), x.

its place as place, as the place one need not go anymore because there is nothing left there to be seen. If Foucauldian writing constitutes the world, makes an "age" by virtue of its being simply there, the existence that marks a place it refuses to name and for which it will not account is the logic that ties language to a particular geographical space, the foundational logic of national culture that arrests the simultaneity of 1881 at the border.

As I have already intimated, the first principle of this book is that the meaning of the "nationalism" of national literature, and more generally of national culture, cannot be understood from within the context of that single national—here, British—culture. Such a claim is more broadly a claim that the history of culture—both the histories of particular discourse and the history of the general concept—needs to be written across national cultures and that it is fundamentally not a single narrative but many, a history of language, the various histories of different languages, the history of the nationalization of language. And if, when writing is what is at issue, the first principle in its axiomatic, philosophical sense is nothing more or less elevated than the mundane and originary compositional decision about what goes in and what must be left out, where we end is both the thing that is read last and the logically inevitable outcome. I end with the history of the making of a language, with the making of a literary tradition—the making of the Hebrew novel—that is separable neither logically nor chronologically from the history of the writing out of which this literature is constituted.

In 1896, when Shalom Yaakov Abramovitch writes מסעות בנימין השלישי (*The Travels of Benjamin the Third*), the Jews of Europe are possessed of, and by, too much language and not enough. Scattered in varying concentrations throughout the populations of most of the countries of Europe, Jews are defined juridically in terms that differ from one state to the next, yet they maintain a sense of their connections to one another across national boundaries by virtue, at least in part, of their relation to a common set of writings—the Hebrew Bible, various rabbinical commentaries like the Talmud, and daily prayers. But the centrifugal force exerted on the dispersed Jews bears an awkward and uncomfortable relation to the logic of Foucauldian discourse. The Hebrew writing that draws these Jews together in the nineteenth century is anything but pervasive, since it coincides with no particular common geographical space and is not spoken regularly even by those Jews who spend their days studying Hebrew writing. Insofar as what these Jews have in common at this moment is exclusively a set of texts, their relationship to one another rests on too much writing; insofar as what the Jews have in common is merely a set of texts, existing in lieu of institutions of state and of other expressive practices, their relationship to one another rests on too little writing. Far from operating either as the engine of or as synecdoche for a clearly delineatable, spatialized national culture, Abramovitch's Hebrew novels need to be read in relation to his own extensive oeuvre of Yiddish writing. I will argue that the particular quality of novelistic fictionality that distinguishes Abramovitch's work from its western European literary forebears finds its echoes in the autobiographical preface to the first modern Hebrew dictionary, a narrative told by a man—Eliezer Ben-Yehuda—who believed he could turn a collection of texts into the spoken language of a national culture by dint of his own strenuous labors. Moreover, this autobiographical writing of Eliezer Ben-Yehuda can be adequately understood only when it in turn is read in relation to Samuel Johnson's "Preface" to his English dictionary, where he expresses his fervent hope that the divisions of labor that threaten to fragment English society might be dissolved into the immaterial unity of a linguistic culture.

Simultaneity, then, insofar as it organizes and figures limits to relations of historical causality, can be understood to constitute a theory of agency, even if that agency is not always simply mapped onto the acts of individual subjects. If a set of events has explanatory relevance, can be called to account for other sets of events, texts, and people only within a certain geopolitical proximity or set of relations, then the categories of agency and historical causality themselves turn out to be intimately connected with both the particular boundaries of particular states and the shifting meanings of nationality more generally construed.

In emphasizing the discontinuity between the nation and what is beyond it, I want finally to propose that the work of nations—and the notions of historical causality implicitly linked to such a conceptual framework—cannot be understood without stepping outside the boundaries of the nation. Such a step is something of a paradox: though my approach in part turns on my willingness to examine novels—and "contexts"—from a variety of national (literary) histories, my stepping beyond the nation is not quite of the order of a border crossing, a movement from one country to another. At the same time, my reading of the relation between nationalism and the novel is wholly informed by the plain historical fact that, as the nineteenth century draws to a close, from the perspective of the Europe that generated the paradigm there are no actual places "beyond the nation," no space that has not in some way been nationalized.

The theoretical imperative to mask discourse's location within and dependence on particular national cultures also sets the agenda for the most influential Foucauldian accounts of the novel. For both Armstrong and Miller, the novel is an instrument by which the political regime called liberalism makes plausible its claim to produce subjects beyond the reach of—or deeper than—politics and economics or, even more fundamentally, beyond the realm of the social discipline produced by various discourses. Within the context of my discussion of discourse's erasure of its own national origins, Miller and Armstrong's critiques of the claim to the outside and their accounts of the ways novels lay claim to such an outside take on a new resonance. Although Miller titles his collection of essays *The Novel and the Police,* it is finally not the police at all that command his attention: "I will argue," he announces in his preface, "that the theme of the police is an 'alibi' for a station-house that now is everywhere" (x). By Miller's account, it is the novel's investment in naming particularities—in representing police as flesh-and-blood people patrolling specific streets—that becomes evidence for the novel's claim to abstraction, to being outside. In representing the police, the novel locates its "carceral restraints" (and by implication itself) in a particular place. To place oneself, or acknowledge one's placement, anywhere is to lay claim to being outside, to fly in the face of the harsh, inescapable truth insisted on by the rhetoric of Foucauldian discourse, the truth of a discipline's inescapability. But if the placedness of the police constitutes an alibi for the discipline that is everywhere, then being "everywhere" turns out to be the condition of being no place at all.

This logic that associates being in culture in the most profoundly constitutive sense (which is finally, we recall, the most superficial) with being nowhere at all is what allows a Foucauldian critic like J. Paul Hunter to oppose reading novels "in culture" to reading novels in different languages together:

> The choice was between an emphasis on the way the novel reflects a particular culture and the way it participates in another kind of context, the commonality of other novels. It seems to me impossible, at this point in critical history, to do justice at the same time to the cultural aspects of origins and to structural questions—those matters that cross national and linguistic boundaries—and I have firmly chosen to anchor my account of the nature of the novel in cultural specificity.[9]

Thus what begins as a gesture of critical modesty—the decision to limit the scope of his project to a "particular culture"—turns out to announce a choice not among different particular cultures, but between different sorts of analysis—between "the cultural aspects of origins" and "structural questions"—a choice that finally enables Hunter to lay claim, "firmly," to cultural specific-

9. J. Paul Hunter, *Before Novels: The Cultural Contexts of Eighteenth-Century English Fiction* (New York: W. W. Norton, 1990), xxii.

ity *in general:* "I have firmly chosen to anchor my account of the nature of the novel in cultural specificity."

Whereas critics like Miller, Armstrong, and Hunter have maintained that the novel and liberalism are most "firmly" disciplinary at the moment they proclaim their distance from the carceral restraints of discourse, let me turn the tables for a moment and propose that such Foucauldian analysts of the novel most decisively reveal their liberal roots at the moment they obscure the way the very category of discourse emerges out of the noncongruence of national boundaries and particular cultures. But while the resemblance of liberalism and Foucauldian historicism might seem to make visible a certain unacknowledged idealism within the concept of discourse, I believe the discovery that both rely on their location within a national culture that is already existing, if not immediately apparent, provides an opportunity for reconceiving liberalism, historicism, and the relation between the two. By acknowledging the ways liberalism's foundational narratives depend on recognizing the particularity of a given national culture and its limits and discontinuities from other national cultures, we can come to see liberalism not as a refusal of the contingencies of history, or of what it means to act as a subject or to create an aesthetic object "in cultural specificity," but as a deliberate and self-conscious negotiation with the fact of historicity. As I hope this book will make apparent, liberalism can be seen as an engagement with the variousness of individual subjects' historical location, but also with the way the process of understanding that variety, created and inflected by expressly *social* categories, might itself become the ground of a new sort of sociality. And in this version of the social constituted out of the common experience of an unpredictable, irreducible historicity, the realist novel, with its fictionalized—abstracted—detailing of particularities, stands not as a symptom of the desire to escape culture but as an instrument producing a subject whose imagining of his or her agency is limited and enabled not simply by its existence at a specific moment in time but by its movement through time.

(Inter)Nationalism and Liberal Space

The nationalism that reaches its apogee at the end of the nineteenth century in Europe and elsewhere at once founds the right of a people to a given geographical space on their shared history (normally) within that space and renders what goes on outside it not quite history, only obliquely related to the hopes and loyalties and fates of members of the national community. As Liah Greenfeld puts it, "nationalism locates the course of individual identity within a 'people,' which is seen as the bearer of sovereignty, the central object of loyalty, and the basis of collective solidarity."[10] The initial concept of the *natio,* derived from the Latin "to be born," was both derogatory and in some sense "international": in Rome, according to Guido Zernatto, the name *natio* was used to designate foreigners coming from the same geographical region, whose status as foreigners deprived them of the rights of state accorded Roman citizens.[11] The rehabilitation of the term nation, part and parcel of modern nationalism's transformation of geographical space into a positive ground of identity, thus involved a certain forgetting of the foreign. But this forgetting was made possible only by introducing an ideology according to which, rather than being positive or negative, the history of one's birth meant nothing at all. The nationalism of the late nineteenth century, then, needs to be understood in the context of the universalist liberalism that preceded it and in some cases coexisted with it: the forms of political subjecthood, historical causality, and cultural authority associated with modern nationalism assume new significance when viewed as the manifestations of certain contradictions implicit within the ideology of Enlightenment and pre-Enlightenment liberalism.[12]

Because the terms of liberalism and modern nationalism not only are difficult to extricate from one another but are mutually constitutive, neither the formalism that seems at first to be liberalism's privileged disciplinary mode nor the historicism that might appear authorized by nationalism is sufficient

10. Liah Greenfeld, *Nationalism: Five Roads to Modernity* (Cambridge: Harvard University Press, 1992), 3.

11. Guido Zernatto, "Nation: The History of a Word," cited in Greenfeld, *Nationalism,* 4.

12. I want to clarify that in emphasizing the discontinuity that modern nationalism sets up between a given nation and what is outside it, I do not mean that individual nations exist without some generally accepted notion of the terms that constitute nationness. Insofar as this consensus exists, I am in agreement with Anderson that the imagined community of an individual nation-state and the imagined "community of nations" are in some way homologous. Indeed, Greenfeld argues, persuasively to my mind, that the spread of nationalism depended on the existence of a "supra-societal system, or shared social space," a common model that allowed the model of the nation to be subsequently borrowed by one culture from another. She writes: "It is probable that initially such shared social space was created by Christianity and, perhaps, the Renaissance. Parenthetically, this may explain why, while individual proto-nations—namely societies held together by solidarities remarkably similar to national, although not called 'nations'—were known in the ancient world, notably among the Jews and the Greeks, nationalism never spread beyond the borders of these individual societies. In distinction, Christianity did create in Europe the supra-societal social space which made such spread possible" (495n). I hope that the significance of this prehistory of the nation for my book's conception of national culture will become clear in my discussion of the relation between Jewish national identity and liberalism. If liberalism became the theory by which the Roman understanding of nationality as foreignness could be forgotten, it was precisely the presence of a forcibly "internationalized" Jewishness—a Jewish nationality not only no longer confined to its own borders but without any borders whatever—that rendered untenable liberalism's claims to universalism.

by itself to discern the history of liberalism. To articulate a national history of liberalism or, alternatively, the universalism that authorizes late nineteenth-century nationalism is in one sense to take neither discourse entirely on its own terms.[13] Nationalism might be understood as the discourse by which liberalism gains both a history and a means of realization, a narrowed conception of political belonging that saves liberalism in its formalist universalism from the triviality of diffuseness.[14] In another sense, however, I hope that by following liberalism in and out of history, my book reveals not only the ways the contradictions distinguishing liberalism and nationalism make each work, but also the way this particular opposition helps produce a relation between the text of the realist novel and its (nationalized) historical context that serves as the paradigm for modern conceptions of history. With this knot of relations in mind, I pair the history of liberalism with the eighteenth- and nineteenth-century history of European Jews—a national group whose members, in lacking a shared geographical space or a common national language, bear crucial formal resemblances to liberalism's universalist subjects.

This spatialized notion of culture characteristic both of the realist novel and of much contemporary new historicism is not simply an isolated phenomenon. Rather, I contend that the presumption that the limits of the nation-state constitute the boundaries of any variety of cultural practices in a way so self-evident that the fact of their coincidence need not be examined at all is absolutely central to the discourse of English liberalism, with its particular emphasis on landed property as the ground of political and social agency. While the centrality of land to English conceptions of citizenship hardly need be argued, I suggest that it is liberalism's complex and intermittent invocation of the *figure* of space—from a description of land to an underlying and mostly unmentioned form of cultural likeness—that is liberalism's most powerfully pervasive legacy. I will discuss a bit later the significance of the process by which the material relations at the heart of liberalism's property-based notion of citizenship get transformed into a decidedly less material

---

13. Etienne Balibar makes a similar argument about the relations between nationalism and racism; for him, nationalism moves from a fictive ethnicity based on shared language to a fictive ethnicity based on race or genealogy because race serves as a necessary supplement within the notion of nationality that endows it with a principle of exclusion, of closure. While our arguments are in many aspects homologous, my interest in the knot of relations linking liberalism and nationalism means that the salient terms of my discussion involve agency and knowledge rather than identity as it is familiarly construed in most contemporary analyses of race. See Etienne Balibar and Immanuel Wallerstein, *Race, Nation, Class: Ambiguous Identities* (London: Verso, 1991), especially chap. 3, "Racism and Nationalism," and chap. 5, "The Nation Form: History and Ideology."

14. I am grateful to Elizabeth Dillon for her help in clarifying the formulation that follows.

concept of culture; for now I am interested in tracing the permutations of the category of space that enable such a dematerialization to take place. To apprehend fully the ideological force of this spatialization of culture, we need to look to those moments, and social relations, in which the expressly political-economic category of land and the less expressly designated "space of culture" do not overlap neatly. Such a history of noncoincidence might be figured within the terms of my critique of Anderson as a history of "internationalism."

I turn to one of the foundational texts of the English liberal tradition, John Locke's *Two Treatises of Government,* to examine the ways the universalism that stands as the ideological cornerstone of liberalism's reimagining of political authority depends on positing a peculiar kind of internationalism. While the nationalism of the late nineteenth century is by no means an inevitable outcome of this latent (inter)nationalist strain within liberalism, it nonetheless illustrates how deeply nationalist particularisms are indebted to apparently incompatible liberal models of citizenship for their concepts and forms of political authority, as well as for the cultural practices used to bring that authority into being.

The historical relation between Locke's composition of the *Two Treatises* and the Glorious Revolution of 1688 has long been a point of fierce scholarly contention:[15] historians who believe Locke wrote his theory of state formation before the fall of James II generally envision a radical Locke constructing a theory of political resistance, defending individuals' right to reject government coercion where legitimate political authority is absent. Those scholars who read Locke as having written the *Two Treatises* after 1688 tend to describe a much more conservative Locke, one concerned primarily with conceptualizing the obligation of subjects to obey the authority of James's successor William III, shoring up monarchical authority in general in the wake of the particular challenge to James. Kirstie McClure has recently and persuasively argued, however, that the political dynamic Locke theorized is neither consent nor obligation but the *transfer* of allegiance (from James to William).[16] That is, the political conundrum facing Locke was not "which rival power had the better claim or title to obedience or whether armed resistance could be justified in the abstract," but whether subjects encumbered by past political loyalties could be understood to retain the right to choose their polit-

15. For a good summary of the controversy see Peter Laslett's introduction to the Cambridge edition of the *Two Treatises*, esp. 41–50.

16. For an account of the history and force of the distinction between consent and obligation in liberal theory, see Jeremy Waldron, "Liberal Rights: Two Sides of the Coin," in *Liberal Rights: Collected Papers: 1981–1991* (Cambridge: Cambridge University Press, 1993).

ical allegiances.[17] In some way, then, we might see the *Two Treatises* as written in response to the emergence of a distinct category of culture, a foundation of social cohesion separable from the institutions of state that juridically defined the geographical space of England.

To gloss the *Treatises* by means of an account of the origins of an expressly political authority, then, is to risk misrepresenting them, since it is a virtual commonplace of Locke criticism to note how little emphasis Locke places on the liberal individual's movement from the state of nature to the civil sphere. For Locke, institutions of state come into being in order to guarantee that individuals can possess undisturbed the property they have acquired while in the state of nature. Locke's narrative of property, which is the centerpiece of his theory of rights, is no doubt familiar: individuals possess their own bodies in accordance with the law of nature; by mixing their bodies with the material world around them in the form of labor, Lockean subjects come to possess objects in the world insofar as these objects are extrapolations from the subjects' own self-possession. The crucial element of this paradigm is its claim that the civil state does not stand as the foundation of individuals' right to property but merely ensures that they can keep what they already naturally possess. First, such a formulation means that individuals' right to property is a natural rather than a civil right and hence that their possessions are not subject to seizure by the government. Second, it implies that though we might be tempted to read the tenuousness of the Lockean subject's hold on his[18] property as evidence of constraint upon that subject's capacity to act as an absolute free agent, to impose his will on the world, we would be mistaken. By associating such tenuousness with the institutional contingency of the

17. Kirstie McClure, *Judging Rights: Lockean Politics and the Limits of Consent* (Ithaca: Cornell University Press, 1996), 116. The political paradigm for such consent is the social contract, which offers a narrative explanation for the way individuals could be assumed to be naturally free and yet at the same time be obliged to obey limitations on their freedom imposed by government authority. If individuals are above all free, then any limitations on their freedom must be understood as an expression of that freedom, limitations imposed by the self. The social contract becomes the instrument by which individuals cede their authority to a civil society that is in turn represented by a government; the laws enforced by the government are thus understood as deriving their authority from the wills of individuals.

18. As Carole Pateman has argued, the Lockean subject not only is always, indeed constitutively, male but necessarily occupies the position of the son. In taking aim against Robert Filmer's identification of the power of the absolute monarch and that of the father, Locke not only makes metaphorical the relation between father and king—they merely resemble one another in form, exercising power in the separate realms of public and private—but implicitly defines the individual subject as a child. But as Pateman astutely points out, the bifurcation of the civil and the domestic realms that underpins Locke's reduction of the relation between father and king to mere figurativity, requires him to ignore the fact that the originary contract is not between subjects, but between husband and wife. Hence Lockean subjects not only are male but turn out to be sons as well. See Pateman, *The Sexual Contract* (Stanford: Stanford University Press, 1988).

second-order sphere that is the government, Locke effectively frees his individuals to be free, even if that absolute, ideal freedom is only contingently
manifest in the actual world.

Thus the making and getting of property becomes for the Lockean subject
the ideal expression of his limitless capacities, a realm in which self and world
become so intimate, so closely enmeshed, as to be virtually indistinguishable.[19] But if self-possession is at once the ground for possessing the world
and the ground of individual subjects' equality, not all possessions are created
equal. Though on the first iteration both movable property like acorns and
apples and immovable property (land) are possessed through the extension
of self-ownership that constitutes Lockean labor—acorns and apples are
gathered and land is cultivated—as Locke's discussion progresses it becomes
clear that their common origin is not adequate to keep the two forms of property identical. "But the *chief matter of Property* being now not the Fruits of
the Earth, and the Beasts that subsist on it, but the *Earth it self;* as that which
takes in and carries with it all the rest: I think it is plain, that *Property* in that
too is acquired as the former."[20] The process of distinguishing between types
of property both depends on and produces a history of property making;
whereas at one time all forms of property were of comparable value (equally
useful? equally plentiful? equally scarce?), one mode of property has become
valued over others—*now* "the chief matter of Property . . . is the Earth it
self." But as quickly as the value of property—and hence, of property making—is historicized, the distinctions associated with this historicizing are
again subsumed in the common narrative of a labor that originates in the
self-evidence, the "plainness," of self-possession: "I think it is plain, that
Property in that too is acquired in the former."[21]

19. However seductive this fantasy of inalienability—what we might term agency of entanglement—
is to Locke, it cannot be sustained for the length of Locke's description. I have discussed elsewhere the
problem of Lockean property and the alienability of identity in relation to copyright and intellectual
property. (See Irene Tucker, "Writing Home: *Evelina,* the Epistolary Novel and the Paradox of Property,"
ELH 60, 2 [1993]: 419–39.) For now I am less interested in the instability of the relation between
property and identity generally in the *Second Treatise* than in the patterns by which Locke invokes specific *kinds* of property.

20. John Locke, *Two Treatises of Government,* ed. Peter Laslett (Cambridge: Cambridge University
Press, 1991), 290.

21. Locke's bivalent notion of space is rendered even more complex by a similarly doubled account
of types of labor. Locke writes: "This *Labour* being the unquestionable Property of the Laborer, no Man
but he can have a right to what that is once joyned to, at least where there is enough, and as good left
in common for others. He that is nourished by the Acorns he pickt up under an Oak, or the Apples he
gathered from the Trees in the Wood, has certainly appropriated them to himself. No Body can deny but
the nourishment is his. I ask then, When did they begin to be his? When he digested? Or when he eat?
Or when he boiled? Or when he brought them home? Or when he pickt them up? And 'tis *plain* [empha-
sis added] if the first gathering made them not his, nothing else could. That *labour* put a distinction

To his by now familiar maxim authorizing property in the fact of self-possession, Locke appends a qualification implying that in some way that identification depends on a condition of infinite plenty. He declares, "For this *Labour* being the unquestionable Property of the Labourer, no Man but he can have a right to what that is once joyned to, at least where there is enough, and as good left in common for others." The world according to Locke is at once a world of infinite abundance and one that is absolutely stable over time, a contradiction that, as we shall see, helps account for the privileged status of landed property within Locke's system.[22] If for Locke land is now "the chief matter of Property" because it is "that which takes in and carries with it all the rest," in what sense does land accomplish this, and how might this capacity enable Locke's version of landed property to overcome the contradictions of his vision of society?

In the most straightforward and literal sense, Locke's land "takes in . . . all the rest" of the forms of property in that owners of land are presumed to own all that exists on that land—all the fruit trees and nuts and beasts that might make their home there. In this conception, land is understood as an object to be owned like other objects, yet possessing, "carrying with it," the peculiar capacity to limit access to other forms of movable property that might otherwise not have been taken from the common. In that it literally and juridically frames and, in some sense, determines the fate of the other forms of movable—and, importantly, *renewable*—forms of property that fall within

---

between them and the common" (288). The previous passage presented a proliferation of types of property that threatened to undermine the subject's capacity to possess that property, which tended, in its variousness, to flaunt property's capacity to remain stubbornly itself. Here, in contrast, it is not the world that is resistant to the willful laboring of the subject but the subject who is inadequate to the task of willing, of laboring in its "plain" sense. Requiring nourishment from the apples on the trees in the woods, Locke's individual engages in a flurry of frenetic activity that has the ultimate effect of reminding him just how dependent he remains on the material world he inhabits. Locke's idealist conception of property—his vision of property as perfect self-representation—is thus threatened from two directions and in two aspects. It is threatened first by a historicism, by the admission of a temporality that shatters the category of "property" into a variety of properties that in their particularity announce the tenuousness of the individual's hold on them. Second, it is threatened ontologically or, more accurately given Locke's naturalist rhetoric, at the level of the definition by the possibility that his liberal subjects simply do not have the autonomy with which he would endow them by fiat. What is for my purposes most significant about Locke's delineation of types of labor is the way it makes evident how his model of space erases the temporality of the liberal subject.

22. The most explicit articulation of this tendency to transform the temporal into the spatial occurs as Locke's notion of tacit consent, where the problem of how political consent can be understood to move from one generation to the next is solved by the invention of a consent marked, to all intents and purposes, by the occupation of a given geographical space. Under this concept of tacit consent, sons are understood to consent to the social contract into which their fathers have "literally" entered at the moment they use public works like roads, inherit property, or in any other way participate in a public sphere that is defined as coincident with the space of the state.

its boundaries, landed property can be understood to perform a stabilizing function. Moreover, because the possession of land has the effect of canceling the separate significances of the movable property contained within it, it effectively turns the different forms of labor that might take place within it into a single abstract concept of labor, a move essential to establishing the absolute autonomy of the Lockean subject.

Landed property thus turns out to function in two ways, to map out two aspects of the subject. First, it operates as a kind of property, a thing to be possessed in itself; second, it operates as a space within which other activities take place, a backdrop that guarantees, at least formally, the autonomy and efficacy of the Lockean agent. This double quality of land is crucial theoretically because it enables a certain kind of indirection: as ur-property, it cancels the temporality associated with the renewability and variety of the movable property that exists within its boundaries; as background, mere unmarked space, land naturalizes this expulsion of temporality that underwrites—and renders transcendent—the Lockean subject's freedom of agency. The experience of abundance offered by the possession of land to which others have no access produces an absolutely free subject within its bounds. Yet in the narrow fact of exclusive possession such land offers the guarantee of stability, the assurance that, once possessed, the movable property will remain the property of the subject. Conceived of as space, then, land becomes the backdrop for a free agency whose autonomy and efficacy it underwrites; conceived of as property, land stabilizes the (movable) property brought into being by the will of the liberal subject by making certain it cannot be seized by someone else.

Students of liberalism such as Hannah Arendt and Sheldon Wolin have long bemoaned the tendency of Locke and his intellectual heirs to collapse the functions of a political sphere—the processes of debate and the deliberate actions of (self-)government—into the productively vague realm of the "social," a conflation, they claim, that makes social and economic relations appear identical and consequently unchangeable.[23] But simply to understand

23. Wolin and Arendt are mostly in agreement in their diagnoses of the problem (the loss of a notion of distinctively political activity) and in their prescription for its solution (the development of a deliberately formal model of political citizenship). They depart from one another somewhat in their readings of the liberal tradition, and consequently in their respective understandings of when and how the distinctively political realm came to disappear. For Wolin, liberalism's error was essentially analytical and ideological: in conceiving of the problem of the subjectivism of monarchical absolutism as the problem of personified authority, Locke and the nineteenth-century utilitarians who were his intellectual heirs turned away from the personalized authority of king or pope, only to yield to the less visible authority of "society."

Arendt, by contrast, traces liberalism's loss of the political back to the mistaken adoption of the

Lockean liberalism as naturalizing a certain set of property relations by authorizing what Wolin calls "the primacy of economic action" (300) is to miss
half the story. It is, in a word, to read Lockean land as property while overlooking its function as space. For the genius—or somewhat less sublimely,
the profound cultural persuasiveness—of Locke's narrative of political consent lies less in its power to justify given social and economic relations than
in its capacity to make the existence of the state mean no more—or no less—
than the existence of the landscape itself. Liberalism's explanatory success, in
other words, lies not so much in its collapse of the political and the social as
in its identification of the political and the *ontological,* an identification that
both "takes in and carries with it" the realm of the historical and finally
renders such historicism critically impotent.[24]

What might it mean, then, to think about the relations of political authority and historical causality from an international perspective, as I believe the
multiple and overlapping meanings of land in Locke bid us do? We might
begin to answer this question by looking to the text of the *Second Treatise*
itself, to the peculiar version of internationalism Locke himself introduces to
his system.

What is striking about Locke's privileging of landed property is that it is
the one form of property that is—by its nature rather than contingently—
subject to scarcity. Whereas apples and acorns and beasts can be consumed
and renewed and thus offer, at least theoretically and over time, "enough
and as good left in common for others," landed property is inherently finite.
(Although land can certainly be cultivated endlessly, it is only the initial act
of cultivation, of mixing one's labor with the soil, that establishes it as private
property. Therefore subsequent acts of cultivation remain irrelevant to the
abundance or scarcity of land in general. There is a finite amount of land on
the earth to be used; once it has been removed from the common, it effectively
has been "used up.") Again, the process of generating distinctions between
types of property historicizes the category, but Locke escapes the destabiliz-

---

economically deterministic paradigm of the French Revolution. In tracing the origins of revolution—
and hence the authority for political action—to the French rather than the American Revolution, the
professional revolutionaries of the twentieth century have rewritten revolution as a kind of biological
necessity rather than a deliberate choice, the biologism associated with the hunger and deprivation that
both motivated the actions of the French revolutionaries and brought about the Terror.

See Sheldon Wolin, *Politics and Vision: Continuity and Innovation in Western Political Thought*
(Boston: Little, Brown, 1960), esp. chap. 9, "Liberalism and the Decline of Political Philosophy," and
Hannah Arendt, *On Revolution* (New York: Penguin, 1965).

24. See Jeremy Waldron's account of the relation between actual and hypothetical consent in liberal
political theory. Waldron is especially interested in the way the "transparency" of civil institutions might
substitute for actual consent. Waldron, *Liberal Rights: Collected Papers, 1981–1991* (Cambridge: Cambridge University Press, 1993), esp. chap. 2, "Theoretical Foundations of Liberalism."

ing effects of such a historicization by positing an internationalism that is curiously both inside and beyond the unmarked space of Lockean civil society:

> This measure [of limiting landed property to what an individual could appropriate] did confine every Man's *Possession,* to a very moderate Proportion, and such as he might appropriate to himself, without injury to any Body in the first Ages of the World, when Men were more in danger to be lost, by wandering from their Company, in the then vast Wilderness of the Earth, than to be straitened for want of room to plant in. And the same *measure* may be allowed still, without prejudice to any Body, as full as the World seems. For supposing a Man, or Family, in the state they were, at first peopling of the World by the Children of *Adam,* or *Noah;* let him plant in some in-land, vacant places of *America.* (292–93)

While the overt goal of this passage seems to be assimilating an increasingly broad temporal sweep into the regularized conditions of universality, what turn out to distinguish the "first Ages of the World" from the pointedly less specified present—and consequently what need to be made regular—are forms of social organization. In the previous narrative land, once possessed, became the space in which an autonomous agent could then freely take possession of a variety of movable properties. What this earlier account pointedly excluded, however, was the possibility that landed property's status as property could remain actively at issue subsequent to its initial creation-possession. Here, with the shift in the order of magnitude from landed property as the space within which movable property might be freely possessed to a form of property in its own right, the universalization of the "space" of civil society threatens to become obviously untenable. The identification of government and space around the invisible middle term of landed property turns out to depend on excluding land from the discourse of property; once it is figured as still in flux itself, "renewable" and hence subject to evaluation in terms of its abundance or scarcity, the gap between historical causality ("what happens") and the worldliness of a given nation-state ("what happens to certain people within certain boundaries") yawns wide.

Locke's solution, as we see in the passage above, is to introduce the space of "America." Neither wholly inside nor wholly separate from the system of nation-states/natural space, "America" offers the quality of abundance that for Locke is both the ground for and the evidence of his subjects' autonomy, while at the same time figuring an absolute break between this "space of abundance" and that space already rendered coterminous with existing nation-states. "America" allows us to discover the concept of the international precisely because it fails to function entirely as a nation itself. What Locke's solution does, in effect, is to detach the abundant and hence freedom-endowing qualities of landed property from those aspects of land that, insofar as they come to be identified with the transparent figure of the nation-state, guarantee the stability of the land that is already possessed. By locating these two qualities of land at different levels of abstraction—that is, by making "America" both continuous and discontinuous with already extant nation-states—Locke stabilizes the existing system of nation-states by relegating the business of making new landed property, and the state making associated with that possession, to a place outside the system of nations. Liberal subjects thus ought not to consider themselves in any way constrained—and hence historicized—by the fact that all the land in England is already possessed, "used up," because they can always go to America where, rhetorically if not actually, there is always land for the taking in infinite plenitude. By the same token, that individuals are understood to have the "natural right" to possess whatever land they need and labor over does not necessarily imply that either the order of possession of landed property already in existence or the political order authorized by these empirical facts of possession need be in any way threatened by this individual freedom to possess.

Such a stratagem is not without its costs, however. In rhetorically disconnecting landed property's function as a guarantor of freedom from its stabilizing, universalizing aspect, the figure of "America" purchases the stability of the existing civil order at the price of being able to represent that order as following naturally from the existence of geographical space itself. The Wittgensteinian quality of the resolutions bodied forth by Locke's concept of landed property ought not to come as a great surprise: the more strenuously the existence and stability of a specific political order is insisted on, the more difficult it becomes to contend that the state in general is the effect of geographical space generally construed. If the Lockean state depends on a universalist, transhistorical conception of the subject, I hope this discussion has made it clear that it is equally invested as a descriptive system in its manifestation as a particular state. Far from marking a liberalism fallen from universalist principles, the particular interplay of the historical and the formal I have sketched out constitutes the foundation of that liberal state. And if, as I maintain in this book, the overtly historicist nationalisms of the late nineteenth century can be understood to emerge from within the terms laid out by Lockean liberalism two centuries earlier, such a nationalist historicism ought to be viewed less as a perversion of the ideals of liberal universalism than as a shift in emphasis within a social vision committed *in theory* to its own civil realization.

Liberalism, Probability, and the Place of the Fictional

As a history of the novel, my book is an anomaly in one quite obvious way: instead of concentrating on the development and consolidation of the novel in the eighteenth century, I focus on realism's end, its dissolution at the close of the nineteenth century. My decision to tell the story of the realist novel from its moment of consummation instead of its earliest appearance is of a piece with my desire to recharacterize liberalism. If the eighteenth century is the era of the emergence of the market, the end of the nineteenth century marks the institutionalizing of a certain kind of historicism, the moment when the existence of cultural particularity is registered by economic, political, and juridical institutions within the nation-state and thus at once set forth as the limit and the ground of social cohesion.[25] But while this project might fairly be glossed "The Decline of *The Rise of the Novel*," this movement from origin to end is, I mean to show, less an abandonment of Ian Watt's long-dominant paradigm than a fulfillment of its inner logic. The power of Watt's book to set the terms of critical discussions of the English novel in the forty years since its publication lies not so much in the descriptive acuity of its thesis as in its absence. Or to be more specific, the insight of Watt's book is to be found not in its thesis but in its refusal to settle on one. *The Rise of the Novel* contains not one argument but two, and while the book's failure to articulate the relation between its two theses can be seen to have generated a particularly broad intellectual legacy, enfolding such suggestive and influential work as that of Michael McKeon, Catherine Gallagher, and Nancy Armstrong, it is the logic implicit in the very irresolution of Watt's two theses that has led me to tell the story of the realist novel from the perspective of its end point.

The doubleness of Watt's arguments lies in his account of just what makes the novel liberal. In the opening chapter, "Realism and the Novel Form," Watt links the emergence of the realist novel to the tradition of philosophical realism associated with Locke, Descartes, and Thomas Reid. Although the emergent moments of philosophical and literary realism do not quite coincide, Watt nonetheless traces the generic particularity of the novel to the philosophical position that "truth can be discovered by the individual through his senses." By this first account, the innovation of the novel is primarily episte-

---

25. By way of example, William Whitney's 1875 *The Life and Growth of Language* emphasized the collective institutional character of language, against the understanding of language as an organic expression of a culture. In chapter 3 I also examine the shifting relation of language and state institutions in the work of Oliver Wendell Holmes. See the account of Whitney in Dennis Taylor, *Hardy's Literary Language and Victorian Philology* (Oxford: Oxford University Press, 1993), 229.

mological, and the social and political transformations that accompany or follow from the emergence of this new literary genre are predicated on its being conceived as a new way of knowing.

In the next chapter, "The Reading Public and the Rise of the Novel," Watt offers an entirely different definition of the novel's "liberalism." Here the novel's rise is connected to the growth of literacy in the eighteenth century and the consequent emergence of a middle-class reading public, an audience of liberal subjects. This latter account conceives of the novel in ontological terms, as a material object—a kind of thing—whose significance lies in the social and economic relations by which it comes to be produced, circulated, and consumed.

As I have intimated, Watt is entirely mute on the question of how the philosophical and intellectual genealogy he presents in his first chapter is related, causally or even chronologically, to the socioeconomic, material description of the novel he presents in the second.[26] And for the most part, the theorists of the novel who have followed Watt have recapitulated the divide generated, if not fully recognized, by *The Rise of the Novel.* In Nancy Armstrong's 1987 *Desire and Domestic Fiction* and Catherine Gallagher's 1994 *Nobody's Story,* the novel—and its authors as complex analogues to the works they produce—come to matter inasmuch as they can be incorporated into, or disrupt, the relations of an emergent market economy. By contrast, Michael McKeon's 1987 *The Origins of the English Novel* is firmly ensconced on the epistemological side of Watt's great divide, tracing the movement of the novel from the seventeenth through the mid-eighteenth century as an ongoing oscillation between ways of knowing, a dialectical movement between "naive empiricism" and "extreme skepticism." Whereas Armstrong and Gallagher see the novel primarily as a made thing, a product of authorial labor to be turned into a commodity, for McKeon, who subordinates acting ("questions of virtue") to knowing ("questions of truth"), the novel is first and foremost an expression of a certain way of understanding the world.[27]

26. Much of the criticism leveled at *The Rise of the Novel* over the years has concerned its dating, and I believe the difficulty of tying Watt's multiple historical causes of the emergence of the novel to one another or to the moment at which Defoe, Richardson, and Fielding were writing is a symptom of Watt's fundamental ambivalence about whether the development that is the novel is best understood within a philosophical and intellectual genealogy or a sociopolitical one. Likewise, Watt's failure to assimilate Fielding plausibly within his own schema while nevertheless retaining a commitment to including him in this developmental narrative suggests that Watt is not entirely at ease with a model that identifies the novel's epistemology with its characters' knowledge and its qualities as a commodity with its readers' reception while leaving the authority of the fictional narrator entirely unaccounted for. See Ian Watt, *The Rise of the Novel* (Berkeley: University of California Press, 1957).

27. Michael McKeon, *The Origins of the English Novel, 1700–1840* (Baltimore: Johns Hopkins University Press, 1987).

The premise of this book is that the most powerful insight of *The Rise of the Novel* is the one it performs rather than articulates. In the chapters that follow I propose that what liberalism and the novel have in common—indeed, what characterizes them as new and significant social forms—is their capacity to bring together the epistemological and the ontological or material, to imagine a relation between the two sides of Watt's divide that nonetheless accounts for the experience of the autonomy—the "thingness"—of the ontological. In my reading, both liberalism and the novel ought to be understood as modes of recognizing and deliberately negotiating with historicity, a set of attitudes regarding the links between knowledge and (historical) agency. I understand liberalism to name a condition of subjectivity in which one's capacity to know and predict the contingent particularities of the material world—including the particularities of other people in specific social, political, and economic relations to one—becomes the ground of one's operation as an agent.

The liberal tradition that begins in the seventeenth century with Locke does not merely posit an ideal, transcendent subject able to impose his will on, and in spite of, the contingencies of the material world. Instead, by embracing a logic of "probability," not empiricism—what one believes might happen rather than what one can see—liberal subjects set as their task the continual recognition and overcoming of historical contingency. In its conception of liberalism as a theory of the relation between knowledge and agency, my book diverges from Foucauldian critics of the novel and liberalism like Armstrong and D. A. Miller, for whom the project at hand is one of identifying the nature of the discourse that might be said to precede the specific individuals who instantiate it. For such critics, the content and relative values of various beliefs become important insofar as they are discursive rather than individual (or discursive and therefore individual) and insofar as the limits of the discourse establish the limits of individuality. What I aim to do, by contrast, is not so much to identify specific sets of beliefs as to identify the basic social and political conditions that make belief possible and, indeed, make beliefs come to look as though they are crucial forms of action.[28]

This book argues that the history of the realist novel comes clear at the moment of its "decline" in the late nineteenth century because that is the moment in Anglo-American culture—and in Anglo-American realist fiction—when the liberal subject's capacity to know ceased to appear adequate to the task of allowing that subject to act freely. In response to this perceived breakdown of individuals' capacity to predict and know the world, institu-

28. I am indebted to Frances Ferguson for this last formulation.

tions of state stepped in, offering everything from new social services to new modes of legal interpretation in order to mark and compensate for citizens' sudden incapacity. So whereas knowing had been a way of expressing one's freedom, in the late nineteenth century it became the condition around which individual subjects came to recognize their links to—and dependence on—the nation-state. Both Watt and McKeon define realist epistemologies that are essentially synchronic. For Watt "the novel is surely distinguished from other genres and from previous forms of fiction by the amount of attention it habitually accords both to the individualisation of its characters [he cites in particular the novel's adoption of nontypological proper names for its characters] and to the detailed presentation of their environment" (17–18). For McKeon, the novel distinguishes itself from earlier forms both by the overt claims to authority articulated by authors in their prefatory material and by the *sorts* of objects they present as evidence: the genre's development is characterized by "the stealthy substitution of physical for intellectual and spiritual proofs as the overarching standard for what might . . . be embraced as truth inviolate" (73).

I contend, by contrast, that the knowing around which the novel is organized is not a knowing that occurs at an instant, and that what is being known likewise extends over time: the relation among events, the persistence or nonpersistence of the material world over time. By this account, knowing is a process with its own causality, and the distinction between knowing and doing, between epistemology and ontology, becomes less and less sustainable. Foucauldian discourse's idealizing insistence on its own placelessness produces a model of culture so pervasive that it comes to assume the quality of a thing itself, an ontology so present at any given moment that it can neither be apprehended over time nor be understood as a framing mode of apprehension, whereas McKeon and Watt offer a definition of a liberal novelistic subject that is statically epistemological. Departing from both these positions, I assert that the culture of liberalism—and the economy of the realist novel that is a constitutive form of such a culture—is primarily *probabilistic,* where the process of knowing the world through time and only incompletely becomes the condition within which individual subjects act and imagine their relations to one another.[29]

---

29. Having just offered an extended account of this book's relation to a history of writing about the novel, I feel compelled at the very least to note what is not here: a similarly detailed reading of my relation to the emerging field of Jewish cultural studies. While I have drawn inspiration from a good deal of the recent work in the field—Michael Ragussis's *Figures of Conversion* and Jonathan Boyarin's *Storm from Paradise* have been especially helpful to my thinking—and while I hope *A Probable State* will be read as a contribution to this burgeoning area of scholarship, precisely what makes this field especially

Those who have remarked on the link between a liberal model of subjectivity and a probabilistic epistemology, most notably Marxian thinkers like Sheldon Wolin and Fredric Jameson, have generally understood the association as a mark of liberalism's quietism. For Wolin, Lockean liberalism's erasure of a formal realm of politics has brought with it a lamentable denigration of philosophy:

> The cramped quarters assigned philosophy by liberals was but the specific application of a general estimate about the human condition which had first been described by Locke and then accepted into the main stream of later liberalism. Where Plato had set as the target of human aspiration "the completest possible assimilation to God" and Aristotle had exhorted men "to put off mortality as far as possible" Locke had confined man to a middling sort of condition, incapable of omniscience or perfection, "a state of mediocrity, which is not capable of extremes. . . . " The philosophy best suited to man's limited possibilities was one which concentrated on "the twilight of probability" between "skeptical despair" and proud presumption. (Lord King, *The Life of John Locke, with Extracts from His Correspondence, Journals and Common Place Books.* 2 vols. 2nd Edition [London, 1830].) This subdued and sober temper had a decisive influence on the way that Locke and his followers viewed the problems of political theory and practice. (296–97)

By this account, Locke's turn to a philosophy of probability, evinced most explicitly in the *Essay concerning Human Understanding,* is part and parcel of his tendency to collapse the political and the social. This conflation, in Wolin's view, produces a conservative politics that constrains itself to what already is, finding its epistemological counterpart in a probabilism within which knowledge is limited to an always imperfect process of predicting the future behavior of empirically present data.

In Wolin's reading of liberalism, a deeply pessimistic politics of diminished expectations cannot think its way outside an unambitious probabilism. "The effect of turning philosophy outwards was to accept existing society as a datum, susceptible to minor modifications but always within the frame of reference supplied by the *status quo,*" he explains. "This, in turn, implied a form of political knowledge in which precision and certainty were neither neces-

---

exciting to work in—its relative newness and its multidisciplinarity—also renders it recalcitrant to descriptive consolidation and to the kind of self-positioning I am attempting here. I plan to think more about the nuances of the discursive logic of "Jewish cultural studies" in the near future, but for the purposes of this introduction such details send me far afield. Also, because my chapter on the emergence of the Hebrew novel and an early Hebrew vernacular culture draws on a history of Israeli literary criticism that is related to, but in no way identical with, the predominantly Anglo-American field of "Jewish cultural studies," I think both my debts and my departures are best acknowledged at the local level of the footnote.

sary nor desirable" (298).[30] For Wolin, the ascendancy of probability over philosophy that accompanies the growing hegemony of liberalism means essentially one thing: that the option of thinking and acting outside the constraints of existing material and categorical frameworks—the option of thinking politically—has been abandoned. Such a reading presumes that probability has always had one meaning and that, insofar as that meaning can be characterized as a certain deference to the "reality" of empirical evidence, it likewise presumes that empiricism has always meant one thing. In contrast, I understand the concept of "probability" to describe not only a mode of knowledge—a bow toward empiricism—but a set of attitudes regarding the possibility and conditions of knowledge. In my chapter on Henry James, "What Maisie Promised: Realism, Liberalism, and the Ends of Contract," I examine the contract—the central rhetorical figure of Locke's story of liberal state formation—as a probabilistic narrative, reading the history of Anglo-American commercial contractual obligation not simply as one manifestation of a more general history of probability but as a set of reflections on the content and the efficacy of probabilistic knowledge. Within this framework, to characterize the discourse of probability as a conservative epistemology of despair, as throwing up one's hands to what is, is to fail to recognize the way probability acts as a self-conscious reflection on the empirical and even, in its most "optimistic" moments, as an attempt to exceed the limits of the world by knowing them.

Indeed, as I demonstrate in detail in the chapter, we can understand contract to be structured around what we might call, taking a cue from Wolin, a tension between the "optimistic" and "pessimistic" aspects of Lockean liberalism. Insofar as contract figures a subject who is sufficiently able to predict both the future and his or her capacity to act in a certain way at that future time, probability can be seen to work in its optimistic mode, as an assertion of the power of probabilistic knowledge to help bring about a certain out-

30. For Wolin the intellectual historian, the mere fact that one can discern resemblances between John Stuart Mill's notion of a government that concerns itself with providing "the greatest happiness for the greatest number" and Locke's majoritarianism offers adequate proof that Locke finds his logical—hence inevitable—fulfillment in Mill or, alternatively, in Bentham. Neither a whole host of countervailing differences between the two sets of thinkers nor the intervening fact of a historical contingency—an economic structure different from the one that emerged in England over the course of the nineteenth century, for example, or in Arendt's understanding of liberal history, a different interaction of French and American revolutionary forms—that might have produced a variety of readings of Locke and hence a variety of "Lockean traditions" is sufficient to convince Wolin that the utilitarian end of liberalism is anything other than necessary. With its peculiar messianism, Wolin's intellectual history replaces the shifts and transformations, the sudden and unexpected irrelevance, of the overlapping sets of ideas called liberalism with an implicitly horizontal, synchronic description of emergent, present, and residual elements conceptually available at any given moment.

come *despite* its partiality, its necessary incompleteness. In the existence of the juridical insistence on contractual *obligation,* on the other hand, we discover the pessimistic underside of probability, the necessity of legal enforcement bespeaking a knowledge and agency limited by and beholden to the material world. Moreover, the relation between these two "readings" of probability structured into the notion of contractual obligation does not itself remain stable over time. Whereas from the mid-eighteenth century through the first half of the nineteenth Anglo-American judges understood obligation to have occurred in the act of promising, thus invoking an "optimistic" reading of probability, by the last quarter of the nineteenth century obligation came to be understood more "pessimistically" (and, it should be noted, more historically), with the actual effects of the partial performance or nonperformance of the contract serving as the evidence of obligation. So while I asserted earlier that Foucauldian discourse analysis reveals its liberal underpinnings when, in insisting on its unlocatability, it erases its links to and reliance on already existing institutions of national culture, here I submit that it is the presence of the national within both liberalism and Foucauldian historicism as a political, contingent, changing, and changeable set of institutions and cultural relations that marks the historicism of both liberalism and the notion of discourse. The liberal subject is neither wholly ontological nor wholly epistemological; rather, it constitutes a condition in which the process of analysis, of knowing, can (within unavoidable, if always changing, limits) be experienced as making the contingency and historicity of one's culture evident.

Once probability has been reconceived in this way—not as a simple or straightforward submission to the exigencies of a material world but as a self-conscious effort to figure knowledge (and consequently agency) as a shifting and transformable relation to those exigencies—"philosophy," in Wolin's sense of the term, also loses its analytical privilege. Viewed within the frame of the conception of probability made manifest in the history of contractual obligation, "the empirical world" no longer appears as an inert datum to be escaped by means of philosophical thought but becomes an object indistinguishable from the modes within which it is known. Just as Locke's doubly valenced rhetoric of landed property produced the appearance of neutral geographical space and historical causality within what was in fact a highly specific organization of social, economic, and political authority, the empirical world that comes to be known within the context of a discourse of probability is a "world" understood as the organization of different kinds of epistemological authority. In this world not philosophy but fiction—specifically the fictionality of the realist novel—stands as the powerfully illuminating and potentially transformative mode of knowledge.

By inviting its readers at once to trace the apparently contingent turns of plot, to evaluate the plausibility of such contingent movements in relation to some always complex web of historical event and narrative convention, and finally to recognize that what they are reading is fictional and hence the product of a wholly controlling authorial will, the realist novel suspends the contradiction between a subject limited by the material world and the buffetings of historical contingency and the ideal liberal subject whose mere willing is presumed sufficient to bring about a desired end.[31] To the extent that readers can be said to choose to understand the novel as *either* fictional *or* plausible and hence (narratively) contingent, the formal quality of the novel seems ultimately to require them to come down on the side of fictionality: a reader is more likely to put a novel down to go get a glass of water than to call the police to report a kidnapping she has just read about. In that this sense of fictionality is paramount, the experience of the ideal liberal subject's efficacy—manifested here as the author's authority to make meaningful fictions—might be understood to prevail; at the same time, what makes the realist novel powerfully, rather than trivially, compensatory is that readers do not experience the novel as forcing a choice at all. After all, if a triumph of the liberal will is made manifest in the capacity of the liberal subject to make up stories, such agency can hardly bring much comfort to readers who no doubt experience manifold limitations on their will each day. It is precisely because the fictionality of the novel makes itself known in the form of the author's control over specific events in some way resembling events in the actual world that the experience of agency produced by the realist novel is worth having. This resemblance between the probabilistic, materially double quality of realist fictionality and a Lockean "America" that functions rhetorically on two levels of abstraction at once suggests that realist representation implicitly turns on the category of the international, however buried such a logic might be. That is, insofar as the realist novel characterizes the boundaries of the realist world as meaningful by virtue of its fictionality, in the peculiar cases where such fictional authority becomes discernible as limited, as historically contingent, then the meaningfulness of the world represented by the novel itself comes to be understood as limited as well. Within this condition of limitation, such novels are experienced as meaningful only in relation to the discontinuous sites of authorities organizing what lies beyond them, either other novelistic "worlds" or the various "historical contexts"

31. Robert Newsom terms this generic doubleness by which a given realist representation is experienced as "true" (that is, plausible) and "not-true" (that is, fictional) "the antimony of fictional plausibility." See Newsom, *A Likely Story: Probability and Play in Fiction* (New Brunswick, N.J.: Rutgers University Press, 1988), esp. chap. 6.

that might be mobilized to account for the meaning of these novels. Of course such a sense of limitation normally remains merely implicit within the fictional logic of realism. What is noteworthy about the particular late nineteenth-century novels I examine here is how far they represent and articulate this limited, constrained "internationalist" fictionality that is normally buried within the logical economy of realism. The space of these novels is experienced by their characters or readers as worldly and complete only tenuously or in passing; the linguistic seamlessness or spatial autonomy signaled by these texts is repeatedly disrupted so as to render the fictional authority that underwrites them limited and contingent.

Because European Jews possessed at the same time the qualities associated with nationhood and the qualities of liberal subjects—they are identified as a group sharing a common culture yet are without a common geographical space, institutions of state, or a common spoken language and thus appear like liberal subjects—they are featured especially prominently in these troubled late-century novels. Indeed, as novels such as *Middlemarch, Oliver Twist, Our Mutual Friend, Vanity Fair, The Golden Bowl,* and Trollope's many novels featuring Jewish usurers attest, Jews often act within Victorian fiction as a kind of principle of accident around which the relatively predictable unfolding of plot events is suddenly made strange and unpredictable.

I begin by reading George Eliot's *Daniel Deronda* as a novel that self-consciously announces itself as the point where the history of English realism comes to an end. The fictional authority of the novel draws the "English" and "Jewish" plots of the novel together only tenuously, presenting the dual narratives less as simultaneously operating elements of a single "imagined community" than as separate cultures jockeying for dominance *across* narrative time. Eliot's narrative authority in *Daniel Deronda* needs to be read, I propose, not simply as a revision of the theory of fiction she offers in her early essay "The Natural History of German Life" but also in relation to the fictionality of Eliot's own pseudonymic authority and the battle over the nature of the links connecting (religious) belief, state institutions, and history waged between John Locke and Jewish Enlightenment thinker Moses Mendelssohn in their debate on religious toleration. Understood within these contexts, the two plots' insistence on being experienced serially rather than simultaneously becomes less the mark of compositional failure or of Eliot's ambivalence regarding the assimilability of Jews into British culture than an attempt to create a new conception of fictionality. This model of fictionality, relentlessly diachronic, turns the novel from an object into an event, an occasion of imagination during which *Daniel Deronda* narrates the process of its own obsolescence.

If *Daniel Deronda* establishes itself as the limit case of realist fictionality, as Eliot's exposure of the diachronicity of novelistic authority and liberal culture effectively allows the imagining that occurs as a consequence of an individual's reading of the novel to supplant the imagining that constitutes the reading process itself, then Henry James's *What Maisie Knew* and the emergent genre of the Hebrew novel exemplified by S. Y. Abramovitch's *The Travels of Benjamin the Third* can be read as two alternative responses to the impasse that is *Daniel Deronda*. In my chapter on *What Maisie Knew*, I link the novel's examination of the limits of a little girl's individual agency and knowledge both to the history of probability and to a late nineteenth-century shift in the Anglo-American notion of commercial contractual obligation that relocated obligation from the act of promising to the historical effects of a promise made. The novel introduces the pointedly *synchronic* category of race, I believe, in order to pry the fictional authority of the narration from the various social relations of power represented *within* the narrative (most particularly, the manipulations engineered against the child Maisie by the many adults in her life) as well as to make conceivable a relation between literary text and historical "context" that is similarly irregular and unpredictable. Abramovitch's novel presents a version of fictionality in which not only are characters and the geographical spaces they inhabit equally mobile and transient, but neither the represented world nor the language in which the representation takes place preexists the other; instead, they come into being at a single moment. Scavenging the classic texts of Jewish religious life for the words to make his fictional characters speak, Abramovitch powerfully transforms Jews' national relation to the texts they read, and in so doing he both points out and moves beyond the implicit nationalism of most versions of historical context. In this act of textual transfiguration, which not only enables made-up characters to speak Hebrew but eventually leads to its full revival as a language spoken by actual Jews and non-Jews, fictionality is neither simply a mode of representation nor an instance of vaguely utopian political imagining. Rather, Abramovitch's Hebrew fiction making becomes the pointedly cautious initiating act of a new politics of history.

This book, then, insists on the meaningfulness of an odd, international simultaneity even as it exposes the concept's status as a convention. In part I am arguing that there exists something like a *Western* crisis of political subjectivity—a crisis that manifests itself variously in the history of contract, in the novel, and in the abandonment of the Jewish Enlightenment. But the awkwardness of the simultaneity I propose also reveals a crisis within the very assumptions underwriting traditional simultaneity, a strain in the fabric of social homogeneity that makes time itself seem both narrow and infinite.

WRITING A PLACE FOR HISTORY

Daniel Deronda and the Fictions of Belief

Coal, like the English language, like freedom,
general intelligence, or piety, is protestant.
HOLLIS READ, THE HAND OF GOD IN HISTORY, 1849[1]

IN 1856 MARIAN EVANS, a translator and essayist of minor renown, took it upon herself to offer the world a theory of fiction. A year later "George Eliot" published her first work of fiction, a novella called "The Sad Fortunes of the Rev. Amos Barton." Its author insisted that the piece be presented in *Blackwood's* as the first installment of a series titled "Scenes of Clerical Life," even though in January 1857, when "Amos Barton" first appeared, the existence of the subsequent installments was little more than theoretical. If we can only speculate on how the theory might have provided its author the credit, both psychological and editorial, to believe in her fiction-making ability before she had *written* a fiction, we take a stand on firmer ground to note that the theory, "The Natural History of German Life," bears the marks of its anteriority to practice. Marian Evans need not have written any fiction herself to set rules for how it might be done because, according to "Natural History," the best model for writing fiction is not to be found in existing works of fiction. The

---

1. Quoted in Richard W. Bailey, *Nineteenth Century English* (Ann Arbor: University of Michigan Press, 1996), 7.

essay, first published in the *Westminster Review,* takes English pastoral writers and painters to task for the romantic excesses of their representation of "true peasantry" and calls for a fictional realism that adopts the methods of "direct observation" found in the sociological writings of German natural historian W. H. Riehl. "The Natural History of German Life" is striking in its bold assertions that rules might be made and that the truth value, and consequently the ethical and political force, of a writer or artist's realist fictions might be linked to their representational fidelity to the known.

Although this optimism regarding the efficacy of rules might be seen as at once a cause and a symptom of the autonomy of Eliot's fictional theory and practice, I believe the optimism of "Natural History" is both more subtle in its operation and more far-reaching in its claims than is implied in this account of the essay as a codification of fictional technique. Framed as a review of and general introduction to Riehl's work, Eliot's "Natural History" traces the ways private experience—from affective and family relations to the perception of other forms of phenomenal or material reality—becomes "common." But while the general contours of Eliot's subject matter clearly conform to the parameters of an emerging "science of society," her decision to link the question of the common to issues of aesthetic representation not only helps determine the specific role of theory in relation to the practice of imagining but also leads her to develop a notion of the common, a category of culture that departs markedly from earlier models. Eliot opens her essay with what appears to be a theory of language and in doing so places herself within a tradition whose members include John Locke and Adam Smith, writers best known for theories of private property, for whom the relations of proper and common embedded in the structures of grammar were understood to be a necessary supplement to a socius overtly structured around property. But though Eliot begins "Natural History" by locating it within this linguistic tradition, as the essay unfolds it distances itself from this discourse, finally transmuting into a theory of fiction by which the novel's claim to be about something other than the language out of which it is constructed, to represent a world of behaviors not reducible to "common meaning," becomes the basis of the genre's power to create commonness. And if Eliot seems from the outset to intuit the significance of this autonomy of the fictive imagination by producing a theory of fiction before she actually writes a novel, this same excessiveness of the imagined novel to its theory will paradoxically operate in her final novel, *Daniel Deronda,* to produce a model of the common that supplants the very theory that predicted it.

I begin this chapter by briefly examining the theories of language developed by Locke and Smith, theories of language designed to resolve, or at least to circumvent, the tension between private property right and the common social consensus that both writers considered in some way necessary to guarantee this right of private possession. "The Natural History of German Life" implicitly offers a critique of these linguistic models of commonness and presents its own model of culture generated out of the workings of the artist's imaginative authority, a model I will explore in relation to the controversies surrounding Eliot's own complex, pseudonymic authority. Given Eliot's established interest in the link between linguistic commonness and the distribution of private property, *Daniel Deronda*'s dilation and worrying of the question of inheritance seems entirely predictable. But if Daniel's search for his father locates him squarely within a tradition of "orphan and revealed identity" plots as old as the novel itself, that the search for his father leads him to his mother implies a fundamental transformation. In place of the query "Who is the father?" (that is, "From whom shall an individual character receive his property?") we are offered a different question: "What are the rules by which not only property but cultural identity is dispersed or passed from one generation to the next?" *Daniel Deronda* engineers this shift in emphasis on a thematic level, but the fact that it is only through the *process* of searching for his father that Daniel discovers he ought to be searching for his mother means the thematic realignment not only is inextricable from the process of telling the narrative but is indeed a consequence of it. In moving from the question of who is the real father to ask what social conditions allow inheritance to take place, Eliot makes *Daniel Deronda* the occasion of a scrupulous anatomizing of the way the representational logic of the realist novel underwrites the logic of liberal property.

Signifying Something: The Language of Property

The English recoinage debate, which began in earnest in 1695, took up the structure of monetary value amid severe economic crisis. With the outbreak of war against France in 1689, the English government was forced to send large shipments of coins to the Continent to pay its soldiers and fund its Flemish allies, sharply increasing the domestic demand for silver shillings, which were already in short supply. Although the English economy of the period was organized on a silver standard, the mint had been issuing gold guineas for nearly thirty years. But whereas the value of silver coins was fixed by law, the price of the guineas was allowed to fluctuate with the market value of gold bullion. As a consequence of this legal disparity, silver became undervalued; that is, the face value or denomination placed on silver coins was less than the value of the raw silver contained in the coins themselves. This gap in value encouraged English people and foreigners alike to melt down English coins and export the bullion to Europe for sale at the higher price. Then the gold could be imported back into England for buying up more cheap silver coins. This disparity between nominal and actual value also encouraged people to clip off the edges of these hammered coins and melt down the clippings, exacerbating the disparity between the two indexes of value.[2]

In an effort to extricate his country from this fiscal crisis, Treasury Secretary William Lowndes prepared a report for the King's Privy Council in which he offered the then startling claim that the exchange value of silver coins does not depend on their silver content but is instead produced as a convention by the process of exchange itself. In a forceful rejoinder to Lowndes, John Locke rejected the idea that the value of silver coins might simply be conventional, insisting instead that they have an absolute value or meaning derived from the "universal esteem" in which silver is held. In positing the existence of a universal esteem for silver, Locke attempted to do for money what his *Second Treatise of Government* had already done for property: create a natural value that by virtue of its naturalness would remain forever beyond the reach of political maneuvering. But while Locke's efforts to naturalize the value of silver followed the same basic logic as his argument for the natural right to private possession, the two naturalizations can quickly be seen to conflict. So long as the value of silver coins exists universally—exists independently of who owns those coins—Locke is hard pressed to explain how the question of private property (who owns what) can be made to signify. In Locke's account, then, the possibility of common value, of agreeing on a common meaning, appears to stand in irremediable conflict with the goal of distributing private property differentially among individual citizens.

This tension between the proper and the common articulated by Locke in particularly compact form—as a theory of signification of money itself—reappears a century later in the work of Adam Smith as a full-blown theory of language. In his essay "Considerations concerning the First Formation of Languages," Smith lays out a narrative of the process by which the private language of primitive individuals becomes common. By establishing an autonomous theory of language rather than simply enfolding language into a

2. For a good summary of the crisis, see Joyce Appleby, "Locke, Liberalism and the Natural Law of Money," in *Liberalism and Republicanism in the Historical Imagination* (Cambridge: Harvard University Press, 1996), 61.

more general theory of signification as Locke had done, Smith does an end run around the Lockean impasse. Since the entity to which he shifts his attention—language—can be said not to exist until it is possessed in common, Smith's insistence on language as the organizing principle of social commonness operates by dematerializing what becomes proper.

In Smith's narrative, particular material objects become possessed in—and as—common by being given a single name:

> Those objects only which were most familiar to them, and which they had most frequent occasion to mention, would have particular names assigned to them. The particular cave whose covering sheltered them from the weather, the particular tree whose fruit relieved their hunger, the particular fountain whose water allayed their thirst, would first be denominated by the words *cave, tree, fountain,* or by whatever other appellations they might think proper, in that primitive jargon, to mark them. Afterwards, when the more enlarged experience of these savages had led them to observe and their necessary occasions obliged them to make mention of other caves and other trees, and other fountains, they would naturally bestow, upon each of those new objects, the same name by which they had been accustomed to express the similar object they were first acquainted with. The *new objects* had *none of them any* name of *its* own, but *each of them* exactly resembled another object, which had such an appellation.[3]

In Smith's story of the origins of language, the movement into (common) language is represented as the shedding of proper nouns; commonness is achieved as *individuality*—the wanderer's wholly private system of names (including, implicitly, his or her own)—is transmuted into the generalized *particularity* of common nouns. Insofar as he eliminates proper names entirely from the world he describes, Smith envisions a common culture created out of the absolute distinction of subjects and objects.

But Smith's account does not so much substitute cultural capital for material capital as the defining stuff of possession as it seeks to hide the way proper and common are established as a direct result of the intervention of some sort of undefined authority. While the story of origin promises to authorize common language as a solution to the problem of social isolation caused by individual experience and private possession by revealing how such a substi-

---

3. Adam Smith, "Considerations concerning the First Formation of Languages and the Different Genius of Original and Compounded Languages," in *Lectures on Rhetoric and Belles Lettres* (Oxford: Oxford University Press, 1983), 203, second set of emphases mine).

tution of language for things takes place, in fact the narrative works only by means of its failure to narrate:

> It was impossible that those savages could behold the new objects, without recollecting the old ones; and the name of the old ones, to which the new bore so close a resemblance. When they had occasion, therefore, to mention, or to point out to each other, any of the new objects, they would naturally utter the name of the correspondent old one, of which the idea could not fail, at that instant, to present itself to their memory in the strongest and liveliest manner. And thus, those words, which were originally the proper names of individuals, would each of them insensibly become the common name of a multitude. (204)

As Smith narrates the process of substitution and resolution, the narration becomes the solution as the grammar of the passage transmutes the beholdings of individual savages into the collectivity that is "their" memory, the argument over possession waged by the syntactic fiat of the genitive. Language becomes common, ceasing to be the accumulation of the particular names an individual bestows on the objects encountered in random wanderings around the countryside, only by passing through a moment of "insensibility," a mysterious and seemingly unnarratable process following which language becomes at once immaterial and common. This moment of "insensibility" evacuates the commonness of any identifiable content by submerging the complex negotiations waged by competing and differently empowered experiencing subjects in a rush of mystically indescribable unity. Common language in this history is not the ground of political authority, or even the medium within which it might be established, but instead is the condition of politics' elimination.

And lest we be tempted to conclude that the anxiety about the reconcilability of common culture and private property that generates Smith's "First Formation of Languages" is merely a symptom of the new proliferation of private ownership in the eighteenth century, we ought to note that this anxiety persists, in somewhat altered form, well into heyday of industrialized England in the work of Eliot's contemporary John Stuart Mill. Whereas Smith's essay worried that a commitment to private property and experience might inhibit the formation of common culture, for the Mill of "On Liberty" (1859) the existence of a common, what he terms "public opinion," poses a real and substantial threat to the preservation of private ownership:

> There is confessedly a strong tendency in the modern world towards a democratic constitution of society, accompanied or not by popular political institutions. It is

affirmed in the country where this tendency is most completely realized . . .—the United States—the feeling of the majority, to whom any appearances of a more showy or costly style of living than they can hope to rival is disagreeable, operates as a tolerably effectual sumptuary law, and that in many parts of the Union it is really difficult for a person possessing a very large income, to find any mode of spending it, which will not incur popular disapprobation. . . . It is known that the bad workmen who form the majority of the operatives in many branches of industry are decidedly of the opinion that bad workmen ought to receive the same wages as good, and that no one ought to be allowed, through piecework or otherwise, to earn by superior skill or industry what others can earn without it.[4]

For Mill, the mere fact of the existence of common value moves from exerting a constraining ideological force on those who would exhibit their wealth to impelling the redistribution of property itself.

Evans does not expressly repudiate language as a model or ground for establishing commonness; instead, she redescribes language in such a way that its rhetorical and analytical force is remade as well. Whereas Smith introduced the category of language in the context of a narrative of origin, and thus configured language as a construct whose constitutive qualities are contained within the logic of the narrative's unfolding, in Evans's redescription language is not so much an immaterial representation overlaying existing relations of property as a thing-in-use, fragmented internally into relations of proper and common. For Evans, the analytical insufficiency of the language paradigm follows directly from this redescription. She invokes this discourse of language in order to cast a critical glance at its logic. It is a mistake to adopt language as a paradigm for common culture because to do so presumes that an individual's behavior counts as participation in a common culture as long as he or she *means* the same thing as others mean when they behave in the same way. Those thinkers who subscribe to a linguistic model of culture effectively turn all activities of common culture into an elaborate symbolic system, by which such activities are discernible as culture only so far as they mean something beyond themselves, so far as they are signs of some generally agreed-on meaning.

By including an account of the operation of common language within a narrative more immediately concerned with the ways individual artists represent the material world, Evans forces a distinction between language and other forms of culture and lays the groundwork for a different conception of culture, one that distinguishes between a given behavior and the meanings

4. John Stuart Mill, *On Liberty*, in *"On Liberty" and Other Essays* (Oxford: Oxford University Press, 1991), 97.

that might be attributed to it. As we shall see, such a distinction complicates the way a category of common culture is understood to mediate between individual subjects' relations to the material world and the institutional or political authority arrayed to justify and enforce particular relations of the social and the material. Moreover, in constructing its argument around the fundamental discrimination between what people do and what is to be made of the fact that they do it, "The Natural History of German Life" apportions a particularly significant role to that discrimination. If, as "Natural History" presents it, the category of culture is able to reconcile the "common" and the "proper" because it articulates, rather than presumes, the connection between how people act and what their actions mean, then the novel, which makes such a distinction its representational principle under the banner of "style," stands to play a crucial role in creating common culture.

The intrusion of an analysis of language into the essay's account of fictional representation is both cautionary and dilatory, at once urging its readers' hesitancy and necessitating it:

> It is an interesting branch of psychological observation to note the images that are habitually associated with abstract or collective terms—what may be called the picture-writing of the mind, which it carries on concurrently with the more subtle symbolism of language. Perhaps the fixity or variety of these associated images would furnish a tolerably fair test of the amount of concrete knowledge and experience which a given word represents, in the minds of two persons who use it with equal familiarity.[5]

Although the passage ends with a standard empiricist elevation of experience over airy abstraction—the essay goes on to excoriate the "man of wide views and narrow observation" (189)—this conventional affirmation is troubled by the incapacity of language to guarantee what it promises, to deliver some reliable common meaning. The artistic imagination that is the essay's putative subject—"the picture-writing of the mind"—exists alongside but is not reducible to "the more subtle symbolism of language." Not only does the delineation of this distinction between language and imagination signal the dangers of assuming that a theory of language might be made to function more broadly as an account of various other aspects of cultural production, but it

5. George Eliot [Marian Evans], "The Natural History of German Life: Riehl," in *Complete Works of George Eliot*, vol. 6 (London: Blackwood, 1883), 188. Page numbers of subsequent citations will be included parenthetically within the text. The most interesting critical account of the essay I have read is Suzanne Graver's, in *George Eliot and Community* (Berkeley: University of California Press, 1984), esp. chap. 2. Graver's book reads the essay as a mediation between two models of social cohesion theorized in contemporary German accounts of community.

also radically undermines the claims of language use itself. Language—its abstract or collective terms, in any case—not only is not necessarily compatible with the operations of imagination but cannot even be trusted to guarantee that the people who use it share a certain state of mind, that they mean the same things when they use it.

But while it is abstract or collective nouns that reveal the nonintersection of language and imagination, Evans is not simply, or even primarily, interested in pointing up the epistemological unreliability of abstraction. In keeping with her interest in language as it is used, she constructs her analysis not around the general idea of abstraction, but instead on the history of a particular abstraction, one that goes by various names: "'the people,' 'the masses,' 'the proletariat,' 'the peasantry.'" Moreover, "Natural History" characterizes the peasantry that is its object of interest in terms of the peasants' peculiar geographical fixity, an immobility suggesting that Evans's argument turns on the plausible substitution of the social unit of "the people" for the landed property whose scarcity poses a threat to the establishment of common authority.

But even as Evans seems to be engineering such a substitution, her elaboration of the specific role of the artist in making the dematerialized object "the peasantry" present and comprehensible to others effectively undermines the opposition between the immateriality of peasant sociability and the inert object world that can function as the grounds of the common only insofar as it remains unpossessed. The peasants occupy a kind of ontological middle ground, somewhere between sociable subjects and wholly inert material objects, a liminality testified to by their names, neither fully proper nor fully common: "The cultured man acts more as an individual; the peasant, more as one of a group. Hans drives the plough, lives, and thinks just as Kunz does; and it is this fact, that many thousands of men are as like each other in thoughts and habits as so many sheep or oysters, which constitutes the weight of the peasantry in the social and political scale" (199). The linguistic inbetweenness of the peasants' characteristic corporatism is made even more evident a few pages later, where their proper names teeter on the verge of becoming common:

It would be possible to give a sort of topographical statistics of proper names, and distinguish a district by its rustic names as we do by its Flora and Fauna. The continuous inheritance of certain favorite proper names in a family, in some districts, forces the peasant to adopt the princely custom of attaching a numeral to the name, and saying, when three generations are living at once, Hans I, II, and III. (201)

Smith's narrative of language formation, we recall, claimed to provide an account of the way proper names become common, but he was able to do so only by mystifying the movement as a moment of "insensibility." In turning her analysis to the hybrid objects Hans I, II, and III, neither entirely proper or common, Evans recovers the moment of transformation from the analytical mists of the insensible in the objective correlative of the peasants. But as the essay's cordoning off of the role of language within the larger argument about the aesthetic might lead us to anticipate, the peasants' hybrid quality is crucial to its theorizing of an alternative to a linguistic model of cultural commonness.[6]

As Evans presents them, the peasants' hybridity is itself twofold: not only are they stuck somewhere between the proper and the common, not quite individual subjects, but in an intersecting but not identical framework they are somewhere between subject and object. That these two analytical frameworks—proper/common, subject/object—are even distinguishable in itself indicates a departure from the discourse of language formation within which we have been reading "Natural History." Indeed, the very ideological force of the language formation discourse lay in its capacity to make the two frameworks look identical: in Smith, the moment when objects become nameable by common nouns was the moment when all subjects were understood to be common in relation to one another, to participate in a common culture by virtue of meaning the same things, *having the same thing in mind,* when they used a word. In this way the mere existence of common nouns was sufficient evidence of the achievement of a broad cultural consensus. By distinguishing between the two *sets* of oppositions even as she challenges the oppositional status of each, Evans takes issue with a foundational presumption of linguistic theories of culture like Smith's, the presumption that the common experience of the material world forms the basis of a common culture.

For in the vision offered by the multiply fractured, complexly liminal figure of the peasant, the experience of a common world cannot provide the ground for a shared culture precisely because what is common cannot be experienced, cannot be the stuff of subjectivity. "Custom with [the peasant]," Evans writes, "holds the place of sentiment, of theory, and in many cases of affection" (205). It is the overwhelming influence of custom, she explains elsewhere, that accounts for the peasants' virtual sameness ("Hans drives the

---

6. Thomas Hardy gestures toward a similar hybridization of the proper and the common in contrasting the nomadic worker with the "serf, who lived and died on a particular plot, like a tree." Thomas Hardy, "The Dorsetshire Laborer," in *The Selected Writings of Thomas Hardy: Stories, Poems and Essays,* ed. Irving Howe (Greenwich, Conn.: Fawcett World, 1966), 130.

plough, lives and thinks just as Kunz does"), nearly turning nouns we would expect to be proper into common ones. Even more significant, in "hold[ing] the place of sentiment, of theory, and . . . of affection," the sameness of the peasants renders them incapable of functioning as subjects. So whereas we were initially led to suppose Evans's choice of the peasantry, rather than possessable material objects, as the foundational objects of a common culture was motivated by a desire to lessen the distance between subject and object, as "Natural History" unfolds it becomes clear that the rhetorical function of the peasants is to make subjects and objects absolutely distinct. Evans's focus on an "object" that is abstract and social rather than material—that is, the peasantry—absolutely differentiates subject and object. But insofar as the condition of sameness in itself is sufficient to reclassify sentient human beings as objects rather than subjects, within the terms of the essay "sameness" becomes a condition unavailable to subjects, unexperienceable by subjects qua subjects.

So although the essay's departure from the conventions of the discourse of language formation starts out as an emphasis on likeness, it ends not only by emphasizing the difference between subjects and objects but by hypostatizing it. "Appeals founded on generalisations and statistics require a sympathy ready made" (193). Because the objects in question—the peasants—resemble subjects so closely, the difference between the observing subjects and the peasants must be established as absolute rather than contingent, following from qualities inhering in the subject and object themselves instead of a potentially shiftable condition of the link between them. "Sameness" must, in other words, be transmuted into a positive content, no longer a relation between categories but a definition of the category itself. And because, within the terms of the essay, to be constrained within a category is to cease to be a subject, sameness must become the definition of the category of objects. To be an object is to be categorical, and to be a subject is to be unable to experience sameness.

Lest this figuration of the peasants' absolute, foundational sameness be taken as mere rhetorical sleight of hand, Evans offers a narrative of how this constitutive sameness came into being:

> Peasants may still be distinguished into groups by their physical peculiarities. In one part of the country we find a longer-legged, in another a broader-shouldered race, which has inherited these peculiarities for centuries. . . . In the cultivated world each individual has his style of speaking and writing. But among the peasantry it is the race, the district, the province, that has its style—namely, its dialect,

its phraseology, its proverbs, and its songs, which belong alike to the entire body of the people. This provincial style of the peasant is again, like his *physique,* a remnant of history to which he clings with the utmost tenacity. (199)

Here the peasants' likeness to one another is clearly inextricable from their location in a particular geographical space. But Evans seems to be making another point as well: that the peasants' sameness is the outcome of their general condition of locatedness as well as their particular location, of their immobility as well as their locality. Thus the history of their sameness is in part a resistance to history, the condition of absolute sameness expressly what cannot possess a history. At certain moments in Evans's account, the physical likeness that links particular peasants to their regions is literally *caused* by the geographical space in which it occurs: "In both these zones, men are hardened by conflict with the roughness of the climate" (225). At other moments, however, the link identifying peasant and region seems symbolic or analogical, the essay culminating with an irresolution that is as apparently unruffling to Evans as it is frankly remarked: "And the analogy, or rather the causal relation, between the physical geography of the three regions and the development of the population goes still further" (228). It seems that insofar as the peasants' sameness can be understood to be the effect of their inhabiting a certain place—muscles knotted, backs broadened by the unremitting necessity of working a given region's rocky soil, of scaling a particular ridge every day—such sameness would be not an absolute quality of the peasants' status as peasants but the contingent effect of their life in that region. On the other hand, insofar as their sameness is simply analogical, marking the peasants' place in the world without offering any explanation for the relation between the particularity of the region and the particular quality of the mark, it seems an inherent quality of their status as peasants.

But perhaps this double characterization of the peasants' relation to the geographical locale that defines them is not a simple oversight on Evans's part. By her seemingly contradictory claims that peasants are linked to the geographical regions they inhabit both symbolically—by way of analogy— and by being "caused" or made over physically by the topography, Evans establishes the space of the peasants' habitation as the literal grounds of their objectification. While the causal account of the link appears to offer a reading of the peasants' culture as contingent, following from the accident of their having begun to labor in a particular place, the peasants are also *disqualified* as subjects by their immobilizing labors. In other words, at the very same moment that the peasants' role in creating both the customs they live by and even their own appearances—their self-cultivation, as it were—is acknowledged, their ongoing work on the land immobilizes them, turns them into embodiments of the topography and virtual copies of one another, and so prevents them from exerting the control over the broader significance of their behavior that is reserved for subjects. The peasants' likeness to one another is produced by their own labor—labor we might conventionally be tempted to classify as an expression of their subjectivity—yet this likeness is simultaneously evidence of their incapacity as subjects, their inability to determine the values of their culture.

But whereas the essay's earlier contention that peasants were not subjects because they were too like one another looked like a kind of semantic violence, a disempowerment by definition, here the essayist can forswear all responsibility: it is the land itself, or rather the condition of placedness, that turns the peasant from protosubject into object. I noted in my introduction that the Lockean labor theory of value must invoke two meanings of land simultaneously: land is at once a kind of free space, enabling the Lockean liberal subject to function as a wholly efficacious agent whose labors allow him to accrue property and, at the same time, a kind of property itself, whose exclusive possession guarantees the free agency of those subjects who act within it. If, as I argued there, such circularity hid the role of state institutions in making certain that landed property remains possessed of and by its rightful owners, here it becomes clear that the very inarguability of its relations of cause and effect is just what renders it vulnerable to reversal. Once the connection between land and its inhabitants has been transformed from the condition to be justified to the point of departure of the analysis, place becomes the mark of its inhabitants' constraint and objecthood rather than the guarantee of their absolute freedom. Whereas Locke's description of liberal space was designed to make the mere fact of the liberal individual's capacity for labor sufficient evidence for his connection to a given place—that is, to make place a natural quality of the subject rather than an effect of political institutions—that same locatedness can be easily transformed into a reason why the peasant has no choice, naturally, but to act where, and in the way, he does.

This self-evidence of place offers Evans a justification for her fiction-making, a naturalizing ground for her imaginative departures. "Art is the nearest thing to life; it is a mode of amplifying experience and extending our contact with our fellow-men beyond the bounds of our personal lot. All the more sacred is the task of the artist when he undertakes to paint the life of the people." She concludes:

> The greatest benefit we owe to the artist, whether painter, poet or novelist, is the extension of our sympathies. Appeals founded on generalisations and statistics re-

quire a sympathy ready-made, a moral sentiment already in activity; but a picture of human life such as a great artist can give surprises even the trivial and the selfish into that attention to what is apart from themselves, which may be called the raw material of moral sentiment. (192–93)

The artist's role is thus twofold. First, since their immobility and geographical isolation place the peasants outside the daily experience of most English men and women, the artist's representations serve the straightforward practical function of bringing a broader population into contact with them. By effectively converting the peasants into texts, the artist is able to overcome the physical distance that separates them from the bulk of the English populace. But artists serve another purpose as well. Since the peasants' sameness to one another testifies to their status as objects and, despite their ongoing labors, renders them absolutely *unlike* other people, and hence beyond the sympathies of the subjects who would seek to know them, the artist's intervention is required in order to make them comprehensible to that distant audience who reads about them or goes to browse among their painted images in a London gallery. It is the intervention of the artist's *imagination* that transforms "appeals founded on generalisations and statistics" into a "picture of human life." Seemingly ineffable but for its capacity to cause "surprise" in readers and viewers, this "imagination" seems nothing more—though nothing less—than the expression of the irreducible individual artistic subjects.[7]

So as Evans describes it, artistic imagination is perfectly equipped to compensate for the two aspects of the peasants' condition that makes them unknowable: their geographical location and their quality as interchangeable objects. But insofar as "Natural History" represents the peasants' likeness to one another, their objecthood, as a consequence of their immobility—they labor endlessly on the same bit of land until the topography of their region remakes their physiognomies—and represents their immobility as a conse-

---

7. Evans elaborates: "When Scott takes us into Luckie Mucklebackit's cottage, or tells the story of 'The Two Drovers,'—when Wordsworth sings to us the reverie of 'Poor Susan,' when Kingsley shows us Alton Locke gazing yearningly over the gate which leads from the highway into the first wood he ever saw,—when Hornung paints a group of chimney sweepers,—more is done towards linking the higher classes with the lower, towards obliterating the vulgarity of exclusiveness, than by hundreds of sermons and philosophical dissertations" (193).

The placement of the passage in the essay seems designed to define the characteristics of "a picture of human life such as a great artist can give," to fill in the details of the distinction between such pictures and those "appeals founded on generalisations and statistics." That the promise of such a definition quickly gives way to a series of examples further underscores my contention that it is the aesthetic particularity of the various objects, their status as the manifestations of imaginative workings of individual artists rather than any generalizable qualities of the objects, that enables these artworks to "link the higher classes with the lower."

quence of their objecthood, the two forms of power embodied in the aesthetic object collapse into one another. If the placedness of the peasants leaves them so remote from the general population of England that the artist's textualizations are required in order for them to be known, the fact that their location in a given geographical region also renders them virtually interchangeable with one another means that the artistic power of imagination, turning the peasants into specifically *aesthetic* objects and making them available as objects of sympathy, becomes indistinguishable from what we might term the power of *reportage,* the power to turn remote objects and their doings into texts. A text reporting the doings of the peasants to an audience of readers not proximate enough for direct observation becomes the same as a fictional narrative about them.

Because Evans represents such geographical distinction as both cause and effect of the peasants' characteristic objecthood, the identification of the artist's aesthetic and reportorial powers transmutes the nature of those being described as well. When the peasants were figured primarily in terms of their *distance* from the rest of the populace, we recall that their objecthood, or more significantly their exclusion from the status of subject, was unstable. It was sometimes presented as a natural and inherent quality of peasants qua peasants but was just as often seen as the result of an immobility itself caused by their failure to own the land they inhabited. Transformed into images in a landscape or characters in a novel, however, the peasants' objecthood becomes unmistakable and irreversible; they cannot act as subjects, cannot describe, represent, or theorize their own conditions, because they do not exist except for the actions of the author or painter. Aesthetic representation thus turns a relation that is contingent and unstable in the actual world—the relation between the remote, immobilized peasants and the writers who report on them—into a relation of absolute, ontological difference—the relation between the artist-subject and the fictional peasant-objects who inhabit that artist's novels or paintings. But because the aesthetic power that creates these ontologically other, fictional peasant-objects has already been equated with the power to report about peasants from a distance—a power that does not figure subject and object as ontologically different from one another, but only as more or less fixed in their places—the absolute, ontologized difference does not remain within the realm of fictionality but is mapped back onto the living peasants. The aesthetic representation of the peasants thus becomes a way of transforming their immobility and lack of subjectivity from a contingent, potentially negotiable condition of social power into a quality of being.

But as my earlier discussion has outlined, Evans's investment lies not so much in determining the true nature of peasants or the methods by which they might most accurately be represented as in articulating the way fictional representation, the product of an individual artist's imagination, might provide the basis for a common culture. Once subject and object are separated, all action need no longer be understood as above all a kind of meaning-making; the person performing a certain action is no longer presumed to have a privileged relation to the meaning of his or her actions or, more fundamentally, to the definition or articulation of his or her identity. Thus the peasant Hans's driving the plow in his characteristic way brings him into commonness not only with Kunz, whose way of driving the plow is identical, but also with the artist who observes Hans and incorporates his plowing, transmuted by artistic imagination, into a novel and, finally, with the readers who encounter the fictional Hans's plowing from afar in the pages of the novel. By bifurcating the authority to lend value or significance to objects from the material presence or the possession of those objects, "Natural History" eliminates the tension between being or possessing an object and participating in a common set of values. The realist novel, in which, crudely put, the behavior of the objects represented is lent significance by the authority of the artist who imagines those objects into being—in which the significance lies in the very fact that those objects are someone else's imaginative production—thus stands as the ideal cultural form for the production of commonness. Indeed, I am arguing that the genre of the realist novel develops and becomes the preeminent literary form of the eighteenth and nineteenth centuries by virtue of its unique capacity to accomplish this end.

But while, by Evans's account, the novel has the power to resolve the tension between commonness and private property to the extent that it makes reportage and fiction the same thing, it does not accomplish this conflation by mere theoretical fiat. Although "Natural History" grounds the logic of its identification of the two representational modes in the claim that both modes are responses to the peasants' objecthood, such a claim is illuminating less as a description of the way peasants "are" than in what it reveals about the process of *reading* and the social functions of such an activity: not what truths novels tell but how they work to seem true. That is, we ought to see the identification of reportage and fiction not as something that realist novels are justified or unjustified in doing but as an attitude directed toward them. For George Eliot, or at least for the Marian Evans who generates a theory of fictional realism before she has ever written a novel, realist novels "work" insofar as readers agree to read fiction as if it were reportage.

The tension between a common culture and private property suddenly becomes a nonissue because the individual subject is constituted around a condition of consciousness, a state of mind, rather than a relation to the potentially unevenly distributed material world. What the realist readers theorized by "Natural History" share is neither the experience of their encounter with the peasants nor their experience of their encounter with an artist's representation of the peasants. What Evans imagines her reading subjects to have in common is the experience of the fictional, the peculiar suspension by which readers, choosing to believe that the world of the novels they read is autonomous and self-sufficient, experience themselves as detached from the limitations of the world they inhabit. That the link between artist-subject and peasant is bridged by a condition of belief, a way of reading assented to rather than verified, is exactly what makes the inequalities that characterize the original relation between artist and peasant disappear.

The Grounds of Belief

In deriving a theory of fiction from the particular circumstances of the placedness of the English peasantry and the language generated to represent those circumstances, Evans effectively reconceives of culture as a shared *structure* of belief in place of the notion of a shared meaning or *content* of beliefs implicit in the earlier linguistic paradigms of commonness. But if the rhetoric of Evans's argument clearly positions her delineation of belief's conditions of possibility as supplanting language models, the category of belief itself has a history within which the discourses of liberalism and state-formation are relevant to Evans herself as well as to those who would analyze her writing.

John Locke's *Letter concerning Toleration,* notable in its own right as one of the founding statements in support of an absolute separation of religious and political authority, is at least as striking in the way it reframes the more familiar terms within which Locke imagines the constitution of liberal political authority.[8] In *A Letter concerning Toleration* (1689), the authority of the state rests on its power to create what society and history foreclose: that is, a realm of absolute subjective freedom, a state in which conviction is selfhood. The business of civil government, Locke writes, is "by the impartial execution of equal laws, to secure unto all the people in general, and to every one of [the] subjects in particular the just possession of these things belonging to this life."[9] Overtly, Locke's goal here is to trace the boundaries of civil power,

8. For a more detailed account of the publishing history of Locke's entire set of *Letters concerning Toleration,* see Alexander Altmann's commentary (158–61) in Moses Mendelssohn's *Jerusalem, or On Religious Power and Judaism,* trans. Allan Arkush (Hanover, N.H.: University Press of New England for Brandeis University Press, 1983).

9. John Locke, *A Letter concerning Toleration,* ed. James H. Tully (Indianapolis: Hackett, 1983), 47. Further citations will be made in parentheses within the text.

defining the function of the magistrate in order to limit government power and, in so doing, make the case for a realm of religious belief outside the control of the state. The letter establishes its argument for separate spheres by beginning with the premise of an absolute distinction between the temporal and the eternal:

> Every man has an immortal soul, capable of eternal happiness or misery; whose happiness depends upon his believing and doing those things in this life which are necessary to the obtaining of God's favour, and are prescribed by God to that end. It follows from thence, first, that the observance of these things is the highest obligation that lies upon mankind, and that our utmost care, application, and diligence ought to be exercised in the search and performance of them; because there is nothing in this world that is of any consideration in comparison with eternity. . . .
>
> But besides their souls, which are immortal, men have also their temporal lives here upon earth; the state whereof being frail and fleeting, and the duration uncertain, they have need of several outward conveniences to the support thereof, which are to be procured or preserved by pains and industry. For those things that are necessary to the comfortable support of our lives are not the spontaneous products of nature, nor do [they] offer themselves fit and prepared for our use. This part therefore draws on another care, and necessarily gives another employment.

As the essay proceeds, however, what becomes clear is how far government authority is justified as an instrument of compensation, a means of making the political subject more like the religious subject. Whereas the coin-clipping debate revealed the way common culture and private property were in tension with one another, in Locke's theory of government it is this tension that justifies the creation of civil authority.

The government comes into being to adjudicate among individuals' competing property claims, which it does by establishing a point of view independent of any identified by the competing individuals. In the terms of our analysis, the impossibility of squaring commonness with private property generates the need for a third perspective—the government's—in order to choose among competing claims. It is important to note that, in the strict terms of Locke's narrative, the government does not produce a new "common" in the linguistic sense of a new shared meaning or value but operates in the gap created by the impossibility of stably and permanently establishing such value. The government is experienced as an *institution* exerting power to organize individuals' relations to the material world, not so much charged with the task of creating commonness as generated in the interstices of the failure of the common.

Faith is distinguished from willed industry and the property that manifests such industry (and removes it from temporality) by its nonfungibility. The point of view from which a common culture might be established need no longer conflict with any unequal distribution of material evidence that would produce such a point of view, because belief is precisely what cannot be distributed.

> The pravity of mankind being such that they had rather injuriously prey upon the fruits of other men's labours than take pains to provide for themselves, the necessity of preserving men in the possession of what honest industry has already acquired, and also of preserving their liberty and strength, whereby they may acquire what they rather want, obliges men to enter into society with one another, that by mutual assistance and joint force they may secure unto each other their properties, in the things that contribute to the comfort and happiness of this life, leaving in the meanwhile to every man the care of his own eternal happiness, the attainment whereof can neither be facilitated by another man's industry, nor can the loss of it turn to another man's prejudice, nor the hope of it be forced from him by any external violence. (47)

Belief can safely be left outside the realm of government power, in part because such power is unnecessary to keep beliefs attached to their believers. Since it does not require this additional institutional force to shore it up, belief both marks and produces the absolute individuality of its subject. The religious subject's freedom from state control is at once presumed, presented as an inherent value, and argued for; here the rhetorical effect of the passage's sequence is to suggest that the value of faith as a category of expression lies in its resistance to being appropriated by others. But belief stands as the ideal expression of the subject in an even more fundamental way: it does not presuppose the existence of a common culture, a more generally accepted set of social values, for its meaning and significance. Belief is eternal rather than temporal not simply because the object of its attention—God—is itself eternal, but because its meaning exists independently of historically local societies or values.

To grasp the full import of Locke's argument about toleration, we need to consider the role his claim for the autonomy of belief plays within his larger system of economic, political, institutional, and social relations. While Locke's insistence on the analogousness of the realms of belief and property reveals the "pravity," the imperfection, of the temporal realm in all its property-centered sociability, his assertion of the two realms' likeness also is a means of justifying government authority. The role of the civil government thus becomes to exercise its policing, judiciary function so as to approximate in the civil realm the nonappropriability of identity that distinguishes the realm of faith. Civil law works successfully when it prevents one political subject from appropriating the industry—that is to say, the property—of someone else. That politics can never achieve its end (politics and belief, after all, have absolutely different relations to time) becomes in itself proof of that end's necessary validity. That the condition of absolute nonfungibility that is constitutive of belief does not and cannot exist within the temporal realm is expressly what defines its value.

Belief thus turns out to be not simply the goal to which political institutions aspire but the mode of argument by which such aspirations are established. If the impossibility of achieving the state of perfect nonfungibility characteristic of the realm of belief by means of the contingent and temporal authority of government institutions testifies to the value of such an effort, it does so because the very analogousness of the relations of the temporal and eternal realms must itself remain a matter of belief. Analogies are structured as a relation of likeness between two objects—between two identities, we might say—where the specific grounds on which the likeness is being asserted are excised from the expression of the relation.[10] In insisting on this identity of terms without articulating the grounds of the connection between them, the analogy demands that those who would understand it take its assertions on *faith;* Locke's analogy functions not simply as an argument for belief but also as an expression of it. Belief—argument by analogy—becomes the means by which the act of persuasion is made to seem like no act at all, the exertion of power cloaked as the discovery of likeness. If the sense of belief's resemblance to private property is a matter of any believer's faith rather than some person's efforts, then private property's resemblance to belief and also the particular civil institutions and acts necessary to maintain and even intensify this resemblance become not policies to be argued for at a particular moment in history, but self-evident truths, good always and forever.

Viewed against this backdrop, Eliot's concept of fiction generates in its

10. As Celeste Langan explains, following Maurice Merleau-Ponty, the failure to understand analogies correctly stems not from a failure of explication but from an insistence on it: "The disabled patient's difficulty with metaphor—the clinical term is *apraxia*—is not a *rational* incapacity; in fact, the dysfunction requires him to resort to reason, to articulate (rather than intuit) the posited identity *as an analogy.* Merleau-Ponty: 'If we described analogy as the apperception of two given terms under a coordinating concept, we should be giving as normal a procedure which is exclusively pathological, and which represents the roundabout way in which the patient makes good the normal understanding of analogy. This freedom in choosing a *tertium comparationis* on the patient's part is the opposite of the intuitive formation of the image in the normal subject.'" Langan, *Romantic Vagrancy: Wordsworth and the Simulation of Freedom* (Cambridge: Cambridge University Press, 1995), 25–26.

readers something strikingly akin to what we find in Locke, a sort of secularized belief. It is the supposed analogousness of the individual artist's imaginative response to the peasants and a kind of transparent reportage that authorizes those acts of imagination that make this imaginative exertion of the artist necessary in the first place. Not only does this dynamic of fictional belief have the effect of assimilating the audience's point of view to the perspective of the more specialized imaginative artist, but it also subsumes the artist's local acts of imagination within the self-evidence of the aesthetic object. The fiction becomes believable only as it ceases to appear to be created at an identifiable moment; the artist's agency becomes continuous with the belief of the audience as "temporal" acts of imagination are apprehended on the evidence of an "eternal" fictional world.

If "The Natural History of German Life" is premature as an account of the social role to be played by the aesthetic in general, and fictional realism in particular, it is also precocious. Composed before Marian Evans began writing novels and became George Eliot, "Natural History" has little to say about how her understanding of what novels do might direct the thousands of decisions, minute and grand, that constitute writing a work of fiction. Indeed, the essay seems barely aware that novels take time to be made; fictions seem instead to spring fully formed from a singular and instantaneous imaginative burst. By adopting the logic of Locke's economy of belief to structure her understanding of the operation of fiction, Eliot makes the privacy and unverifiability of her poetic imagination the ground of its value. But in that this private experience of *reading* fiction makes the reader's sense of the material world drop away, the resemblance to one another of subjects individually engaged by these fictions not only is unverifiable but is without content as well. In making the disappearance of the material world the ground of common experience, Eliot achieves a commonness only by acknowledging that that sameness will not matter in the world. By the time she publishes her final novel, *Daniel Deronda,* in 1876, such commonness has become a bargain she is ready to renounce.

The Subject of Overhearing

Yes, I expected more aversion than I have found ["to the Jewish element in Deronda"]. But I was happily independent in material things and felt no temptation to accommodate my writing to any standard except that of trying to do my best in what seemed to me most needful to be done, and I sum up with the writer of the Book of Maccabees— "if I have done well, and as befits the

subject, it is what is desired, but if I have done ill, it is what I could attain to." GEORGE ELIOT,
LETTER TO HARRIET BEECHER STOWE, 29 OCTOBER 1876[11]

It was recently stated, within the hearing of the present writer, that the longstanding social preju-
dice against persons of Jewish race, although somewhat modified by the march of civilization, still
exists in many quarters, in spite of numerous evidences to the contrary. Whether this be or be not
the case it is difficult for Jews themselves to determine; but if this purposeless prejudice still linger
in the minds of any of our cultured compatriots, it is certain that nothing that can be done by
Jews towards its removal could possibly be so effective as that which "George Eliot" has done
by the production of "Daniel Deronda." UNSIGNED REVIEW OF *DANIEL DERONDA*, *JEWISH*
CHRONICLE, 8 SEPTEMBER 1876[12]

We are meant to be grateful, George Eliot would have us suppose, that her
final novel was authored by a person "independent in material things." Eliot,
by the time of its composition professionally and financially secure in her reputation as the foremost novelist of her day, need no longer conform her representations to the standards of popular prejudice but might direct her efforts
toward a more elusive, if more pressing, representational standard: "what
seemed to me most needful to be done." George Eliot having become "George
Eliot," she is free to be governed by moral rather than material necessity.

When in the final months of 1859 "Marian Evans Lewes" took deliberate
steps to reveal herself as the author of novels heretofore attributed to "George
Eliot," her goal was not to free herself of a reputation, of the limitations of
an actual past, but to assert her possession of one. Earlier that year a man

11. David Carroll, ed., *George Eliot: The Critical Heritage* (London: Routledge and Kegan Paul,
1971), 405–6.

12. The *Jewish Chronicle*, founded in 1841, quickly became one of the most influential popular
organs of Anglo-Jewish opinion. For a history of the publication, see *The Jewish Chronicle, 1841–1941:*
A Century of Newspaper History (London: Jewish Chronicle, 1949). A helpful (though frustratingly
lacking a bibliography) survey of Jewish reaction to the publication of *Daniel Deronda* is "The Jewish
Reception of *Daniel Deronda*," by Minna Givton, Aviva Gottlieb, and Shmuel Werses, in *"Daniel De-*
ronda": A Centenary Symposium, ed. Alice Shalvi (Jerusalem: Jerusalem Academic Press, 1976), 11–43.
The most detailed and sustained contemporary Jewish response to the novel is David Kaufmann's *George*
Eliot and Judaism: An Attempt to Appreciate "Daniel Deronda," published in German in 1876 and
translated into English the following year (reprinted New York: Haskell House, 1970).

Noteworthy recent criticism on the politics of Jewishness in the novel include Bernard Semmel,
George Eliot and the Politics of National Inheritance (Oxford: Oxford University Press, 1994), esp.
chap. 5; Patrick Brantlinger, "Nations and Novels: Disraeli, George Eliot, and Orientalism," *Victorian*
Studies 35, 3 (1992): 255–75; Susan Meyer, "'Safely to Their Own Borders': Proto-Zionism, Feminism
and Nationalism in *Daniel Deronda*," *ELH* 60 (1993): 733–58; Catherine Gallagher, "George Eliot and
Daniel Deronda: The Prostitute and the Jewish Question," in *Sex, Politics and Science in the Nineteenth*
Century Novel, ed. Ruth Bernard Yeazell (Baltimore: Johns Hopkins University Press, 1986), 39–62;
Amanda Anderson, "George Eliot and the Jewish Question," *Yale Journal of Criticism* 10, 1 (1997):
39–61; and most important, Michael Ragussis's powerful *Figures of Conversion: "The Jewish Question"*
and English National Identity (Durham, N.C.: Duke University Press, 1995).

named Joseph Liggins had permitted people to believe that he had written *Scenes of Clerical Life* and *Adam Bede;* when the ruse developed to the point where concerned members of the novels' reading public began organizing a charity drive for Liggins, who, not unexpectedly, had not been paid for his authorship of either novel, Eliot informed her publisher Blackwood of her plan to, in his words, "withdraw the incognito."[13] If, as Eliot asserts in her letter to Harriet Beecher Stowe, it was her "independen[ce] in material things" that allowed her to reject the standard of mimetic fidelity to the material world in the name of a more pressing moral necessity, the Joseph Liggins episode implies that the freedom to fictionalize engendered by such material independence itself depended on Eliot's power to convert the fictionalized identity of her pseudonym into the name of an actual past—almost, if not quite, a material thing.

Thus, as she transformed herself from the Marian Evans who theorized fictions into the George Eliot who wrote them, the alignment between her aesthetic authority and the fictionality of her novels was anything but neat. Whereas the fictional "George Eliot" initially appears to authorize the fictions of the novels on which the name would appear, Eliot's demand that her fictionalized writing self be rendered sufficiently real for material recompense forces her to disrupt the analogousness of the two kinds of fictions.[14] In the

---

13. Alexander Welsh, *George Eliot and Blackmail* (Cambridge: Harvard University Press, 1985), 123–31.

14. Although Eliot does not here explicitly link her pseudonymic authority to her assertion of her fictions' power to bring about politically or morally desirable goals (as opposed to strictly representing empirical truths), she frequently associates her novelistic and pseudonymic fictions elsewhere. Most often, as Alexander Welsh has argued, the link between the moral good of her fictions and the fictionality of her pseudonymic authority is triangulated around the transgression of her "irregular" liaison with George Lewes. Even after her death, the falsehood of her pseudonymity continued to be tied to the falsehood of her marriage, with a reviewer of Johnny Cross's *George Eliot's Life* observing wryly in 1885, "It is no more true that the author of *Adam Bede* was Mrs. Lewes than it is true that the author of *Adam Bede* was Mr. Liggins" (*Saturday Review* 59 [1885] quoted in Welsh, *George Eliot,* 129). In 1880, in a letter to her new sisters-in-law following her legal marriage to Cross, Eliot refers to herself as "the criminal usually known under the name of George Eliot. If she was not quite "Mrs. Lewes," being not quite "George Eliot" enabled her to produce fictions whose positive effects would counterbalance the moral dubiousness of her unorthodox marriage. Writing as "Pollian" to Sara Hennell immediately after the publication of "Mr. Gilfil's Love-Story" and the adoption of her pseudonym, Eliot uses syntax strongly echoing the moral/fictional balancing act she returns to in her letter to Stowe: "If I live five years longer, the positive result of my existence on the side of truth and goodness will outweigh the small negative good that would have consisted in my not doing anything to shock others, and I can conceive of no consequences that will make me repent the past" (To Sara Sophia Hennell, 5 June 1857, in *George Eliot Letters,* 2:342), quoted in Welsh, *George Eliot,* 126).

Catherine Gallagher persuasively links Eliot's pseudonymity to the general scandalousness of female authorship in the nineteenth century, which associated fictionality with prostitution. See Gallagher, "George Eliot."

representational economy of "Natural History," the absolute distinction between writing subject and fictional objects that defined the conditions of belief underpinning the realist novel produced a common state of consciousness
that could not be instantiated in the material world. In the letter to Stowe, as
Eliot shifts her representational interest from the analogousness of mimetic
accuracy to the accomplishment of "what is most needful to be done," the
logic of the pseudonym, which insists on the imbrication of (fictional) subject
and object, comes to the fore. Eliot's letter—which in its reference to independence *in* material things also might imply independence *of* material things,
that is, of the obligation to representational fidelity—might be said to announce a rejection of the earlier analogy between imaginative and reportorial
authority that constitutes fictional belief in "Natural History."

The power of the pseudonym to articulate a different model of fictional
authority rests on its synthesis of two sorts of authorial identity: anonymity
and reputation. The anonymous quality of Eliot's pseudonym—the notion
that anyone might be the author of *Daniel Deronda*—associates the possibility of things' being otherwise with fictional authority in the present. But the
pseudonym does not just assert that *anyone* could become an author; it also
asserts that *someone*—some quasi-fictional entity—has actually done so,
someone whose power to create fiction in the present has, in effect, been created in the past. Reputation does not so much evaluate the specific example
of the present work as a plausible or implausible extension of the author's
oeuvre as take the place of that present work; a given novel must be good
(or must be published or must be bought) because it is the work of Well-
Respected Author X. Such a substitution renders effectively simultaneous the
moments of writing and of reading or evaluation. The indisputable fact of
authorship takes the place of the doubly contingent quality of literary value,
doubly contingent in that it depends not simply on the vagaries of literary
production but on the vagaries of literary evaluation as well. Such contingency is absorbed by the narrative of the author's biography and stabilized by
the assertion of identity around the historical fact of authorship. Simply put,
that a particular author has written a work subsumes both its narratively
particular meanings and the audience's evaluation in the present of those
meanings. This temporal conflation transforms aesthetic value or imaginative
fiction into historical fact, with the authority of reputable authorship grounding both the quality of the individual work and the plausibility of the imagined fiction. At the same time, that the existence of the history of writing is
testified to by a present fiction—the fiction of the authorial name—has the
effect of turning the pastness of the historical past into a condition that might

be acceded to or resisted rather than simply standing as the inert data of the given.

For Eliot, then, discovering the "usefulness" of novels depends on theorizing a category of fictional making, of action in the material world, neither wholly subsumable within nor wholly distinguishable from the authority of the fiction produced. The letter to Stowe might lead us to assume that Eliot, armed with her newfound sense of the transformative power of realist fiction, sets out, like Dorothea Brooke, in search of "something needful to be done." But if Eliot exhibits little of Dorothea's characteristic tentativeness in identifying an appropriate outlet for her political energies, I propose that Eliot's certitude results less from any profound characterological differences between the two than from her turn to the Jews. Addressing the condition of Jews in contemporary England is for Eliot that "most needful" thing not so much because the Jews lie on the far end of some objective misery index as because, from the early part of the century through the decade in which Eliot composes *Daniel Deronda,* the "Jewish question" functioned as the discourse within which the meaning of "politics" itself began to change. Just as the element of fiction in Eliot's pseudonym offers evidence of an ongoing "material"—economic—power that underwrites her authority to create a seemingly transparent, wholly autonomous fictional world and at the same time prevents that fictional authority from being entirely absorbed into the world it creates, the parliamentary debates surrounding the removal of Jewish political disabilities that raged from the 1820s through the 1850s can be understood largely as motivated by the emergence of a new, pointedly *economic* power that did not seem immediately assimilable to the transparent institutional power conventionally associated with English political authority.

In 1830, when the British Parliament first took up the issue of political rights of Jews settled in England, the question of how "Jewish" were "Jewish civil disabilities" was the subject of considerable controversy, both historical and political. Because the readmission of the Jews to England by Oliver Cromwell in the middle decades of the seventeenth century followed the failure of the 1655 Whitehall Conference to reach any agreement as to the official terms of Jewish residency, the Jewish presence in England received its legal recognition as a patchwork of local, limited regulations and informal executive tolerations.[15] As a consequence, when Parliament voted in 1828 to

15. On the readmission of the Jews to England, see David Katz, *Philo-Semitism and the Readmission of the Jews to England, 1603–1655* (Oxford: Clarendon Press, 1982), and Katz, *Jews in the History of England* (Oxford: Clarendon Press, 1994). For a comprehensive history of the legal status of Anglo-Jewry, see H. S. Q. Henriques, *The Jews and the English Law* (London: J. Jacobs, 1908).

remove certain old restrictions imposed on non-Anglican Christians—that is, Protestant Dissenters and Roman Catholics—it was not clear whether this relief ought, at least in the name of consistency, to be applied to Jews as well, in large part because it was not clear what restrictions *did* apply to the Jews.[16] According to Henriques, at the time of the Act of 1828, Jews' legal status was virtually identical with that of Dissenters and Catholics, with two notable exceptions: Jews were prohibited from engaging in retail trade in the City of London, and there is some doubt whether they were able to own land.[17] Thus the notion of particularly *Jewish* disabilities—as well as the feasibility of launching a political campaign deliberately designed to remove such disabilities—first came into being when the House of Lords introduced a measure into the 1828 Act pointedly differentiating between Catholics/Christian dissenting sects and Jews.[18] Once identified, these particularized disabilities quickly gained a tenacious political life of their own; not until 1858, thirty years after the question of a *political* Jewish particularity first emerged and nearly twenty years after Lionel de Rothschild was elected to Parliament but prevented from assuming his seat because he refused to take the accepted oath, did the House of Lords finally join the House of Commons in agreeing to allow Jews to swear allegiance to Parliament without alleging their faith in Christ as well.

Even as the Act of 1828 eliminated the demand for institutional affiliation with the Church of England as a precondition for citizenship, the rhetoric of the Jewish emancipation debate took up the issue of the essential Christianity, if not the essential Anglicanism, of English institutions.[19] For High Tory protectionist Henry Drummond, "the intense interest which the discussion of

16. Nor is this merely a question of legality. In May 1830 Sir Robert Wilson told the House of Commons that Jews habitually voted in parliamentary elections in the south part of London because no one bothered to insist that they take the Christian oath. The Liverpool Poll Book of 1832 lists Rabbi Asher Ansell as a voter as well. See Geoffrey Alderman, "English Jews or Jews of the English Persuasion? Reflections on the Emancipation of Anglo-Jewry," in *Paths of Emancipation: Jews, States and Citizenship,* ed. Pierre Birnbaum and Ira Katznelson (Princeton: Princeton University Press, 1995), 128.

17. Henriques, *Jews and the English Law,* 199–201.

18. The most interesting account of the emancipation campaign I have encountered is David Feldman's *Englishmen and Jews: Social Relations and Political Culture,1840–1914* (New Haven: Yale University Press, 1994), which places the debates about the removal of Jewish disabilities in the context of shifting models of Englishness as well as in relation to the huge immigration of Jews from eastern Europe later in the century. See also M. C. N. Salbstein, *The Emancipation of the Jews: The Question of the Admission of the Jews to Parliament, 1828–1860* (Rutherford, N.J.: Fairleigh Dickinson University Press, 1982), and Israel Finestein, *Jewish Society in Victorian England* (London: Vallentine Mitchell, 1993).

19. For the developing relationship between Anglicanism and liberalism, see J. P. Parry, *Democracy and Religion: Gladstone and the Liberal Party, 1867–1875* (Cambridge: Cambridge University Press, 1986), and Richard Brent, *Liberal Anglican Politics: Whiggery, Religion and Reform, 1830–1841* (Oxford: Clarendon Press, 1987).

this question excited did not regard the Jew, but the Established Church."[20] While the Whigs characterized their opponents' resistance to Jewish relief as motivated by a residual antisemitism that would inevitably be swept away by the progress of reason, Conservatives figured themselves as protecting the fundamental Christianity of Great Britain.[21] At issue was whether the Crown ought to continue to be understood as deriving its authority from its connection to the Anglican Church, a link that had been axiomatic ever since the 1688 Act of Succession mandated that the monarch be Anglican. Such an account of the Jewish disabilities debate effectively turns the dispute into a replaying of the Burke-Paine debate of the previous generation; in this light the question whether Christianity was enshrined in English institutions can be understood to be as much about the nature of the power of English citizens as about the proper hierarchy of English institutions.

But while the Jewish emancipation controversy in many ways replicated the lines of division of earlier debates about English institutional authority, the translation of such debates into the terms of religious belief nevertheless can be seen to have powerfully reframed and transformed the very topic of government power. I believe this relocation of the debate revealed and continues to reveal its implication within a variety of seemingly remote controversies. The emergence of discussions about government authority in the context of questions about the nature of religious belief suggests that, despite Conservative MP Drummond's assertions to the contrary, the "Jewishness" of the Jewish disabilities debate was hardly incidental. Far from operating as one site among many where an ongoing conversation about English governmentality might be endlessly reiterated, introducing the possibility of Jewish political power in England fundamentally transformed the way British civil authority and its relation to British history might be imagined.

Strikingly, the significance of this translation of the debate over institutional authority becomes most apparent at the moments the discussion strays from the established opposition between natural rights and the heritable power of institutions. What is perhaps the single most famous contribution to the Jewish disabilities debate—Thomas Babington Macaulay's—is also its most anomalous. For Macaulay, making his maiden appearance before Parliament on 5 April 1830, the issue was not the origin of English political power or whether one understanding of institutional authority rather than another might offer a better foundation for opening the English civil sphere to Jews but the relation of political power to other forms of social power,

20. Drummond, 17 December 1847, quoted in Feldman, *Englishmen and Jews*, 32.
21. Feldman, *Englishmen and Jews*, 28.

most notably economic. Political power must be extended to the Jews for no other reason than that they already commanded formidable economic power; in maintaining too absolutely the distinction between the political and the economic, Parliament ran the risk of rendering its own narrowly conceived political compass ineffectual and finally beside the point:

> Jews are not now excluded from political power. They possess it; and as long as they are allowed to accumulate large fortunes they must possess it. . . .
> What power in civilised society is so great as that of the creditor over the debtor? If we take this away from the Jew we take away the security of his property. If we leave it to him, we leave him a power more despotic than that of the king and all his cabinet.[22]

Whereas the Jews' supposed propensity for "nonproductive" economic pursuits like usury had, within the German Enlightenment tradition of *Bildung*, long been seized on as evidence of their unfitness for emancipation, here Macaulay transmutes the Jewish concentration in economic professions into a reason for institutionalizing Jewish political power.

A variety of contemporary critics and historians of Jewish culture have noted the contradictory demands frequently made of Jews as they moved to gain entry into modern, "secular" European societies: Bryan Cheyette, for example, sees the simultaneous construction of the Jews as both "spectacularly civilized" and "an unchanging semitic other" as a "product of the competing needs of the liberal nation-state which situates 'the Jew' in both a particularist 'English' community and an assimilating universalist [natural rights] framework."[23] While this ambivalent opposition—what Cheyette terms "semitic discourse"—lines up roughly with the main fault lines of the Jewish disabilities debate, the example of Macaulay's idiosyncratic contribution to the dispute ought to be a salutary reminder of the dangers of accepting the terms of the debate at face value. Macaulay insists on analyzing the political sphere in general, and institutional authority more specifically, not simply in terms of the shifting boundaries of the polity—that is, in terms of the extent and character of the space, and of the populace, that can be brought within

---

22. Thomas Babington Macaulay, "Civil Disabilities of the Jews," in *Essay and Speech on Jewish Disabilities,* ed. Israel Abrahams and S. Levy (Edinburgh: Ballantyne, Hanson, 1910), 24, 25.

23. Bryan Cheyette, *Constructions of "the Jew" in English Literature and Society: Racial Representations, 1875–1945* (Cambridge: Cambridge University Press, 1993), 13. For other articulations of this primary "ambivalence" of European host cultures toward the Jews, see Jacob Katz, ed., *Toward Modernity: The European Jewish Model* (New Brunswick, N.J.: Transaction Books, 1987), and Jonathan Freedman, "The Jew in the Museum" (unpublished manuscript).

the sweep of English law—but also in terms of the shifting and incompletely legible relations between the political and the economic.

Emerging as British wealth becomes less and less easily translatable into the foundational category of landed property, this notion of a distinctly economic power announces the passing of the fundamental analogy linking political and novelistic representation up until that point: the analogy between English political institutions and the literal geographical space of England. Once the power of English political institutions is no longer conceived to be most formidable at the moment they disappear, that is, once the authority of Englishness is no longer to be discovered in the very hedgerows and vistas of the English landscape, the entire aesthetic system built around this analogy— the realist fictionality theorized in "Natural History"—is remade as well. The artist's imaginative encounter with the peasants can no longer be rendered equivalent to reporting about them from a distance because the meaning of being in English space can no longer be assumed to be the same everywhere. The appearance of a distinct category of economic power means that the unequal distribution of (landed) property among individuals is no longer mitigated by the meaningfulness of occupying a geographical space rendered homogeneous by political authority. Consequently the existence of an autonomous novelistic world no longer testifies to the necessary freedom from material things of its author or the fundamental likeness—material or otherwise—of its various readers. And while Jews, long prohibited from owning land in England, were obvious beneficiaries of this trend toward recognizing nonlanded, overtly "economic" forms of authority, Eliot's interest in them is not limited to their status as representatives of a new form of wealth. Eliot makes the Jews the aesthetic and political objects of the new activist fictional authority she claims in her letter to Stowe not because their plight is in most dire need of amelioration, or because Jews are powerful members of a newly powerful "economic" middle class, but because, by inhabiting the space of England while participating neither in its political institutions nor entirely in the common language by which that space may be named, the Jews become the subjects around whom Eliot's new fictional authority becomes conceivable. If Eliot's "independen[ce] in material things" allows her to make the Jews the subject of her novel without worrying about her audience's "aversion" to her subject matter, we might say that it is the Jews who make Eliot the author she imagines herself to be.

Eliot's reengineering of the meaning of fictionality identifies the political efficacy of such a representational practice with its assertion that world-making is an ongoing, present activity, made manifest as a temporalized, contingent fictional authority. Only by seeing the realist novelist's authority to create fictions as constrained by and vulnerable to local and temporal forces of the material world, Eliot avers, can we understand this authority as having the power to transform that world. But as we will see, Eliot bases her expansion of her authorial power on its alignment with the fictionality of her pseudonym. Such circularity, eschewing as it does the demand for evidence, runs the risk of replicating the structure of prejudice it has been enlisted to combat. By her own account, her representation of Jews gains the authority of fact not because it is plausible, for plausibility of representation as a criterion of evaluation is foreclosed by the structure of "social prejudice," which makes its judgments in spite of evidence rather than in accordance with it.[24] Eliot's evaluation of Jewish life is most compelling at the very moment we are forced to see it as Eliot's, as a fictional production of her imagination, since the fact of her authorship carries a historical indisputability unmatchable by any evaluation of the plausibility of the representation of the Jews, which, even if it were not ruled out by the existence of social prejudice, would always remain in the realm of opinion.

If Eliot's emphasis on the significance of reputation constrains individual agency by tying it to events that are already over and done with, that the reputation in question is pseudonymic enables it to slip out of the manacles of established social values. By tying the pseudonym's anonymity—the possibility that anyone might have been the author—to the individual author's imaginative authority, the Stowe letter implies that anyone could and would have done what the author did. In this way the values of the common are made wholly compatible with the imaginative acts of the individual artist by being rendered *indistinguishable* from those acts. Whereas the model of fiction in "Natural History" eliminated the constraining pressure of politics or ideology by valuing the power of the imagination to do anything as opposed to any specific imaginative effect, Eliot's letter to Stowe presents a model of fictional imagination within which the compatibility of common values and the values of individuals goes without saying—because the imaginative effects could have been anyone's. Indeed, the very power that Eliot suggests is implied by her pseudonymic reputation—the force of the moral imperative to make over the existing conditions of the world into desired ones, to assimilate fact to value—turns on the presumption that all members of a given population are, or can be, made interchangeable, that each of them could have been the person to produce the fiction that one of them has produced. Thus, for the Eliot who pauses to take stock of her career by considering the way her

24. For a related account of the evidencelessness of judgment by analogy, see David Lloyd, "Race under Representation," *Oxford Literary Review* 13 (1991): 62–94.

final novel has come to matter in the world, people become like one another in their common embrace of the power to imagine and, in so imagining, to bring about a world aligned by their values. Populated by citizens made common by their common belief that they can make the world as they would wish it, Eliot's is a world in which politics is renounced in the name of politics.

Whereas Eliot's letter to Stowe acknowledges her own dependence on the complex of social forces that constitutes her reputation but then immediately moves to assimilate such forces to her own imaginative power, Eliot's canniest *readers* turn out to be better positioned to envision a role for the novel—and to discern this power in *Daniel Deronda*—in producing some sort of cultural commonness that does not depend on turning an imagining author and an entire audience of readers into potential versions of one another. In a review of *Daniel Deronda* in the *Jewish Chronicle,* the official weekly publication of the London-based Jewish Board of Governors, the unnamed writer reframes the relations of imagination, political agency, and fictional representation so as to account for the *uneven* distribution of social and political power. As if to preempt even the thought that the writing or reading of novels might lift those who partake of them from the petty divisions of their mundane social existence, the review begins not with an account of the novel but with a description of that same sort of anti-Jewish prejudice that Eliot says she has written *Daniel Deronda* to repudiate:

> It was recently stated, within the hearing of the present writer, that the longstanding social prejudice against persons of Jewish race, although somewhat modified by the march of civilization, still exists in many quarters, in spite of numerous evidences to the contrary. Whether this be or be not the case it is difficult for Jews themselves to determine.

Here, the *Jewish Chronicle* reviewer, who like the pseudonymous "George Eliot" is anonymous, directs his or her energies to theorizing an account of the realist novel's power to intervene politically that does not depend on transforming all involved into interchangeable subjects. *Antisemitism* is here first of all a discursive system, less a common ideology than a structure of relations between subjects and objects. That it "is difficult for the Jews themselves to determine" whether "the longstanding prejudice against persons of the Jewish race . . . still exists" is not simply the condition of analysis but the condition to be analyzed; it is this three-way disjunction separating speaker, object, and audience—the idea that gentiles might speak about Jews without the Jews' themselves knowing about it—that constitutes the "longstanding prejudice" under discussion. But having defined antisemitism this way, the writer immediately goes about challenging the stability of the discursive terms. While antisemitism is distinguished by Jews' lack of access to what others are saying about them, the reviewer is in a position to report on speech that is not necessarily intended for his or her ears ("It was recently stated, within the hearing of the present writer . . ."). And although the speech the writer overhears[25] initially appears to be speech concerning the existence of antisemitism rather than antisemitic speech itself, the writer's attempt to ground the report in specific evidence ("despite numerous evidences to the contrary") renders ambiguous exactly what is being discussed. Here the ideology whose tenets remain intact in spite of contravening evidence can with equal grammatical plausibility be understood as a belief in the continuing existence of antisemitism or as antisemitic beliefs themselves.

But even while arguing for understanding the relations among subject, object, and audience of antisemitism not simply as discursive roles inhabited or shed at will but as positions linked to a variety of nondiscursive social relations, the reviewer points out the relative instability of those positions. In fact the anonymity staged in the passage enables a kind of discursive mobility that paradoxically makes the social differences from which the speech issues all the harder to ignore. Without knowing for certain who hears what, one cannot determine whether antisemites are functioning as subjects or objects, whether they are speaking (the case if what the writer overhears is antisemitism) or spoken about (the case if what the writer overhears is a discussion about the incidence of antisemitism). Logically, the possibility that the reviewer might have overheard antisemitic speech, even though the position of audience to such speech would be barred by the rules of the discourse, appears to turn on his or her anonymity, an anonymity that carries with it the chance, if not the promise, of slipping into places unseen.

Lapping over the boundaries of self-ascription, the *Jewish Chronicle* reviewer's anonymity touches Eliot's authorship as well, giving the pseudonymity of "George Eliot" the cast of its own complexion. The discursive relations

---

25. The *Jewish Chronicle* reviewer recalls and revalues John Stuart Mill's notion of "overhearing" in Mill's 1833 essay "What Is Poetry?" "Poetry and eloquence are both alike the expression or utterance of feeling: but, if we may be excused the antithesis, we should say that eloquence is *heard;* poetry is *overheard.*" For Mill, "overhearing" served as the mark of an aesthetic that is nonperformative and hence nonpolemical. Mill's overhearing essentially depends on a naturalized proximity of poet and audience. Robert Browning vehemently rejected Mill's formulation and developed his dramatic monologue form as an exploration of the limitations of Mill's model. For an interesting, if somewhat factually flawed, discussion of the history of this concept of "overhearing" in Victorian poetry, see Isobel Armstrong, *Victorian Poetry: Poetry, Poetics and Politics* (London: Routledge, 1993), 137, passim. See also J. S. Mill, "What Is Poetry?" in *Essays on Poetry by John Stuart Mill,* ed. F. Parvin Sharpless (Columbia: University of South Carolina Press, 1976), 3–22.

that constitute antisemitism are incorporated into the strategy of their fictional overcoming:

> Whether this be or be not the case it is difficult for Jews themselves to determine; but if this purposeless prejudice still linger in the minds of any of our cultured compatriots, it is certain that nothing that can be done by Jews towards its removal could possibly be so effective as that which "George Eliot" has done by the production of "Daniel Deronda."

The particular efficacy of writing by "George Eliot" seems to be her own non-Jewishness, her distance from the Jews she takes as her objects ("nothing that can be done *by Jews* toward its removal could possibly be so effective as that which 'George Eliot' has done"). But this diagnosis is haunted by the specter of its opposite, that the anonymous author who goes by the name "George Eliot" might not be so far from the Jews after all. Indeed, if we look at the passage again, we will notice that Eliot's efficacy is merely hypothetical, framed within the subjunctive of the ambiguity that structured the passage's opening: "*if* this purposeless prejudice still linger in the minds of our cultured compatriots." As the anonymous quality of Eliot's pseudonym pries biographical identity apart from fictional authority, the success of Eliot's project to remove the purposeless prejudice of antisemitism comes to rest on the capacity of the *Jewish Chronicle* reviewer to apprehend the phenomenon. If authorial anonymity allows that Eliot herself might be Jewish, it does so insofar as it renders her own discursive authority inextricable from that of the Jews. For the reviewer, Eliot's fictional authority relieves the condition of the Jews to the extent that it makes both her own authorial subjectivity and her fictional texts unimaginable except in relation to the Jews' authority.

Within the reputational paradigm Eliot herself laid out, the fictional representation of Jews she offered was convincing because it had been written by Eliot, not because it conformed to any standards of evidentiary accuracy or narrative plausibility with regard to actual Jews. The *Jewish Chronicle* challenges Eliot's account of her own authority. Here the ontological and temporal ambiguity of the pseudonym "George Eliot" is made to neatly parallel the eponym "Daniel Deronda." The titular function of the name, which locates Eliot's authority in the act of writing in an isolated moment in the past, slides without a perceptible break into the story of Daniel Deronda the character in all its narrative particularity, with Eliot's authorial identity made as contingent and difficult to discover as Daniel's own. The authority signified by the name "George Eliot" can be wholly identified neither with the pastness and consequent immutability of the already completed text *Daniel Deronda* nor with Daniel Deronda himself, a character whose identity, both formally and by virtue of the particular plot of the novel in which it is embedded, is not knowable before or apart from the process of being read.

The *Jewish Chronicle* reviewer sees in the pseudonym "George Eliot" a fictional authority identified in some shifting and ambiguous relation between the completed text of *Daniel Deronda* and the plotted contingencies of Daniel Deronda's own search for identity. In this ambiguity we discover a model of authorship in which the function of writing cannot be easily or productively distinguished from the function of reading. The "George Eliot" whose authority is made manifest in the fact of the material text *Daniel Deronda* is an author entirely absorbed into the historical act of writing, whereas the "George Eliot" whose authorial identity can only be assembled, bit by bit, in the process of uncovering Daniel Deronda's genealogy is an identity conceived as and brought into being by the actions of the reader. Insofar as the authority figured in "George Eliot" is equally produced by the acts of reading and writing, the two positions become occupiable by the same people only so long as their differences are retained. The pseudonym suggests not that the positions of reader and writer are essentially the same, but that they can be occupied sequentially. Writers may become readers not because the roles of writer and reader are essentially interchangeable abstractions, but because the reader can come to occupy his or her position as a result of having read and learned what the writer had to say.

Moreover, once we understand the authority of "George Eliot" to come into being not simply at that isolated moment in the past in which she wrote *Daniel Deronda* but over the time it takes, has taken, and will take a variety of readers to read and learn about Daniel Deronda's identity, not only does the force and quality of *Daniel Deronda*'s textuality change, but the meaning of being a reader—more specifically, an anonymous reader—is transformed in important ways as well. The reviewer, anonymously "overhearing" what he or she might not be deliberately told, gained an oddly free access to the kinds of speech that Jewishness might have been expected to preclude. But the power of the anonymous audience to affect profoundly the authority of "George Eliot" emerges from relations much more generalizable than the reviewer's own admittedly anomalous case.[26] The greatest change wrought by

---

26. In *The Lifted Veil*, the highly uncharacteristic ghost story whose title, Gordon Haight has argued, refers to unraveling the secret of her pseudonym, Eliot explicitly associates narrative authority with the capacity to distinguish Jewish and non-Jewish space. The narrator of this tale claims the often painful power to penetrate the consciousness of other people. Such a claim positions the events both as supernatural and as the products of a psychotic imagination. The story promises that its narrator's sanity will be established by a tour of the streets of Prague, since he has never before visited Prague but has

the development of technologies for the mass production and distribution of written material over the course of the eighteenth and nineteenth centuries was to replace the relation of the writer and a private, local audience comprising socially equivalent, if not necessarily like-minded, people with a relation to a far-flung audience for whom no particular likeness might be presumed. For the *Jewish Chronicle* reviewer, this new anonymity offers the prospect of remaking those social relations, like antisemitism, that are predicated on controlling the distribution of particular information. Insofar as antisemitism is conceived as a system of relations where Jews are objects of representations to which they are denied access as audience, print culture might seem, by turning all audiences into anonymous ones, to produce a kind of mass "over-hearing," a promiscuous mixing of audiences, subjects, and objects that would make the discursive relations constituting antisemitism impossible to sustain.

Nor are the effects of print culture limited to allowing people to find out what others are saying about them. The review proposes that the mass circulation of novels produces a situation in which "George Eliot" is effective as an author both because she is not Jewish and because she might be. Print culture not only provides access to representations, like those of Jews by non-Jews, that might otherwise have been withheld but introduces the chance that audiences might encounter representations they had no particular desire to see, hear, or read. The social efficacy of Eliot the gentile does not preclude or contradict the social efficacy of Eliot the crypto-Jew because it is the very impossibility of predicting what sorts of representations one might bump up against—the chance that an encounter with a Christian might suddenly turn out to be an encounter with a Jew—that enables the anonymity of mass circulation to leave its imprint on those who have no desire for political transformation as well as on those who do.

For the *Jewish Chronicle* reviewer, then, the anonymity of authors and readers is significant not because it means that everyone might be the same, but because it maintains the differences among and between writers and those readers who pick up printed texts either deliberately or unknowingly. This description of the encounter between artist and audience as one that depends on the past and present differences of the parties rather than on their fundamental or potential likeness not only marks a departure from the principles Eliot articulates as underlying her own fiction but also registers

---

experienced it only through his access to others' memories. But the expected moment of corroboration is interrupted, leaving the question of the narrator's reliability to rest on whether the Jewish quarter of Prague (which the visitors *do* see) is understood to be synecdochal for the city as a whole.

an important shift in the constellation of relations in which the sameness or differences of subjects, their representations, and those readers are measured. What was significant about the theory explicated in "The Natural History of German Life" was not simply that common culture was conceived to be the experience of like individuals out of time, but that this experience of commonness was keyed explicitly to a condition of geographical proximity. So while one can see the artist's fiction as providing an *alternative* to the experience of the local—after all, the artist's imaginative representation of the otherwise immobile peasants made them available to an audience outside their immediate geographical ambit—it is perhaps more accurate to describe Eliot's imaginative fictions as offering a *replication* of a condition of geographical proximity.

Thus when the reviewer seeks to reread the reception of the text *Daniel Deronda* as a coming together of author, textual authority, and audience that articulates and produces the very real social differences among those various positions, this recharacterization of the operation of Eliot's final imaginative fiction is significant not only because it challenges the fundamental premise that the commonness of a culture is defined by the likeness of its members, but also because it rejects the presumption that such commonness is fundamentally the outcome and condition of sharing a common geographical location. In asserting that the textuality of the imaginative fiction functions not to equalize the sharply different levels of social and political power held by those who write, read, and are written about but in fact depends on those differences for the novel's political effect, the anonymous reviewer, tracing out the logic of his or her own palpably indirect experience of antisemitism, forcefully disrupts the notion that those who are most likely to act, think, speak, and mean in the same ways are those people who live near one another.

But while the *Jewish Chronicle* review both reveals and rejects the way geographical location operates as the largely unacknowledged deep structure of thinking about culture in nineteenth-century England, it pulls up short as the task of critique is about to give way to the creation of a new account of culture. The review's uncoupling of culture and space is part and parcel of its demand that the authority of the printed, circulated fiction be seen as an entirely contingent, context-determined outcome of the relation between differently positioned writer and reader. But the relentlessly agonistic quality of the model makes it difficult for the review's own readers to figure out how this clash of unequal forces might ever produce a condition in which the antagonists might come to understand one another.

To discover the theoretical underpinnings of what we might call the *Jewish*

Chronicle reviewer's "poetics of antisemitism," we need to turn to a source whose relevance to the topic of novelistic fictionality and common culture might initially appear oblique. George Eliot read Moses Mendelssohn's 1783 treatise *Jerusalem, or On Religious Power and Judaism* sometime in 1872,[27] as part of the extensive, and extensively publicized, research she undertook in preparation for writing *Daniel Deronda*. Even the sketchiest intellectual biographies reveal Eliot and Mendelssohn to be kindred spirits: Mendelssohn, writing in Berlin, and Eliot, writing in midcentury London, Surrey, and Homburg, place themselves at the margins of their respective intellectual cultures by their common efforts to bring together two traditions usually understood to be at odds with one another—German idealism and English empiricism. Mendelssohn composes *Jerusalem* as a direct response to Locke's *Letter concerning Toleration* and, like Locke, takes up the question of the proper relation between state power and religious worship. But *Jerusalem* addresses this question from the perspective of Judaism, a religious system at once conventionally understood to be unwedded to any *principled* separation of religious worship and state institutions and at the same time lacking any state power. Although by the moment of *Jerusalem*'s publication the Jews had been without state power for well over a millennium and a half, Jews continued to adhere to an extensive set of laws that in large part (though not entirely) presumed a community living in a shared geographical space under that community's own political control.

Writing from a perspective where the opposition between the authority of the state and the wholly private beliefs of individual subjects is theologically irrelevant, Mendelssohn is virtually unique among Locke's commentators in understanding Locke's writing on religion to be not so much an analysis of the power and limitation of civil government as a theory of culture. Viewed from within a context of Jewish religious and social history, the most visible legacy of Mendelssohn's writing on religion doubtless lies in his challenge to the axiom—until Mendelssohn, shared by Christians and Jews alike—that Jewish religious practice was fundamentally national, composed primarily of laws governing communal relations (ideally institutionalized by way of some autonomous national authority) rather than subjective relations between individual believers and a divine authority. Nevertheless, in making the case for a division between religious practice and state authority, Mendelssohn continues to insist on the "Jewish" quality of his notion of religion.

By theorizing a version of religious practice that is something other than

27. See Jane Irwin, ed., *George Eliot's "Daniel Deronda" Notebooks* (Cambridge: Cambridge University Press, 1996), 233, 508.

the absolutely inaccessible private consciousness of an individual free of state constraints, Mendelssohn slides free of the opposition between a monolithic institutional authority and a commonness of mutually inaccessible, formally identical subjects. In rejecting the sanctity of individual consciousness, Mendelssohn effectively rejects a model of belief that does not and cannot matter in the world, and in so doing he allows religious practice to become not only a kind of culture but a kind of authority as well. Although the *Jewish Chronicle* reviewer was unable to explain how the social and political heterogeneity that fueled the power of these fictions might ever produce anything resembling a common culture, Mendelssohn's insight is to transform immanence from a description of the way fictions work into a model of culture itself. For Mendelssohn, the difference between writers and readers does not simply result in a common culture but constitutes culture in itself. By converting language from a meaning—an achievement of the past around which authority might be consolidated and upon whose representations a common culture might be created—into an ongoing activity that itself might be called culture, Mendelssohn undoes the opposition between the proper and the common by conceiving the relation between the two as fundamentally *temporal* rather than *spatial.*

Mendelssohn announces his departure from Locke by rejecting the fundamental postulate of Lockean toleration, the absolute separation of the temporal realm of the state and the eternal realm of belief:

> It is, in the strictest sense, neither in keeping with the truth nor advantageous to man's welfare to sever the temporal so neatly from the eternal. At bottom, man will never partake of eternity; his eternality is merely an *incessant temporality.* His temporality never ends; it is, therefore, an essential part of his permanency and inseparable from it. One confuses ideas if one opposes his temporal welfare to his eternal felicity. And this confusion of ideas is not without practical consequences. It *shifts the borders* of the sphere in which man can act in accordance with his capacities, and strains his powers beyond the goal which Providence has so wisely set for him. (Emphasis added)[28]

In rejecting Locke's model of analogous religious and civil realms, Mendelssohn does more than merely recharacterize belief. For Locke, the analogy between possessing belief and possessing property—they were figured as absolutely distinct but entirely comparable versions of one another—not only justified the separation of the two realms but also rendered timeless and indisputable the argument for their likeness and, by extension, for the institu-

---

28. Mendelssohn, *Jerusalem,* 39. Subsequent passages will be cited parenthetically within the text.

tional power necessary to maintain the analogy. Mendelssohn's assertion that
religious practice be understood as taking place within time thus implicitly
redescribes the power of the state as well; in retemporalizing religion, Mendelssohn retemporalizes civil authority. No longer defined by its aspiration
toward a condition of self-evident, immutable godliness, the authority of the
state becomes expressly historical, constituted and expressed in each of its
acts.

Moreover, Mendelssohn does not simply assert the validity of his redefinition of religion by authorial fiat; he roots his recharacterization—and the
redefinition of civil authority implicit in such a recharacterization—in the
differences between Judaism and Christianity:

> Judaism knows of no revealed religion in the sense in which Christians understand
> this term. The Israelites possess divine *legislation*—laws, commandments, ordi-
> nances, rules of life, instruction in the will of God as to how they should conduct
> themselves in order to attain temporal and eternal felicity. Propositions and pre-
> scriptions of this kind were revealed to them by Moses in a miraculous and super-
> natural manner, but no doctrinal opinions, no saving truths, no universal proposi-
> tions of reason. These the Eternal reveals to us and to all other men, at all times,
> through *nature* and *thing,* but never through *word* and *script.* (89–90)

Whereas being Christian is defined as accepting a set of beliefs ("doctrinal
opinions," "saving truths"), to be Jewish is to act in a certain way, to follow
laws, commandments, and rules of life without believing or *meaning* anything in particular by one's actions—in other words, without understanding
those actions as a form of expression of a common meaning or value established at some moment in the past. Once religion is understood as a kind of
behavior rather than as a state of consciousness or the expression of that
state of consciousness, it becomes a condition of *action* rather than *belief;* its
significance is made up and made authoritative at the moment it is apprehended rather than being discovered after the fact, as a thing already written.
For Locke possessing belief and possessing property functioned as an analogy
or expression for one another and at the same time *justified* one another. For
Mendelssohn, by contrast, belief is the *consequence* and expression of a certain already established, and consequently indisputable and immovable, organization of authority.

But whereas for Locke the writtenness of the revealed meaning—its appearance as "word and script"—constituted it as a kind of belief and also as
the expression of an established authority, Mendelssohn redefines textuality,
transforming it from an expression of existing authority that is meant to

guide belief and behavior into an assertion of the ongoing quality of signification. Textuality is no longer to be associated with literal writtenness but is
related to what Mendelssohn terms "ceremonial law":

> The written as well as the unwritten laws have directly, as *prescriptions for action*
> and rules of life, public and private felicity as their ultimate aim. But they are also,
> in large part, to be regarded as a kind of script, and they have significance and
> meaning as ceremonial laws. They guide the inquiring intelligence to divine truths,
> partly to eternal and partly to historical truths upon which the religion of this
> people was founded. The ceremonial law was the bond which was to connect action
> with contemplation, life with theory. The ceremonial law was to induce personal
> converse and social contact between school and teacher, inquirer and instructor,
> and to stimulate and encourage rivalry and emulation. (128)

In ceremony, Mendelssohn not only discovers a way to make sense of history
by transforming it into a symbolic system but also finds a system that is forever being produced. The performance of a ceremony simultaneously means
in its own right—as a single, unrepeatable happening at a particular time and
place in history—and means as an instance of a series of formally identical
events that have occurred in the past and likely will continue to occur in the
future. We will recall that Mendelssohn earlier differentiated "knowledge"
from "belief" in terms of the temporal relation between subject and object
each described: whereas knowledge articulated the simultaneous copresence
of the subject in the process of knowing and the object being known, belief
described a condition in which the evidence of an object or event and the idea
of it were separated in time, space, or both. If we remember as well that
writing served as both the sign and the instrument of this temporal disjunction, we can see that in the simultaneity of ceremony Mendelssohn finds a
mode of representation that captures the relations of knowledge without rei-
fying them into belief. Whereas writing both produces and marks the condition of belief, ceremony produces and marks the condition of knowledge. By
maintaining a tense equilibrium between its meaning as a single historical
event ("action") and its symbolic meaning as an iteration of a series (representation or "a kind of script"), ceremony blocks the consolidation of authority into a single site. In each ritual they perform, Jews are acting historically,
acting within a particular set of unrepeatable conditions, and at the same
time acting as a kind of script, repeating and transforming a set of gestures
whose significance lies in its extension through time, from one iteration to
the next. In acting through time, Jewish ceremonial law refuses the consolidation of authority around space. In this way, meaning itself is distributed

among the performers who at once act and are read as signs that render the actions of others as meaningful representations, continually produced and reproduced through time. By redefining textuality as a set of social relations extending though time, Mendelssohn is able to offer a model for imagining commonness as being constantly made and remade through time, out of the very historicity and difference of its makers. *Daniel Deronda* becomes both the instrument for discovering such a temporalized commonness and the occasion of its enactment.

Daniel Deronda: Origins and Foundations

Daniel Deronda begins, famously, with an epigram about the impossibility of beginning. And if we were to take the stolidly unveiled contextlessness of the epigrammatic form, ever unbegun, as an invitation to take Eliot at her word, we might read this lament at the necessity of the "make-believe of a beginning" as an expression of authorial humility in the face of too much pastness. But while Eliot's meticulously elaborated self-consciousness is certain to alert us to the difficulty of incorporating all that has come before into the force of that starting off ("No retrospect will take us to the true beginning and whether our prologue be in heaven or on earth, it is but a fraction of that all presupposing fact with which our story sets out"), it is likely to do so at the cost of our noticing what has not yet been said. What is missing from the beginning of *Daniel Deronda* is, quite simply, Daniel Deronda. With the movement into the narrative proper, the humility about the task of beginning that we find in the epigram immediately segues into a much more complex crisis of narratorial confidence, where the narrative's apparently unmoored anxiety of its evaluations turns out to belong not to the timeless, placeless narrative voice of the virtually authorial narrator of the epigram but to the eponymous Daniel Deronda himself:

> Was she beautiful or not beautiful? And what was the secret of form or expression which gave the dynamic quality to her glance? Was the good or the evil genius dominant in those beams? Probably the evil; else why was the effect that of unrest rather than of undisturbed charm? Why was the wish to look again felt as coercion and not as a longing in which the whole being consents?[29]

29. George Eliot, *Daniel Deronda*, ed. Terence Cave (New York; Penguin, 1995), 7. Subsequent passages will be cited parenthetically within the text.

Just at the moment when this slide from an epigrammatic narrative consciousness to a narrower, characterological one encourages us to identify the vision of *Daniel Deronda* with that of its titular protagonist, Daniel Deronda virtually disappears from the novel. Gwendolen Harleth, the gambler whose "dynamic . . . glance" turns back at the gaze directed toward her, draws that gaze into the narrative frame. By chapter's end, Deronda has become the novel's structural principle by virtue of his absence, as the narrator, once again firmly ensconced beyond the purview of the novel's characters, informs us with a reportorial flatness that "Gwendolen did not make Daniel's acquaintance on this occasion" (14).

Daniel's absence did not pass unremarked by the earliest readers, who first encountered the novel in serial installments and thus were made all the more aware of his disappearance. Whereas the reviewer for the *Sunday Times* remained sufficiently convinced of the reliability of the conventions of novelistic titling simply to mark the delayed information—"As yet, the hero is scarcely seen" (*Sunday Times*, 20 February 1876)—others saw Deronda's absence as posing a challenge to the interpretive conventions of the form. Writing in the *Guardian* on 2 February 1876, one reviewer complained, "Why call the book *Daniel Deronda*? That [gambling incident] is all we hear about him for the present: if we want to know anything more, we are reduced to guessing at the meaning of the odd-looking name." Over the course of the next fifteen chapters during which Daniel Deronda remains entirely offstage, we are likely to experience his absence as a decreasingly pressing matter. If we, like Gwendolen, depart the Leubronn casino scene actively wondering when we will next encounter Deronda, as Gwendolen's story becomes increasingly complex and absorbing, the full-scale absence of Daniel Deronda from the novel *called Daniel Deronda* comes to feel less a determining condition of the narrative than a vaguely unsettling oddness.

But though we may not read the novel merely waiting for the time to pass until we meet Daniel again, the earliest reviews also suggest that readers experienced the first installments as transforming the act of reading into an experience of the passage of time. Eliot's particular accomplishment in *Daniel Deronda* lay in her capacity to turn the material necessity of publishing in serial installments to positive narrative effect. The 13 February 1876 *Weekly Dispatch* commented that while for volume readers of the novel "the first impulse" would probably have been "to rush to the end to see what becomes of Gwendolen Harleth," serial readers are better able to discern "the gradual development of characters." Likewise, Henry James, reviewing the first installment (of twenty-four) in the February 1876 *Nation*, noted that insofar as the novel offers the opportunity of experiencing another, fictional world, it is a world experienced and known through time: "We must express our pleasure in the prospect of the intellectual luxury of taking up, month after month, the little clear-paged volumes of Daniel Deronda. . . . For almost a year to come the lives of appreciative readers will have a sort of literal extension into another multitudinous world" (362–63).[30]

Although James, writing after only one installment, would have had no way of anticipating the multiple registers within which his comments would resonate, his formulation makes apparent how Eliot is able to use the experience of reading as an experience of the passage of time to introduce readers to "worlds"—that is to say, cultures or populations—with which they are otherwise unfamiliar. Whereas Eliot claimed it was her reputation—her "independen[ce] in material things"—that enabled her to do "what was needful to be done" by presenting Jews in such a light as to overcome the entrenched habits of English antisemitism, the means she uses is quite literally her manipulation of the very material circumstances of the time required for her novel to be published and read. Most straightforwardly, where her usual readership would be likely to resist, or at best be indifferent to, a novel devoted entirely to the Jewish world she represents within *Daniel Deronda,* by beginning with Gwendolen Harleth's narrative and then gradually supplanting her story by both Daniel's search for his origins and the accompanying awakening of his Jewish national aspirations, Eliot forces readers invested from the novel's outset in discovering the fate of Gwendolen and her family to take an interest, however pragmatic, in the fate of the Jews as well. The "other multitudinous world" James catches sight of as it flashes into being in the early chapters of *Daniel Deronda* is thus not merely the finely wrought fictional world of Gwendolen's bourgeois England. Since the fictional world of the novel, assembled out of words that must be read linearly, registers its fictionality as the necessity of being apprehended over time, the other multitudinous world becomes the heretofore mysterious environs of London's Jewish East End. By transforming the time it takes to read the novel—the temporal dilation born both of its writtenness and of its seriality—from a condition to be forgotten or ignored into a central element of the conscious experience of novel reading, Eliot makes the banal fact of the novel's fictionality into the condition of its political efficacy.

But the opening lines of *Daniel Deronda,* and the temporalized reading process set in motion by those lines, accomplish more than simply authorizing the logic by which novelistic fictions can become instruments of political

30. My account and citation of these early reviews is indebted to Linda K. Hughes and Michael Lund, *The Victorian Serial* (Charlottesville: University Press of Virginia, 1991), 155–68.

change. In that these initial lines link the novel's reworking of the concept of fictionality to a notion that relations between subjects and objects are shifting and contingent, the opening of *Daniel Deronda* recalls the complex subject position articulated by the anonymous *Jewish Chronicle* reviewer. In so doing, these lines imply that the novel's grapplings with fictionality are part of a broader historical concern in rethinking the relations between individual subjectivity and common culture. If, as the novel's earliest readers attest, it is the gap between the expectations generated by the title and Daniel's virtual absence from the early books that creates the experience of reading as an experience of the passage of time, it is likewise the shifting and uncertain relations between *Daniel Deronda* and Daniel Deronda that generate the evaluative crisis of the novel's opening and the disintegration of an eighteenth-century notion of commonness grounded in an aesthetic subject announced by this crisis. For the *Jewish Chronicle* reviewer, the fiction of George Eliot's pseudonym not only had prevented character and novel—or, more strictly, the points of view of character and narrator—from being wholly conflated, it also prevented the author's act of imaginative fiction-making from being wholly absorbed within or naturalized by the "worldly," timeless, fictional world produced by that act of imagination. The impossibility of identifying author and fictional text means that the text of the novel, its circulation, and its transmission neither presume nor produce a condition of likeness among author-subject, character-object, and an audience of readers, but insist on the ongoing differences among those positions, relations to reading crosshatched by historical differences in social and political power.

Although the novel opens with an attempt to assign value ("Was she beautiful or not beautiful?"), the difficulty of making such an assignment seems as much the result of the difficulty of determining whether value resides in subjects or objects as it is a problem of deciding what the content of the value might be: "What was the secret of form or expression which gave the dynamic quality to her glance? Was the good or the evil genius dominant in those beams? Probably the evil; else why was the effect that of unrest rather than undisturbed charm? Why was this wish to look again felt as coercion and not as a longing in which the whole being consents?" When the "she" who may or may not be beautiful has the temerity to look back at the transcendent narrative gaze that would seek to assign her value, the effect of the returned glance is not to create a likeness or mutuality between subject and object but to escalate differences. Indeed, the relocation of value from subject to object, a relocation here marked as the shift from aesthetic to ethical value, blurs the distinction between subject and object, which turns out to vary from one context to the next. But this revaluation of the reversibility of value produces not concord or commonness but irresolvable difference. The very necessity of tracking the relative positions from one context to another rather than relying on a stable authority to set value produces a kind of "unrest" that transforms even the heretofore untroubled experience of the unmoored evaluating looker into a fraught contest of competing claims to power. If Gwendolen's dynamic return glance is enough to disabuse us of the hope that we might remain perched, omniscient and unmoved, on some outcropping of an originary fictionality, we are nonetheless left with the chance of escaping the vicissitudes of the ever mixing and remixed relation between looker and looked upon by viewing any particular relation as though it is likely to change in time.

The opening chapter of *Daniel Deronda* thus lays out the case, here backed only by the affect of a vague anxiety, for a new kind of reader, a reader who understands his or her knowledge of the fictional world of the novel—and effectively, the very existence of that world—to be accumulated only bit by bit, in the time it takes to read from the beginning of the novel to the end. Read this way, the characters of Eliot's imaginings bear the marks of the piecemeal and imperfect attention of those who would know them, the intervals not only of pages turned but of meals prepared and eaten, diaries put down and taken up again, trips made to town. But if the opening chapter offers an argument for learning to read anew, Eliot remains cognizant of the persistence of old habits of reading. As I have proposed, the novel's diverting our attention away from Gwendolen toward the largely unfamiliar rituals and domestic habits of Daniel's slowly widening community of Jews marks the moment when the dilation of the reading process reveals its political promise. But Gwendolen's role in bringing about right reading neither begins nor ends with the overshadowing of her story. For at least one element that gets pushed to the edges of the novel is the story of Gwendolen as reader; as we cease to read about Gwendolen, we cease to read like her as well.

Indeed, what makes Gwendolen a reader—or, more precisely, what makes her a bad reader, is that she insists on reading herself to the exclusion of all else. Consider the account of her initial meeting with Grandcourt, arguably the novel's most formally unconventional episode. As the two make conversation, Gwendolen tirelessly stages and represents the scene she is bringing into being:

"I suppose you are a first-rate shot with a rifle."

(Pause, during which Gwendolen, having taken a rapid observation of Grandcourt, made a brief graphic description of him to an indefinite hearer.) "I have left off shooting."

"Oh, then, you are a formidable person. People who have done things once and left them off make one feel very contemptible, as if one were using cast-off fashions. I hope you have not left off all follies, because I practise a great many."

(Pause, during which Gwendolen made several interpretations of her own speech.)

"What do you call follies?"

"Well, in general, I think whatever is agreeable is called a folly. But you have not left off hunting, I hear."

(Pause, wherein Gwendolen recalled what she had heard about Grandcourt's position, and decided that he was the most aristocratic-looking man she had ever seen.)

"One must do something." (112)

Satisfied with the progress of their conversation, Gwendolen ends the tête-à-tête after having provided herself with the interior assurance that she need not fear rivals for Grandcourt's attention:

(Pause, wherein Gwendolen was thinking that men had been known to choose some one else than the women they most admired, and recalled several experiences of that kind in novels.) (114)

Eliot is here at her most unrestrained in lampooning Gwendolen's illimitable self-absorption, but even as the episode pokes fun at Gwendolen, its deliberate highlighting of readers' access to her consciousness formalizes and hence generalizes both the temptations and the dangers of Gwendolen's relentless self-reading. The passage not only makes it evident that her interiority consists overwhelmingly of ruminations concerning her own behavior as a social being but also displays her unwavering faith that the meaning of her own behavior lies in what she thinks about what she has done. From her perspective, since she is her own best reader, she need be nothing more than a reader. But we might have just as accurately said that Gwendolen is her own best writer or imaginer; because she conceives of the positions of subject, object, and audience as ideally identical to one another, she is at once author, creation, and audience of herself. What matters is not what she does, but what she imagines herself doing.

Daniel Deronda's opening presented a model of sociality, and a mode of reading, in which the prospect that subjects and objects might occupy one another's roles produced a sense of the ongoing differences among the positions rather than a sense of the fundamental identity of the various occupants. In Gwendolen's worldview, by contrast, one need not take time to trace the oscillations of power, the jockeyings and counterjockeyings of subjects and objects, because one need only look to one's consciousness to know how one means in the world, how one is valued. In her faith that the private imaginings of an individual are sufficient to produce a host of identical consciousnesses, to turn imagining subject, object, and audience into different manifestations of a single common subjectivity, we can discern the echoes of the aesthetic imagination theorized in "The Natural History of German Life."

These resonances offer clues for discovering the particular pitfalls associated with the sort of reading Gwendolen indulges in. In "Natural History," recall, it was the *mutual inaccessibility* of the individual aesthetic consciousness, the peasants who were the ur-objects of this consciousness and the spatially remote readers, that licensed the imagining of the individual artists—a sort of belief—to serve as the ground of common culture. While Gwendolen's initial encounter with Grandcourt demonstrates her unruffled assurance that all that matters is what she thinks about what she does, the passage also provides the origins of Gwendolen's certainty that what she thinks may be kept secret from other people as long as it does not manifest itself in what she does. When Gwendolen pledges to Grandcourt's mistress Lydia Glasher that she will refuse Grandcourt's offer of marriage and later, having told no one of the agreement, reneges on her pledge, her belief that she can reverse herself with impunity rests on her assurance that her secrets are inaccessible to others, indeed, that the definitive quality of her consciousness—like the aesthetic imagination of "Natural History"—is its inaccessibility. What Gwendolen does not realize, of course, is that she has been made object as well as subject, that Grandcourt's lackey Lush has *overheard* (in a way reminiscent of the *Jewish Chronicle* reviewer's overhearing) Gwendolen making her pledge, and that Grandcourt will turn his knowledge of her knowledge to brutal account after their marriage. Although Grandcourt appears to seek to reduce his activity to a bare minimum ("One must do something"), he chooses his goal not because, like Gwendolen, he assumes that what he does is less important than what he knows, believes, or means about what he does but because he recognizes that knowing, believing, and meaning constitute actions in themselves, constitute the most significant social acts there are. What Gwendolen fails to recognize, but Grandcourt sees all too plainly, is that her knowledge of what went on between her and Lydia Glasher in the forest that afternoon is not absolutely meaningful, possessing a value for her to invoke or make disappear, but has meaning and value that change as they interact with other people's—here, Grandcourt's—knowledge and the use they decide to make of it.

Moreover, if the oddness of the novel's representation draws our attention not merely to Gwendolen's strikingly absorbing—and peculiarly accessible—consciousness but also to the author who would direct and monitor our attentiveness, we might be tempted to return our glances to the text and read in its strange parenthetical asides not simply the outward signs of a character's interior but the marks of the novel's own production. The parentheses that both define Eliot's view of conventional narrative authority and, through Gwendolen, dramatize the dangers of a naive acceptance of such an authority also read like nothing so much as Eliot's compositional notes for the conventional realist novel she can no longer bring herself to write. In this way Eliot offers a version of fiction-making in which the creation of the fiction is not isolated in a moment of composition always already prior to a particular act of reading but acts, as James might put it, as "a sort of literal extension into another multitudinous world." We learn to be cognizant of the time it takes us to read by noticing the time it has taken Eliot to write, by recognizing that she is still in effect writing as we read.

Of course, one might object that even if we agree to the resemblance of the parentheses that graphically trace the bounds of Gwendolen's inner musings and those we would find in Eliot's notes for a novel, the parentheses we find in *Daniel Deronda* are less elements of an ongoing compositional process than symbols of a fiction-making that is over and done with. I would respond that so far as the responsibility for interpreting the parentheses metafictionally falls to the reader, the fiction of the novel continues to be created, to become meaningful, over the course of our own acts of reading. The paradox of such a project (as we shall see, it is a paradox whose implications will require the great length of *Daniel Deronda* to be worked out) is that the more strongly we understand Eliot to be intending us to read the parentheses in such a way, the less we are able to say she succeeds. Indeed, even with the terms she lays out in the novel, Eliot maintains a certain investment in *not* succeeding. In so emphasizing both the production and the materiality of the novel, she attempts to use her autobiography—in essence, to introduce history, the history of her writing process—as a means of avoiding what she clearly sees as the immorality of Grandcourt's nihilistic reduction of meaning to a random play of social positions, to a contest of who best can know without being known, while at the same time avoiding Gwendolen's error of embracing too readily the false compensations of conventional realism. Faced with the specter of Grandcourt, who jettisons the ontological otherness of the authority of the realist narrator and thus subsumes the realist novel's distinction between the true and the not-true within an infinite array of equally (in)valid systems of meaning, Eliot here responds by tipping the balance toward an assertion of the priorness of her own authority, her power to control the quality of reader response on which the meaning of her fictions depends.

What might seem to be a disinterested juxtaposition of the fictional (Gwendolen and Grandcourt's conversation) and the historical (the passage as autobiography, as a historical record of her process of writing the novel) is established and then, at least at this early point in the novel, abandoned so that Eliot can assert the indisputable aspect of historicity, the pastness of her act of fiction-making. She uses the person of her own fictional creation Grandcourt as the occasion to reconsolidate the fictional authority she nonetheless continues to feel moved to distribute. Eliot begins *Daniel Deronda* by articulating this impasse as implicit in the form of the realist novel and, as we shall see, uses her own final novel as a means of staging a series of alternative versions of realist fictionality in the effort to work herself, and the novel form, beyond this impasse.

Moreover, as I hope was foreshadowed by the genealogy of "commonness" I presented at the beginning of this chapter, the novel becomes the locus for the articulation of this historical difficulty of imagining commonness because it represents the likeness of individual subjects as following from their location in a common geographical place. Oddly enough, for Eliot it is expressly because the realist novel represents this principle of spatial proximity as if it were the novel's own principle of organization (narrator's and reader's perspectives are blurred into Daniel's as he stands at the side of the room observing Gwendolen), at once cloaking and removing from history the work of the author herself, that the genre can be used as an instrument for countering that very principle of spatial organization of commonness. *Daniel Deronda* stages the transformation of the novel from a representation of relations— the relations of people who live in the same geographical place—into a protracted process of learning by demonstrating the strenuous difficulties writers and readers encounter in their efforts to make sense of one another. In her writing of the novel, Eliot challenges the transparent self-evidence of geographical location by turning the interchange between author and reader from an encounter whose rules of engagement are presumed by both parties into an awkward, chancy series of negotiations, the wary, watchful circlings of historically particularized subjects who discover how and what they know and believe by the very difficulty of learning it from others.

To suggest, as I mean to do, that George Eliot intends her novel as anything other than an affirmation—indeed, a celebration—of the power of geographical locale to shape the most intimate subjective contours of its inhabitants is almost certain to provoke a second look, less one of curiosity directed toward a familiar text made new than one of incredulity, the incredulity reserved for the critic who indulges herself without limits. Because for a moment, at least, it seems as though a moment is all we need to know what Eliot, clad in only the flimsiest of first-person narrative veils, believes about the proper relation between the landscape and those people who inhabit it:

> Pity that Offendene was not the home of Miss Harleth's childhood, or endeared to her by family memories! A human life, I think, should be well rooted in some spot of a native land, where it may get the love of tender kinship for the face of earth, for the labours men go forth to, for sounds and accents that haunt it, for whatever will give that early home a familiar unmistakable difference amidst the future widening of knowledge: a spot where the definiteness of early memories may be inwrought with affection, and kindly acquaintance with all neighbours, even to the dogs and donkeys, may spread not by sentimental effort and reflection, but as a sweet habit of the blood. At five years old, mortals are not prepared to be citizens of the world, to be stimulated by abstract nouns, to soar above preference into impartiality; and that prejudice in favour of milk with which we blindly begin, is a type of the way body and soul must get nourished at least for a time. The best introduction to astronomy is to think of the nightly heavens as a little lot of stars belonging to one's own homestead.
>   But this blessed persistence in which affection can take root had been wanting in Gwendolen's life. (22)

In its barely discernible address to the reader, the invitation to pity at once acknowledges the necessity of appeal, the consent underwriting the likeness, and records it as a condition once and always brought into being. Truncated into ambiguity, the gently imperious command to the reader, "You pity," glides into the blithe narratorial description, "It is a pity," and with this halting of appeal, there seems to end our cause to look a second time.

Taken on its own, the disquisition appears to make a generalized case against a vaguely defined universalist cosmopolitanism with what might be termed a geography of memory, a "blessed persistence" of experience that is associated with a given geographical space without being simply the literal fact of that space. Like Adam Smith, the passage figures placedness against the fundamental incoherence of "abstract nouns," turning the temporalized "sounds and accents that haunt" and thereby layer themselves into the "blessed persistence" of childhood memories into a sort of infinitely expandable property: "The best introduction to astronomy is to think of the nightly heavens as a little lot of stars belonging to one's own homestead." We might read this passage as an attempt to revise away the contradictions that plagued Eliot's attempt in "Natural History" to describe the nature of the ties linking humans to the geographical spaces they inhabit. No longer need the choice be between a constitutive relationship to the land where one lives and the capacity for self-reflection; here an individual's power of memory, indeed, his or her subjectivity, at once makes and is made by the continuous inhabiting of a place. Place is no longer absolutely constitutive of its inhabitants, as it was for Riehl's peasants, but neither is it wholly imaginary; rather, the effect of remaining continuously in a place is entirely real, if not wholly material.

The passage seems equally straightforward read within its more local narrative context. At the conclusion of the chapter immediately preceding this passage, Gwendolen, having lost the last of her money at roulette, returns to her room to discover a letter from her mother, informing her of the sudden demise of her family's fortune and recalling her home. The chapter closes: "In this way it happened that Gwendolen never reappeared at the roulette-table, but set off that Thursday for Brussels, and on Saturday morning arrived at Offendene, the home to which she and her family were soon to say a last good-bye" (21). This turn of events provides adequate occasion for the narrator's reflection on the quality and force of place, or its memory, in creating a self: Gwendolen has been called home suddenly from Leubronn, she is faced with the threat of imminent eviction (so the end of the previous chapter tells us), and her lack of early memories for the place—an absence of ties generally—robs her return even of the comfort of familiarity. Or alternatively, the passage could be understood as a narrative attempt at mitigating the starkness of Gwendolen's situation: though she will soon be forced to leave her home, things might have been worse; she might have had to leave a place to which she had real attachments. New shelters can be found, but childhood homes with their attendant memories are irreplaceable.

What the passage leaves crucially unclear is that the events of the plot it initiates come much earlier chronologically than the incident at Leubronn that sends Gwendolen home to that countryside to which she had appeared to have only the most tenuous connection. That is, the novel's opening episode—the exchange of glances between Gwendolen and Daniel at the roulette table at Leubronn—actually occurs chronologically well *after* Gwendolen's return to her family's residence at Offendene, although we are not likely to become aware of this narrative break until much later, when the flashback closes as the narrative returns to the moment of Gwendolen's arrival at Leubronn. What enables such a misreading is the continuousness of Gwendolen's presence at Offendene or, more precisely, her power to leave the estate and return to it again. We read the events of the two chapters as continuous at least in part because the content of the second passage informs us that Gwendolen has lacked the kind of persistent presence at Offendene that might have allowed her to form an emotional attachment to it. The episodes' discontinuity from one another—and the "blessed persistence" at Offendene implied by recognition of such discontinuity—becomes perceptible only when we as readers experience the repetition of the gambling episode at Leubronn, only, that is, when we become conscious of memories outside the chronologically ordered events of the plot. Not only does our discovery of the discontinuity jar us into recognizing that reading takes place over time, but it illustrates in no uncertain terms that what we think a given passage in the novel means depends on when we read it and what we already know at that moment. It is this experience of the separability of our affective state (memories, interests, aversions) and the temporality of our learning from the temporality of the events of the novel that enables us to understand the true chronology of Gwendolen's activities.

But as I have hinted already, Eliot's insistence that we consider the role of the reader—the particularized, historically situated reader—in constituting narrative meaning is not motivated simply by her interest in imagining the way the novel might produce common knowledge and values among writers and readers by detaching that knowledge from the contingencies of the material world. Instead, it is part of a much more pointed attempt to challenge the assumption that people are who they are because of where they live—and, by implication, the presumption that individuals are likely to share common knowledge, values, and interests, to be part of a common culture, because they live in the same place. Here the evidence regarding Gwendolen's ties to Offendene offered at the level of narrative content (she has not lived at the estate continuously enough to have been made by it) seems to directly contradict the evidence offered by the novel's form (that the continuity of her presence at Offendene was sufficient to span the temporal discontinuity of the two episodes). These two sets of apparently contradictory data are, of course, both right; they simply describe Gwendolen's condition at different chronological moments, with the description of transience applying to an earlier period in her life and in the novel's plot. We misread because we tend to read the narrative's transparent conditions as conditions that are ongoing, existing beyond time, and consequently more fundamentally defining of the subjects marked by them, leading us to understand Gwendolen's transient relationship to Offendene as permanent. These passages indicate not necessarily that Gwendolen's ties to Offendene are more fundamentally transient than they are persistent but that our sense of the permanence, the unchangeability, of an inhabitant's relationship to land—whether that relationship is one of persistence or transience—is the mark of our willingness to forget who and where we are when we read. For Eliot, the realist novel conventionally accedes to the authority of the imaginative fiction so as to subordinate its readers' sense of the changeability of an individual's relation to a given geographical space to a sense of the necessity and permanence of the relation.

The effect of the Offendene scene is to create an experience of reading that is wholly assimilable neither to the authorial consciousness that imagines the details of the novel into being nor to the sort of consciousness produced by the "blessed persistence" on a single spot of land or by a character-defining geographical transience. The readerly subjectivity that emerges from this early scene and that is refined and elaborated on over the course of *Daniel Deronda* is presented not as an alternative to experiencing oneself as located in a particular geographical place, but as an alternative means of experiencing one's relation to that place. Although the emphasis of the scene is be on distinguishing its readers from these differently constituted forms of subjectivity, the subject Eliot envisions emerging out of the difficult, knotty labor of making sense of the narratorial ruminating on Offendene is an occasion for imagining a new sort of sociability. In pointing out a readerly subjectivity in which selfhood is generalized through time, *Daniel Deronda* begins to make available a kind of personhood conceivable not as a collection of attributes but as the accumulating of knowledge, a selfhood at once particular and contingent. For Eliot, the subject who comes into being over time begins to lose its edges in the accumulation of a lifetime; the knowing that constitutes a self becomes the knowing that constitutes a string of selves, an assemblage. In *Daniel Deronda* the subject is discernible as an autonomous individual only in that he or she is identified with a particular geographical place, but the recognition of individuals on the evidence of the space they occupy is, in a way at once trivial and profound, a misrecognition. The assertion that an individual *belongs* to a particular space, that the place occupied tells us something deep and true, is necessarily an assertion of a belief rather than a kind of knowledge; it is likewise the constitution of that subject as someone who believes rather than knows. Within this context, the gradual occlusion of Gwendolen's narrative—the stories of her locatedness, her marriage, her power to make promises and keep secrets—by Daniel's inadvertent yet seemingly inevitable discovery of his genealogy can be seen not simply as a politically savvy sleight of hand by which readers who start off reading about a spoiled young Englishwoman unwittingly discover themselves engaged in the lives of a group of Jews. It also announces a fundamental transformation in the terms around which narratives are organized. Whereas the stories that compose Gwendolen's narrative presume an autonomous subject and then follow that subject to its dissolution, in Daniel's genealogical narrative the very existence of the autonomous subject becomes the stuff of storytelling, the search for the relations between Daniel and his parents structured as an attempt to discover *what* they are as much as who they are.

Daniel Deronda begins his search for his parents by accident; with the terms of his search themselves to be searched out, he literally does not know what he is asking. Earlier, as we followed Gwendolen from the casino home again to Offendene, the unexpected discovery that we had been reading a flashback jarred us into recognizing our power to know independent of the fictional events of the narrative. Here we are invited to "imagine" the portentous moment in Daniel's past life, the novel making no effort to present the personal history of the individual subject as something that exists prior to the creative efforts of the reader. We are asked to imagine an "epoch[al]" moment long ago, when the thirteen-year-old Daniel pores over Sismondi's *History of the Italian Republics* and, confused by the text's repeated references to various popes' nephews,[31] politely asks his tutor to explain "how it was the popes and cardinals always had so many nephews" (164). Daniel "starts up" "as if something had stung him." Because Daniel has always referred to his guardian Sir Hugo Mallinger as his "uncle," suddenly "the uncle whom he loved very much took on an aspect of a father who held secrets about him" (167).

But the narrative immediately complicates the epiphanic, singularly "momentous" quality of Daniel's insight. Rather than elaborating by specifying the content of the knowledge into which young Daniel is stung, the narrative instead offers us the details of habitual behavior—"He had always called Sir Hugo his uncle" (165)—a description of the ongoing state that in its own dilating presentation of details dramaturgically overwhelms any sense we might have had of the eventfulness of the revelation. The dramatic effect of the apparent new knowledge is subverted by the nondrama of its narrative consequences, as the elaboration of Daniel's past habits, poised ambiguously in relation to present behavior, quietly slides the narrative energies backward into the untroubled past: "He was too fond of Sir Hugo to be sorry for the loss of unknown parents" (165). Daniel thus effectively subordinates, at least temporarily, a notion of identity associated with the acquisition and evaluation of knowledge at a single, identifiable occasion—the sort of knowledge that might be experienced by readers forced to recognize that the same passage can mean very different things depending on when they read it—to a selfhood rooted in the ongoing experiences of everyday life. Compensation

---

31. The reference to popes' nephews recalls Browning's 1844 dramatic monologue "The Bishop Orders His Tomb at Saint Praxed's Church," where the dying bishop addresses "Nephews—sons mine." Robert Browning, *The Poems* (New York: Penguin, 1981).

here is quite literally local, a connection to a place, "one of the finest in England, at once historical, romantic and home-like," whose power as an alternative source of identity emerges directly from its capacity to seem foundational, to appear to exist prior to and as the ground of any historically specific experience of discovery.

Left markedly ambiguous is the description's status as history and, not unrelatedly, its status as evidence. Although its logical context seems to identify it as an extension and elaboration of the discussion about subjectivity that precedes it, and consequently to adopt that earlier discussion's point of view and narrative occasion as its own, the passage's introduction of a variety of temporal markings neither clearly reconcilable with one another nor clearly assimilable with what has come earlier challenges such an assumption. As we have seen, what begins as a clearly delineated narrative incident (Deronda's reading of *Sismondi's History* as the moment of discovery of the "truth" of his parentage) is quickly followed by a far less localizable description (his musings about his attachment to Sir Hugo's estate). We are likely, then, to read this initial movement from a narratively specifiable incident to the description of a sustained state of mind within the context of the initial incident. ("And at that time, he did not mind learning more, for he was too fond of Sir Hugo to be sorry for the loss of unknown parents. Life was very delightful.") Hence we see the shift from the temporally local to the general as an indication of Daniel's psychic maneuverings, maneuverings clearly distinguishable from the narrative's own epistemological position. Daniel's turn to a sense of placedness as an absolute ground of identity is, however, contextualized by the novel in such a way as to refuse the reader the resolution Daniel himself so eagerly seeks. The absoluteness of his relation to place is asserted, then immediately complicated by the elaboration of his experience of the home:

In Sir Hugo's youthful portrait with rolled collar and high cravat, Sir Thomas Lawrence had done justice to the agreeable alacrity of expression and sanguine temperament still to be seen in the original, but had done something more than justice in slightly lengthening the nose, which was in reality shorter than might have been expected in a Mallinger. Happily the appropriate nose of the family reappeared in his younger brother, and was to be seen in all its refined regularity in his nephew Mallinger Grandcourt. But in the nephew Daniel Deronda, the family faces of various types, seen on the walls of the gallery, found no reflex. (166)

Both the occasion and the point of view of this extended rumination are tricky to pin down. Are we to understand the portraits to offer evidence affirming Daniel's discovery of his real relation to Sir Hugo, made just moments earlier? We might then read the opening of the chapter up through the description of the portraits as the narratively local elaboration of a specific incident, with the disruption produced by Daniel's realization first mitigated by his efforts to shift the ground of his identity to a relation to place, then confirmed by the additional visual evidence of consanguinity offered by the portraits. But what of that evidence? The description of the portraits seems to dispute more than to support Daniel's sense that Sir Hugo is his real father, yet the novel fails to register any sense of confusion produced by the evidence of the portraits. Perhaps, then, we are instead meant to understand the portraits as a further elaboration of the sense of place presented by the description of the house rather than as evidence confirming Daniel's new, narratively local discovery. Within this line of interpretation, the portraits might even be understood as offering a partial explanation for why the truth of his relationship to Sir Hugo did not occur to Daniel earlier (they don't look alike), as well as further indication that the new discovery, set against the more permanent identity of place, is not likely to matter much. In short, placing the incident temporally becomes the same as determining its logical or evidentiary function within the narrative. This circularity ought to introduce the idea that what is at stake here is less an unambiguous determination of the knowledge Daniel gains from looking at the portraits on the walls of Sir Hugo's manor house than a demonstration of the process by which such knowledge is produced.

What, then, do the intertwined ambiguities surrounding the scene's narrative occasion and its status as evidence reveal about the social relations at the heart of Daniel Deronda's misreading? Inasmuch as this extended passage counterposes a model of a subject forged out of the ongoing relation to place against that of a subject formed temporally, by knowledge, it reprises the tension articulated with such startling efficiency in the Offendene scene. But with the introduction of the wall of portraits as an element of the geography of "home" to which Daniel feels himself attached, the relatively straightforward opposition between placedness and a temporalized, cumulative knowledge is rendered more complex. By linking the tension between these two versions of subjectivity not only to the operation of an aesthetic, imaginative authority but to questions of genealogy as well, the portrait scene works to make visible how the particular modes of realist representation—the ways novels represent people, space, and the relations between them—develop as a means of creating commonness in the face of uneven distribution of material property. By delineating the exact representations that allow the novel to appear as though it is adequate in itself to create its readers' likeness, Eliot uses the portrait scene as the first step in her effort to marshal the realist novel as the instrument for its own undoing. Once we recognize the novel's representation of the paintings to be articulating a fantasy that the relations of paternity—the links between father, son, and the land they inhabit—might be known absolutely rather than remaining at the level of mere belief, we can see that the novel's peculiar positioning between the proper and the common—between Daniel Deronda the character and that text called *Daniel Deronda*—is the source of both its greatest social and political power and its greatest instability.

In one sense the problem of determining the relative priority of narrative event and evidence that makes the meaning of the scene so difficult to fix might be understood as following the form of the paternal relations that are its thematic concern. Within the larger context of the novel, Daniel's error lies in mistaking nothing for something, that is, in understanding Sir Hugo's ongoing silence to mark a deliberate withholding of acknowledgment of their relationship, a refusal to own, rather than a decision to announce no relationship at all or, more accurately, not even to announce.

Central to the novel's interest, as well as to the narrative form of Daniel's misreading, is the way the "act" conferring *illegitimacy,* the *refusal* to own, can be seen to stand as the foundational gesture of the conception of paternity within a liberal state. The cultural force of legal paternity in nineteenth-century England rests at least in part on its status as ideal, a speech act absolutely independent of the contingency (and unknowability) of material bodies. Such a notion of an ideal legal paternity can be said to come into being only at the moment it is refused, that is, the moment when the overlap between biological paternity and the social and juridical relation of inheritance linking father and son is itself demonstrated to be contingent rather than necessary. For Eliot, the curious aspect of the concept of illegitimacy is that it implies two contradictory relations—connectedness and unconnectedness—at once. The lack of connection asserted by a father's refusal to own his son depends on, and must implicitly reinvoke, the logical priority of their connectedness. Moreover, the fact that the "act" supposedly marking the unconnectedness—a deliberate silence of refusing to name—is empirically indistinguishable from no act at all, from the unmarked passage of time, means that identifying a single moment when the status of illegitimacy becomes an isolatable historical act is unlikely, if not strictly impossible. The outward effects of a will, merely contingent within the terms of liberalism, happen to be indistinguishable from the appearance of no act of will at all; the father's withholding of the paternal name is able to hide its contradictoriness because it comes into being at liberalism's vanishing point, at the moment when meaning something and doing something—producing effects in the material world—become indistinguishable.

The ideological overlapping of this textual moment is complex: the contradictoriness implied by the imputation of illegitimacy is sustainable because the referents of connection and disconnection occur at different levels of abstraction. That is, illegitimacy is seen to escape internal contradiction because its simultaneous claims of connection and disconnection are seen to name different sorts of relations: connection describes the biological, material link, whereas disconnection describes the juridical immaterial relations that govern the transfer of property. At the same time, the connection *between* these two sorts of relations—merely contingent connection between the biological and the juridical versions of paternity—is naturalized, made to seem absolute by being marked by signs that resemble each other absolutely (the sign of silence). What these separate meanings of silence accomplish by virtue of their contingent intersection is to make the claims of connectedness and nonconnectedness appear to occur in a single level of abstraction, as possible relations of likeness and difference rather than within a binary economy governed by the presence or absence of a name. The "likeness" created by painting supplants the name. By means of this translation into signs that at once mean something and mean nothing, the theoretical tension at the heart of the concept of paternity is both sustained and naturalized.

Exactly how do the portraits achieve this reconciliation? In appending the description of the portraits lining the walls of Sir Hugo's home onto the narrative of Daniel's discovery, then, Eliot creates a situation within which description can be mustered as evidence in support of two opposed notions of identity, depending on whether it is understood to occur as a specific narrative event or as a state of sustained experience without discernible beginning or end. The series of portraits itself claims to take the place of the patronym as a model for determining lineage, with the implication that the paintings offer merely an alternative system of signifiers marking an identical set of relations. But is this in fact the case? Whereas the patronym is either given or withheld, with the portraits we are shown a model of relatedness in which the relation of likeness and difference is a matter of degree. While this substitution of an economy of resemblance for the patronym's system of identity and absolute difference effectively eliminates a relation of absolute identity, what it accomplishes more significantly is to eliminate the option of absolute difference. Daniel's crucial error, we will recall, was to mistake the silence of absolute unrelatedness—a silence without meaning—for the silence meant to signal Sir Hugo's withholding of his name. Within the portraits' system of resemblance, there is no comparable space of absolute irrelevance, no space that remains unmarked by some degree of relatedness to the family. No one can be said not to resemble the portrait of Sir Hugo in some way, to be absolutely "unlike" him. As a result, paternity's conventionality, normally perceptible in the possibility of absolute difference, is rendered inconceivable at the moment the portraits become the evidentiary ground on which Daniel evaluates his relation to Sir Hugo.

The portraits are able to accomplish what they accomplish in naturalizing paternity because they can account for certain problems regarding the narrativity of paternity that the patronym on its own is unable to make disappear. In a sense, the portraits transform paternity into a synchronic rather than a diachronic relation, since, at least in Daniel's experience of the wall of portraits, the family line is traced not from one generation to the next but from resemblances of feature apprehended at a single moment.

What exactly is at stake in this transformation? In this substitution of a synchronic system of resemblance for the diachronic relations of probability that more accurately describe at least the biological aspect of the relationship in question, the ontologically and epistemologically threatening infinitude of probability's future-directed temporality—the chance that anything might happen, that sons might not be, much less look like, sons—becomes the source of the paternity's all-inclusiveness within the portraits' horizontal web of resemblances. The paternal horror that anyone could be the father becomes, by miraculous sleight of hand, the certainty that everyone—or at least everyone pictured—is somehow related to him.

Or at least everyone pictured. Temporality cannot finally be fully excluded from the system, and it is at just those moments when the portraits are shown to exist through time that we can see both the line of their intersection with the real world and the terms of their complicity with the novel's own representational forms. Let us return to the first part of the passage in question:

> In Sir Hugo's youthful portrait with rolled collar and high cravat, Sir Thomas Lawrence had done justice to the agreeable alacrity of expression and sanguine temperament still to be seen in the original, but had done something more than justice in slightly lengthening the nose, which was in reality shorter than might have been expected in a Mallinger.

The passage introduces a number of different relations of resemblance: between Sir Hugo and his present if undescribed relatives; between "the original" Sir Hugo and his portrait; and less explicitly, between the youthful Sir Hugo and the somewhat more worn version with whom Daniel himself is acquainted. What the description leaves crucially unclear, however, are the

relations governing these different—and differently connected—terms. Given
the information offered in the description, we cannot know with certainty,
for example, whether Daniel is persuaded by the resemblance between Sir
Hugo's youthful portrait and those representing the other members of his
family (which, after all, exhibit a remarkable likeness, right down to the
length of the figures' noses) or, instead, by the connections between Sir Hugo
"the original" and the family portraits, which reveal a decidedly less convincing similarity. As we have seen, the function of the portraits was to eliminate
the sense of arbitrariness the patronym left untouched through its incapacity
to define all acts in relation to paternity. Here that arbitrariness—the arbitrary willfulness of representation—threatens to show itself, leaving undone
the ideological tasks that the portraits' signifying system of resemblance had
been brought in to perform in the first place.

Enter temporality. I have been proposing that the portraits were effective
in transforming the contingency that plagues paternity's claims to authority—and the partiality that contingency implies—into necessity insofar as
they were able to turn the diachronic aspect of probability into the synchronicity of resemblance. While the portraits do in fact transform a series of relationships occurring through time into a single moment of resemblance, what
the passage illustrates is that they are able to accomplish this transformation
by *separating* the salient temporal relations from the epistemological limitation associated with nineteenth-century notions of contingency, of chance.
The passage of time is discernible at two locations within the structure of
kinship relations implied by the portraits: first, in the fact of Sir Hugo's aging
(perceptible, somewhat ambiguously, in the relation of difference and likeness
between the youthful portrait and the considerable more aged "original"),
and second, less obviously, in the process by which the portraits are created.

The description of Sir Hugo's portrait blurs the contours of the dual influ-
ences of time and artistic intervention. But this instance of something like too
much representation invites us to analyze it in relation not simply to the thing
itself—Sir Hugo in the flesh—but also in the context of that thing over time.
The passage begins to undo this naturalization by representing representation
as itself a historical process. In identifying Sir Thomas as the subject of the
sentence in place of Sir Hugo, the process of representation takes up the uncertain and consequently destabilizing aspect of temporality and relocates it
wholly in the past, leaving the organizing ground of likeness firmly centered
in Sir Hugo's capacity to remain himself over time.

Here is how this works: by making the effect of convention—that is, of
mere representation—inextricable from the effect of the passage of time,
which turns out to be no meaningful effect at all, representational effects are

rendered irrelevant as they are implicitly contained by Sir Hugo's presumed continuity as a subject. "In Sir Hugo's youthful portrait . . . Sir Thomas Lawrence had done justice to the agreeable alacrity of expression and sanguine temperament still to be seen in the original." "Still" is the rhetorical key here; with a single stroke, it invokes a narrative foreclosed, probability that has resolved itself into identity. That the alacrity of expression still exists implies that it might not have, but its potential for being otherwise, its threatening unknowability, is located entirely in the past. Moreover, by rendering the effects of representation indistinguishable from the passage of time in this first section, Sir Thomas Lawrence's arbitrariness gets likewise contained within the frame of Sir Hugo's continuity as a self, even when, as toward the end of the passage, it seems "something more than just."

The contingency of history is narrated on the model of aesthetic choice, not so much erased as appropriated, with the fact that something might have turned out differently in the past lending necessity to the way things did turn out. Not only does this effect depend on circumscribing the effects of representation within the unmarked temporality of the identity of a continuous subject (as with Sir Hugo's portrait), but it relies equally, if incoherently, on transforming history into a set of artistic choices justified—and ended—by the artifact with which they culminate. In order for the contingency of history in the past (the possibility of things' having been otherwise) to be evidence of anything other than the contingency of the present (the possibility of things' being otherwise now), it has to be, like the imaginative choices that result in an artwork, something that occurs in the past and whose traces are available in the present only in the artwork itself. As he stands in Sir Hugo's hallway trying to make out the truth of his past, Daniel does not read the portraits according to the model of the world he occupies—if he did, he might notice that he is not pictured—but instead reads the world according to the model of the portraits. Once what is there becomes the basis for evaluating what ought to be there—once, that is, the plausibility or likeness of a representation is evaluated independent of its status as representation—the contingency of history has been transformed into something like realist narrative.

Insofar as the portrait scene suggests that the description of paintings on a wall traces the same web of relations that it is conventionally the task of the patronym to name, the passage equates the common descriptive language by which the portraits mark likeness with the "proper" noun that is the patronym. But Eliot's claim that the common language of the portraits and the proper language of the patronym are interchangeable does not simply multiply the idioms with which a given set of relationships can be articulated; it changes the very nature of the relationships themselves.

Whereas the common inhabitancy of land is conventionally understood to mark the link between father and son by way of analogy—the inheritance by sons from their fathers is invoked as a sign of the biological link precisely because the existence of that connection cannot be determined for certain—the literalization of the link between shared geographical space and the connectedness of the father and son who inhabit it transforms the meaning of that space. Rather than functioning as a sign—a representation in the juridical and social realm that such a biological relation exists—inhabiting the same geographical space comes to serve as empirical evidence of the relationship. With this detailed description of the wall of portraits, the condition of being in a common space and the likeness of the people who "inhabit" that space are not merely evidence for one another but are absolutely identical. The likeness of Sir Hugo and the people pictured around him works as evidence for their inhabiting the same geographical space because the likeness of Sir Hugo and his cohort are very literally part of the same geographical space. Their resemblance to one another can be read in where they are because their resemblance to one another literally constitutes where they are.

To the extent that looking alike and being in the same place are not simply signs of one another but instead are absolute identical, the link between geographical space and identity need not be circumscribed within the limits of private (landed) property and the relation between father and son. The portrait scene thus eliminates the tension between the proper and the common that dogged thinkers from Locke onward not merely because it substitutes the common language used to describe the paintings for the patronym but also because, in literalizing the link between spatial proximity and resemblance, it generalizes the connection between the private property inhabited by fathers and their sons to embrace any geographically delimited space and its population.

But the striking idiosyncrasy of the representation required to bring about this reconciliation—the verbal representation in a work of fiction of a visual representation whose exact relation to its objects of representation and to the temporal moment of creation is pointedly ambiguous—ought to alert us to the difficulty of the task, and to the very particular social, political, and economic demands to which the novel is responding. In the first place, despite its overt claims to the contrary, the seamlessness of the connection between the resemblance of the pictured individuals and their place of habitation turns out to rest on a causal link between the two rather than their literal identity: the paintings all seem to bear a likeness to Sir Hugo *because* they are near one another. At the same time, the infinitude of the web of resemblance connecting Sir Hugo to everyone who might theoretically inhabit the same geographical space—the infinitude that reconciles the proper and the common and leads Daniel to think that he too resembles all the others by virtue of his spatial proximity, even though he is not pictured—rests on the presumption that the "common" social group identified by their inhabiting a common geographical space and the common social group identified by its members' likeness to one another are the same. What this slippage reflects is that the portraits' capacity to reconcile the proper and the common depends at least in part on the willingness of their audience to view the works of art as if they are complete in themselves, as if they constitute a world.

While it might be tempting to gloss the strategy of the passage by saying that it succeeds in reconciling the common and the proper by making the portraits and the patronym equivalent, such a characterization would be only partly true. For what this gloss leaves unclear is whether what is being equated are the patronym and the portraits or the patronym and the *verbal description of the portraits*. This ambiguity is key to the passage's apparent power to eliminate the tension between proper and common and is crucial to understanding both why Eliot sees the realist novel as particularly able to effect such a reconciliation and at what ideological price such a reconciliation is purchased. If we understand the passage to be equating the patronym with the paintings themselves, that equation circumvents the difficulty of establishing a common meaning or value according to which the likeness—the "commonness"—of the people pictured might be ascertained. That is, insofar as the visual nature of the portraits enables onlookers to apprehend the resemblance among the people pictured in a way that is immediate and self-evident, their visuality eliminates the need for figuring out a process by which meaning might be made common; the likenesses of the portraits are common because they are self-evident.[32] But the problem with this "solution" is that it severely limits what gets to count as "common": only those people and objects who seem to resemble one another self-evidently are understood to be alike. So although the paintings' onlookers may be said to resemble one another inasmuch as they recognize the connectedness of the people in the portraits, the parameters of their shared knowledge are so narrow that they can hardly ensure the onlookers' likeness to one another.

By contrast, if we understand the passage to be equating not the patronym and the paintings but, instead, the patronym and the verbal description of the paintings, the means for generalizing the reconciliation of proper and com-

---

32. Although I am not arguing for any inherent self-evidence of the visual—we might say that there are of course visual languages—I nevertheless believe that the logic of the passage asserts a difference between the immediacy of the visual and the diachronic quality of the verbal.

mon are more apparent. The evidence for the equivalence of the two verbal representations, and for the reconciliation of common and proper that verbal equivalence announces in this case, is the audience's capacity to understand the "common" language (as opposed to the patronym) used to describe the portraits. Yet as with Adam Smith, this second reading of the portrait scene as a relation between two sorts of verbal naming offers no clue as to how the common verbal meaning might ever be established, no guarantee that readers understand the same things by the words they read.

What this account ought to make clear is that the portrait scene "succeeds" in rendering the proper and the common noncontradictory by refusing to allow itself to be read as either an exclusively visual or an exclusively verbal artifact. Insofar as its mode of representation is visual, it offers a version of commonness that is self-evident and immediately apprehensible by all; insofar as it is verbal, the commonness made self-evident by the portrait's visual aspect is extended by fiat to the language used to constitute that aspect, generalized into a condition of common meaning. Once we recognize how the not quite visual, not quite verbal quality of the portraits works to bring together the proper and the common, not only can we begin to explain the particular efficacy of the realist novel as an instrument for bringing about this end, but we can also refine the definition of novelistic authority upon which this efficacy rests. The realist novel's capacity to reconcile proper and common depends on its ability to subordinate the linguistic identity that makes it legible to its power to represent specifically visual effects. By presenting its readers with the visual spectacle of people and places made out of words, the fiction of the novel creates the conditions within which people—the characters in the novel—can mean the same thing without ever agreeing on, or for that matter even *using,* the same language, the conditions within which they can become one with the geographical places they inhabit without having any economic or political control over these places. So long as we as readers agree to suspend our notice of the wordiness of the novel's people and places by attending instead to their visual presence and self-evidence, then the realist novel offers its readers the ground for believing in their own commonness.

But even as *Daniel Deronda* constitutes the venue within which Eliot is able to offer her most detailed account of the way fictional authority conventionally creates a common culture, that her theorizings occur within a narrative provides the condition of its undoing as well; the novel is anatomized and turned against itself. Whereas subordinating the reader's sense of the novel's writtenness to the experience of the visual implies a definition of novelistic fictionality in which the world of the novel is apprehended immediately, in an instant, we have already seen how the novel's account of Gwendolen's "return" to Offendene temporally dilates the reader's experience of the novel's fictionality. As the narrative presses toward Daniel's discovery of his parentage, another narrative is set in motion as well, one in which the dominant economy of the visual explicitly gives way to the experience of hearing sounds. Having traveled to Frankfurt as part of his effort to search out the remaining family of Mirah, the young Jewish woman whose suicide attempt he has thwarted, Daniel wanders into a synagogue to observe a Friday night service:

> Deronda, having looked enough at the German translation of the Hebrew in the book before him to know that he was chiefly hearing Psalms and Old Testament passages or phrases, gave himself up to that strongest effect of chanted liturgies which is *independent of detailed verbal meaning*—like the effect of an Allegri's *Miserere* or a Palestrina's *Magnificat*. The most powerful movement of feeling within a liturgy is the prayer which seeks for nothing special, but is a yearning to escape from the limitations of our own weakness and an invocation of all Good to enter and abide with us; or else a self-oblivious lifting up of gladness, a *Gloria in excelsis* that such Good exists; both the yearning and the exultation gathering their utmost force from the sense of communion in a form which has expressed them both, for long generations of struggling fellow-men. The Hebrew liturgy, like others, has its transitions of litany, lyric, proclamation, dry statement and blessing; but this evening all were one for Deronda: the chant of the *Chazan's* or Reader's grand wide-ranging voice with its passage from monotony to sudden cries, the outburst of sweet boys' voices from the little quire, the devotional swaying of men's bodies backwards and forwards, the very commonness of the building and shabbiness of the scene where a national faith, which had penetrated the thinking of half the world, and moulded the splendid forms of that world's religion, was finding a remote, obscure echo—all were blent for him as one expression of a binding history, tragic and yet glorious. He wondered at the strength of his own feeling; it seemed beyond the occasion—what one might imagine to be divine influx in the darkness, *before there was any vision to interpret.* (367–68, emphasis added)

Most straightforwardly, the passage stages the unfolding of a new economy of value as Daniel, poring over a translated prayer book, is converted from a consciousness through which the novel's readers forget they are reading words rather than watching a spectacle into a reader himself. Daniel's experience of the writtenness of the text, which the passage follows by a description whose details are overwhelmingly aural, culminates in the wholesale rupture of vision and value: "He wondered at the strength of his own feeling; it seemed beyond the occasion—what one might imagine to be divine influx in the darkness, before there was any vision to interpret."

But what transpires in the space between Daniel's refiguration as reader at the beginning and the demotion of visual perception with which the passage ends is a realignment at once more complex and more theoretically far-reaching than a simple substitution of aural for visual detail. Although he is consigned to overhearing a swirl of words through a double layer of translation (as an English reader of the German translation of the Hebrew liturgy), Daniel, like some proleptic avatar of his own best reader, the anonymous *Jewish Chronicle* reviewer, claims a privileged access to the spectacle's true meaning, a meaning available to him specifically because he is not burdened and distracted by the literal meanings of the Hebrew words. He is paradoxically distinguished from the Jews "for whom the service was [perhaps no] more than dull routine" (368) by his incapacity to distinguish among the different forms of prayers, since by his account the most compelling value these prayers might express is the one that puts aside valuing altogether, "the prayer which seeks for nothing special." Prayer does not resolve the ongoing historical tension between proper and common so much as it *dissolves* it, with the failure of common meaning announcing the disappearance of the proper, the private, a "seek[ing] for nothing special" rather than an accession to its terms. The passage is rent neatly in two by syntactical ambiguity:

> The Hebrew liturgy, like others, has its transitions of litany, lyric, proclamation, dry statement and blessing; but this evening all were one for Deronda: the chant of the *Chazan's* or Reader's grand, wide-ranging voice with its passage from monotony to sudden cries, the outburst of sweet boys' voices from the little quire, the devotional swaying of men's bodies.

This sentence appears designed to distinguish the narrator's knowledge from Daniel's, since, while Daniel experiences the service as a blur, the scene's separate elements bleeding into a single "expression of a binding history," the narrator carefully renders the details that are inaccessible to Daniel. Operating as a kind of grammatical enactment of analogical form, the colon at the center of the sentence announces an equivalence of the terms on either side while refusing to make explicit the grounds of the equivalency. The various categories of discriminations Daniel fails to make become "all . . . one" for the narrator, as Daniel's incapacity to name the items composing the narrator's lists is replaced by the narrator's blurring of the boundaries separating one list from its lack. To the extent that the passage associates the lack of discrimination with the elevation of sound over sense, the triumph of the aural marks the triumph of the (non)logic of the analogy as well. The passage begins by emphasizing the distinction between Daniel and the narrator, since the latter is able to specify the distinctions to which Daniel, as a non-Hebrew-speaking observer, has no access. But by the time we reach the oddly divided midpoint the narrator has come to bear a striking resemblance to the character whose differences she documents: no longer can the narrator discriminate among the various lists of discriminations Daniel fails to make. And as Daniel claims a certain insight arising from his failure to make fine generic distinctions, we might discern an invitation to extend to the narrator's blurrings a similar insight. In failing to distinguish among Daniel's various failures to discriminate, the narrator reveals to us a more essential truth about Daniel than would any pedantic documenting of details.

Still, we would be mistaken, I think, to consider the passage an unambiguous endorsement of Daniel's claim of superiority, both because the surrounding evidence is at best equivocal, marking the narrator's difference from Daniel as much as their likeness, and because the larger movement of the narrative educates Daniel out of his complacent belief in the salutary effects of disengagement. Because our verdict regarding the sameness of Daniel and the narrator rests entirely on what principle of organization we choose to measure such things, we can see that the passage does not endorse the kind of inattention to detail Daniel celebrates so much as it reveals how the meaningfulness of the common nouns that make up the details to be distinguished or ignored rests with the authority to determine what categories matter. By representing the power to determine categories as what is ambiguously a point of convergence or divergence for narrator and character, the novel at once identifies this power as the conventional authority of fiction and at the same time renders it contingent, arbitrary, the sort of authority possessed by a character with limited, interested knowledge. Once the process of making details significant is pointedly distinguished from imagining them into being—that is, once language and fictionality are represented as two related but not necessarily identical or even homologous sets of practices—it becomes possible to understand the process of attaching significance to the (fictional) material world as something that occurs within and over the course of the novel rather than prior to it.[33]

The subordination of visual to aural detail implies a shift from an immediacy of perception to a perception that takes place over time, a perception that thus might assign to the material detail a variety of meanings. Whereas Daniel assumes that discriminations are either noteworthy or entirely ignorable, the passage as a whole raises the prospect that the process of discrimination

---

33. We recall that it was this move to distinguish the authority of making fiction from the authority of making meaning that marked Eliot's departure from her forebears Locke and Smith.

is not an oscillation between the binaries of mattering and not-mattering but a weighing among and creation of a variety of conceivable sorts of mattering. This account of Daniel's visit to the Frankfurt synagogue, in describing a new model of reading, thus offers a different vision of the way the realist novel can intervene in and produce meaning in the world.

In the reference to the "*Chazan* or Reader," the undiscriminated sound that Daniel celebrates as expressing the true spirit of Jewish history—untranslated Hebrew—is evoked and then replaced by the signification of the English, as the novel's readers find themselves at once named and deflected. They are brought into being by learning to attach meaning to what first existed as merely unintelligible sound, but their arrival at a point of recognizable signification, at the name "Reader," is accompanied by a set of associations—both the retrospectively comprehensible meaning of the Hebrew original and the narrative context of the scene more generally—that makes the words mean something very different even as it names them. They are made readers by coming to understand what being a reader means, in the movement from the sound *chazan* to "reader." In this way the process of reading becomes not simply the immediate apprehension of established common meaning but the experience of meaning coming into being, a creation of a new sense that is always in the process of transmuting existing significances, closing off options even as it creates new ones.

Moreover, while the novel's audience is defined here as those who do not know how to distinguish but learn to do so, the sound that becomes meaningful is already in a sense marked *as distinguished* by its very presence as part of the description. To understand *chazan* as already distinguished, even before its English translation has been offered, is effectively to recognize the fictionality of the scene, to recognize that its particular details are included because an author has chosen them and not some others. Yet the word in its moment of sounding before being understood can be seen to mark the world's resistance to being known, but the resisting ground is in this instance the materiality of language, its status as a particular historical instantiation. The untranslated word is thus the place where the linguistic and the material world come together, the "reader" defined as the position that sorts through the indistinguishable terms. In the translated Hebrew word, the text registers an unknowability that is acknowledged from the outset to be contextually specific: *chazan* is not equally opaque to the praying Jews and to Daniel in his act of sublime overhearing. With the description of the "*Chazan* or Reader," we get the story of a process of coming to know in which the knowledge arrived at is knowledge only to the extent that we as readers are able to maintain our recognition of its contingency, the narrowness of its significance. Because the still untranslated word is nonetheless implicitly distinguished by the mere fact of having been selected by the author to appear in the description, our sense of its being only contingently known or not known is itself indistinguishable from, though not absolutely identical to, our recognition of the entire scene's fictionality. In Eliot's vision, a kind of overhearing, we discover fictionality and the nationality of languages together.

So whereas the portrait scene, with its emphasis on visual detail, presented a model of a reading subject whose immediate apprehension and discrimination of the common details of the local space and people bespoke the existence of common meaning and value while suppressing the process by which such commonness is achieved, the shift to an aural model of reading presents the experience of reading as the process of discovering meaning in sounds of phonemes. What the conclusion of the episode makes evident is that the transformations produced in and around *Daniel Deronda* not only produce a new understanding of the novel's capacity to make meaning in the actual world but announce and produce a broader transformation of the subject who reads and becomes "common." The portrait scene not only showed the way a certain model of reading and conception of realist fictionality produces an apparently immediate and self-evident commonness but made the world generated out of such a reading process one in which the fact of being in a certain geographical place was sufficient to make one like everyone else in that place. The episode at the Frankfurt synagogue, which closes by staging inconclusiveness, the failure of common speech, uncouples the identity between faces and spaces established in the portrait scene and thus undermines the reliability of space as an indicator of likeness of identity.

Daniel has just left the service he has found moving, if incomprehensible, when he is accosted from behind:

> He had bowed to his civil neighbor and was moving away with the rest—when he felt a hand on his arm, and turning with the rather unpleasant sensation which this abrupt sort of claim is apt to bring, he saw close to him the white-bearded face of that neighbor, who said to him in German, "Excuse me, young gentleman—allow me—what is your parentage—your mother's family—her maiden name?"
>
> Daniel had a strongly resistant feeling: he was inclined to shake off hastily the touch on his arm; but he managed to slip it away and said coldly, "I am an Englishman." (368)

As Deronda internally justifies his reaction immediately after the encounter, "He could not have acted differently. How could he say that he did not know the name of his mother's family to that total stranger?—who indeed had taken an unwarrantable liberty in the abruptness of his question, dictated probably by some *fancy of likeness such as often occurs without real significance*" (417–18, emphasis added). He does not answer Joseph Kalonymos's questions because, in a sense, he does not understand them. It does not occur to Daniel that "the stranger" might have specific information to offer him about his personal history because he does not think that he and a white-haired, German-speaking Jew could possibly have shared a world.

Daniel's moment of revulsion makes clear the way this concept of potentially infinite likeness implicit in liberal paternity's constitutive moment of silence, as well as the novelistic description associated with it, can do the cultural work it is meant to do only when it is understood metaphorically rather than literally. The potential for infinite resemblance that the portraits reveal to be at the conceptual heart of a naturalized paternal authority might be registered in the form of a certain kind of narrative description. But such description represents not so much the material as the idea of materiality, a prospect of resemblance that is meaningful only as long as it remains potential.

For Daniel, then, the scandal of Joseph Kalonymos[34] is that he takes paternity's appropriation of the literal literally. If the portraits on the wall transformed paternity from a condition of belief, a likeness that must be taken on faith, to a likeness that might be known for certain, they did so by exchanging the proper patronym for the evidence of the "common" visual details of the portraits, a commonness that produced a potentially infinite web of resemblance. While the commonness of the meaning is rendered self-evident by the visual details of the portraits, the dependence of this correspondence between spaces and faces on a self-evident common language produces the paradox that is the system's undoing as well as its enabling condition. Insofar as the commonness of the "language" testified to by the portraits is self-evident and beyond question, it can *guarantee* the likeness between space and inhabitant only at the cost of not being able to *limit* that correspondence. That is, the web of resemblance created by the portraits can make the connection between people and space—and among those people as well—absolutely knowable, but it marks a condition of literal common knowledge only so long as the web of resemblance is understood to be infinitely open. It is this contradiction that Kalonymos works when he insists that the logic of the portraits and the infinitude of resemblance they argue for must be taken literally, when he insists that Daniel's visual likeness to Kalonymos's implied acquaintance must

---

34. Kalonymos, which in Greek means "good name," is also the name of an early writer of Hebrew prayer books.

be taken seriously—even though Daniel and Kalonymos seem to have, or know, nothing in common.

Let us look again to the language of their encounter. In some sense we can understand Kalonymos to be speaking German and not-German at once; we read his words in English, but if we accept the narrator's authority, we are meant to imagine that the conversation is taking place in German, much as we might understand a scene to be probable and hence to seem real even as we know that what we are reading is fictional—that is, in some sense not true within the world we inhabit. But the parallels between the structures of language and fictionality begin to collapse as we move on in the passage. At the level of the plot, Daniel's response to Kalonymos's repeated pressings has the quality of a non sequitur, tempting us to read it as psychological symptom. In the context of the linguistic dynamic already established, however, Deronda's response is not so much unmotivated as redundant. To announce that one is an Englishman when one is speaking (presumably unaccented) English is effectively to say the same thing twice. But if we look at the passage again, we will notice that it is not at all clear that Daniel is, in fact, speaking English: while the sense of his utterance would be reinforced by being spoken in English, both the fact that Kalonymos has addressed Daniel in German and the evidence of narrator's last descriptive tag imply that he answers in German.

What is crucial about this moment of undecidability is not how much it disrupts an uncritical reading of the scene but how little it does. Even though, according to the claims of narrative authority, Daniel's answer is rendered in no determinate language whatever, we are able to read it as though he were speaking English because we are reading English. Kalonymos cannot simultaneously be speaking both German and English not because the levels of narrative abstraction at which the two languages are supposed to be operating are too different from one another, but because they are too much the same, because they are both language. This opposition between the two languages acts in striking contrast to the dynamic of illegitimacy where, we recall, connectedness and disconnectedness were understood to be noncontradictory because they described different sorts of relations, the biological and the legal. At the level of the plot, Kalonymos's forwardness is untoward in Daniel's eyes because he claims a common history; by subsuming the contingencies of his individual history within the model of an absolute national identity, Daniel rejects those claims, a rejection that depends on the principle that one cannot simultaneously be both English and not-English, just as one cannot speak English and German at once. Because he and Kalonymos do not speak the same language, they can have nothing to say to one another. Just as Kalo-

nymos calls liberal paternity's discursive bluff by seeing in the claim of potentially infinite relations of resemblance the intersection of his and Daniel's life
histories, here the novel brings its own linguistic presumptions into crisis by
the very act of representing its language as language. Whereas the portrait
scene implicitly defined paradigmatic novelistic "language" as the language
that produced visual images, here, outside the synagogue as within, the language of the novel is first and foremost *speech*. Language is not so much
literalized as moved inside the narrative to become an object of description
with edges and a beginning and an end, something to be chosen or abandoned, if not quite at will, then not wholly by the whim of birth either. That
Kalonymos speaks German can be evidence that he could not have anything
to do with an Englishman only if individuals are identified as speaking only
one language *or* another—if national language is taken to be absolutely syn-
onymous with national identity. The realist novel becomes the instrument for
accomplishing this conflation to the extent that it can make the fact of its
being written in a particular language absolutely coterminous with the fact
of its fictionality. Our sense of the novel as a seamless, "real" world depends
on our being able to suspend the fact that it is a world made entirely of language, and we can do that only insofar as the language in which it is written
appears to us as no language in particular.

But of course Daniel's language cannot remain stably unmarked, even
within the novel's own terms of fiction, because his words are distinguished
from the words that describe the pressure on his arm and the words that name
the language of Kalonymos's question by being identified *as language*. The
presence of dialogue—of language unambiguously labeled as language—
blurs the boundary separating the frame of fictionality (and the unmarked
language of world-making) from the individual elements of that represented
world, and in so doing it places the language of the novel itself under the
logical demands of a real world of always-inflected national languages. The
moment the project of rendering language unmarked is represented explicitly
within the narrative, not only does this project fail to achieve its goal of con-
flating national language and national identity, but it ends up demonstrating
just the opposite: the contingency of the two terms' intersection. We read
in the linguistic indeterminacy of Daniel's answer not the possibility of an
absolutely transparent, world-defining language but the considerably more
mundane, yet here quite disruptive, fact of his capacity to speak *both* German
and English. If Daniel is an Englishman, by novel's end it turns out he is a
Jew as well.

According to the model of realism anatomized in the portrait scene, conventional novelistic fictionality substitutes the common language constituting

the fictional material world for the actual private property that had made legible the relation between father and son, while maintaining the existence and symbolic continuity of private property. Only within the oddly paradoxical logic of novelistic fictionality can the representation of the physical resemblance between father and son, the "consequence" of their constitution out of common details in a putatively common language, become the mark of a more general state of likeness and shared value. It is this strange balance struck by the novel, offering itself as at once made up in (common) language and apprehensible prior to any mediation by language, that appears to allow individual readers to value individuals and their private property at the same time as they value the broader cultural and civil authority that may or may not support those particular individuals' claims of possession. The novel's success in resolving the tension between the proper and the common is registered in the emergence of a third term, a new sort of relation between individuals and the ur-property that is land: the nebulous "belonging," of people to place and of place to people, that goes by the name of culture.

The portrait scene makes evident the particular power of the novel not only in forging this mediating category of culture but in producing that nebulous sense of likeness among individual subjects—of belonging to each another—that is the way culture manifests itself as affect in the daily life of its subjects. But having painstakingly delineated the representational logic of common culture and the role of the novel in producing that culture, Eliot launches what is both a critique of the uses she sees such a notion of culture being put to and the first steps in dismantling them. Kalonymos and Daniel, a Jew and a man in search of his father who does not know he is a Jew—two men whose resemblance to one another must be worked out over time, by way of narrative, rather than being perceived instantaneously—disrupt the model of common culture produced by the novel because the geographical places they inhabit are not places to which they "belong" or that belong to them in any strong sense of the term. Because they belong to no geographical place that can be represented in language, using language does not place them in any particular locale but becomes an activity that can be done anywhere. Once Jews are discovered in the midst of the boundaries of England, the space of culture that produces the likeness of its subjects known as Englishness, being located in a certain place comes to mean nothing more than being located in a certain place. Shriveled into pale literalism, being in England becomes entirely self-evident and thoroughly uninteresting.

Almost. Although much, even most, of *Daniel Deronda* concerns itself with the task of delineating how the notion of English "common" culture comes into being and what is wrong with it, the novel nonetheless moves beyond critique in an attempt to articulate both a new relation of culture to space and also a different kind of subject, as well as a new role for the realist novel in producing that culture and that new subject. Although the Frankfurt episode operates most immediately and explicitly to disrupt the correspondence between geography and identity locked in by culture, it also initiates the swerve of plot that leads Daniel to discover something quite different from what he thinks he is looking for: his mother. Nowhere is the fundamental unassimilability of English and Jewish cultures articulated more economically than in the reality that, since Jewish identity is transferred matrilineally whereas English identity passes from father to son,[35] Daniel literally cannot know what he is looking for until he finds it. That is, he cannot know he is Jewish and therefore needs to be searching for his mother and not his father until he finds his mother and discovers he is Jewish.

This infinite regress, which a number of critics have noted,[36] is most interesting here for the way it pointedly refuses at the level of form the model of immediately apprehensible identity implied by the visible, visual novel. In place of the believing subject whose identity signifies and is recognizable in an instant, the matrilineally defined subject is one that comes into being by learning about and experiencing the world over time, one whose temporally dilated accumulation of knowledge continually remakes the identity of the subject doing the learning. But the novel's shift from patrilineality to matrilineality does not simply exchange one model of identity for another, a move that would be as unpersuasive as it is ungeneralizable. If the associations of patrilineality with an immediate, self-evident identity and matrilineality with a temporally dilated, incomplete one seem counterintuitive, it is likely because these associations reverse the conventional genealogical discourse in which the relation between fathers and their children is supposed to be unknowable while the relation between mothers and their children is self-evident. In representing a logic in which the opposite set of relations not only appears descriptively persuasive but also seems to hold a great deal of cultural authority, the authority of the category of culture itself, *Daniel Deronda* demonstrates that these associations cannot be considered in isolation from the modes of social representation established to render them legible. Just as Moses Mendelssohn

35. Whereas participants in the Burke-Paine debate seemed to take opposing positions on the fundamental "Englishness" and heritability of English culture, my argument recharacterizes the relation between the private property that defines the Whiggish liberalism of Locke and Paine and a heritable national culture in ways that relegate the differences between the arguments of Burke and Paine to their details.

36. See especially Cynthia Chase's brilliant deconstructive reading of the dynamic in "The Decomposition of the Elephants: Double-Reading *Daniel Deronda*," *PMLA* 93 (1978): 215–27.

used the inarguability of divine revelation occurring at some point in the past to insist on an understanding of historical action as contingent and diachronic, in which action and representation are inextricable from one another, Eliot seizes on the self-evidence of the relationship between mother and child at a particular point in the past—the moment of birth. She emphasizes this moment at which likeness is absolutely knowable not in order to cordon off a realm of absolutely knowable experience prior to language but to demonstrate the way even the immediate and knowable ought to be seen as existing through time and as a form of representation, a symbol of immediacy and self-evidence.

The correspondence between location and identity that the novel both represents and helps bring about—the correspondence cemented by and as culture—takes the form it does because it generalizes the link between fathers and sons conventionally marked by the transfer of private landed property from one generation to the next. If thus far I have treated this cultural authority as though it were identical to the authority of civil institutions, this is in part because the efficacy of culture as a unifying force rests heavily on its capacity to appear as though it creates its own law, as though it offers both the motivation and the means for bringing about the common behavior and shared values that manifest its existence. But such a conflation of culture and state institutions also makes it well-nigh impossible to register the shifting meaning of the category of culture itself, as the state appropriates the odd double structure of culture in order to authorize a new sort of institutional practice.

We might say, on the evidence of the portrait scene, that "culture" works to make the authority of the government seem unobjectionable by making it appear that it is doing nothing at all (or, more accurately, that what the government has done was done entirely in the past). While the category of culture inscribes an idea of a government that deserves its authority because it will use its power only to articulate and guarantee existing social relations, the civil authority born of "doing nothing" and empowered to do more of the same is likely to face a good deal of difficulty justifying specific laws designed to bring about social relations presumed already to exist.

In 1834 the Poor Law Commission Report, notorious for establishing a national system of workhouses in place of the parish-based patchwork of informal charity and "outdoor relief," proposed the most sweeping changes to the legal definition of bastardy since the government began regulating such behavior. The new regulations radically redefined the sort of data that could be made to stand as evidence of a relationship between parent and child, and in so doing it not only transformed the particular family relationships deemed paradigmatic of a more general cultural commonness but also changed the nature of the relation between the familial and the cultural. What is most remarkable about the 1834 Poor Laws is how efficiently they rewrote the most fundamental grounds of civil power by reconceiving the basic relations of culture and the state. The newly active, if sometimes actively neglectful, national government that emerged as a consequence of Reform did not simply announce its arrival by passing laws broadening its provenance. I contend that, by means of such provisions in the New Poor Laws, the government retheorized the basic terms of its own authority.

In reformulating the evidence by which kinship could be proved, the new regulations governing bastardy profoundly altered both the meaning of culture and its relation to civil authority. With culture no longer defined as the logic that generalized the passing of private landed property from fathers to sons into the likeness of citizens inhabiting the same geographical space, civil authority ceases to figure itself as the institutionalizing of culture's reconciliation of the proper and the common. Instead, the bastardy clauses of the New Poor Laws create a form of institutional authority that figures itself as an alternative to culture, taking over the functions of culture rather than building on them. The new regulations governing bastardy authorized a more activist government by enabling that government to monopolize the power to determine who belonged in which geographical space, a monopoly that fundamentally transformed that space's meaning. Recognizing the profound shift in the relations of culture, space, and institutional authority engendered by the new laws, George Eliot turns these juggled relations to her own effect and in so doing allows a new kind of authority to accrue to novelistic fictions. Freed from the task of rationalizing the connection between people and space, in a way that recalls her status as "independent in material things," and therefore, as it were, free from the operation of the Poor Laws, Eliot offers her final novel as the ground of a new sort of social relatedness.

Before 1834, both the mother and the putative father of a bastard child could be compelled to maintain the child by weekly payments under threat of imprisonment, though such punishments were rarely enforced.[37] What especially disturbed the drafters of the 1834 reforms were the provisions of an act of 1809 (49 Geo. 3 c. 68) that allowed a single woman who declared herself pregnant to charge any man as the father of the child-to-be, with the mere accusation sufficient for the court to issue a warrant for the man's arrest

---

37. I am deriving my account of the prehistory of the 1834 laws both from the 1834 commissioners' report itself and from U. R. Q. Henriques, "Bastardy and the New Poor Law," *Past and Present* 37 (July 1967): 103–29.

and to commit him to jail for the duration of the woman's pregnancy so as to ensure his financial support for the child. Normally the courts would make their final decision as to who was responsible for maintaining the child when the infant was a month old, with the justices looking to discern family resemblance. The uncertainty of paternity, the commissioners complained, effectively aligned the entire force of an abstract, wholly formal law behind the word of the mother, who was not required to offer any material evidence in support of her charge:

> If there were no other objections to these laws, than that they place at the mercy of any abandoned woman, every man who is not rich enough to give security or find sureties, that they expose him to be dragged, without previous summons, on a charge made in his absence, before a tribunal which has no power to examine into the merits of the case; if these were their only faults, we should still feel it our duty to urge their immediate abolition.[38]

The 1834 commission recommendations repealed all laws enabling a woman or a local authority to charge a man with being the father of an illegitimate child or allowing the magistrate to arrest the putative father or make him liable for child support.

But since the government was no longer going to compel fathers, whether actual or merely putative, to maintain their children, it needed to develop an alternative system of financial support. Under the old laws, not only were federal justices compelled to imprison those accused fathers who could not provide assurances of their future financial support, but in the years following the birth of the child and the establishment of paternity, the state would continue to act as an agent for the mother, collecting the payments from errant fathers and subtracting such payments from the regular government allowance paid for the child's support. Having gone out of the business of compelling unwilling fathers to support their bastard children, the commissioners now demanded that mothers assume financial responsibility for their children's upbringing; those who could not were to look to their parents or husbands (even if those husbands were not the fathers of the children in question) for whatever additional financial support was necessary, and those people, through their relationship to the bastard's mother, were deemed legally culpable. Even as the bastardy clauses absolved the government from legal responsibility for maintaining the children of unwed mothers, they offered detailed provisions for determining which local administrations would assume

38. *His Majesty's Commissioners' Report for Inquiring into the Administration and Practical Operation of the Poor Laws* (London, 1834), 166–67.

the duty of supporting those children whose unwed mothers could not or would not do so. If this odd disclaiming and embracing of responsibility seem to be acts of lawmakers unsure of the nature of the institutional authority they were executing, an authority that alternately commands and knows but never does both at once, the baroque complexity of these provisions for determining settlement stands as both a symptom of that confusion and the vehicle by which the authority of these institutions is transformed.

In the "Remedial Measures" section of the 1834 Poor Law Commission Report, the commissioners lay out the merits and demerits of two alternative settlement schemas: one would assign government responsibility according to the *residence* of its indigent citizens; the other would assign responsibility according to *birthplace*. Settlement by residence might seem the most straightforward and easily administered method for establishing municipal jurisdiction: "Its adoption," the report concedes, "would often prevent inconvenience to particular parishes, from the return, in old age and infirmity, of those who have left them in youth and vigour, and inconvenience to the paupers themselves, from being removed from friends and residences to which they have become attached, to places in which they have become strangers" (343). Despite these manifest advantages, however, the commissioners are forceful in rejecting the settlement-by-residence model, arguing that such a system of jurisdiction would negatively restrict the flow of labor, with workers declining to move frequently in search of work for fear of losing the security of accumulated municipal benefits.

Somewhat contradictorily, the commissioners also argue that the residence schema prevents women from working by making them too mobile. "Know[-ing] that if a child is born in their parish" they will be "responsible for its support throughout life and for the support of its posterity," local government officials employ all the resources in their power to prevent women from giving birth within their jurisdiction. Such harassment not incidentally prevents the pregnant woman from laboring to support herself and her child independently of the financial support of the government, effectively splitting women's status as laboring subjects from their condition of being known. So whereas the regulations governing bastardy before 1834 identified the unmarried mother's absolute, government-sanctioned authority to name a father (an agency of knowing) with her absolute legibility as an object (her maternity is entirely visible), the new laws split laboring agency absolutely from the condition of being known.

With the debate over the bastardy clauses, then, the political geography of geography—the overlapping of space, government authority, and kinship—is altered fundamentally. The most obvious and remarkable change wrought by the new laws is to make individuals' spatial locations wholly unreliable as signs of their identity. Although it is the mother whose physical location is made the object of the new law's scrutiny, the self-evidence of the mother's connection to her children allows her geographical uncertainty to proliferate, with everyone potentially out of place and the very metaphor of "being in place" at once literalized and eviscerated of meaning. The new laws split spatial location understood as a description from spatial location understood as a sign: location becomes a name for the resemblance of parent and child rather than evidence of that connectedness. With this split, the laws effectively redivide proper and common and bring about the end of culture as we have come to understand it in *Daniel Deronda*. Culture disappears both in an immediate sense and in a more fundamental way: in the most immediate sense, the connectedness of individuals is no longer discernible in the language they use, or in the space they inhabit, or by virtue of the ways they behave in that space, but becomes simply a matter of bureaucratic record, a list of which women were born where. The authority of the state here rests not on its capacity to appear continuous with the authority of the culture, a mere recognition of relations that already exist, but on its ability to keep comprehensive records. In the broader sense, inasmuch as this transformation of government authority into the power to know depends on mandating an absolute division between women as subjects—subjects with the power to labor and to identify the fathers of their children—and women as wholly legible objects, the bastardy laws end the chance, at least for women, of any sort of public self-representation.

But if the bastardy laws produce a new kind of bureaucratic government power that authorizes itself by displacing the claims of culture, the displacement acts like a dissection, as the laws undo the association of likeness and space by adhering to the very logic of the connection. In the portrait scene, culture came into being as a way of making paternity wholly knowable; in replacing the uncertain connection between father and sons marked by the patronym with the display of resemblance indicated by the wall of portraits, the episode transforms paternity into a version of maternity, with the link between parent and child immediately self-evident. The likeness of fathers and sons was made knowable by being generalized; insofar as it turned inhabiting the same land from a symbol of an otherwise unknowable relation between father and son into direct evidence of the resemblance of a common group, culture was able to offer unassailable proof for the existence of the relationship because the relation is not figured as having preexisted the evidence that renders it knowable. In the genealogy of culture enacted by the portrait scene, then, English culture comes into being in order to make a relationship that exists without ever being known (the relationship between father and son) and a relationship that does not exist until it is known (the relationship between people who live in the same geographical place) look like the same thing. The desire articulated by the category of culture is thus the desire that people who are alike should know the same things—that knowing becomes an aspect of who one is. But as was made apparent by the novel's incorporating Daniel's encounter with the painting of Sir Hugo within the larger trajectory of his search for his origins, the emergence of this model of "knowing" subject from within the context of social relations organized around the distribution of property means that the category of culture is designed to make what one knows the result of who one is, and not the other way around. Culture must therefore be profoundly amnesiac, creating subjects with the power to know and create as if they were not themselves created.

While the goal of culture is thus to make who you are and what you know indistinguishable, it is also to make both qualities seem wholly self-sufficient, entirely meaningful and legible in themselves. Less abstractly, this means that people are who they are because of their culture—because of the place they live—but that this local culture has marked these individuals so absolutely at some point in the past, made them so wholly who they are, that they remain unchanged whether or not they continue to inhabit the space of this constitutive culture. By this logic, however, the same independence of the descriptive and constitutive qualities of the culture of geographical proximity that allows people to continue to resemble one another whether or not they live in the same place also allows the geographical place to mean what it means whether or not people described and made over by it inhabit it. In other words, if "culture" is invoked as the force that turns geographical location from merely the place an individual happens to be into a deep quality of who that subject is, then it seems to constitute the sort of identity that at some point ceases to depend on being in the particular space, at some point to become "deeper than that." The very claim that geographical place constitutes identity becomes the grounds for absolutely separating the two.[39]

It is just this contradictory logic of culture, a contradictoriness that turns on the category of culture's origins in the uncertain relation between fathers and their children, that the 1834 bastardy clauses seize on in order to replace the force of culture with a new sort of government authority. In ruling that the

---

39. For a wonderful textually and historically nuanced account of the changing legal and rhetorical status of English landed space in a colonial and postcolonial context, see Ian Baucom, *Out of Place: Englishness, Empire, and the Locations of Identity* (Princeton: Princeton University Press, 1999).

identity of a mother and her child is to be constituted legally not according to where both are at the moment of birth, which is the moment at which their resemblance to one another is self-evident, but according to where the mother herself was born, these bastardy regulations literalize the distinction between the sign of that constitutive culture—geographical space—and the subject constituted by that space. Because, unlike paternity, the link and the likeness between mother and child can be discerned with absolute certainty at a particular moment in a particular place, the double, contradictory logic of culture no longer comes together to produce an identity at once created and made apparent by a given geographical space but instead produces a condition in which the power to constitute likeness and the power to know that likeness are absolutely distinct both temporally and ontologically. Because the likeness between mother and child is unambiguously knowable at a particular place and time, there is no need to look to any evidence beyond the birth itself to discover the resemblance. Nor is it possible, as it had been in the case of paternity, to conflate the process of coming to *know* who is like whom with the process of creating that likeness, a conflation that goes by the name of culture.

By insisting that the limited, literal, self-evident relation between *mothers* and their children be adopted as the fundamental paradigm of social likeness, the 1834 bastardy laws dissolve the category of culture altogether and, having done so, stake the government's power to attach such likeness to a particular geographical locale, as well as the power to make such likeness meaningful, on the very self-evidence of the link. The bastardy laws, in other words, reconfigure the meaning of "commonness" in two ways. First, they redefine the source of commonness from culture, or "nation," to the state—to institutional power as such. Second, the laws establish the state's authority, an authority whose technology is the comprehensive residency records to which municipal relief is linked, by tying that authority to the self-evidence of the information—likeness—being tracked. Rather than rendering any sort of external authorization unnecessary, the self-evidence of maternal likeness lends *its* authority to the bureaucratic institutions of the state. The likeness of mothers and their children thus turns out, within the logic of these bastardy laws, not only to be self-evident but to be a *figure* for self-evidence generally construed.

The 1834 laws, with their displacement of patrilineal in favor of matrilineal likeness along the axis of geographical location, reflect a context within which we might read *Daniel Deronda*'s similar shift in narrative emphasis as evidence of the novel's ongoing engagement with the deep structures of contemporary English politics. But the canniness of Eliot's representation of matrilineality here rests not on its recapitulation of the contemporary controversy but on the ways it is able to appropriate the terms by which the bastardy laws dismantle the category of culture and replace it with the authority of a state system of knowing, not in order likewise to do away with culture but to radically transform its definition. If the large trajectory of the novel takes Daniel from an unsuccessful search for his father to an unexpectedly significant discovery of his mother, the book's account of the social meaning of matrilineality is noteworthy for its departure from conventional representations. That mothers can be searched for just like—indeed, in place of—fathers, means that the "self-evidence" of matrilineal likeness is not all it appears.

Here the shadow of the bastardy laws reveals the contours of Eliot's project. In offering a narrative in which maternity becomes as uncertain as paternity, Eliot intimates that the self-evidence of maternity might act in ways other than mere description. In the bastardy laws, the self-evidence of maternity not only provided the grounds for determining which woman and which parish ought to assume financial responsibility for a given child but also functioned as a figure, a sign of self-evidence whose authority the bureaucratic state borrowed in order to become equally inarguable. What *Daniel Deronda*'s matrilineal narrative makes apparent is that the likeness of mother and child is self-evident and absolutely certain only for an instant—the moment of birth. Like the authority of municipal bureaucrats to record the identities of the mothers who give birth within their municipality's borders, the self-evidence of the link between mother and child beyond that moment of birth is figurative. That Daniel stops knowing who his mother is once they stop living in the same place means that though maternity may begin as an entirely self-evident, immediately knowable condition, he, and we, must look to a different kind of evidence to discern the relation between mothers and their children later on. Just what would constitute such evidence is left largely undefined within the novel, imaginable only negatively, by its difference from Daniel's (non)history with the Alcharisi, but whatever the specific details of its content, this postpartum link is a matter of behavior rather than identity. And if Daniel's uncertainty concerning his mother seems a consequence of their not having remained geographically proximate, their physical difference matters not because a common geographical location would have been an unassailable sign of the resemblance of mother and son, but because it might have enabled the kind of ongoing behavior that constitutes the relationship. In defiguralizing the "self-evidence" of maternity, then, *Daniel Deronda* not only presents a narrative in which who one's mother is can be as much a question as who one's father is but also empties of significance the geographical location that in the paternal paradigm of culture worked to compensate

for genealogical uncertainty. Once the evidence of being a mother rests on acting like one—behaving in such a way as to extend the momentary certainty
of birth eternally onward—inhabiting the same geographical space comes
to mean nothing in itself.

Insofar as the new bastardy laws emphasize the moment (and place) of
birth over the mother and child's subsequent place of residence in determining
where their resemblance to one another will matter, these laws appear to acknowledge the limited legibility of maternity; but to the extent that the regulations insist that the conditions of the moment of birth continue to be legally
meaningful even after they cease to be descriptively accurate, the bastardy
laws make matrilineality figural. But by emphasizing the limited, literal quality of maternal likeness while eschewing the compensatory powers of the
state, *Daniel Deronda* turns the historical precedent of the bastardy laws'
dissociation of commonness and geographical proximity to its own account.
The novel refuses to follow the laws' example of offering civil authority as a
compensation for the loss of the fantasy of a geographically grounded culture,
leaving the odd relationship between Daniel and his Jewish mother Leonora
Halm-Eberstein to serve as the vague, preliminary outline of a new model
of culture.

At its most pessimistic, *Daniel Deronda,* by insisting that the connectedness of mothers and children can be ensured only at the moment of birth, puts
forth a vision of English culture as hopelessly antiquated, with the grounds of
cultural commonness vanishing to a point in the distant past, to be compen-
sated for by the empty formalism of the state. But although the scene at the
Frankfurt synagogue announces a fundamental change in the way the novel
invites itself to be read, not until much later, after Daniel's genealogical search
has ceased to drive the plot, do the stakes of this redescription of novelistic
fictionality become apparent. And though it is the narrative ascendancy of
the Jewish Daniel—polyglot, matrilineal, only contingently connected to the
geographical space of England—that marks the supplanting of the old notion
of fiction by the new, the effects of the transformation are signaled more
readily in the ragged remnants of the plot that so dominates the novel's early
chapters: Gwendolen's.

We recall that Gwendolen, *Daniel Deronda*'s most avid (and most uncritical) reader of novels, enthusiastically embraced the detemporalized, visual
paradigm of novelistic authority—to her detriment. In her initial encounter
with Grandcourt, Gwendolen kept up an interior running commentary on
her own conversational salvos, which was introduced into the text of the conversation as parenthetical interjections. In their resemblance to an author's
compositional notes, these interjections invited us to counterpose Gwendo-

len's misguided belief in the privacy and autonomy of her own interiorized subjectivity against a model of fictional authority that was not presumed to have occurred entirely in the past but continued into the reader's own present. For Gwendolen, the interiority of her imaginings ensured that they took place outside time and could be kept secret as long as they were not manifested in behavior.

Within this context, Gwendolen's final encounter with Grandcourt—or, more accurately, her narration of that encounter to Daniel—is striking as a repudiation of the detemporalized model of fictional imagination. Grandcourt, having forced Gwendolen to accompany him in a sailboat off the port of Genoa so he might exercise his authority over her without interference, is suddenly cast overboard. Gwendolen narrates the series of events to Daniel after the fact:

> "I remember then letting go the tiller and saying, 'God help me!' But then I was forced to take it again and go on; and the evil longings, the evil prayers came again and blotted everything else dim, till, in the midst of them—I don't know how it was—he was turning the sail—there was a gust—he was struck—I know nothing—I only know that I saw my wish outside me. . . .
>
> "[. . .]'The rope!' he called out in a voice—not his own—I hear it now—and I stopped for the rope—I felt I must—I felt sure he could swim, and he would come back whether or not, and I dreaded him. That was in my mind—he would come back. But he was gone down again, and I had the rope in my hand—no, there he was again—his face above the water—and he cried again—and I held my hand, and my heart said, 'Die!'—and he sank; and I felt 'It is done—I am wicked, I am lost'—and I had the rope in my hand—I don't know what I thought. I was leaping away from myself—I would have saved him then. I was leaping from my crime, and there it was—close to me as I fell—there was the dead face—dead, dead." (695–96)

Here, as Gwendolen's racing imagination makes the visible world disappear—"blot[s] everything else dim"—and the drowning Grandcourt calls out "in a voice not his own," Gwendolen narrates the horror of the realization of her version of private, wholly interior novelistic imagination. The passage's conflation of the event and its narrative representation—"he called in a voice—not his own—I hear it now" might seem to collapse the distinction between author and character established early on by the double meaning of the parentheses and consequently to undermine the privacy and autonomy of the imagination. But that Gwendolen's account here registers this imagination as mattering only so far as it is realized means that she remains within the logic of her original novelistic paradigm. Struggling for a response to Gwendolen's confession of guilt, Daniel pointedly rejects the novelistic imaginative economy Gwendolen would embrace—"I saw my wish outside me." But while Daniel resists Gwendolen's idea that she has somehow imagined Grandcourt's accident into being, the passage nonetheless falls short of exculpating her entirely. Her narration of the moments surrounding her husband's death includes in equal parts a moment-by-moment account of Grandcourt's slide beneath the waves and Gwendolen's terrified, desperate imaginings, imaginings that make it difficult for her to distinguish between his renewed pursuit of her and her terror of that pursuit. What makes Gwendolen's imagination dangerous here—and what allows some degree of culpability to be attributed to her for these imaginings—is not that it has the power to make private subjective visions real but that it operates through time. And the time Gwendolen spends imagining appears to prevent her from doing other things, things like throwing Grandcourt the rope that might have enabled him to pull himself to safety. Gwendolen's imagination matters not because it makes ideas real, makes words into visible things, but because it makes history.

So if by its insistence that the likeness of mothers and their children is discernible only at a single moment in the past *Daniel Deronda* seems to be representing just one more instance of a broadly Victorian sense of cultural belatedness, a sense that the conditions that once made English people like one another have now disappeared irretrievably into the past, the model of imagination set forth in the passage I have been examining complicates the pessimism of this sense of belatedness. A number of critics have remarked on the vehemence with which the novel heaps opprobrium on the Alcharisi for her failure to act as a mother to Daniel; most have read the novel's outsized passion on this score as a mark of George Eliot's effort to distinguish the Alcharisi's nonreproductive artistic ambition from her own. But I submit that if the novel pulls no punches in attributing full moral responsibility to the Alcharisi for her decision not to continue to act as Daniel's mother, the moral outrage it invites from its readers is designed less to distinguish her from other, more dutiful mothers than to differentiate her from those "nonmothers" who cannot choose—those unmarried women described by the new bastardy laws who cease to be legible as mothers as soon as they give birth. While these newly designated unwed mothers effectively cease to act as mothers (at least within the narrow definition of the term produced by the statutes) because their power to mark resemblance has been appropriated by the civil bureaucracy, the Alcharisi, by contrast, stops acting as a mother because she chooses to. And whereas the bastardy laws' bureaucratization of maternity ensures that we can tell nothing about who resembles whom from noticing

where individuals live, no matter how often we look, in the case of the Alcharisi we can know whether she is continuing to fulfill her role as Daniel's mother
only so long as we keep looking—or reading.

This clarification is important, because while it was matrilineality's self-
evident literalism, however fleeting and limited, that established the authority
of bureaucratic institutions as similarly self-evident, this same literalism made
maternity problematic as grounds for establishing a commonness that extends beyond the particular dyad of mother and child. In intimating that the
Alcharisi remains Daniel's mother and can be supposed to resemble him—to
share a common culture in its narrowest compass—only so long as the two
of them remain geographically proximate and have the same experiences,
come to know the same things, *Daniel Deronda* redefines "commonness" as
a kind of behavior, or the knowledge produced by and gleaned from behavior,
rather than as a kind of identity. But the novel hardly presents such a redefinition as a solution, and not merely because the Alcharisi is less than adequate
as a mother. Indeed, we might see this bifurcation between knowledge and
identity as merely a translation of the social, political, and economic crisis
with which we began into epistemological terms, yet another discovery of the
persistent unassimilability of proper and common.

But though redefining "commonness" as an effect produced through time
does little to ensure its extension, the novel does offer a specific temporalized
behavior, a particular experience of coming to know in time, as the ground
of a common culture: the experience of reading and the process of imagining
generated by that reading experience. Critics from Henry James to F. R.
Leavis have lambasted *Daniel Deronda* for its lack of unity, with Leavis going
so far as to recommend that the "Jewish plot" be excised entirely and the
novel renamed "Gwendolen Harleth."[40] But *Daniel Deronda*'s multifarious-
ness, I believe, lies less in the lack of connection among its various events and
characters than in the terms within which it presents itself as an object to be
read. As we read the novel from beginning to end, the text before us becomes
something else entirely, so that our process of reading registers its movement
through time not only by its interaction with other sorts of local activities but
by its rendering itself obsolete. By the time we close the book and allow its
final images to fade into recollections, the gathering together of something
never quite here, *Daniel Deronda* has become a novel no longer capable of
being read as it was at that first beginning. And if this is in essence always the

40. F. R. Leavis, *The Great Tradition* (New York: Anchor, 1954). Of course Leavis and James are
effectively in sympathy on this final point as well, since in offering a generalized exhortation to the
production of a *Daniel Deronda* without Daniel, Leavis was merely calling for what James had already
done in *The Portrait of a Lady*.

case—if the fact of having read any novel once precludes our ever returning to it in the condition of our first reading—George Eliot's masterstroke lies in transforming this progressive obsolescence from an inescapable and thoroughly unnoteworthy condition of reading into a structural principle of her narrative as well as its condition of political possibility.

Like some hybrid shorthand of two centuries of novel history, *Daniel Deronda* ends with a death and a marriage: Daniel's fellow Jew and spiritual progenitor Mordecai slips into silence and then death in Daniel's arms, consumed by some unspecifiable combination of tuberculosis and spiritual fervor, and Daniel marries Mordecai's sister Mirah. But this excessive closure undoes the novel's ending as much as it ends it too much, as though piling up so many concluding conventions eviscerates the ending of all but its conventionality. This nonending of so many endings is granted the authority of logic within the novel as Daniel and Mirah await their departure "to the East," and our discovery that there are no more pages of *Daniel Deronda* left for us to read is transformed into an interlude. In positing a novelistic afterward, in inviting us to imagine Daniel and Mirah's life in Palestine as they labor to establish a Jewish "commonness" at some specific geographical place, *Daniel Deronda* gives that thoroughly inevitable, thoroughly unnotable fact of ending a novel a positive content, turns the halting of signification into a kind of significance. The fading images of the novel we have only just finished, and our imaginative efforts to recollect those images as the content of our experience, thus merge with our efforts to imagine what has not yet been written.

Daniel Deronda is, in the most literal sense, a utopian novel. And operating on the premise that it is not utopian but pragmatic to give a utopia a name, Eliot names her utopia, not-yet-placed, Jewish. But the Jewish utopia of *Daniel Deronda* is not, or at least not in any straightforward sense, the land in Palestine where Daniel and Mirah might be supposed to settle, or the community, with its farms, its small shops, its rules of self-governance, that we presume they will set up there. What is remarkable about what George Eliot does at the end of *Daniel Deronda* is not that she invites her readers to imagine a world that does not exist, since in a certain sense we might say that this is what all novelists, writing fictions, do. Rather, what is remarkable about the end of *Daniel Deronda* is that Eliot invites her readers to imagine a world that she has not yet *written*. In concluding her novel so many times that effectively it fails to conclude at all, Eliot redefines what it means to "read" a novel. Whereas we as readers spent most of the novel turning the words we read into the visual images of people and streets and lines of portraits on a wall, as *Daniel Deronda* ends we are invited to imagine a place that does not yet exist and about which no words, no common language, have been written. Reading is thus converted from the imaginative acts that turn words on a page into a visible world as they are understood to the imagining of alternative worlds that the reader is impelled to produce as a *consequence* of having read.

The significance of this redefinition of reading readily becomes apparent when we recall that, according to the "theory of the novel" presented by the portrait scene, it is the novel's capacity to generate the translation of language into self-evident, immediately "perceptible" images that underwrites its claim to be constituting a common culture and to be tying that culture to a specific geographical place—to reveal culture to be the consequence of inhabiting a common place. By redefining reading from the imaginative process that takes place as one encounters a novel to the imaginative process that takes place after one has put it down, *Daniel Deronda* not only rejects a notion of a common culture constituted out of a common language or by the inhabiting of a common geographical space but insists on understanding culture as a process whose commonness remains contingent and changeable into the present. For Eliot, then, realist novels generate a common culture not simply because they make their readers speak a common language or experience the language they *do* speak as common, or simply because they make their readers imaginatively "inhabit" a common geographical space or understand the space they *do* inhabit as common, but because they allow their readers to experience the material world they inhabit as a made world, created in the past and present and capable of being made anew in the future. *Daniel Deronda*'s injunction to its readers to imagine Mirah and Daniel's life in Palestine asserts that the process of reading novels should be recognized as the process of making the novel one is reading disappear. To the extent that novels become, in this view, readable only once, *Daniel Deronda*'s highlighting of the novelistic afterward is a highlighting of the moment of that novel's disappearance, the final moment of the feasibility of a certain kind of reading and a certain kind of imagining. In this moment, novel reading becomes the experience of what Christina Rossetti calls "not-returning time,"[41] the process by which readers come to discover their own irreducible historicity.

By projecting readerly acts of imagination as the consequence of the details of its own text, then, *Daniel Deronda* makes itself over into the occasion of its apprehension—a halting that is a knowing—and becomes an event rather than an object. As an occasion of reading, the text becomes forever unrepeatable at the moment we imagine a time-after and a place that we, and the

---

41. Christina Rossetti, "Goblin Market," in *Norton Anthology of English Literature*, ed. M. H. Abrams et al., 5th ed. (New York: W. W. Norton, 1986), 2:1508–20.

characters described to us in "common language," have never been. In abandoning the representational logic of the portrait scene in order to enjoin its readers to imagine what comes beyond it, *Daniel Deronda* turns the realist novel from a created thing into an activity. But by suggesting that its readers' process of imagining this novelistic afterward bears some relation to what they have read within it—that the lives we imagine for Daniel and Mirah in the East are historically connected to the acts of imagining themselves—George Eliot resists the temptation to think of the literary text as a kind of blank, undifferentiated locus of undecidability, the slim pretext upon which its readers' imaginative freedom might rest. If reading beyond the ending of *Daniel Deronda* effectively means we can read the novel only once, and if this unrepeatability makes novel reading the occasion for discovering the historicity of our various acts of imagining, it likewise insists on the irreducible particularity of the text's details: the novel available to be read at a certain time and place by a certain reader within a given set of social relations must be written by a writer likewise marked, and as *Daniel Deronda*'s anonymous *Jewish Chronicle* reviewer first insisted, it is the unassimilability of these two clusters of particularities that makes novel reading a profoundly social act.

What *Daniel Deronda* accomplishes, then, is a redefinition of the sort of "commonness" of culture novels create. According to the model with which the author can never, by definition, quite conclude, people have a common culture because they have read and continue to read the same literary texts. In elevating a common culture based on the reading of a shared set of texts over the unifying terms of language and land, Eliot may appear to be calling "English" the textualized model of culture associated with Jews at the very moment she represents these Jews as poised to trade in such a model of culture for a more conventionally national, landed form of identity. But it is paradoxically her insistence for the duration of *Daniel Deronda* that a textualized "literary" culture be recognized as particularly Jewish that gives her call for such a literary culture any political purchase within the context of the institutional politics of the English state. That is, only by representing a literary culture in an unevenly overlapping, embattled, and finally *changing* relation to forms of commonness organized around language, land, and the authority of the state does Eliot invest the vision of textual culture offered by *Daniel Deronda* with the potential to make social relations anew. By insisting that we cannot separate the power of the category of the literary from the representation of the shifting fate of such a textualized culture within the particular novel *Daniel Deronda*, George Eliot keeps us reading, ceaselessly, over and again.

2

WHAT MAISIE PROMISED

Realism, Liberalism, and the Ends of Contract

IN ITS BAREST OUTLINE, the celebrated 1864 case *Raffles v. Wichelhaus* appears an entirely unremarkable occasion of breach of contract: the plaintiff, a cotton seller with operations out of Bombay, sued the defendant for refusing to accept or pay for a delivery of cotton contracted "to arrive ex Peerless"—that is, on a ship called the *Peerless*—in Liverpool. What made this case noteworthy was not the defendant's desire to escape from the contract but the ingenious, elaborately implausible legal means his lawyer employed in the effort to allow him to do so. Counsel did not deny the allegations against his client but instead argued that the *Peerless* the defendant "meant and intended" was a ship that had sailed from Bombay in *October*, whereas the ship the plaintiff's cotton had arrived on "was another and different ship, which was also called the Peerless, and which had sailed from Bombay, to wit, in *December*."[1] Even odder, counsel for the plaintiff was quick to agree.

Parts of chapter 2 have been previously published as Irene Tucker, "What Maisie Promised," *Yale Journal of Criticism* 11, 2 (1998): 335–64 © 1998, The Johns Hopkins University Press.

1. *Raffles v. Wichelhaus*, cited in Grant Gilmore, *The Death of Contract* (Columbus: Ohio State University Press, 1974), 35–43, quotation on 36. Both Gilmore and P. S. Atiyah identify *Raffles v. Wichelhaus* as a turning point in the history of Anglo-American contract law. See Atiyah, *The Rise and Fall of Freedom of Contract* (Oxford: Oxford University Press, 1979). See also Oliver Wendell Holmes Jr., *The Common Law*, ed. Sheldon M. Novick (New York: Dover, 1991), lecture 11, "Void and Voidable Contracts," 309. For a reading of the decision as an affirmation of a wholly formal conception of contract

True, he granted, it was possible, even likely, that the plaintiff and the defendant "meant and intended" different ships by the phrase "arrive ex Peerless," but establishing that both parties meant the same ship when they said *Peerless* was crucial only if the particular identity of the ship mattered to the sense of the contract. In this case, he argued, that the ship was called the *Peerless* was a contingent rather than a necessary element of the contract, indicating only, as was the convention of the period, that if the ship was lost on the voyage the contract would be at an end—the seller would bear the loss, but the buyer would not be able to claim damages for nondelivery.[2] Even if the seller had been mistaken in sending the cotton on the December instead of the October *Peerless,* such a mistake was not sufficiently central to the performance of the contract to justify the contract's recision.

Accepting the defendant's contention that although no departure or anticipated arrival dates had been specified within the text of the contract the ship's identity was nonetheless a crucial condition of the contract, the *Raffles* judges concluded that because buyer and seller had intended two entirely different meanings by the use of the term "*Peerless,*" there had been no "meeting of the minds," and hence no contract had ever existed to be broken. The buyer had intended the meaning "a ship sailing in October," whereas the seller meant "a ship sailing in December." The contract law at issue was thus revealed to be incoherent, since agreement was defined as a condition of interi-

---

as promise, see Charles Fried, *Contract as Promise* (Cambridge: Harvard University Press, 1981), 59–60. A. W. Brian Simpson provides a fascinating reading of the canonizing of the *Raffles* case itself—its movement from relative obscurity to the status of "leading case" in American legal education—arguing that this canonizing has required abstracting the case from the particular economic circumstances that made its controversies legible. This piece also offers the most detailed historical account of the case I have found. See Simpson, "The Beauty of Obscurity: *Raffles v. Wichelhaus and Busch* (1864)," in *Leading Cases in the Common Law* (Oxford: Clarendon Press, 1995), 135–62. Another helpful account of the place of contract within the history of Anglo-American law is Morton J. Horwitz, *The Transformation of American Law, 1780–1860* (Cambridge: Harvard University Press, 1977).

2. Both Simpson and Gilmore propose that the 1864 date might explain the precipitous drop in the price of cotton that generated the dispute over delivery dates. During the early years of the United States Civil War, the effective Northern naval blockade prevented cotton from being shipped out of Southern ports, resulting in what came to be known as the Lancashire Cotton Famine. The Lancashire cotton industry was the largest in the world by the time the Civil War began, and it relied almost exclusively on cotton produced in the American South. According to Simpson, "It was widely thought that there remained in the southern states a huge stock of cotton, which would be released onto the market once the war ended and collapse the price; hence any rumor of peace caused sharp falls" (Simpson, "Beauty of Obscurity," 145). As a consequence of these volatile economic and political conditions, speculation in cotton was a lucrative but hazardous trade. Simpson's and Gilmore's accounts of what we might call the "politics of probability" suggest the ways the economic relations between England and the United States, as well as the imbrication of British and American legal traditions, were tied up with the narratives of cultural autonomy and race relations that, as I hope to show, haunt James's fictional interventions into these probabilistic politics.

ority—a "meeting of minds"—yet the achievement of such an internal condition was measurable only through external signs that the case revealed to be only contingently and ambiguously linked to these internal mental states. What is striking about this decision is how easily—indeed, how much more easily—it might have been otherwise: a cursory reading of the case offers ample evidence that a sudden decline in the price of cotton had simply made the terms the defendant had negotiated economically unadvantageous to him. Insofar as they admitted as plausible the defendant's suspiciously baroque account of how he had come to believe he was not obliged to accept the cotton delivered to him on the *Peerless,* these judges displayed a willfulness of their own, a willfulness derived from, though certainly not reducible to, the pointedly *narrative* willfulness of the defendant's claim that what motivated his refusal to pay was not the precipitous drop in cotton prices but confusion over how and when that cotton was to be conveyed to England. By rejecting the seemingly straightforward conclusion of breach of contract in favor of a verdict that became precedent setting for Anglo-American contract law by revealing that law to be incoherent, the *Raffles* judges transformed a single lawyer's momentary and apparently desperate manipulation into a rule of law.

It has by now become conventional in Foucauldian accounts of culture to read such causal hiccups, moments in which the outcome of a given incident seems far in excess of the event that supposedly produced it, as evidence of the broad pervasiveness of the given cultural paradigm being described. By this reckoning it is a particular act's quality of undermotivation, of being unexplained or unjustified by the most immediate conditions of subjectivity invoked to account for it, that lends a particular artifact or an isolated agent's behavior its significance. The moment of willfulness thus becomes evidence of the impossibility of individual acts of will, the moment at which individual subjects turn out to be acted through rather than willing, spoken through rather than speaking. The defense attorney's brazenly convoluted, almost literary account of why the *Raffles* contract ought not to be binding and the judges' surprising acceptance of the defense's logic not only gain the force of law but are ascribed the force of culture as well. The "contingent" legal positions set forth by the lawyer and the judges—that quality of willfulness that might seem to announce their autonomy, their freedom as liberal subjects—thus are not so contingent after all but the necessary, ineluctable expression of a pervasive cultural logic.

That such a model of culture is monolithic and atemporal are charges frequently—and not unjustly—lodged against it. The *Raffles* case allows us a way of reframing these charges in much more specific terms, however, terms that would allow them to become something other than an absolute refusal of such a paradigm of culture. To the extent that this Foucauldian conception of culture turns the defense lawyer's and the judges' manifest willfulness into evidence of the monolithic, will-canceling power of modern culture generally conceived, it makes the experience of willfulness—an individual subject's sense of accession to or deviation from his or her surrounding social norms— not simply invalid but indiscernible as an object of analysis. I mean to demonstrate that this quality of an apparent freedom of contingent action that becomes meaningful at the moment it is shown to be neither contingent nor free ought not to be understood simply as the paradigm for the operation of modern culture in general. It should be seen as the particular condition of liberal subjectivity in England and the United States in the second half of the nineteenth century, a condition whose paradoxes are made especially apparent by the fact of its historical embattlement. From its origins in the writings of Locke and Rousseau, liberalism has taken up the figure of the contract as the mark of its own discursive originality, with the social contract generally read as asserting the individual's new power to order his[3] social and political relations against the pressure of inherited social status and the divine right of kings. Liberal subjects are thus understood to live where they live, buy and sell the property they buy and sell, and hold the political allegiances they hold not because their fathers engaged in these same relations, but because the liberal subjects contracted to do so. By conventional readings of the social contract, then, liberal subjects are first and foremost *agents*—abstract bearers of a will whose particular historical circumstances reveals something about who they are not because they enable or constrain what such a subject can do, but because they have been chosen by that subject. As industrialization and urbanization disrupted systems of social hierarchy whose relations had previously been understood as givens, contract became the paradoxical instrument by which owners and laborers came to share in the task of forging the new relations—normally relations of inequality—by which they were to be governed.

For historians of Anglo-American contract law, the odd outcome of *Raffles v. Wichelhaus* has long been seen to mark a turning point in the history of contract law, with the case's multiple challenges to the self-evidence of the act of promising working to transform courts' understanding of precisely *when* in the sequence of events initiated by contracts the people who sign them

---

3. Carole Pateman argues that the subject of the Lockean social contract is necessarily male, since the social contract's constitutive division between public and private rests upon a prior, and only intermittently acknowledged, sexual contract. See Pateman, *The Sexual Contract* (Stanford: Stanford University Press, 1988).

become obligated to do what the contracts say they will do. As promising came to seem less transparent and unambiguous an act, judges began to look elsewhere in the contractual process to find the moment at which obligation is created, away from the promise and toward historical effects resulting from the contract's existence. This shift in the conception of contractual obligation can be seen in broad terms as part of a more general transformation of the nineteenth-century individual from an ideal bearer of abstract rights and powers organized around a "will" to a more historical subject, understood to be legible in relation to the local and particular conditions within which he or she happens to be situated and the local and particular effects of their presence in the world.

As I will explain, contract law clearly functions in this era as a discursive instance by which this paradoxical conception of culture manifests itself. But more important, it is also one of the central instruments available to individuals to rationalize and hence stabilize their experiences of the unpredictability of the social and material world around them—to rationalize historical contingency. Another major cultural instrument by which this rationalization of accident takes place, I propose, is the realist novel. Offering a formal logic by which apparently contingent details of the material world and turns of plot are understood to be meaningful—interpretable—by virtue of being authored, the realist novel represents characters whose freedom, whose capacity to will, is demonstrated by the nonnecessity of their actions. At the same time, it is the fictionality of the representation, its being the product of an authorial will, that operates as the "pervasive cultural logic" of the world that is the novel, that makes meaningful these accidental, contingent behaviors of the characters represented. Accordingly, the novel acts out the tension within liberalism between agency and cultural determination.

But I am not merely arguing for the existence of a formal homology between the novel and the contract form. Henry James's *What Maisie Knew* powerfully links its thematic concern with the possibilities and limits of liberal knowledge and agency together with a formal elaboration of the range and the ethics of fictional authority. In this novel, adults manipulate and coerce a nominally "free" child by their very insistence on her freedom to choose, while James renders such behavior continuous with, and sometimes even indistinguishable from, the ways authors control the behavior of characters they represent as acting by the characters' own volition.[4] In connecting

---

4. Although *What Maisie Knew* has recently become the object of a good deal of critical scrutiny, it is not one of James's better-known works. At the risk of vulgarity, I offer the following summary of the plot of the novel, with the caveat that, as always in James, what happens is hardly what matters. Maisie's parents divorce and are awarded joint custody of her, with Maisie directed to split her time between the

the formal logic of the realist novel with the volatile—and historically contingent—relations among the capacities of its various characters to assert their wills upon one another and upon the material world, James at once historicizes his own fictional authority and draws the crisis of this authority signaled by *Maisie*'s formal self-reflexivity into relation with the newly apparent incoherence of liberalism marked by the *Raffles* case.

I begin by analyzing the "crisis" that is *Raffles:* what is revealed by the particular terms of the contract's sudden unenforceability is the way liberal subjectivity generally and Anglo-American contract law as the paradigmatic instantiation of that liberal subjectivity are generated out of the very tensions that ultimately lead both to seem descriptively unconvincing in the last third of the nineteenth century. I trace the discourse of contractual obligation through the two alternative "solutions" to the epistemological, moral, and political difficulties posed by *Raffles* that emerged in the wake of the case: a newly historicized, contingent notion of contractual obligation posited by the measurement of "reliance" or "benefit" and Oliver Wendell Holmes's attempt to imagine a version of contractual obligation that does not depend on the states of mind of the contracting parties. By following the conundrums articulated by *Raffles* through their variously problematic and incomplete resolutions to their much more aesthetically and socially enabling manifestations in *What Maisie Knew,* I hope not only to show that the novel and the contract draw from a common discourse of an embattled nineteenth-century liberalism, but also to demonstrate how both forms helped produce the very category of culture by which they might be linked. But instead of being a kind of all-purpose analytical category by which the behavior of individual subjects, apparently aberrant, can be considered evidence of some larger social phenomenon, Foucauldian "culture" turns out to be the product of a particularly liberal—and finally unstable—tension between autonomy and

---

two households. She is made the mostly unwitting medium by which the two parents can continue to exchange barbs. Maisie's father, Beale Farange, employs a governess, Miss Overmore, whom he later marries, at which time she comes to be known as "Mrs. Beale," while Maisie's mother, Ida, takes up with a man known as Sir Claude. The most onerous responsibilities for Maisie's upbringing are assigned to a governess, Mrs. Wix. She begins as Ida's employee, but when Beale and Miss Overmore marry she shuttles between the two households along with Maisie. As Maisie's parents lose what little interest they initially had in keeping track of her fate, responsibility falls to the two stepparents, Mrs. Beale and Sir Claude, who use the opportunity afforded by their meetings on her behalf to begin a dalliance of their own. By novel's end, Sir Claude proposes that Maisie abandon Mrs. Wix entirely and live with him and Mrs. Beale so as to legitimate their relationship. Maisie, who has by this time matured sufficiently both to understand the ends to which she is being employed and also to desire to possess Sir Claude's affections exclusively, offers a counterproposal by which she will leave Mrs. Wix if Sir Claude will leave Mrs. Beale. Sir Claude effectively, if never explicitly, rejects Maisie's proposal, and Maisie and Mrs. Wix are left to fend for one another.

historical contingency, with the "context" normally invoked as an explanatory ground of the realist novel itself dependent on the representational relations of the novel.

Raffles's dueling attorneys set two questions in play. First, they introduced the question of the necessity of the relation between inner states of mind and externally perceptible behaviors. The terms of the controversy presume that contractual obligation is understood to be established by an act of promising, and promising is understood to take the form of an internal act of will— a mental state—only contingently connected to its outward manifestations. (What did the two parties *mean* when they *said* "*Peerless*"?) What happens to such a notion of contract when the nonnecessity of the link between inner and outer renders external behavior (the speech act "*Peerless*") inadequate as evidence of a particular mental state? ("*Peerless*" could refer to the October or the December *Peerless*.) Second, even if the parties who said "*Peerless*" could be understood to have meant the same thing, what is to ensure that they meant it in a strong way, as a necessary component of the contractual agreement?

The extraordinary range of claims regarding just what constituted the "promise" of *Raffles* heralds the case as a moment of crisis in the history of Anglo-American contract law. The peculiarity of the ruling bespeaks in no uncertain terms the contradictory quality of the prevailing "promissory" doctrine of contractual obligation: agreement depends entirely on the intersection of two wills at the moment of promising, yet the fact of such an intersection, like the content of either of the individual wills, seems fundamentally unknowable. Judges had sidestepped the difficulty by locating evidence of such subjective comings-together in a series of external signs of agreement. But in *Raffles v. Wichelhaus,* that both parties had in contracting said "*Peerless*" was deemed not to constitute sufficient evidence that they had intended the same thing by their use of the term. With their decision that articulating a set of syllables no longer proved any determinate intention, the *Raffles* judges revealed the epistemological incoherencies of a conception of contractual obligation founded in the promise as inner will, and in so doing they abruptly ended the legal principle's relatively untroubled, century-and-a-half-long tenure.

The two issues raised by *Raffles*—the nature of the link between internal mental states and outwardly perceptible behaviors and the relative "strength" or "weakness" implied by the mere fact of inclusion in a description—both entail concerns about the relation of knowledge and accident. But as I will show, only when we understand contract itself to be structured as an instrument for both acknowledging and controlling the uncertain relations of knowledge and historical contingency do the two questions become inextricably linked, discernible less as distinctions than as emphases whose aspects shimmer into visibility and fade again as the contradictory impulses implicit in the contract form generally shift around the courts' changing understandings of obligation.

The "reliance" and "benefit" notions of contractual obligation that emerge in the years following the crisis in legal description articulated by *Raffles* locate obligation not in the act of promising but in the effects produced on the contracting parties as a consequence of their having promised—how far either of the parties has actually "relied on" or "benefited from" the existence of a contract. Such an understanding might seem to be a throwback to an era even before the reign of the promissory contract, an era in which, in the famous phrase of the nineteenth-century anthropologist Henry Maine, "status" took precedence over "contract,"[5] so that agreements were understood to articulate existing social relations rather than to offer a means of transcending them.[6] But whereas eighteenth-century courts saw contract as a mere marker, an invocation, of existing social relations and the responsibilities attendant on them, the late nineteenth-century reliance contract retained the potential of creating obligations while at the same time complicating presumptions about the means by which such agency to choose might be produced. The courts were no longer content to assume, as they had at the height of the period of promissory freedom, that parties to a contract made their promises based on all the information theoretically available to them. Instead, courts began to see it as their responsibility to investigate what information the contractors *actually did* acquire before making promises.[7] By acknowl-

---

5. Henry Maine, *Ancient Law* (New York: J. M. Dent, [1861]).

6. Under this system, practitioners of a wide variety of services deemed essential for the functioning of the community were expected to provide these services to all who required them and were able to pay what custom determined to be a "just price." Under this system, an innkeeper with an establishment on a well-traveled road could not reserve the last available room until several potential occupants had arrived and then award it to the person willing to pay the highest price. Rather, the innkeeper must rent the room to the first person able to pay the just price; issues of scarcity and demand had no place in determining cost. Over the course of the first half of the nineteenth century, these same practitioners became increasingly free to accept and refuse clients as they saw fit, with clients' fitness largely an issue of their capacity to compete in the market.

7. What needs to be made clear is that promissory and reliance/benefit understandings of contractual obligation are not, strictly speaking, so much different forms of contract as different interpretations of the meaning of the contractual relationship. Contractors at a given historical moment are not in the position of *choosing* to enter into either a promissory or a reliance/benefit contract, though their sense of how the courts are generally interpreting contractual obligation might well affect the circumstances surrounding contracts and the ways the parties use them. Both Gilmore and Atiyah argue for a discontinuity in Anglo-American courts' behavior in evaluating obligation from the middle of the century to its close. My reading of the history of contractual obligation, while concurring that a change does take

edging the subject's knowledge and decisions to be conditional, the courts make the contingent empirical circumstances of the subject, not his or her ideal freedom, the measure by which the justice of a given contract is evaluated.[8]

Henry James's 1897 novel *What Maisie Knew* can likewise be understood to grow up in—and out of—the shadow of *Raffles*. Out of the raw stuff of an anecdote about joint child custody told in passing at a dinner party hosted by James Bryce, Regius Professor of Law at Oxford,[9] Henry James fashions the story of a little girl with so many parents and stepparents that her ties to none of them—or their obligations to her—go without saying. The occasion of the novel's beginning is an unnarratable series of broken contracts order-

---

place, emphasizes how far the notions regarding identity, agency, and temporality that the reliance/benefit understanding of obligation attempts to describe can be discerned in the incoherencies and instabilities of the earlier, more idealist promissory form of obligation.

8. The most explicit literary registration of this change in working notions of contractual obligation is Wilkie Collins's *The Woman in White*. Published in 1860, the novel is coeval with the most heated legal battles over the issue. "The second question, concerning the nature of the legal contract by which the money was to be obtained, and the degree of personal responsibility to which Laura might subject herself if she signed it in the dark, involved considerations which lay far beyond any knowledge and experience that either of us possessed." Wilkie Collins, *The Woman in White* (New York: Penguin, 1985), 274–75.

9. Although I will be arguing that the late nineteenth-century shift in prevailing Anglo-American notions of contractual obligation whose contours I outline below is part of a general cultural realignment of models of citizenship, legal authority, and political and social obligation, James's relation to contemporary discussions about contract was both particular and personal. That James first heard the anecdote that inspired *What Maisie Knew* at a dinner party hosted by Bryce is only the most direct link between James and contemporary discussions about contract and citizenship (Henry James, *The Complete Notebooks of Henry James,* ed. Leon Edel [Oxford: Oxford University Press, 1987], 71). For an account of Bryce's role in the British idealist movement that advocated and theorized this new model of citizenship, see Peter P. Nicholson, *The Political Philosophy of the British Idealists* (Cambridge: Cambridge University Press, 1990), and J. W. Burrow, *A Liberal Descent: Victorian Historians and the English Past* (Cambridge: Cambridge University Press, 1981).

Furthermore, one of the two biographies James wrote (the other being a biography of Hawthorne), *William Wetmore Story and His Friends* (Boston: Houghton Mifflin, 1903), details the career of William Wetmore Story, the son of Joseph Story, who in 1837 wrote and published the first code of American contract law. The younger Story abandoned a promising legal career to travel to Europe and work as a sculptor, a career trajectory that bears obvious resemblances both to James's own biography in general and, more specifically, to the complex interplay of contract and art in the establishment of legal authority and national cultural identity in the period. Finally, James makes most explicit the association between the social disempowerment and limited consciousness of a child and the shifting notions of contract in his short story "The Pupil," which he links to *Maisie* in his earliest notebook entry on the novel. In "The Pupil," first published in 1891, James tells the story of a tutor who remains in service to his young student because he is never paid, the shifting and paradoxical nature of contractual obligation having made it impossible for him to close a deal with his young charge's parents. I am grateful to Tami Yaacobi for bringing this story to my attention. For an interesting account of the relevance of contract to James's work in a specifically American history context, see Brook Thomas, *American Literary Realism and the Failed Promise of Contract* (Berkeley: University of California Press, 1997).

ing, variously, Maisie's parents' marriage, the terms of their guardianship, and their very obligation to honor the contracts to which they have agreed:

> The litigation had seemed interminable and had in fact been complicated; but by the decision on the appeal the judgement of the divorce-court was confirmed as to the assignment of the child. The father, who, though bespattered from head to foot, had made good his case, was, in pursuance of this triumph, appointed to keep her. . . . Attached, however, to the second pronouncement was a condition that detracted, for Beale Farange, from its sweetness—an order that he should refund to his late wife the twenty-six hundred pounds put down by her, as it was called, some three years before, in the interest of the child's maintenance and precisely on a proved understanding that he would take no proceedings: a sum of which he had had the administration and of which he could render not the least account.[10]

Both syntactically and semantically, the passage resists a reader's attempt to "render the least account," demanding, as it does, that we know everything at once before we can begin to know anything at all. The custody appeal recedes before the judgment it reconfirms; the judgment of the divorce court recalls the marriage whose cancellation it is meant to mark. If we patch together a rough chronological narrative of the events alone, we are still left with some nagging puzzles about just who does what. The Faranges divorce; custody of the child Maisie, along with £2,600 of Ida's money, is awarded to Beale in exchange for his agreement not to take further proceedings, that is, not to break the contract. But while we might succeed in putting together a plausible account of what took place, the difficulty of attaching that history to a set of interested contracting agents threatens to undermine the plausibility of even the barest chronology of events. To whom, for example, ought we to attribute the initiation of the second round of "proceedings"? Does the pronouncement returning the money to Ida, a condition associated with Beale's agreement to engage in no further litigation, suggest that Beale has in fact broken that contract and begun a new round of legal action? What might we understand his interest to be in initiating those proceedings, if he is said to "triumph" on an appeal that merely confirms the original decision? If, alternatively, we understand Ida to be responsible for the second round of court battles, then how do we make sense of her imposing a moratorium on legal action as a condition of the prior agreement? The swirl of questions generated by our attempt to transform the passage's disjunct beginnings and endings into a narrative and its contracts, obligations, and breaches into a line of interest and agency settles itself into a single, uncompromising ques-

---

10. Henry James, *What Maisie Knew* (New York: Penguin, 1987), 35. All further page references to the novel will be cited in parentheses within the text.

tion: Do Beale and Ida Farange want to keep Maisie, or do they want to get rid of her?

The temptation to turn from narrative as account to list as account is telling, since it seems to mean that chronological clarity, a certain logic of historical causality, is discernible only by ignoring the distracting claims of individual agency—interest, motivation. If this opening links Maisie's fate unmistakably to the fate of contract, it at the same time predicates the intertwining of their destinies on the impossibility of aligning the unfolding action of the various contracts to the wills of individuals. And the passage's relentless thwarting of our attempts to figure out why Beale Farange and his wife make and break the contracts they do warns that if we understand the history of contract as mattering to *What Maisie Knew* only at the moments when contracts are explicitly represented in the novel, we do so at our own peril, at the risk of producing consequences neither intended nor anticipated. For the more strenuously Beale and Ida Farange resist our efforts to make their behavior make sense, the more they gain the substance and opacity and unassimilability of real people, their very irrationality and unpredictability apparently freeing them from their fate as mere counters in some grand authorial master plan.

Maisie's parents repeatedly demand that she be the one to decide which of them she will be entrusted to, and in this demand lies the novel's poignancy and moral force as well as its thematic link to the contract debates. In attributing to Maisie the capacity to make such choices despite her obvious financial, emotional, and intellectual dependency, Maisie's various "guardians" cynically and self-interestedly invoke the discourse of the liberal, promissory contract, which presumes a wholly autonomous and efficacious subject. Yet by imposing such a model on a child who clearly cannot fulfill or embody it, *What Maisie Knew*—like the new reliance/benefit conception of contractual obligation—can be seen to represent the patent falsity of the promissory contract's presumptions. Both the new model of contractual obligation and James's novel show that the subject's conditions, historical and material, severely limit his or her ability to be a traditional "liberal" agent.

The Strange Career of Nineteenth-Century Contract

In 1830 a writer in the influential law journal the *American Jurist* described the emergent intellectual system of contract law:

> Under a free and natural system of laws, men have a right to make any agreement they please, however contrary to the usual custom, [and where not contrary to the

original social contract] this agreement will be recognized as the law to them. [Only] an unnatural and artificial extension [of public institutions could create a] power to overrule the express agreements of individuals . . . since whatever men have consented to, that shall bind them, and nothing else.[11]

As it emerged from the tradition of English customary law in the late eighteenth century, contract law was characterized by its emphasis on the right of the parties to an agreement to determine the terms by which they are to be bound. In creating what P. S. Atiyah has called "an instrument of private planning"[12] that allowed parties to articulate and create detailed private agreements within the parameters of standing law, contract shifted the focus of legal relations to individual will—the right to make an agreement—and away from both the legislative processes of the state and social custom. According to Atiyah, the idea of an *ordinary* contract as the creation of a voluntary agreement, produced by a conscious and deliberate act of will that did not depend on existing rights or duties, was still emerging in the eighteenth century. Even more radical was the idea that the rights and duties generated by a contractual agreement were themselves products of the will irrespective of existing duties or rights.[13]

But by 1880 the era of the promissory contract had begun to wane. In his influential article "Liberal Legislation and Freedom of Contract" (1881), T. H. Green, an Oxford law professor who tutored a succession of liberal legislators from the 1860s until his death in 1882, challenged the primacy of the principle of freedom of contract. The extension of the suffrage brought about by the Reform Bills had resulted in the election of a critical mass of liberal legislators who not only set about upsetting the terms of contracts and leases between (for example) landlord and tenant but sought to reconceive the very terms of civil freedom. Green writes:

11. *American Jurist* 28 (1830): 35, quoted in Horwitz, *Transformation of American Law*, 203.

12. Atiyah, *Rise and Fall of Freedom of Contract*, 420.

13. Although the new emphasis on voluntarism was most explicit in the contractual form, the same elevation of a will presumed able to control its environment sufficiently to commit itself to future action was discernible in the emergence of credit and insurance as instruments of commercial expansion. Atiyah argues that the general social stability that characterized eighteenth-century England was crucial to allowing insurance to emerge without having the implicit contradiction of its structure become disablingly visible. The establishment of the gold standard in England in 1717 created the kind of monetary stability necessary for the growth of a credit economy, and the intersecting functions of insurance, as well as its coincident spread, seem to establish credit, insurance, and promissory contracts as parallel developments. But unlike credit, both insurance and contract displayed a certain ambivalence about the capacity of present acts to ensure future events, even as their structures seemed designed to bring into being the capacity they were figured to presume.

When we . . . speak of freedom, we should consider carefully what we mean by it. We do not mean merely freedom from restraint or compulsion. We do not mean merely freedom to do as we like irrespectively of what it is that we like. We do not mean a freedom that can be enjoyed by one man or one set of men at the cost of a loss of freedom to others. When we speak of freedom as something to be so highly prized, we mean a positive power or capacity of doing or enjoying something worth doing or enjoying, and that, too, something that we do or enjoy in common with others. . . .

. . . If I have given a true account of that freedom which forms the goal of social effort, we shall see that freedom of contract, freedom in all the forms of doing what one will with one's own, is valuable only as a means to an end. That end is what I call freedom in the positive sense: in other words, the liberation of the powers of all men equally for contributions to a common good.[14]

In his reconceptualization of freedom as positive content—the power to accomplish certain social goals—rather than the classic liberal notion of freedom as freedom from restraint, Green articulated the connection of such shifting conceptions of the proper relationship between the individual and the state to a transformation in the dominant conception of contract.[15] Green's

14. T. H. Green, "Liberal Legislation and Freedom of Contract," in *Lectures on the Principles of Political Obligation and Other Writings,* ed. Paul Harris and John Morrow (Cambridge: Cambridge University Press, 1986), 198, 200.

15. Consider the following example: Gloria, the owner of an attractive three-bedroom bungalow, puts her house on the market. On Tuesday afternoon she receives calls from two people interested in buying the house. She agrees to show the house on Wednesday morning to the first caller, Malcolm, and also makes an appointment for early Friday morning with Doris, the other interested caller. On Wednesday at noon, immediately after seeing the house, Malcolm agrees to purchase it at the price Gloria is asking and puts down a deposit of $2,000 to hold the property. Three hours later Malcolm calls Gloria and tells her he is no longer interested in buying the house.

Under a strict notion of promissory obligation, such as the one that dominated Anglo-American through the first half of the nineteenth century, Malcolm would lose his entire deposit. His obligation is based simply and solely on his promise to buy the house, and on this basis he is guilty of breach of contract. On the other hand, a court attempting to determine the extent of Malcolm's liability under a reliance/benefit understanding of obligation would need to ask more questions. What did Gloria do immediately after Malcolm signed the paper agreeing to purchase the house? Whereas within a promissory understanding of contract Malcolm's obligation occurs before his cancellation, under reliance/ benefit a court would want to determine whether Gloria (a) did nothing, so that Doris, the other willing buyer, came to her appointment as scheduled, agreed to purchase the house, and made a down payment; (b) canceled the Friday morning appointment with Doris, who immediately found another house to buy; or (c) canceled the appointment with Doris but then called her and rescheduled a few hours later, after Malcolm had called to say he was no longer interested.

In case (a), whereas Malcolm has promised to purchase the house and is therefore liable for the deposit within a context of promissory obligation, in a legal context in which a reliance/benefit notion of contract holds sway he might not be liable at all, since Gloria apparently did not rely on his agreement and, as a result, was not harmed by his failure to live up to his promise. In case (b) Gloria very definitely relied on the fact that Malcolm had signed the paper and suffered discernible harm as a result of that reliance. Still, it is important to keep in mind what becomes evident by a comparison of cases (b) and (c)—that the conception of positive freedom can be partly understood to announce a shift in emphasis toward historical contingency, a sudden slipping of the tension between an autonomous, ideal will (and the knowledge that would make such a will efficacious) and the unexpected historical contingencies that would limit the exercise of such a will. The reliance/benefit notion of obligation solves the problem of the incoherence of the "act" of promising by doing away with the significance of promising altogether: what matters is no longer the abstract fact that a promise has been made, and thus a will expressed. Instead, what is to be measured are the consequences resulting from a contractual agreement. In relocating the evidence of contractual obligation from this problematic act of promising to more easily discernible effects of agreement, reliance/benefit conceptions of obligation not only transform the contract into an openly historical effort to grapple with (historical) contingency but effectively historicize the contracting subjects.

The form of the contract across its different historical manifestations can be understood as a deliberate attempt to rationalize and gain a measure of control over historical contingency, partial knowledge, and the precarious relations between them. The courts' gradual abandonment of a promissory notion of obligation in favor of a conception of obligation based on the social position of the contractors and the contract's actual effects thus was less an absolute break from the more idealist promissory obligation than a shift in emphasis. Through the lens of *Raffles* we can see contract to be a narrative form, an instrument that constructs a concept of an individual subject's agency and knowledge as *probable* rather than as ideal and certain. Such

---

fact of reliance does not necessarily imply the presence of harm. This is not to say that Gloria suffered absolutely no harm in case c; she can likely make a compelling argument for having been inconvenienced by Malcolm's change of heart and claim at least some portion of his deposit as reparation for this harm. Because, unlike promissory obligation, the doctrine of reliance draws its evidence from the contingent circumstances surrounding the performance of contracts, the extent of any harm can be determined only by examining the particular circumstances of a case.

Let's add another complication. Suppose Malcolm demands his deposit back, claiming he decided to renege on his agreement only after being tipped off by a neighbor that the house was infested with termites and likely to collapse to its foundations within six months. Once again, within a strict promissory reading of contract Malcolm would have no recourse to the law, since parties to a contract are presumed to be in possession of all information necessary to evaluate the wisdom of the contracts they enter into. A promissory understanding of contract would place the burden for investigating potential fraud on the parties themselves; contractors are assumed to have the wherewithal to protect themselves from making bad contracts. On the other hand, courts adhering to a reliance/benefit interpretive scheme would be forced to investigate what and how much information each party to the contract had at the time of the agreement. Did Gloria take steps to prevent Malcolm from discovering the termite infestation? Did Malcolm take reasonable steps to inspect the property? Was he somehow pressured to sign the contract more quickly than he might have liked, leading him to overlook something he would otherwise have noticed?

a probabilistic conception of knowledge acknowledges and overcomes the limitations placed on the idea of an autonomous liberal subject by the vagaries of history. The probabilistic, narrative quality of contract, a crucial element of *What Maisie Knew*, should be understood as an attempt to grapple with the challenge historicity poses to the prospect of individual subjectivity.

Consider the central premise of contract in its most general, formal conception, one that describes contract under both understandings of obligation I have identified: two parties enter into an agreement designed to guarantee that both will behave in a certain way in the future (e.g., pay a certain price on the delivery of a given piece of merchandise; pay a certain wage at the completion of a designated period or amount of work). The structure of contract is such that both parties are assumed to believe that the terms of the contract benefit them at the time they enter into their agreement, and both are similarly assumed to believe that the terms will continue to benefit them at the time they will be called on to perform. The practical value of contract as an instrument of private planning, as well as its moral status as an expression of individual freedom, depends on the assumption that one can make reasonably accurate judgments about the likelihood that certain relevant future conditions will prevail. Implicit in the model of the contract, then, is an affirmation of the epistemological usefulness of probability. To this extent the contract stands as an assertion of an individual's capacity not only to predict correctly that certain conditions will prevail in the world, but to act as he or she has promised in having assumed these conditions—in effect, to impose his or her will upon the world.

But contract labors under the force of a contrary impulse as well. The paradox it poses is apparent: if contract presumes that its parties can predict that the conditions will prevail under which they would benefit from fulfilling its terms, what interest can they have in making contracts? Why promise to do something in the future if you would want to do it then anyway?

Clearly, there is an element of having it both ways about the contract. While the tenets of freedom of contract presume that the parties to a contract will desire to perform the acts they have agreed on, the notion of contractual *obligation* suggests something else entirely. In their obligatory aspect, contracts seem designed to compel people to perform acts they might otherwise be unwilling to perform. Conjured by this sudden unwillingness is a narrative of probability gone awry. In contractual obligation, we can perceive the threat of contingent, mundane history: say, the unexpected, apparently inexplicable shift in the market that leaves us saddled, despite our most careful calculations, with an obligation to buy cotton at a cost wildly out of line with prevailing market prices. The contract form thus makes two seemingly contradictory statements at once. First, it asserts that the parties to the contract would behave a certain way in the future notwithstanding the intervention of unforeseen events. Second, it says that precisely *because* unforeseen events might intervene between the moment of promising and the time the promise can be carried out, contracts are necessary to *compel* the action that one of the parties to the contract might otherwise no longer perform.

Contracts thus constitute at once an acknowledgment of the power of historical contingencies to limit a subject's knowledge and a structure for overcoming such limitations by the act of acknowledgment itself. In the emphasis of promissory obligation on the promise made on the strength of probabilistic knowledge, we can read an optimism about the adequacy of such knowledge to enable contracting parties to know and to do what will be beneficial to themselves. In the conception of obligation incurred after the fact, on the other hand, we might discern a certain caution, an unwillingness to hold people to promises based on knowledge that is, after all is said and done, *merely* probabilistic. The promissory form of obligation turns the structural contradictions underlying contract to good account: the condition of knowing only partially is redescribed as a specific knowledge technique—knowing probabilistically—and this redescription, insofar as it guides the contractors' behavior in relation to one another, produces the outcome it presupposes.[16] But the confusions articulated by *Raffles* demonstrate that the unexpected vagaries of history cannot, at midcentury, be quite so easily rationalized. No longer are the contracting parties assumed to be sufficiently alike that their "not knowing" can be turned into a shared condition of subjectivity. Rather, with the explosive recognition produced by *Raffles*'s multiplying ships—that subjects might not even have the same knowledge about the present—the promissory contract's largely temporal, equalizing notion of historical contingency is replaced by the idea that the contracting subjects are themselves ineradicably marked by contingency. People can no longer be held to their promises because they have nothing in common to promise, because they have

16. Lorraine Daston has recently made the case that we cannot understand the concept of classical probability that emerged in the seventeenth century without recognizing its roots in contract law: "Seventeenth-century legal practices and theories shaped the first expressions of mathematical probability and stamped the classical theory with two of its most distinctive and enduring features: the 'epistemic' interpretation of probabilities as degrees of certainty; and the primacy of the concept of expectation [that is, the idea that probability measured the likelihood of events' happening to different people rather than the likelihood of their occurring at all]. Moreover, legal problems provided the principal applications of the classical theory of probability from the outset. Even the earliest problems concerning games of chance and annuities were framed in legal terms drawn from contract law." See Daston, *Classical Probability in the Enlightenment* (Princeton: Princeton University Press, 1988), 6.

no common set of interests, or even common language, from which to create relations of mutuality or exchange.

I propose that the kind of knowledge presumed and produced by the realist novel was organized so as to stabilize just these contradictions manifested by the liberal, contracting subject. In his account of the operation of probability in the reading experience of novelistic fiction, Robert Newsom recalls Aristotle's pointedly antimimetic description of the relation between poetry and history. In Aristotle's view, poetry is a more philosophical undertaking than the writing of history because it concerns itself not with the wholly contingent particulars of what actually happens but with what could happen.[17] Poetry, dealing as it does with probabilities rather than the events of history, paradoxically represents events that can happen but likely never will, because events in real life rarely occur with the neatness and regularity of universals.

What is innovative about the realist novel, in Newsom's view, is the way the novel (like the contract) formalizes this bipartite quality of probability. The reader of realist fiction experiences the text through two frames of reference at once, one that places the evidence of the text in relation to evidence from the "real" world and one that places textual evidence in relation to the fictional world. We know that Maisie is a fictional character and thus in some sense can be understood to be not true—wholly improbable—at the same time as we pass judgment about the different degrees of probability of moments within the fictional narrative. Such a stance can accommodate entirely contradictory evidence (Maisie can be understood at once both to exist and not to exist), but the experience of literary probability requires that the tension between the two frames of reference be maintained rather than resolved. This tension—what Newsom terms "the antinomy of fictional probability"—helps show the ways realist novels and contracts might operate in alignment with one another to produce in liberal subjects a belief that they can do what they want in their environments, although they live in worlds of which they have only partial knowledge, over which they have only partial control. Whereas the contract offered a paradox of degree, the antinomy of fiction Newsom describes stabilizes these relations insofar as it balances the partial (the events of the narrative) and the absolute (the wholly fictional quality of the novelistic world). The realist novel thus offers a cultural instrument for bolstering the far less stable contract: the reader well schooled in engaging with only partially knowable characters buffeted by unpredictable twists of

17. Robert Newsom, *A Likely Story: Probability and Play in Fiction* (New Brunswick, N.J.: Rutgers University Press, 1988), esp. chaps. 1 and 6.

plot while at the same time remaining certain that these people and events are ultimately knowable as "not-true"—that is, fictional—is likely to be more optimistic about his or her capacity to make contracts work.

Not only does Newsom's theory of fiction describe a general relation between a single event and like events within each of the frames of reference, then, but it describes as well the position of the reader of fiction *between* frames of reference, an oscillation between the general condition of absolute difference of the real and the fictional and the contingent local relations of resemblance joining the details of the two frames. Given this unresolved tension, the real does not simply serve as the context within which a reader's belief in the fictional world is to be evaluated; the two contexts provide evidence for the evaluation of one by the other. While the reader's beliefs regarding the real become the ground according to which a judgment of fictional plausibility is rendered, this ground is itself unstable, subject to constant remaking in response to the pressure of the fictional world. The bodies of evidence that produce the beliefs within each frame of reference accumulate separately and thus remain in a contingent relation to one another; the effect a given fictional representation will have on the long-held beliefs of a given reader can be predicted only probabilistically, but the transfer of evidence from one frame of reference to the other presumes that a condition of probability has already been established. This stabilizing category of realist fictionality seems inadequate to the task of resolving the problem raised by *Raffles,* the problem of subjectivity at a moment where it is no longer self-evident that probabilistic knowledge is sufficient to make the world predictable. Not only does the compensatory power of the realist novel no longer seem enough to ameliorate the threat posed to the ideal of individual autonomy by the experience of historical unpredictability and social heterogeneity, but this growing sense of the pressures of the contingent will fundamentally alter the category of novelistic fictionality as well.

When Maisie Knew: James's Narrative Temporalizing

As the novel's introductory expository section draws to a close, Maisie's family, disrupted at the outset, is reassembled across time as Beale, unable to account for the whereabouts of the money Ida has contributed to Maisie's expenses, is ordered by yet another legal decision to give Maisie to her mother for six months of the year. Although Maisie once again finds herself with both father and mother, Maisie's nuclear family-in-time is something less— and more—than a family. To the extent that Maisie understands who she is and what she is capable of doing as being linked to who her parents are and the sorts of demands they make on her, such an identity is suddenly no longer discernible at any given moment. It must, like the contractual subject implied by the reliance model of obligation, be discovered over time both by the novel's readers and by Maisie herself as the child is shuttled between her parents' households. And such a subject is not simply knowable through time but is itself diachronic, less given than produced, a subjectivity constituted out of its relation to the passage of time.

It is from within this context of a newly diachronic conception of subjectivity that the novel figures an institutional bureaucracy to emerge:

> What was to have been expected on the evidence was the nomination, *in loco parentis,* of some proper third person, some respectable or at least some presentable friend. Apparently, however, the circle of the Faranges had been scanned in vain for any such ornament; so that the only solution finally meeting all the difficulties was, save that of sending Maisie to a Home, the partition of the tutelary office in the manner I have mentioned. . . . Their rupture had resounded, and after being perfectly insignificant together they would be decidedly striking apart. Had they not produced an impression that warranted people in looking for appeals in the newspapers for the rescue of the little one—reverberation, amid a vociferous public, of the idea that some movement should be started or some benevolent person should come forward? (36)

Beale and Ida cannot be compelled to act as parents despite their having contracted to do so; the fact of the contract's existence testifies to this social truth more powerfully than the specific terms of agreement it contains. The transformation to the contractual realm results in the elevation of a principle of substitutability, leaving the choice to be made among a range of resemblances. The spectrum of simulacra ranges from Beale and Ida themselves, who from the outset act only vaguely "like parents," to the threatening specter of the depersonalized "Home." The entire turn of events implies that the sort of civil bureaucracy that flickers into momentary visibility and then disappears comes into being not as a consequence of a stripping away of cultural particularity but as a result of a saturation by particularity. The chance that Maisie's interests will be protected by an institution fades with the dimming of the prospects for discovering that "proper third person"—the third person who might signal the terms of Beale's and Ida's battlings to be less a domestic pathology than a cultural norm.

The state socializes its individual actors so they become effectively interchangeable without having itself to create a wholly unfamiliar institution as substitute: "A good lady came indeed a step or two: she was distantly related to Mrs Farange, to whom she proposed that, having children and nurseries wound up and going, she should be allowed to take home the bone of contention and, by working it into her system, relieve at least one of the parents" (36). When Ida objects that if this adoption plan were to go through she would lose her right as a mother to make her case before her child, the relation retreats and Maisie is "abandoned to her fate." This failure of substitution, a failure in which the novel finds its impetus, is the outcome of a kind of failure of social context, the failure of the collective to offer a set of social conventions sufficiently stable to authorize substituting the behavior of the collectivity for that of the individual. Maisie is consigned to her fate because she has the misfortune to occupy a moment of transition between two of the structures Pierre Bourdieu calls the "habitus."[18] Ida has the authority to reject the relative's offer to assume custody of Maisie because she is able implicitly to invoke an apparently waning system of relations in which parents' ties to their children are absolute. At the same time, however, Ida participates in—indeed, helps to produce—a set of cultural assumptions according to which the relationship between parent and child is contractual, voluntary.

If this opening section is organized by its disorganization, drawn toward its inconclusive conclusion by entropy rather than narrative causality, the social chaos it describes might seem to follow upon the section's generic ambiguity. Located between James's "Preface" and the first numbered chapter and set in some temporally indeterminate period before the events of the narrative begin, the section takes as its task to describe the conditions, the necessary prehistory, out of which the events of the narrative must precede. Thus tagged generically, this opening interlude announces more than its local incoherence, signaling a crisis in the reliability and predictability of the very structure of the prehistory, of "context," as a conceptual category as much as it marks the dissolution of this particular cluster of conditions.

Whereas this beginning section resists comprehension even within its own narrative confines (the difficulty of understanding why Maisie's parents do what they do being sufficient in itself to obscure the literal chronology of events), the unintelligibility of the novel's initial chapters is of a different or-

18. Bourdieu defines "habitus" as "systems of durable, transposable *dispositions*, structured structures predisposed to function as structuring structures, that is, as principles of the generation and structuring of practices and representations which can be objectively 'regulated' and 'regular' without in any way being the product of obedience to rules, objectively adapted to their goals without presupposing a conscious aiming at ends or an express mastery of the operations necessary to attain them and, being all this collectively orchestrated without being the product of the orchestrating action of a conductor." See Pierre Bourdieu, *Outline of a Theory of Practice* (Cambridge: Cambridge University Press, 1989), 72.

der, a matter of making sense of the relations among episodes rather than between them. The difficulty of reading the first three chapters of the novel[19] is not simply a matter of their local syntactic opacity; unlike the opening pages, the literal meaning of these chapters is fairly accessible. Rather, they present us with the difficulty of reading before our accession to this fiction's claims of probability—the problem of making sense of evidence that resists accumulation. The difficulty of reading these early chapters is that they at once demand and refuse to be put in relation to one another; the piling up of narrative information between episodes subverts rather than contributes to a belief that the process of reading will bring us toward a certain, or even a probable, knowledge of either real or fictional worlds.

> The child was provided for, but the new arrangement was inevitably confounding to a young intelligence intensely aware that something had happened which must matter a good deal and looking anxiously out for the effects of so great a cause. It was to be the fate of this patient little girl to see much more than she at first understood, but also even at first to understand much more than any little girl, however patient, had perhaps ever understood before. (39)

"Looking anxiously out for the effects of so great a cause," Maisie inhabits the time, the epistemological and juridical position between promise—that "great cause"—and performance, around which the paradox of contractual obligation is constituted. If the logical contortions of the *Raffles* judgment are any indication, Maisie is not alone in "looking anxiously out" from that position. This moment, of course, is the place where the contract becomes a form of ideology and is also the place where its rhetorical and logical contradictions emerge: the possibility of willing one's own and someone else's future performance by a simple act of promising is what establishes the contract as a mark of freedom, while the necessity of invoking a civil institutional power to enforce conformity to the contract—to bring about the identification of promise and performance—reflects the constraints on the exercise of that freedom created by partial knowledge and limited agency.

That the passage identifies this moment as a position out of which narrative, and Maisie as the subject of that narrative, is generated makes it evident that the narrative epistemology of the promissory conception of contractual obligation is no longer to be taken for granted. By contrast, because the older promissory obligation had measured contractual obligation in the single instant of the promise, it had understood the period of time between promise

---

19. I am excluding from this designation the opening, unnumbered section, which I have already discussed at length.

and performance, in all its narrative and historical contingency, to be juridically irrelevant. But if the passage insists on the significance as well as the unpredictability of this period, it seems equally cognizant of the difficulties attending the sort of historicism implied by the reliance or benefit standard of obligation. Whereas the promissory conception of obligation presumes contracting subjects unmarked and unconstrained by their local conditions, or at any rate sufficiently capable of predicting the conditions that will obtain at the moment of performance so as to make accommodations for them, the reliance/benefit model does not presume in its contracting subjects a given knowledge or capacity. Instead, it examines exactly what the subjects knew or were capable of knowing when they contracted, and what sorts of obstacles they faced in performing the tasks they agreed to. But in locating the obligation in historical effects, the benefit contract recognizes that the "same" act can have different meanings—can create different benefits and hence obligations—depending on the social conditions of its recipient. The reliance/benefit model is thus fully oriented in the present; its legal meaning comes into being at the moment of its execution, and it cannot create future obligation. What ought to be obvious from such a description is the difficulty of establishing, without any future orientation, the benefit contract as a form of promise at all. Since the obligation produced by the act of promising does not become binding until it has been acted on, it is difficult to see why one would bother to make a promise before the act itself.

As a practical alternative to this kind of radical pragmatism by which the absoluteness of subjects' constitution by their local conditions makes them incapable of imagining themselves or being imagined in any other contexts, and hence incapable of promising, late nineteenth-century Anglo-American courts begin to generalize contracting subjects' likely behavior and knowledge according to a system of social typology.[20] Thus if we are unable to know specifically how a given individual might have relied on a particular promise until after that promise has been fulfilled (or not), we are able to surmise within general terms how a child or a poor, uneducated factory worker or a cotton trader might be likely to rely on a given event and consequently to engage in different sorts of agreements with these various types of people. But James immediately makes apparent how tenuous this stopgap measure is as a way out of the logical circle of historicism: "It was to be the fate of this patient little girl to see much more than she at first understood but also even at first to understand much more than any little girl, however patient, had perhaps ever understood before." If it is Maisie's fate as a "little girl" to be

20. See Mary Poovey, *Making a Social Body* (Chicago: University of Chicago Press, 1995).

incapable of understanding all that she sees—and, we might surmise, to be in a relatively disadvantaged position as a contractor—the very historical specificity of her condition dislodges her from the category within which her contracting capabilities, and hence her degree of obligation, might be measured. It is "also even at first" "her fate" "to understand much more than any girl had ever understood before." Thus a commitment to the power of historical context to constitute subjects is a commitment to a force that undoes even as it describes Maisie's status as a "little girl."[21] To the extent that Maisie's engagement with the world is defined by her childishness, such a definition ensures that the category that structures this engagement will at some point—"even at first"—no longer be descriptively accurate. Although Maisie's status as a little girl might allow us to anticipate probabilistically how she knows the world, her process of knowing transforms what it means to be a little girl, turning the experience into what it means to be Maisie.

Indeed, as the language of the passage makes evident, the Maisie who is caught within the historicist circularity hinted at in the second sentence finally need not look anxiously on anything at all: if her "fate" is already available in the passage's present (and consequently need not be anticipated anxiously by the novel's narrator and readers), this is because, in the terms laid out, Maisie's "fate" is to be incapable of having a fate. She is less caught within a logical regress of reliance historicism than subsumed entirely, made to disappear within her historical context. Constituted entirely by her immediate environment, Maisie is incapable of knowing her fate—or knowing enough to act in the present in order to make a contract that will compel her to act in the future—because she cannot exist outside the immediate context that produces her.

But if this dramatization of the historicist logic of late-century notions of obligation like "reliance" and "benefit" thematizes a theoretical and juridical impasse, it does not quite perform one: Maisie, rendered logically incapable of bearing a fate, goes on to be the object of a narration that presumes she has one. Or to be somewhat more exact, the narrator is able to continue

21. In his most recent book on James, John Carlos Rowe argues that James's abiding interest in representing children is merely one manifestation of a more general interest in the epistemology of the socially disempowered, which takes the form of representations of women and sexual minorities elsewhere in James's oeuvre. For Rowe it is this engagement with disempowered subjects that identifies James as a "cultural critic" in the (not yet established) tradition of the Frankfurt school, despite his failure to produce plausible working-class characters. While I do not disagree with the resemblances Rowe identifies among these different sorts of disempowered characters, I mean to argue that James's representation of the child Maisie is structured not simply around her relative powerlessness but also as an exploration of her education, an exploration of a subject in flux. See John Carlos Rowe, *The Other Henry James* (Durham, N.C.: Duke University Press, 1998), esp. chap. 5.

telling Maisie's story despite the socioontological impasse described within the passage, suggesting that the conditions governing the narration are not entirely conflatable with the conditions of the world represented within the narration. At the same time, if we are tempted to conclude as a consequence of the previous observation that Maisie can possess a fate insofar as what is told about her is different from what she does, we might consider that the "Maisie" whose fate is narrated is one who does not quite exist. If the second half of the passage presents a taxonomic universe in which being constrained by one's historical context precludes being constrained by one's fate—an analytical field in which subjects are conceived (and understand themselves) to be defined *either* by their moment in time *or* by their movement through it—the passage offers, slyly, another model of constitution and constraint: "The child was provided for but the new arrangement was inevitably confounding to a young intelligence intensely aware that something had happened which must matter a great deal."

This sentence initially appears to undertake the same project as the sentence that concludes the passage: to describe the local, historically particular conditions—the "arrangements"—out of which Maisie's subjectivity emerges. Such "arrangements" might be glossed in terms extending from the general, and straightforwardly generalizable (she is financially dependent), to the peculiarly arcane (she is assigned to the joint custody of her parents, who immediately couple up with other people only to have their new partners pair off with one another). It is in the articulation of what we might call a politics of "necessity," a consciousness not simply of the existence of varieties of constraint but of the variety of ways these varied descriptions might be deployed, that this alternative conception of the relation between historicity and subjectivity begins to emerge. "Something had happened which must matter a great deal." Here we are presented with Maisie's sense of a world that impinges on her, in which the necessity of the force of the external is part and parcel of the limitation of her understanding. What happens "must" matter precisely because Maisie does not know how it does. In this context "must" becomes the marker of free indirect discourse, signaling not one voice or subject but two. The "must" announces both Maisie's sense of the inescapability of her only partly understood fate and the narrator's reading of Maisie's sense of her own fatedness, a reading that leans on the wide-eyed bafflement expressed but not intended by Maisie's "must" in order to insist on the discrepancy between what Maisie means and what the passage's representation of what Maisie means. Given the passage's more general engagement with the question of necessity, the free indirect discourse at once offers us the option of understanding the novel's account of the force of the external world and knowledge or of understanding that world as strictly a matter of the relations it represents—Maisie's sense of "must"—and demonstrates the inadequacy of such an account.

But lest we be tempted to assume that the narrator's knowledge trumps that of the characters in some straightforward and predictable way, with the constraint visited on fictional characters by virtue of their fictionality and their limited knowledge subordinated to a kind of transcendent narrational voluntarism, the opening of the next chapter takes up and reshuffles the contested terms. "In that lively sense of the immediate which is the very air of a child's mind the past, on each occasion, became for her as indistinct as the future: she surrendered herself to the actual with a good faith that might have been touching to either parent" (42). In this reprise, not entirely assimilable to what has come earlier, "must" becomes "might." This shift loosens the probabilism by which the degrees of knowability and constraint seem, contra the logic of the contract, to undercut one another: the more legible a given set of conditions are, the more determinately they constrain those who know them. As a consequence, the weakness of the probabilism marked by "might" is linked to an absolute freedom. Here the free play of "might" is associated both with the narrator's ironizing of the parents' flippant indifference to the specific evidence of Maisie's activities (and by implication, to Maisie herself) and with that indifference itself. While the "might" of this second passage seems to echo the earlier "must" with an intensity of compulsion several degrees removed, in point of fact the "might" invokes an understanding of agency and fictional representation different in kind as well as in degree.

Maisie's childishness is here figured as canceling access to her past experiences rather than as marking their power to define her present subjectivity. The "might" that glosses such an account of the subject entirely detaches the probability of the events' occurrence from any kind of temporality or from the sort of knowledge that would accommodate itself to that temporality. The probability that the events that "might" happen will happen has nothing to do here with how much the subjects can know about events in the future beyond their absolute control, or with how their partial knowledge might define or help extend their limited agency. Rather, the likelihood seems to rest entirely on the desire and will of Maisie's parents. Associating the narrator's freedom with irony appears to extend the logic of the "must" passage to its necessary conclusion by intimating that the object of representation can be entirely distinguished from—and subsumed within—the narrator's perspective toward and knowledge of that object. In linking the narrator's irony and Ida's careless willfulness, the passage establishes irony as the paradigm for fiction's authority and articulates the fantasy that fictions express the fiction writer's absolute independence both from the social context within which he or she writes and from the objects represented. But that the passage links the indifference implicit in the structure of irony to the very object being ironized works to disable this voluntarist conception of fictional agency even as it is being articulated.

Taken together in all their unassimilability to one another, these two passages can be seen to invoke the shifting, contested logics of late nineteenth-century commercial contract law as a context for understanding the relation between individuals' capacity to know an always changing external world and their capacity to act within that world. At the same time, this discourse of contract offers a structure for thinking about the very move to invoke such cultural contexts as modes of explanation, a way of understanding such invocation not simply in terms of the exigencies of contemporary critical practices but as an undertaking with deep intellectual roots in the collection of institutions, laws, and ideas called liberalism, particularly as that collection is challenged and modified in the second half of the nineteenth century. As we shall see, insofar as the realist novel and Anglo-American contract law can be seen to illuminate one another, they do so by virtue of their differences as well as their likenesses. I mean by this a good deal more than the formalist truism that the structural homologies such comparisons usually rest on function by revealing differences as well as similarities. If indeed, as I have been proposing, what contracts and realist novels share is their engagement of an epistemology of probability, then both presume the relation between deliberate acts like contract making and novel writing and the external "contexts" that inspire, illuminate, enable, and constrain those actions to be itself contingent, not so much a relation but an infinite and overlapping series of relations. This contingency extends to the relation between realist novels and contracts as well. The juxtaposition of novels and contracts reveals a great deal about what sorts of cultural work each is accomplishing at century's end not because the two discourses can be collapsed into one another, but because they cannot. Insofar as *Maisie*'s expression of both the thematic traces and the epistemological structure of the debates regarding the nature of contractual obligation positions the novel as a theory of history much like the contract, the historicity of both discourses is discernible in their independence from one another, a state of resemblance that falls short of identity.

The Holmesian World as Text

In 1881 Oliver Wendell Holmes reinterpreted the original judgment of *Raffles v. Wichelhaus* and placed this redaction at the center of *The Common Law,* his attempt to theorize and systematize Anglo-American case law.[22] Although Holmes begins his discussion of the case by reaffirming the decision of the *Raffles* judges, his justification of the outcome bears little resemblance to the one they offered. Whereas the *Raffles* judges had attempted to retain the subjectivism of the promissory contract while sliding around the issue of how that subjective will or intent was to be known, Holmes proposed a formal, external notion of contractual meaning that would resolve the difficulty of knowing the contractors' wills by rendering their content legally irrelevant. Holmes writes:

> The law has nothing to do with the actual state of the parties' minds. In contract, as elsewhere, it must go by externals, and judge parties by their conduct. If there had been but one "Peerless," and the defendant had said "Peerless" by mistake, meaning "Peri," he would have been bound. The true ground of the decision was not that each party meant a different thing from the other, as is implied by the explanation that has been mentioned [the rationale put forth by the *Raffles* judges], but that each said a different thing. The plaintiff offered one thing, the defendant expressed his assent to another.[23]

Holmes's rewriting of *Raffles* draws elements from the two kinds of contractual obligation between which it is positioned chronologically: between the willful "transcendence" of the promissory contract and the historicism of reliance, from a conception of the promise as will that is necessary and com-

---

22. In a letter to James Bryce, the host of the dinner party at which James heard the anecdote that was the germ of *What Maisie Knew*, Holmes described his projected *Common Law* as "a scheme to analyze what seem to me the fundamental norms and principles of our substantive law" (Holmes to James Bryce, 17 August 1879, Holmes Papers, Harvard University Special Collections or University Microfilms, Inc., quoted in G. Edward White, *Justice Oliver Wendell Holmes: Law and the Inner Self* (Oxford: Oxford University Press, 1993).

23. Holmes, *Common Law,* 309. Holmes's personal connections to the James family have recently been the subject of significant controversy. Holmes, who was slightly older than Henry James, was initially the friend and intellectual confrere of William. Until 1870 Holmes frequently attended William James's lectures on pragmatism at Harvard and considered himself something of a disciple. According to Holmes's biographer G. Edward White, the commission Holmes received in 1880 to give the Lowell Lectures, which provided the core of material for *The Common Law* published the following year, marked his final and decisive intellectual split from William James.

Leon Edel's massive biography of Henry James, which until recently was considered definitive, cast Henry James and Holmes as friends and romantic rivals, writing of James's discouragement at the apparent ease and success with which Holmes courted James's beloved Minnie Temple. Sheldon M. Novack's 1996 biography forcefully rejects the biographical tradition that reads James as celibate and sublimating. Novack offers convincing, though not wholly unambiguous, evidence that Holmes himself was James's first lover (Novack, *Henry James: The Young Master* [New York: Random House, 1996], 110 and passim). See Edel, *Henry James: A Life* (New York: Harper and Row, 1985), and White, *Justice Oliver Wendell Holmes.* White's biography provides an especially insightful reading of the tensions structuring *The Common Law* in the chapter by that title.

plete unto itself to its conception as a contingent, potentially mistaken speech act. In his interpretation of liability, Holmes is both as absolute and as "promise centered" as the *Raffles* judges; he simply reformulates the notion of "promise" to signify wholly external speech acts instead of a finally unverifiable subjective intent. His emphasis remains on resolving the crisis of causality at the moment of promising, not on accommodating the crisis haunting the relation between promise and performance. Holmes's "solution" implicitly redefines the problem of historical contingency that troubled the original *Raffles* decision as *essentially* a linguistic problem, one that, by virtue of being linguistic, need not bear on the contracting subject's power as agent. In the original *Raffles* verdict, the difficulty of unambiguously linking a given external behavior with a particular internal mental state could be read paradigmatically, as evidence of a more general cultural crisis of confidence in the capacity of internal acts of will to bring about specific external effects. In Holmes's redaction of *Raffles,* by contrast, the question of contingency is separated entirely from the issue of whether individuals can be presumed to say—or do—what they mean; since what matters is what people say rather than what they mean (to say), the contingency associated with what Holmes's contractors say becomes the enabling condition of their agency rather than its limit.

The central reformist claim of Holmes's formalism is that the meaning of promises is legible expressly by *not* reading *through* external behavior in order to discern something like the contractor's will or intention. Yet this claim depends on a highly idiosyncratic understanding of what it means "to say a different thing." For the terms of the *Raffles* contract came under dispute because both parties seemed to be "saying" the same thing: they both uttered (or wrote) *"Peerless."*[24] Holmes apparently accords quite a different meaning to "saying": he could understand the act of reference to include its object, for example; but such a definition, its idiosyncrasy aside, would not so much solve the problem of reference as relocate it.

By insisting that there is nothing behind the words individual subjects speak that matters to allowing those individual to make contracts—no inaccessible "deep" self whose will or intention is expressed in the act of promising—Holmes effectively turns his contracting subjects into something like novelistic characters: they are, in the juridical sense at least, made up entirely of words. The judges who rule on whether these "characters" are liable for

---

24. That Holmes's revision of *Raffles* apparently depends on a misrepresentation of the facts of the case has been noted by many historians of contract law. See, for example, Melvin Aron Eisenberg, "The Responsive Model of Contract Law," *Stanford Law Review* 36 (May 1984): 1123.

the contracts they have agreed to likewise become something like novel readers at the moment they agree to accept a surface of words as sufficient to make a self work as though it were real. But Holmes's new performative notion of obligation depends on its resemblance to the realist novel in another, less straightforward way as well. With its continued emphasis on the significance of the moment of promising, Holmes's formulation presumes, however implicitly, that the same authority that underwrites the language constituting the individual subject and that subject's promise will also determine what happens to that subject. The words of the promise are understood to be adequate to guarantee the performance of the contract because they are generated from a single authorial source. No unanticipated or contingent events that would in any way interfere with the promise's authority can intervene because what "causes" the promise is the same authority that "causes" the events.

In implicitly introducing a novelistic structure of authority as a means of getting around the difficulty of knowing just what parties to a contract have promised, Holmes's new theory of contractual obligation turns not simply on the homology of the realist novel and the contract—their relation of likeness and difference—but on the consistency and predictability of that homology, its constancy over time. But as I proposed, insofar as we understand novels and contracts to be linked by their probabilistic logic, a logic that identifies both as theories of history, it is the changefulness of the relation between the discourse of contract and the novel, the unpredictability of the relation between aesthetic object and historical context, that constitutes the revelation of their juxtaposition. If we begin by reading *What Maisie Knew* as one of Holmes's judges might, by assuming that Maisie's fictionality, her condition of being made up out of words, guarantees that what Maisie can and will do is what the author who creates her wants her to do, by the time we finish the novel *Maisie* has fundamentally transformed the terms by which it invites itself to be read. In so doing, the novel makes the case for an entirely different understanding of the liberal contracting subject.

In *What Maisie Knew,* Maisie's parents repeatedly demand that she assume responsibility for obligating herself to them—that she choose, as though she has the economic, social, or emotional wherewithal to do so, exactly the option they would be forced to compel her to take if she did not choose it "freely." As I have already noted, Maisie's double bind is part and parcel of her location at a moment of historical transition; her parents are able to free themselves from their responsibility for her by invoking the presumptions of the ideal, autonomous promissory subject who can choose without reference to the particularity of his or her social position, but the novel poignantly registers the desperation with which Maisie attempts (and largely fails) to play the part of such a knowing subject. Those moments when Maisie is faced with the paradoxical imperative to "choose one" are moments when the terms of the novel's fictional authority are brought into question as well. The ethical problem surrounding Maisie's coercion (How can Maisie be understood to choose freely, to choose as a liberal subject, when she must do so from within a condition of profound dependency?) is generalized formally as a problem of novelistic representation: How can Maisie, or any other character, for that matter, be understood to choose freely when all their "choices" occur within the frame of the novel's fictionality, when all their choices, that is, are essentially the author's? For James the solution lies in addressing the second representational issue that is in crisis in *Raffles*—in invoking the variable strength or weakness with which details of a description of the world might mean:

The unconsciousness gave Mrs Beale time to leap, under her breath, to a recognition which Maisie caught.

"It must be Mrs Cuddon!"

Maisie looked at Mrs Cuddon hard—her lips even echoed the name. What followed was extraordinarily rapid—a minute of livelier battle than had ever yet, in so short a span at least, been waged around our heroine. The muffled shock—lest people should notice—was violent, and it was only for her later thought that the steps fell into their order, the steps through which, in a bewilderment not so much of sound as of silence, she had come to find herself, too soon for comprehension and too strangely for fear, at the door of the Exhibition with her father. He thrust her into a hansom and got in after her, and then it was—as she drove along with him—that she recovered a little what had happened. Face to face with them in the Gardens he had seen them, and there had been a moment of shocked concussion during which, in a glare of black eyes and a toss of red plumage, Mrs Cuddon had recognized, ejaculated and vanished. There had been another moment at which she became aware of Sir Claude, also poised there in surprise, but out of her father's view, as if he had been warned off at the very moment of reaching them. . . . Reconstructing these things later, Maisie theorized that she at this point would have put a question to him had not the silence into which he charmed her or scared her— she could scarcely tell which—come from his suddenly making her feel his arm about her, feel, as he drew her close, that he was agitated in a way he had never yet shown her. It struck her he trembled, trembled too much to speak, and this had the effect of making her, with an emotion which, though it had begun to throb in an instant, was by no means all dread, conform to his portentous hush. The act of possession that his pressure in a manner advertised came back to her after the longest of the long intermissions that had never let anything come back. (144–45)

Maisie's consciousness remains, if not strikingly absent from the entire passage, then radically postponed, displaced ("It was only for her later thought that the steps fell into their order"), and the narrative force that thrusts Maisie from her narrative place is unmistakably associated with the fragmented conspiracy of forces that shove her into the hansom as she desperately tries, along with us, to discover exactly what is to be narrated. "He thrust her into a hansom and got in after her, and then it was—as she drove along with him—that she recovered a little what had happened." As the carriage races off, leaving Maisie to her thoughts, the narrative displacement that is occurring is literalized, but this very act of narrative literalizing postpones and displaces Maisie's articulation yet further. The "later" from which Maisie's retrospective reconstruction might occur is pushed ever further into the future until it occupies a time altogether outside narrative time. As readers, we are denied access to the content of Maisie's tenuously recovered and reconstructing consciousness; instead, we are given notice again and again that, sometime hence, Maisie was to come to know, each announcement recapitulating and extending her temporal and authoritative removal from the passage. "Reconstructing these things *later*, Maisie theorized that she at *this* point would have put a question to him had not the silence into which he charmed her or scared her—she could not tell which—come from his suddenly making her feel his arm about her, feel, as he drew her close, that he was agitated in a way he had never yet shown her" (emphasis added). The absolute narrative incompatibility of Maisie and the narrator is made most explicit in this passage, where the narrator's representation of Maisie's retrospective use of the present tense "this" produces a narrative no place of time and point of view. Even more significant is that this deferral has the ultimate effect of rupturing any necessary connection between text and reader by transferring all interpretive responsibility outside the text of the novel.

If Maisie's silence seems in equal parts the result of her father's physical coercion and the narrator's representational violence, neither violence is made available to the reader without complication. Instead, the question of how the content of Beale's physical force is to be read at least partially relocates responsibility for this narrative violence. As the delicate balance of mutually agreed on silencing bursts into a narrative flurry of violence and repression, Maisie is no longer simply excluded as a passively observant subject. Here we as readers are asked to recognize in the decidedly eroticized images of Maisie's carriage ride with her father a level of knowledge from which she is excluded yet in which she is nonetheless implicated. To the extent that it participates in Maisie's exclusion from the knowledge that would define her behavior de-

spite her lack of awareness, the act of reading is itself complicit in the assault
on her, an assault produced not by the delineation of a boundary separating
the knowledge she possesses from that of the narrator but by the erasure of
any such boundary, the forcible supplanting of one interpretive matrix by another.

Yet the fact that there is no place where the edges of the two interpretive
matrices may be discerned, where the assumptions that would authorize a
sexual reading of the encounter come up against those that would foreclose
such a reading, means that readers are not allowed the reassuring option of
moving back and forth between consciousnesses but must choose one. But
what would it mean in this instance to "choose one"? While the differences
between the narrative positions described are clear—Maisie's naïveté is distinguished from a sexual knowledge that is able to recognize the eroticized
imagery of pulp romance in the description of a father's carriage ride with his
daughter—the capacity to make the distinction between alternatives effectively renders the choice already made. For Maisie, who quite literally does
not know what she is missing, there is no choice. On the other hand, it is
impossible to speak of *choosing* a naive reading of the scene while retaining
any conventional understanding of the term; although one may certainly
choose to behave the way someone who does not recognize the description's
erotic overtones might be expected to act, such behavior would be anything
but naive. Thus the effect of this scene—the force of its violence—is to compel readers to assume the position Maisie has been forced to assume throughout the novel, the position of "choosing one," of being attributed the social
meaning—and the moral responsibility—of free agency without being accorded real choice.

With the introduction of Maisie's body in all its liminal prepubescence,
then, the meaningfulness of will gives way to the willfulness—the violence—
of meaning. Insofar as we as readers can distinguish Maisie's understanding
of the meaning of her body from our own, we conceive of our interpretation
of that meaning as interpretation, that is to say, as a choice among options;
yet it is just this capacity to understand the concept of choice that forecloses
our choosing. The intrusion of Maisie's ambiguous body thus radically splits
the principle of choice from real, historically meaningful choices. Here,
knowing what Maisie does not—making her encounter with her father mean
something she does not intend or recognize it to mean—aligns our knowing
with Beale's violence, yet our understanding that we only *seem* to be choosing
that knowledge mitigates our responsibility for its violence. The violence associated with our positions as readers plays a certain role, produces a discernible effect in our experience of the represented world of the novel whether or

not we intend it to. Thus to beg off responsibility for the effect of our choice, to contend that we have produced the appearance and effect of choice without intending to do so, is to claim innocence by elevating the importance of intent. If the condition of being a reader is to know without being able to act on one's knowledge, then not only does a kind of reliance meaning become impossible, but the distinction between knowing and willing within the promissory realm disappears as well. We cannot be responsible for our knowing, nor can our knowing make us responsible, but such a rupture frees our knowing from moral sanction only by rendering it trivial. Such is the condition of the readers of *What Maisie Knew.* Having argued against the possibility of a meaningless, morally neutral desire in the squaring narrative, the novel offers its readers a freedom denied its characters, the freedom of not mattering that accompanies, like a shadow, the state of not being matter.

In the scene that follows, Maisie's father, Beale Farange, having all but exacted a promise from her to renounce yet again her poignantly unenforceable filial claims on him, admits to Maisie that if she gives him up to allow him to travel to America, she will never see him again.

"Then I can't give you up."

She held him some seconds looking at her, showing her a strained grimace, a perfect parade of all his teeth, in which it seemed to her she could read the disgust he didn't quite like to express at this departure from the pliability she had practically promised. But before she could attenuate in any way the crudity of her collapse he gave an impatient jerk which took him to the window. She heard a vehicle stop; Beale looked out; then he freshly faced her. He still said nothing, but she knew the Countess had come back. There was a silence again between them, but with a different shade of embarrassment from that of their united arrival and it was still without speaking that, abruptly repeating one of the embraces of which he had already been so prodigal, he whisked her back to the lemon sofa just before the door of the room was thrown open. It was thus in renewed and intimate union with him that she was presented to a person whom she instantly recognized as the brown lady.

The brown lady looked almost astonished, though not quite as alarmed, as when, at the Exhibition, she had gasped in the face of Mrs Beale. Maisie in truth almost gasped in her own; this was with the fuller perception that she was brown indeed. She literally struck the child more as an animal than as a "real" lady; she might have been a clever frizzled poodle in a frill or a dreadful human monkey in a spangled petticoat. She had a nose that was far too big and eyes that were far too small and a moustache that was, well, not so happy a feature as Sir Claude's. (156)

The encounter that follows virtually reprises Maisie's discussion with her father, with the crucial differences that in this case Maisie's interlocutor is the

Countess and, strikingly, that she appears to entertain seriously the idea that Maisie might join her and Beale. By the end, Maisie has determined to flee both the current entanglement and the possibility of any future entanglements:

> She was able to guess later on that her father must have put it to his friend that *it was no use talking*, that she was an obstinate little pig and that, besides, *she was really old enough to choose for herself*. It glimmered back to her indeed that she must have failed quite dreadfully to seem ideally other than rude, inasmuch as *before she knew it she had visibly given the impression* that if they didn't allow her to go home she should cry. Oh if there had even been a thing to cry about it was being so consciously and gawkily below the handsomest offers anyone could ever have received. The great pain of the thing was that she could see the Countess liked her enough to wish to be liked in return, and it was from the idea of a return she sought utterly to flee. (158, emphasis added)

The relation between two encounters lays out its difficulties within the terms of conflict of narrative authority we have been examining. Maisie, having been offered yet another opportunity to "choose one," to go about the by now almost ritualized behavior of choosing without the possibility to select freely among the proffered options, is poised for the first time to call her father's bluff and assert the right to free choice she has supposedly had available all along. Just as she is about to make her choice, however, the plot veers suddenly with the arrival of the Countess, and Maisie abruptly finds herself "before she kn[ows] it, visibly" conveying that she wants to break off any residual claims to Beale's guardianship. Maisie thus once again finds herself choosing what her parents want her to choose.

But while Maisie makes the choice that turns out to be the compliant one, the scene is nonetheless presented as something of a departure from the pattern already established in the novel, most obviously in that Maisie does not conceive of this decision as motivated by a desire to comply. She perceives— and the otherwise relentlessly suspicious narrator says nothing to hint that her perceptions here ought not to be trusted—that "the Countess like[s] her enough to wish to be liked in return." This sense of mutuality, as both the ground and the end of exchange, suggests that for the first time in the novel, Maisie both is perceived as and perceives herself to be an authentically autonomous partner to a potential "contract." This particular "compliance," moreover, is brought about by a shift in the plot—an isolatable "event"—rather than by her father's tacit pressure. The novel's structure of fictional authority allows the movement of plot to appear at once contingent and the necessarily meaningful product of authorial intention. Hence the freedom Maisie demonstrates by her contingent—that is, plot-driven—compliance with Beale's desires begins to seem not very free at all. The author who finally places Maisie in the position of choosing freely only to have her choose exactly as her father would wish bears a suspicious resemblance to the endless procession of parents and quasi-parents who have done the same.

If this coincidence of novelistic and parental tacitness ought to raise our suspicions about just how freely Maisie chooses, so too does it raise the more general question of what it would mean for Maisie, or any character for that matter, to do something other than what "the novel" or "the author" would want. If Maisie's constraint is merely a thematizing of the formal predicament of realism, ought we then to understand the genre simply as a means, or an expression, of liberal freedom *as* mystification?

What story does *Maisie* tell? Maisie plans to choose to stay with Beale; the Countess arrives; Maisie decides—or, better, discovers that she desires—to leave Beale and the Countess and return home. In one sense Maisie's volition is demonstrated by the reversal; we understand her to be choosing freely because we are offered evidence that she might have chosen otherwise. At the same time, the contingency of her choice runs the risk of making it appear undermotivated. Like Mrs. Wix, Maisie's sole remaining guardian at novel's end, we are left with "room for wonder" at just what it is about the intervening encounter—what it is she "knows"—that makes Maisie change her position so radically. This particular problem of narrative motivation is not specific to fiction; historical narratives likewise often move uneasily between causal determinism and looser forms of historical relatedness. What *is* particular to the novel is the way even the quality of undermotivation is framed by the meaningfulness, albeit the tacit meaningfulness, of its having been authored. So if in one sense Maisie's reversal seems undermotivated and consequently suspicious, in another sense it is suspicious because it could not possibly be undermotivated.

The novel thus articulates a constraint that, as long as it remained tacit, masked itself as the freedom that would claim to be the governing trope of both its protagonist's relationships and its own formal operations. *What Maisie Knew* establishes as its ethical and formal imperative the exploration of how one might articulate within the fictional text a meaning independent of the text's fictionality. For though we may be hard pressed to identify a particular happening that motivates Maisie's sudden change of heart, our difficulty stems in part from the way the shift is rendered self-evident, authorized in itself. It is as though the mere sight of the Countess is sufficient to make up Maisie's mind. That the Countess in some fundamental way matters is initially registered by Maisie's observing Beale's observing her arrival. ("But before she could attenuate in any way the crudity of her collapse he gave an impatient jerk which took him to the window. She heard a vehicle stop; Beale looked out; then he freshly faced her. He still said nothing, but she knew the Countess had come back.") Here, watching moves from a behavior that is part of a range of other activities to a fully absorptive occupation (Maisie watching Beale watching) and then to a quality that resides in the object observed (Beale presenting himself to Maisie's gaze as an object that has seen and in so doing making any further verbal exchange unnecessary). Transparency is thus implicitly defined as a kind of self-presentation by the objects being observed, with the fact of self-presentation—a kind of intending—isolating the object from any narrative or interpretive context.

In the description that follows, objects do not remain stably objects, nor do they have only one meaning. On a first reading, what is profoundly discomfiting about the description of the woman is the problem of literalism. ("She was brown indeed. She *literally* struck the child more as an animal than as a 'real' lady; she might have been a clever frizzled poodle in a frill or a dreadful human monkey in a spangled petticoat"; emphasis added). The discomfort issues from a literalism implicitly defined by the preceding section as a kind of interpretive and contextless univocality. The insistence in this passage on the literalness of Maisie's vision serves mainly to throw that literalism into question, since it is on the issue of the literalness of the imagery that the point of view seems to split, yet literalism has just been defined as a descriptive condition that brooks no question of perspective or point of view. The brown woman is brown "indeed"—that is to say, both literally brown and very brown—and this conjunction suggests that literalism is never quite merely so: to insist on the literal quality of something is to insist on its opposite, to maintain that in truly or literally or transparently possessing a quality—say, the quality of brownness—an object comes to possess or be more than that quality itself, to possess the value of truth or literalism or transparency as well. Moreover, we might understand the horror and the offense of the images that follow—the brown lady as "poodle" and, even more complexly, the brown lady as "*human* monkey" (emphasis added)—to be the product of this instability of literalism. The very quality of "more than" that attends the literal is what enables the yoking of such obviously unlike "things" as people and objects, humans and monkeys and poodles at the same time as it makes the insistence on similarity matter in the face of the undeniable differences. This insistence that things are what they are and are meaningful by virtue of being so has the paradoxical effect here of opening the way to an endless variety of comparisons that—and here is the horror—are always poised to literalize their relationship by transforming the like things into one another.

This passage is difficult to read not simply because things refuse to stay what they are but also because this instability of meaning produces an equally unstable narrative point of view. It is this complex conjunction of unstable objects and unstable narrative perspectives that ultimately offers Maisie the chance of doing something other than what the novel "wants" her to do and thus allows the novel itself to represent the operations of its own fictional authority within a broader historical context of the legal and epistemological meanings of authority. At the same time, by insisting on the centrality of the category of fiction for the production of these "extratextual" modes of authority, *What Maisie Knew* radically complicates the relations between text and (historical) context normally presumed and produced by the realist novel.

In one sense the passage would seem to ask to be read as solving the problem of undermotivation by invoking the category of race:[25] Maisie changes her mind about staying with her father when she discovers that the "American Countess" is black. Or more accurately, when she discovers the Countess to be "brown indeed."[26] For this notion of being "brown indeed"—of a literalism that becomes more than itself by insisting on being merely what it is—provides a "motivation" for Maisie's compliant choice, which paradoxically becomes sufficient at the moment it ceases to be identifiable as narrative cause and becomes simply a description of what is. In this sense James's invocation of the category of race here is significant not simply because what it connotes is more meaningful than the qualities it names or describes, but because it challenges the fundamental taxonomy of knowing. Whereas the portrait scene in *Daniel Deronda* revealed how the worldliness of the novel followed from its capacity to suspend the location of its meaning somewhere between

25. The most powerful and sustained account of the role of race in James's work and, just as important, the function of realism for the reimagining of race relations in the wake of Reconstruction is Kenneth Warren's *Black and White Strangers* (Chicago: University of Chicago Press, 1993). I agree with Warren that the categories generated by contemporary race relations are central to James's fiction and also that politics are central to his understanding of consciousness; my account emphasizes race as an organizing structure of novelistic *form* to a greater extent than Warren's does. The critical tendency to associate James's race consciousness with his nonfiction is especially apparent in the debate among Ross Posnock, Sara Blair, and Warren in a special issue of the *Henry James Review*, vol. 16 (1995), on James and race, where the project of determining James's "position" on race is indistinguishable from the project of determining the "position" within his oeuvre of his works of nonfiction like *The American Scene*. See also Sara Blair, *Henry James and the Writing of Race and Nation* (Cambridge: Cambridge University Press, 1996).

26. For a detailed account of the development of Victorian categories of race, see George Stocking, *Victorian Anthropology* (New York: Free Press, 1987).

the immediately perceptible visual world and the time it takes to read the verbal description of that self-evident world, here James uses the category of race to challenge that world's self-evidence, and in so doing he brings the logic of the realist novel's authority under his scrutiny. We might note the way race undoes the self-evidence of self-evidence, turning an immediacy of apprehension and comprehension into a mark of the process by which subjects produce the material world rather than a refusal to note that production.

Yet we are never allowed to be certain that Maisie herself understands the racial overtones of the descriptions filtered through her consciousness; for her, "brown indeed" could quite well mean "very" or "truly" brown. We have difficulty knowing for certain whether Maisie intends, or even knows, what we might call (adopting from our discussion of *Raffles*), a "strong" meaning of brownness or of the metaphors she adopts. On the one hand, Maisie certainly behaves like a racist; one glance at the brown lady is adequate not only to reverse her commitment to defy her father but to render insignificant all the Countess's notably sincere efforts at friendship. On the other hand, the narrative itself has given no prior indication of her racial attitudes or her acquaintance with categories of race. That Maisie "recognizes" the Countess from a past encounter instead of responding solely to the immediacy of her current physical presence further emphasizes the suspension of this moment between the two novelistic modes. Simply to attribute Maisie's reaction to racism, be it hers or James's, is to overlook the narrative complexity of the moment—as well as its cultural force.

Can we bring these two readings of "brownness" into relation with one another, or are we to understand the novel as leaving the terms of the connection undecidable? The two accounts seem more unassimilable than they may in fact turn out to be because they derive their authority (or its absence) from different sources: our inability to know whether race matters for Maisie results from an absence within the fictional narrative, while our suspicion that it might matter depends on our willingness to read extratextual habits of thought and behavior—whether ours or those of James and his contemporaries—into Maisie's otherwise unaccountable reversal. At first glance this contest of authority appears to be yet another example of the pattern of "tacit" authority made thematically and formally prominent throughout the novel, as the authority associated with narrative causality is apparently rendered subordinate to the kind of descriptive meaning that inheres in the designation of the object. However, the representation of the "brown lady" works not by displacing the "weak" meaning established by the plotted events with the "strong" meaning of the fictional frame but by invoking both meanings at once. Whereas Beale operates by means of tacitness, Maisie's encounter with the brown lady works, in contrast, according to the structure of *euphemism,* within which, notably, the brown lady does not cease to be brown—merely and in passing—at the moment she becomes "brown indeed," at the moment, that is, her brownness is racialized.

Indeed, it is this "both/and" quality associated with euphemism that for James makes race the category by which he is able to unmake and complicate the conventions of fictional authority. James invokes race as a practice of representing the behavior of knowing. This conception of race produces a newly mobile concept of fictionality that might help reimagine the relations of identity, knowledge, and legal obligation whose historical instability became evident in our reading of *Raffles*. I have been arguing that, insofar as Maisie's sudden change of heart can be seen as a response to the "meaningfulness" of race, her response depends on meanings that are imported from outside the text as opposed to being specifically associated with the Maisie we have come to know through the narrative. The particular content of this meaningfulness that could bring about such a powerful and immediate reversal is never specified by the text of the novel, and this is crucial. Its absence obviously identifies the meaning as extratextual, but this extratextuality matters because, oddly enough, it offers a way for Maisie to do something other than what the novel wants her to do. Given the representational conundrum set up by this scene (in seeming to offer Maisie a choice, then introducing the sudden plot twist that leads her to choose the option that normally marks her constraint, James the fiction maker ends up looking a lot like Beale the manipulator), this use of race highlights the limits of the authority of fictionality.

But if the category of race becomes the means by which Maisie might escape James, what would she escape to? Since James, like Holmes before him, is concerned with knowledge as an element of human freedom, it seems odd that the such freedom would be demonstrated as a reaction to an undefined category so immediate and powerful that it forecloses choice or agency altogether. Furthermore, the power of the category of race does not appear easily extricable from the formal use to which James puts it; its capacity to mean outside the specificity of any particular narrative is what gives the category its quality of immediacy and inevitability. For James, euphemism is the way out inasmuch as it is the way back in. Because euphemism functions by floating the strong and weak meanings of a given reference rather than by forcing a choice between the two—because, in other words, we can retain the possibility that, in keeping with her childish diction elsewhere, Maisie is merely noting that the Countess's skin is brown, or that the Countess looks like a poodle without necessarily knowing or intending the various invidious social meanings that otherwise attend these designations—it grants Maisie (and crucially, her readers as well) a measure of freedom by allowing her to avoid, at long last, the imperative of "choosing one." In its excessiveness to the fictional narrative presented, brownness as race offers both character and readers a way of experiencing their respective relations to the text as not wholly generated from within the authority of the fictional frame. In its status as just one element of a specific world brought into being by the language of the fictional narrative, brownness as description reminds us that the apparently transcendent "racial" meaning might be otherwise.[27]

The fictional text thus becomes a means of historicizing the very social categories that might be expected to constitute a historically explanatory context, even as the pressure of these categories gives notice of the limits within which fictional authority must operate. In *Daniel Deronda*, Daniel mistakes a silence that has no meaning at all—that is strictly speaking not quite a silence—for a silence meant to signal his putative father's withholding of the patronym. In its focus on nothing made something—an insignificant silence misread as a withholding—*Daniel Deronda* implicitly concerns itself with the constructedness of fictionality as a category, with the social effects of the novel's drive toward transparency. How is it possible, that novel seems to ask, that we can understand the mere fact of being in a certain place at a certain time to be meaningful? For the James of the last part of *Maisie*, in contrast, the point of departure is not a silence that could be nothing but instead a quality—the quality of brownness—that, whether it is understood to be

27. Walter Benn Michaels, whose "Jim Crow Henry James?" was published as part of the special issue of the *Henry James Review* on James and race (16 [1995]: 286–91), structures his discussion of this scene as a direct rebuke to Toni Morrison, who, in her *Playing in the Dark: Whiteness and the Literary Imagination* (Cambridge: Harvard University Press, 1992) decried the fact that it is "possible . . . to read Henry James scholarship exhaustively and never arrive at a nodding mention, much less a satisfactory treatment, of the black woman who lubricates the turn of the plot and becomes the agency of moral choice and meaning in *What Maisie Knew*" (13). Michaels takes Morrison to task for her readiness to make "the brown lady" over into a "black woman," since such a conversion allows her to overlook the way James's representation resists the logic of Jim Crow inasmuch as it *equates* the American Countess's "brownness" with her vulgarity, her *arrivistement*. According to Michaels, Jim Crow established a category of race only so far as it succeeded in distinguishing phenetic marks of physical difference from class status, in "identify[ing] such women as black *instead of* vulgar" (288). While I agree with Michaels that "the brown lady" of *Maisie* is not wholly reducible to a stably racialized blackness, what I hope my reading of the euphemistic quality of her brownness has made clear is that her brownness is not wholly distinguishable from race either. As I will elaborate in a moment, James is able to imagine his fiction making to be socially productive only by tracing the limits of such authority, and he constitutes these limits as the meaningful substantiality of the Countess's appearance. Only because it is a category whose meaningfulness is part and parcel of its substantiality does race offer James a limiting ground against which he is able to imagine that the meanings of his fictional texts might extend beyond them to transform the culture in which he writes.

"merely," descriptively itself or deeply invested with racial meaning, is to him visibly, irreducibly something.

Consequently, the question for *Maisie* is not how meaning can be built from nothing but how it matters for the conception of history and of fictionality and for the relations between the two that the same things have many meanings, both in and through time. Thus the novel's breaking of the frame of fictional authority does not occur as the revelation of the device of its making: we are not suddenly confronted, for example, by the fact that Maisie is mere language. If the linguistic quality of the novel matters, it matters not according to a structure of tacitness but as one of euphemism; it matters, in other words, not because meaning is "made up" but because it is historical, so that any given meaning must be wrought in some relation to a variety of other meanings.[28]

Strikingly, then, the power of *What Maisie Knew*'s insight into the quality of realist historicity lies less in the way it registers the pressure of social context as either a reinforcement or a complication of the terms of a given textual moment than in its refusal to privilege absolutely the authority of either the literary text or the historical context. The novel at once establishes Maisie's encounter with Beale and the Countess as the moment of her ascendancy to the condition of liberal agency and challenges such an account, but what is at least as important as the general fact of this challenge is that it is mounted

28. The question whether James intended this doubleness is of course inextricable from—though not identical to—the question of what Maisie means by "brown indeed." Considered at the level of authorial intentionality, the paradox is that the more deliberately James created the ambiguity I have identified—the more he meant for Maisie's behavior to be undecidable in a way that would allow both her and her readers to avoid "choosing one"—the more he fails in his efforts. The more Maisie's freedom not to choose is understood to be a deliberate effect of James's authorial design, the less it becomes a demonstration of her freedom and the more it is yet another instance of Maisie's being attributed agency only so as to lend a kind of moral authority to circumstances to which she has no option but to accede. But described this way, the paradox makes it clear that while Maisie's agency is indeed constrained by James, James's agency is also constrained by Maisie. Fictional authority is in this way redefined as the manipulation of the relations of various constraints to one another.

Of course this paradox remains paramount only so long as we choose to address the question of what James intended by privileging the logic of the literary text. There are a variety of other "extratextual"— "contextual"—ways the question could be answered: by examining James's other novels, his notebooks addressing the composition of *Maisie,* his recorded statements to other people; by tracing seemingly racialized uses of animal imagery in the culture at large. Although I am arguing that *Maisie*'s euphemisms present an account of the relation between literary text and historical context in which neither can be established as *necessarily* determining of meaning, such an argument does not imply that either the literary text or the historical context cannot be *contingently* determining. The text or the context *can* be definitive, depending on the circumstances in which the question is being asked, who is doing the asking, why it is being asked, and the kind of authority that is attributed, for whatever reasons, to one sort of evidence or another.

equally compellingly, if differently, from "textual" and "contextual" sources. We come to look suspiciously on the novel's assertion of autonomy both because the "contextual" category of race acts so powerfully and immediately as to limit her actual freedom to choose and because the text itself highlights its own formal resemblance to the patterns of manipulation abundantly practiced by Maisie's parents. If the novel reflects on the relation of history to its own narrative, such a historicizing involves the recognition that sometimes historical meaning is *not* paramount. By the end of *Maisie*, neither the historical nor the fictional is given precedence in its challenge to fictional authority. The variability of the connection between text and historical context is what constitutes the historicity of the novel's fictional authority. To historicize fictionality is, for James, to recognize that the relation between history and fiction is not simply one thing.

And to recognize the volatility and contingency of the relation between the aesthetic object and the historical "context" is effectively to intervene in prevailing accounts of both the contract and the novel. Holmes's performative redaction of the *Raffles* case presented a notion of contractual obligation that turned on the stability of the homology between contracts and novels: that a subject uses a certain language can guarantee his or her capacity to act a certain way in the future only so long as contracts can reliably be understood to operate in a world organized around the representational logic of realist novels. By disrupting the constancy of this homology, this scene in *What Maisie Knew* both registers the tenuousness of the cultural support for such an understanding of obligation and, in some subtle, diffuse, and probably incalculable way, exacerbates this tenuousness.

When all is said and done, it is impossible to figure out what "happens," either thematically or formally, in the encounter between Maisie and the Countess. We don't know specifically what makes Maisie change her mind—what Maisie knows about race in general or about the American Countess in all her particularity—nor are we given any evidence that might allow us to surmise what would have happened had she chosen differently. What is striking about the particular terms of the passage's unknowability, however, is the way the evidence for free agency offered by "history" and "fictionality" cannot be easily correlated as long as the relations of text and context remain intact, that is, as long as they are taken as givens. I maintained earlier that it is possible to read *What Maisie Knew* as a text both emerging from and intervening in the history of Anglo-American contract law, at a moment in the late nineteenth century when the deliberately idealist promissory understanding of contractual obligation that had held sway since the eighteenth century began to give way to the more historically attentive notion of obligation known as reliance/benefit. Within this context, Maisie is rendered powerless by the transitional historical moment she occupies, since her parents are able to invoke a promissory understanding of subjectivity—one that presumes her to be capable of knowing and choosing freely—at the same time that her childishness (the kind of historically specific subjectivity that only the emergent reliance/benefit could recognize) makes her unable truly to consider the full range of offered options. As soon as we more explicitly "textualize" the context, however—by moving from the large historical development of contractual obligation to the specific case of *Raffles,* as well as Holmes's rewriting of that case—the relation of the text of *Maisie* to its putative context becomes more complex.

If we understand Maisie's language in the encounter with the American Countess as merely descriptive, we most likely understand both the diction and the imagery as the result of her childishness and everything associated with it. To read her language as mere description is thus to recognize Maisie as the kind of historicized subject accounted for within a reliance notion of obligation, one whose capacity to intend—here, as in *Raffles,* an intention registered in the naming of objects as description—is constrained by the limits of knowledge attendant on her social position. Yet such a reading, in contrast to the alternative "racial" meaning, has to take for granted the authority of the fictional frame to stave off any incursions of the historical, that is, to limit once and for all the context that may legitimately be deemed pertinent to interpreting the text. Once it engages the issues *Raffles* associated with a distinction between strong and weak meanings, however, *What Maisie Knew* undoes any easy correlation of the fictional with the textual, of the historical with the contextual. But such an undoing ought to be cautionary as well, to warn against the assumption that the fictionality that troubles the correlation of the historical and the contextual is located only within the literary text.

To summarize: Holmes rewrites *Raffles* to emphasize the moment of promising while at the same time reconceiving the promise as an externally perceptible speech act instead of an internal mental state, a quality of intention or will. Such a reconceptualizing is designed to preserve the authority of the promise to obligate while solving the evidentiary problems associated with promissory obligation. How can we know what the parties to the contract "meant and intended" when their external behavior, the designation of the ship *Peerless,* indicates a variety of incompatible mental states? As Holmes's own account of the case indicates, however, the external behavior of speech does not refer to the world any *less* ambiguously than it stands as evidence of contractors' otherwise inaccessible promissory intentions. Furthermore, the historical "context" in which a given speech act takes place is insufficient to stabilize that speech act's meaning. First, these contexts are no less ambiguous than the descriptions included in the "text"; second, the relation between text and context may not always be the same (Maisie could be invoking a racialized "extratextual" meaning in her description of the Countess or she could be merely describing her). What James's powerfully destabilizing use of euphemism indicates by way of negative counterexample is that the establishment of an unambiguous and transparent social text—a notion of the norm[29]—depends on just those rationalizing and synchronizing fictions, the novel and the contract, that the normative context is meant to authorize.

To understand how this circular relation between institutional authority and cultural norms functioned outside a pointedly literary realm, I turn briefly to Holmes's construction of contract in relation to his discussions regarding the institution and application of law in general found in *The Common Law*. Holmes's introduction of a concept of the norm seems to be a response to the problems that plagued *Raffles* as an example: while Holmes had to insist, in pointed refusal of the facts of the case, that what mattered was what the contractors *said,* not what they *meant,* the notion of the norm would seem to limit and confirm what is "said" without resorting to a problematically inaccessible "intention." By examining the literary status of contract in connection with Holmes's understanding of law as a cultural and, finally, constitutively *national* norm, I hope to show how *What Maisie Knew*'s complication of the terms of its own fictionality might be understood to comment on and offer alternatives both to Holmes's "norm-based" conception of law and to its correlate, the juridical understanding of national culture.

The overriding conceptual emphasis of the essays that constitute Holmes's *Common Law* is to transform legal liability from a kind of *moral* failure to a behavioral failure, from wrong thinking to wrong acting.[30] The primary pur-

---

29. This concept of a communal norm bears particular relevance to the *Raffles* case. Because of the highly variable character of cotton, purchasing and sampling were regularly left to expert brokers, who would grade it on a scale from "fine" to "ordinary." ("Middling fair," the grade assigned to the *Raffles* cotton, fell toward the low side of the middle of the scale.) Since this system used fairly arbitrary criteria, the Liverpool Cotton Brokers' Association, which was originally established in 1841 to collect statistics on cotton sales and arrivals, instituted a highly regulated system for arbitrating disputes over cotton grades and prices. As a result, the number of cases brought to litigation in the enormous nineteenth-century cotton trade is strikingly small. Daniel Wichelhaus and Gustav Busch, the two defendants in the *Raffles* case, were doubly excluded from the community, being neither English nor cotton brokers. According to Simpson, the very fact that the case appeared in the courts rather than being settled by the rules of arbitration set up by the Cotton Brokers' Association testified to the breakdown of the brokers' "normativizing" procedures of self-government. In this case at least, then, the establishment of juridical, national norms produced by litigation depended in part on the dissolution of competing communities.

30. A promissory understanding of obligation can likewise be seen to invoke such a moralized notion of law in that it takes as paramount the quality of an internal will—the "goodness" of a subject's intentions.

pose of the law, in Holmes's view, is to induce external conformity to the law rather than to indicate or guarantee an individual's attitudes toward given relations or behaviors. What people think does not matter as long as they do not the right thing but the normal thing, the behavior that is standard by virtue of its social acceptance rather than because of any transcendent moral value.[31] The aphoristic debunking of legal foundationalism found in Holmes's 1920 *Collected Legal Papers* is characteristic: "The prophecies of what the courts will do in fact, and nothing more pretentious, are what I mean by law."[32]

What is significant here is that the standard behavior in question is not that of the citizens who will be judged by the law but of the judges who interpret the law. By this account, if the behavior of those people liable under the law is significant, it is only so after the fact, a norm produced in reaction to the institutionalizing *as law* of the probable behavior of the judges who interpret the law. That the content of the law within Holmes's system remains contingent (no one knows for certain "what the courts will do in fact") is of secondary importance, since the law must be followed, its content notwithstanding, simply by virtue of its institutional—formal—authority as law. Within this context of a nod to the legal authority of normativity that is revealed as prescriptive—institutional—rather than descriptive, Holmes's account of the role of the normative in creating contractual obligation becomes particularly instructive. His 1899 essay "The Theory of Legal Interpretation" at once recalls and clarifies the issues raised in his revision of *Raffles* eighteen years earlier:

31. As Ian Hacking argues in *The Taming of Chance,* the nineteenth century witnessed the gradual replacement of the Enlightenment's cardinal principle of "human nature" with a conceptual system in which what is common to individuals is not an effect of their common nature but is discoverable by statistical accounts of norms and deviances established for a group. The Enlightenment's representative individual is supplanted by the "average" national subject, a subject who, crucially, does not exist in the real world but is extrapolated from the characteristics of a given population. Implicit in this elevation of the statistical is a notion of probability that would understand the probable behavior of individuals not within a system of causality—not, that is, in terms of their inherent, or even their historically contingent, capacities or desires as individuals to perform certain acts—but after the fact: it is probable that a given individual will behave in a certain way because most people in the group behave in a certain way. Why or how a given set of conditions has come to exist is granted less predictive significance than the mere fact that the conditions do exist. The emergence of statistical analysis as a method for understanding the characteristics of a population is coincident with the emergence of the notion of population itself. The nation—now understood as a population characterized, rather than joined, by common behavior and attributes—is no longer conceived of primarily by virtue of occupying a shared geographical space. See Hacking, *The Taming of Chance* (Cambridge: Cambridge University Press, 1990).

32. Holmes, *Collected Legal Papers,* 173, quoted in Jan Vetter, "The Evolution of Holmes: Holmes and Evolution," in *Holmes and "The Common Law": A Century Later,* ed. Benjamin Kaplan, Patrick Atiyah, and Jan Vetter, Holmes Lectures, Occasional Pamphlet 10 (Cambridge: Harvard Law School, 1983), 75–101.

Even the whole document [of a contract] is found to have a certain play in the joints when its words are translated into things by parol evidence,[33] as they have to be. It does not disclose one meaning conclusively according to the laws of language. Thereupon we ask, not what this man meant, but what those words would mean *in the mouth of a normal speaker of English, using them in the circumstances in which they were used, and it is to the end of answering this last question that we let in evidence as to what the circumstances were.* But the normal speaker of English is merely a special variety, *a literary form,* so to speak of our old friend the prudent man. He is external to the particular writer, and a reference to him as the criterion is simply another instance of the externality of the law.[34]

Holmes's creation of the figure of the "normal speaker of English" seems to be of a piece with the movement of *The Common Law* as a whole to transform legal liability from the evaluation of internal mental states to the evaluation of externally perceptible behaviors. Within this model, we not only are required to substitute "normal English" for private meanings but are asked to elaborate the sense of this normal English so that it becomes the words of a normal speaker "using them in the circumstances in which they were used."

But once the qualification of the "circumstances of use" is added to the notion of normal English, it is difficult to understand what "normal" would mean or to know what evidentiary advantages such a norm would offer once it has been defined so narrowly. Holmes is able to use the form of the contract as a means of overcoming the secret, barely articulated danger at the heart of *The Common Law:* the threat that, once legal authority is represented as wholly conventional, the norm that is the basis of its authority will be too narrow, since it will be the implicitly coercive normal behavior of judges rather than the normal behavior of the population to which the law is meant to apply. As Joseph Vining has noted, contracts are exceptional within legal discourse both for comprising an identifiable text and for being written at the behest of the agents to whom they will apply.[35] If we recall that the wholly institutional—and hence ideal—authority of the judges was rendered merely probable insofar as it had to be applied to specific historical situations ("The

33. "Parol evidence" refers to the rule whereby once a contract had been put in writing, parties to the contract were not able to modify or amplify its terms by oral evidence regarding what they "really" meant. According to Simpson, this rule was strictly enforced in the Victorian period, though it has been much relaxed since that time (Simpson, "Beauty of Obscurity," 137).

34. *Harvard Law Review* 12 (1899): 417, quoted in Vetter, "Evolution of Holmes," 89; emphasis added.

35. Joseph Vining, "Generalization in Interpretive Theory," *Representations* 30 (spring 1990): 1–12 (special Issue, "Law and the Order of Culture," ed. Robert Post).

prophecies of what the courts will do in fact, and nothing more pretentious, is what I mean by law"), then we can see that when the problem of "specific application" is refracted through the lens of contract, the norm of law is at once, however paradoxically, generalized and rendered ideal. Insofar as contract is understood to rationalize—and in rationalizing to overcome—the constraints placed on the individual subject's knowledge and autonomous agency by the fact of historical contingency, it becomes an instrument for rendering identical the normative behavior of judges and the population at large by symbolizing contingency as the capacity to speak English normally.

One of the most notable aspects of Holmes's rewriting of *Raffles* for the history of contract, we recall, was the way it emphasized the act of *promising* at the same time that it sought to relocate the evidence of that promising from an internal state of consciousness to an externally perceptible behavior—from intention to speech. In theorizing a notion of contract where the subject is sufficiently autonomous for obligation to reside in the promise at the same time that that subject's will is demonstrated as speech, Holmes elevates the linguistic quality of contracts from the status of a passing accident to the instrument that produces the autonomous contracting subject. By redefining contracting from an act of will into a speech act and then, in his late work, transforming the authority to contract from an isolated speech act into an act of speech made forceful by its relation to other people's speech, Holmes makes contract an instrument for bringing about the very (linguistic) cultural agreement it presupposes. By turning the linguistic habits of an individual contractor into the mark of his or her capacity to predict "what the courts will do in fact," he makes contract a means of relocating the authority of law from institutions to culture. Not only does Holmes's contract subsume within its own probabilistic structure the problem of applicability, of the contextuality of norms, then, but by identifying the contracting subject with the normal speaker of *English,* it establishes legal authority as essentially cultural.

In the mysterious reversal produced by her encounter with the brown lady, Maisie's agency was constrained as much by the powerful and immediate "extratextual" racial meaning that would account for her otherwise unaccountable change of heart as she was by the apparent authorial conspiracy that plotted the Countess's serendipitous arrival with a timing Beale himself could not have outdone. The euphemism aligned the simultaneity of the fictional and the historical with the diachronicity implicit in the oscillation between childish literalism and "adult" racial overtones, suggesting that the developing Maisie, whose cognizance of racial meaning cannot be unambiguously determined, can be represented only within a narrative forged of elements of the fictional and the historical. James associates the turn to a notion of history wholly detached from fictional authority with a model of reified racial identity and in so doing drives home the limitations of synchronic, stabilized identity that might be overlooked in the context of more benign manifestations.[36] To the extent that history is conceived simply as the literal events of the past, it produces a subject indistinguishable from the world in which he or she acts, a kind of Holmesian utopia in which the "circumstances" within which people act normally have become all there is.

We can see, then, that despite Holmes's self-professed goal of demoralizing the law by replacing the standard of absolute righteousness with that of normal behavior, his desire to locate that normal standard within a particular set of legal institutions capable of ensuring its authority leads him to establish institutionally produced norms that act as morals by virtue of their institutionality. But whereas Holmes invokes the representational presumptions of the realist novel as a means of naturalizing and generalizing the moralized particularity of the institutional norm, James represents the effort to associate absolutely a moral discourse and the unmarked—that is, normal—conditions circumscribed by contract as necessarily doomed to failure, dependent as it is on temporally freezing both the contracting subject and the contractual narrative itself.

Consider the most explicit treatment of moral discourse in *What Maisie Knew*, the "moral sense" of Maisie's governess Mrs. Wix, whose loyalty to her charge in the face of Maisie's parents' multiple betrayals seems in equal parts the result of a transcendent sense of duty and the lack of anything better to do. Maisie and Mrs. Wix, having been showered with gifts meant to pledge the return of Maisie's stepfather Sir Claude from his latest excursion to England, turn to the question of Maisie's moral sense as they await Sir Claude's return in a Boulogne park. Frequently invoked without ever being quite defined, the narrative of this moral sense follows the formal contours of Maisie's efforts to behave as though she knows, efforts that articulate and reveal a representational economy in which the relation between inner and outer is at once rendered absolutely contingent and reliably identical.[37] Such an econ-

36. In a recent essay on James and race, Beverly Haviland traces W. E. B. Du Bois's famous conception of "double consciousness" to Du Bois's teacher at Harvard, William James. In his 1890 *Principles of Psychology*, William James writes that the brain could allow "one system to give rise to one consciousness, and those of another system to another *simultaneously* existing consciousness." Du Bois's translation of William James's psychophysiological understanding of "simultaneity" into social and racial terms finds an echo in Henry James's use of the brown lady euphemism, where the terms of the euphemism turn on a tension between an identity constructed wholly out of existing norms and the imagination of particularity of identity as a kind of aesthetic looking forward. See Beverly Haviland, "'Psychic Mulattos': The Ambiguity of Race," *Common Knowledge* 3 (winter 1994): 127–43.

37. "It seemed to [Maisie] while she tiptoed at the chimney-glass, pulling on her gloves and with a motion of her head shaking a feather into place, to have something to do with Mrs Wix's suddenly saying, 'Haven't you really and truly *any* moral sense?' Maisie was aware that her answer, though it

omy, I have been arguing, characterizes both the classical promissory contract and the realist novel. In the figure of Mrs. Wix, James represents the effort to moralize a set of circumstances that, in being evoked as explanatory without ever being described, recall both Holmes's norm and the authority of the novel:

> The bathers, so late, were absent and the tide was low; the sea-pools twinkled in the sunset and there were dry places as well, where they could sit again and admire and expatiate: a *circumstance* that, while they listened to the lap of the waves, gave Mrs Wix a fresh support for her challenge. "Have you absolutely none at all?"
>
> She had no need now, as to the question itself at least, to be specific: that on the other hand was the eventual result of their quiet conjoined apprehension of the thing that—well, yes, since they must face it—Maisie absolutely and appallingly had so little of. (212, emphasis added)

What this passage reveals so stunningly is the almost triumphant tautologism of realist sufficiency and the morality of the normative that underwrites Holmes and that James here sets up as the limits of conventional novelistic representation. Mrs. Wix is authorized—"given fresh support for her challenge"—by a "circumstance" that includes the entire description preceding this designation. That absent bathers and twinkling sea pools appear, within the established terms of the narrative, pointedly irrelevant to the establishment of any familiar moral code is just the point: what is is what matters. This norm of "circumstances" at once authorizes and takes the place of any articulation of an actual content of morality, as the designation of the moral emerges from and disappears back into its circumstances. Within the analytical terms laid out in *Raffles*, Mrs. Wix's moral sense makes "strong" the heretofore "weak" meaning of the seashore description, but that very same description is cited as authorizing the moral sense that creates this strong meaning. Moreover, this circular relation between descriptive "circumstance" and the authority of the markedly unspecified moral sense is further complicated by the idea that the lack of specificity of Mrs. Wix's question concerning the state of Maisie's moral sense is itself authorized by the pair's tacit agreement—their "quiet conjoined apprehension of the thing"—concerning Maisie's *lack* of a moral sense.

---

brought her down to her heels, was vague even to imbecility, and that this was the first time she had appeared to practise with Mrs Wix an intellectual inaptitude to meet her—the infirmity to which she had owed so much success with papa and mamma. The appearance did her injustice, for it was not less through her candor than through her playfellow's pressure that after this the idea of a moral sense mainly coloured their intercourse. She began, the poor child, with scarcely knowing what it was; but it proved something that, with scarce an outward sign save her surrender to the swing of the carriage she could, before they came back from their drive, strike up a sort of acquaintance with" (211).

The circularity of the norm and its moralizing is thus justified from a point outside the circle. But such a principle is not as counterintuitive as it may seem if we consider that the tautological linking of terms can be meaningful, can tell us something we did not already know, only insofar as we remain outside the system of equivalence. Within the relations of the passage itself, the conditions before Maisie can be the conditions of a moral sense—can be something more than they appear, in their weak meaning, to be—only if the person doing the apprehending does not know what she is to know, if she does not already possess a moral sense. Paradoxically, then, the power of the circularity is available only at the moment its descriptive limits come into view; only to the person who must at some moment *learn* the relations deemed to be self-evident can the force of that self-evidence be made manifest.

To the extent that the normal behavior in question was perceived to be that of only a small portion of the population whose normative claim on the remainder was extended by means of institutional authority, that prescriptive, implicitly moralized normativity would be experienced as coercive, as something that was not known or given but that needed to be learned. Thus the experience of institutionality for the individual citizen within Holmes's system of overlapping legal norms is the experience of being taught, of experiencing the norm over time as something one does not yet do but must come to do in the future.

In *Maisie*'s narrative elaboration of the nature of the moral that culminates in the scene at the seashore, both the narrative and the ethical conundrum of the "moral sense" concerns exactly how it might be taught. For the citizen subject to the Holmesian system of legal norms, the experience of the norms as institutional, as something one learns to do because one is required to, is necessarily an experience of the law through time. By formulating the political problem of teaching the norm encountered in Holmes around the figure of the maturing child, *Maisie* generalizes the political and ethical (and implicitly narrative) difficulty, transforming the question of coercion from an issue concerning the extent of the norm to an issue of socialization. For children experiencing a set of behaviors for the first time or, more to the point, experiencing for the first time a set of other people's behaviors as something that ought to be binding on their own, the norm feels coercive, even if such behavior statistically reflects the normal behavior of the population at large. Indeed, insofar as a given behavior is experienced as having the *force* of the norm, it is felt to be something one otherwise would not necessarily do.

But even as the novel generalizes the problem of representing the fact of a self-evident social norm, it demonstrates its own generic predisposition to do that generalizing. If the paradox associated with the circularity of normative authority means that the moral force of normativity is experienced only by those who begin outside its circumference, James narrates that formal paradox by making the condition of outsideness part of the content of the norm. To the extent that we glean any specific idea of the values that constitute Mrs. Wix's "moral sense," that moral sense involves the capacity to discriminate: specifically, the capacity to distinguish between the adulterous and nonadulterous behaviors of her various pairings of parents and stepparents and their various consorts. So the moral sense involves the ability to discriminate between categories, a formal capacity. At the same time, however, the categories Maisie is meant to distinguish between are hardly incidental. The difficulty for Mrs. Wix—the reason she cannot simply and straightforwardly instruct Maisie on the differences of which she would like the child to be cognizant, but must proceed by means of indirection and allusion—seems to be that she cannot teach Maisie about the sexuality that would enable her to separate the adulterous from the nonadulterous without in some way rendering Maisie herself sexual. In part this situation can be understood as simply a restatement—from the normative point of view, rather than that of the not yet normal/knowing subject—of the problem of establishing a norm that is at once authoritative and self-evident.

But let us consider more closely how this dynamic of adultery works. In part, James's sketches of the various trysts of Beale and Ida, Sir Claude, Miss Overmore, and the host of other paramours partake of the representational economy I have associated both with Holmes's *Raffles* and with Maisie's early encounter with the American Countess. Recognizing that the surprise meetings, exchanged glances, and flashing teeth are signs of the existence of sexual relations between a given unmarried pairing requires that Maisie append a "strong" meaning to what would otherwise qualify as mere description. But for Mrs. Wix intuitively and for James the author more self-consciously, these activities do not simply stand as *signs* of adulterous behavior but in an important way come to constitute the behavior itself. It is crucial within the terms of both the novel and my discussion of it that what Maisie is meant to recognize in developing a moral sense is not merely sexuality but adultery. In learning to identify adultery, Maisie is required to see the existence of behavior that falls explicitly beyond the compass marked out by the terms of a contract (the marriage contract whose dissolution was the enabling condition for the novel as a whole). Adultery thus challenges the sufficiency of Holmes's version of contract, a vision of contract as realist novel in which the "circumstances" that make up a given contextual moment guarantee the normality of the behavior in question. That Maisie initially has difficulty recognizing the adulterous behavior she encounters suggests that she is not aware of a specifically sexual aspect of parental behavior either. For Maisie, to be married, to be party to a marriage contract, requires, in a sense, that one "do what parents do." In her mind, the descriptive sufficiency of the marriage contract prevents her from recognizing the existence of other types of behavior. The very possibility of extracting a separate category of "sexual behavior" from the general description of what parents do is shown to be the condition on which adultery turns.

By insisting, through the category of the adulterous, on the diachronicity of the norm, the novel demonstrates that establishing the boundaries of "what parents (or Holmesian normal speakers of English) do" depends not only on erasing the history of the creation of that norm, but also on canceling the individual "normal" subjects' transformations over time. That the category of adulterous behavior becomes distinguishable from "what parents do" for Maisie only as she changes and is transformed by her recognition of it intimates that the constitution of a Holmesian, novelistic (though not fictional) self-evidence has as much to do with the constitution of a certain kind of subjectivity as it does with the production of normative social authority. Indeed, what this scene from *What Maisie Knew* itself makes evident is how establishing the authority of the normative depends on canceling any experience of point of view, or, more accurately, on identifying one's experience of the world with lack of a point of view.

The stakes of such an identification with nothing and nobody in particular might become clearer if we look to the closing moments of this scene. Mrs. Wix presses Maisie to confess her jealousy of Mrs. Beale's intimacy with Sir Claude, and Maisie, hoping to lay to rest any remaining doubts as to the existence of her moral sense, expresses her outrage at the prospect of Mrs. Beale's unkindness to Sir Claude:

> Maisie met her expression as if it were a game with forfeits for winking. "I'd *kill* her!" That at least, she hoped as she looked away, would guarantee her moral sense. She looked away but her companion said nothing for so long that she at last turned her head again. Then she saw the straighteners all blurred with tears which after a little seemed to have sprung from her own eyes. There were tears in fact on both sides of the spectacles, and they were even so thick that it was presently all Maisie could do to make out through them that slowly, finally Mrs Wix put forth a hand. It was the material pressure that settled this and even at the end of some minutes more things besides. It settled in its own way one thing in particular, which, though often between them, heaven knew, hovered round and hung over, was yet to be established without the shadow of an attenuating smile. Oh there was no gleam of levity, as little of humour as of deprecation, in the long time they now sat together

or in which at some unmeasured point of it Mrs Wix became distinct enough for her own dignity and yet not loud enough for the snoozing old women.

"I adore him. I adore him."

Maisie took it well in; so well that in a moment more she would have answered profoundly: "So do I." But before that moment passed something took place that brought other words to her lips, nothing more, very possibly, than the closer consciousness in her hand of the significance of Mrs Wix's. Their hands remained linked in unutterable sign of their union, and what Maisie at least said was simply and serenely: "Oh I know!" (217–18)

The passage literalizes Mrs. Wix's figuration of moral sense as a generalization of point of view, a generalization that in diffusing from a single subject to subjects in general becomes the impossible perspective that announces the ideal of the total disappearance of point of view. Maisie's empathy ("she saw the straighteners all blurred with tears which after a little while seemed to spring from her own eyes") is followed almost immediately by an odd blurring of perspective as Mrs. Wix's tears begin to cover both sides of her spectacles, which in turn results in her transplantation to the place of Mrs. Wix, as the governess's tear-soaked glasses make it impossible for Maisie herself to see. ("It was presently all Maisie could do to make out through them [the spectacles] that slowly, finally Mrs Wix put forth a hand.") This constitution of Holmesian normativity—the novel as the condition of point of viewlessness created by the impossibility of a literal "normal" perspective—halts abruptly with the reembodiment, the materialization of the individual protagonists.

In Maisie's tearful encounter with Mrs. Wix, the ambiguous relations between different levels of narration have been replaced by the blurring, synthesis, and finally disappearance of different perspectives within a *single* level of narration. Within the context of Holmes's normative contract, particularity of perspective is not rendered unmarked by the intervention of an idealizing fictionality but is made to disappear as a result of the narrative establishment of a norm. Inasmuch as this apparent disappearance of point of view is figured as the outcome of both the establishing and the impossibility of establishing norms within an actual population, the reembodying of that population announced by the "material pressure" Mrs. Wix and Maisie exert upon one another asserts—against what we might imagine to be Holmes's protestations to the contrary—the *fictionality* of the normative.

But while this moment of bodily contact halts the dissolution of perspective that precedes it, the scene does not end with this reembodiment but goes on to challenge the sufficiency of the mere fact of embodied particularity to undermine normativity. When Mrs. Wix declares to Maisie that she adores Sir Claude, the narrative "events" that follow link the difficulty of bringing inner mental states and externally perceptible speech acts into clear relation with one another to the difficulty of deciding on the meaningfulness of their touching. Maisie is moved by Mrs. Wix's confession, so the passage tells us, to make a confession of her own; what intervenes between this unusual impulse to confess ("So do I") and the laughably familiar outcome ("Oh I know!") can be an event as imperceptible as the shift it is meant to account for. ("But before that moment passed something took place that brought other words to her lips.") We can understand the three responses ("So do I," "Oh I know!" and last, the virtually unaccountable shift from the former to the latter that is finally represented) to constitute three alternative readings of the trajectory of Maisie's development. Mrs. Wix finds herself stymied by the contradictory imperative to teach Maisie to have a moral sense; not only does temporalizing the normal moral sense reveal that it is prescriptive rather than merely descriptive, but the fact that its content was defined as something like the capacity to recognize adultery means the condition of knowing becomes nearly indistinguishable from the behavior that was to be known. At the same time, because the identity of behavior and knowledge in question concerns adultery, the condition of being prior to and beyond the self-evident norm (the "circumstances" of the marriage contract as "what parents do") are not simply epistemological but social and political as well.

The Maisie who would match Mrs. Wix's confession with a confession of her own bespeaks a crisis of the normal subject at once revealed and rendered safely past. In announcing her own sexual interest in Sir Claude, this Maisie hints that the threat posed by the development or historicity of individual subjects can be resolved by the endless multiplication of norms, as the contextuality implicit within the concept of the normal makes imperceptible the historicity of the movement from one norm to the next. The Maisie who answers with blithe, almost blank confidence "Oh I know!" on the other hand, is a Maisie we have encountered numerous times before, a child who trades on the liberal split between internal mental states and externally perceptible behavior to create, if not quite liberal autonomy, then at least the strategically useful form of it. As has been the case throughout the novel, this Maisie is able to be a subject because she cannot be known by others within a liberal economy of evidence and interpretation. But this unknowability, the gap between inner and outer that animated Holmes's legal formalism and led him to posit normal language as an externally perceptible evidentiary ground, is an unknowability that is essentially epistemological, a problem concerning the opacity of individual subjects to one another.

Within the context in which it is finally presented, however, Maisie's "Oh I know!" pointedly marks its deviation from the narrative patterns it nonetheless echoes. In the most literal sense, that her familiar assertion of knowledge follows, we are told, quite a different impulse suggests that this Maisie just might be significantly more canny than the Maisie we thought we had come to know; we might suspect, for the first time, that in not knowing in detail what Maisie knows we risk missing something. For most of the novel, to the extent that Maisie was able to take advantage of the constitutive nonequivalence of inner and outer, she revealed and critiqued the terms of promissory subjectivity while at the same time (insofar as we as readers were able to conclude that Maisie did not in fact have the knowledge to which she pretended) the incoherencies of such a subject could still be accommodated within and by means of the fictionality of realism. Here, however, both the evidentiary instability associated with the bifurcated promissory subject and the embodiment that elsewhere realized the otherwise idealist qualities of a prescriptive normativity are themselves represented as constitutionally, not just contingently, unknowable. Whereas in earlier moments the causal relations between inner impulses and outer effects were either presumed (sometimes against the force of evidence) or figured as narratively inaccessible, here narrative inaccessibility ("nothing more, *very possibly*, than the closer consciousness in her hand of the significance of Mrs Wix's"; emphasis added) is made equivalent to a kind of ontological unknowability ("But before that moment passed *something* took place that brought other words to her lips"; emphasis added). Since the difficulty of understanding how subjects come to act in certain ways is no longer a problem of gaining access to their inner will or of understanding the relation between that will and external behavior effects, such a difficulty is not resolved by the authority of the fictional narrator.

Moreover, insofar as the relation between Maisie's two possible responses asks to be mapped onto two stages of her development—a canny, sexual Maisie set against the Maisie who compensates for her radically constrained agency and lack of knowledge by behaving as though she knows—the passage's reformulation of unknowability as an ontological (or, as I will show, historical) rather than simply an epistemological condition functions implicitly as a reformulation of the historicity of the subject. By refusing to settle on either the sexually knowing, even adulterous "So do I" or the unstably compensatory "Oh I know!" the passage suggests that a subject's knowledge cannot be gauged not because it is inaccessible but because, strictly speaking, there is no one thing, one stable body of knowledge, to be known.

What James reveals here, contra Holmes, is that the moment of imposing coercive, prescriptive authority of institutions is not in fact the condition in which the norm proves itself sufficient—a sufficiency Holmes argued was testified to by the behavior of using the English language normally—but depends on a condition of unknowability. If the structure of the promissory contract is an argument for the capacity of individual subjects to know and control the world in which they act, the institutions necessary to guarantee such a capacity—the legal, generic, and linguistic interrelations that constitute Holmes's norm—end up belying the contract's very claims to sufficiency. In a sense, we can understand James to be taking a lesson from Maisie: not the logic but the paradoxes, the gaps and unaccountabilities of the contract offer the potential, always limited, for individual freedom. Whereas Maisie herself, at least for most of the novel, can imagine an agency created only by hiding her otherwise insurmountable childishness, James sees her childishness, or more precisely the ephemerality of subjectivity that he understands to constitute that childishness, as the condition of a (limited) child's freedom that stands as the model for freedom generally.

For Ann Douglas, who draws on the critical essays of D. H. Lawrence and H. L. Mencken for her analysis,[38] the fin-de-siècle turn to euphemism announced even as it tried to overcome a general American anxiety about the country's cultural beholdenness to the past, about the force of a national history that disappeared as it was asserted. In her reading, the proliferation of euphemism registered the divided quality of the cultural work the figure was assigned to perform. It marked the attempt to achieve a kind of cultural respectability conventionally associated with cultural autonomy at the same time that it registered the tenuousness, the derivative quality of the authority to make such a claim. James reorders this double quality of euphemism to raise the possibility that an individual use of language might be sufficient to shift, if not entirely overcome, the weighty history of cultural norms, even as it is the turn to literalism that paradoxically asserts linguistic freedom. (That he chooses the particularly American "innovation" of race as the figure for the insurmountability of cultural history further emphasizes James's sense that the cultural and linguistic instruments by means of which the past might be shed can be discovered only with cultural terms laid out in that past.)

For James, then, euphemism makes evident how purely conventional is the

---

38. Ann Douglas, *Terrible Honesty: Mongrel Manhattan in the 1920s* (New York: Farrar, Straus and Giroux, 1995), 59, 167, 521, 557–58.

association that would tie transparency of representation to the normal use of language. It is just the presumption of the transparency of this link, recall, that provided the epistemological and political payoff of Holmes's elevation of the norm. By making the "normal" use of English inextricable from the circumstances in which such language is used, Holmes established the norm as evidence of an individual subjectivity that was externally perceptible—behavior in the real world—at the same time it remained unconstrained by the historical particularity of that world. In representing in the fortuitous arrival of the woman who is "brown indeed" the prospect that a deviation from the norms of social use might take the form of literal description, James forcib'y disrupts the naturalizing of the authority of the norm, a naturalizing that itself depends on the construction of fictional authority as the absolute separation of the fictional and the historical. Moreover, insofar as the authority of the norm rests on its formal translation of a diachronic narrative of behavior into a model of stable, synchronic selfhood, James's reconceptualizing of an authorship constituted out of the shifting relations of history and fiction figures the disruption of the identification of the normal and the literal with the acknowledgment that both are experienced over time.

～

I conclude by looking briefly at one final scene in which James at once brings together the terms of his critique of the epistemology of realist normality and posits an alternative conception of the political possibilities of realism. Having spent the afternoon together, Maisie and Sir Claude briefly discuss breaking their ties and escaping together to Paris by train:

> She showed their two armfuls [of luggage], smiling at him as he smiled at her, but so conscious of being more frightened than she had ever been in her life that she seemed to see her whiteness as in a glass. Then she knew that what she saw was Sir Claude's whiteness: he was as frightened as herself. "Haven't we got plenty of luggage?" she asked. "Take the tickets—haven't you time? When does the train go?"
> Sir Claude turned to a porter. "When does the train go?"
> The man looked up at the station clock. "In two minutes. *Monsieur est placé?*" "*Pas encore.*"
> "*Et vos billets? — vous n'avez que le temps.*" Then after a look at Maisie, "*Monsieur veut-il que je les prenne?*"
> Sir Claude turned back to her. "*Veux-tu bien qu'il en prenne?*"
> It was the most extraordinary thing in the world: in the intensity of her excitement she not only by illumination understood all their French, but fell into it with

an active perfection. She addressed herself straight to the porter. *"Prenny, prenny. Oh prenny!"*

"Ah si mademoiselle le veut — !" He waited there for the money.

But Sir Claude only stared—stared at her with his white face.[39] (253–54)

In a moment of marked implausibility ("it was the most extraordinary thing in the world"), Maisie is shown developing, effortlessly acceding to a (linguistic) norm that is neither hers nor that of the novel. Figured in opposition to her new consciousness of the "whiteness" of her face and Sir Claude's, Maisie's movement into French speech announces a Holmesian mending of the liberal, promissory split between inner mental states and the external behaviors conventionally—if not always with good reason—presumed to be evidence of those states. No longer do we see a Maisie who knows only enough to "behave" the knowledge she lacks; here the potential for ambiguity that would exist in the child who might appear to understand French without producing irrefutable evidence of her comprehension is pointedly resolved by the "active perfection" of Maisie's use of the language. Moreover, this active language use that closes the split in the promissory subject is associated with Maisie's most forceful act of the novel, an act that not only stands as the expression of an unmistakable desire but reframes Sir Claude's "liberal" inaction.

Although this representation of Maisie's moment of learning bolsters Holmes's account of how a shift to an evidentiary economy of linguistic use can clarify, even constitute, the willful action of an individual subject, that she is learning *French* radically reconceives the social meaning of this evidentiary transformation. If the linguistic quality of Maisie's behavior means that such behavior becomes meaningful in relation to established linguistic norms, the fact remains that the norms in question are neither Maisie's nor the novel's. And if the apparent effortlessness of her movement into the language makes it look like the unwilled outcome of some culturally produced developmental trajectory, that she moves from her language to another means that her development cannot quite be assimilated to a model of learning in which the difficulty of discerning just what an individual subject knows stands as proof

39. The French of the passage is translated as follows according to the notes of the Penguin edition of the novel:

Monsieur est placé? / *Pas encore* / *Et vos billets — vous n'avez que les temps.* ["Have you got seats, sir?" / "Not yet" / "And your tickets—you've only just got time."]

Monsieur veut-il que je les prenne? ["Would you like me to get them, sir?"]

Veux-tu bien qu'il en prenne? ["Do you really want him to get them?"]

Prenny. [(Maisie's version of *prenez*): "get them."]

Ah si mademoiselle le veut — ! ["Ah, if the young lady wants me to—!"]

of the "normality" of that knowledge. While the form of Maisie's transition partakes of the effortlessness of normal development, its content implies the presence of will, if not willfulness. The implausibility of the moment reminds us of the presence of James the author, but the interesting point is that authorial presence here takes the form not of metafiction but of implausibility, not of a sign of the historicity of the author or the language of the text but of a sign of the historicity of the narrative itself, a rendering "simultaneous" of the movements of narrative and history that are conventionally held apart by the generic markers of realism's fictional authority.

Whereas for Holmes the existence of a normal, national language traced the limits of individual subjects' possible behaviors, James, in the unlikely moment in which Maisie begins, miraculously, to speak French, imagines the linguistic quality of the world to offer the limited possibility of individual freedom. That Maisie's fluency in French is insufficient to get her what she wants in the face of Sir Claude's refusal to hand over the money is only the most obvious sign of her constraint. Counterposed against the model of a literal history, the paralysis of a racialized subjectivity comprising nothing more than the events of the past, the wildly implausible Francophone who emerges at the end of *What Maisie Knew* is free not because she behaves as "normal speakers of English" behave in the same "circumstances," or because she escapes being constrained by norms altogether, but because the norm she enters into—that of the French national language—is one she "chooses" all the time knowing that such a choice can never be wholly, or even mostly, free. And if this implausible Maisie brings us back to the James who stands behind her spinning fictions, she (and he) lends us hope not because she is made up, but because she is made up in a particular language.

3

SPEAKING WORLDS

S. Y. Abramovitch and the Making of Hebrew Vernacular

TO CLAIM THAT THE REALIST NOVEL is a book about talking is to risk stating the obvious. Such a risk, it might be said from the outset, is not at all foreign to the genre's own interests, for the kind of talk with which the novel concerns itself is not any talk but ordinary talk, the tabletime niceties and passing observations of forcefully average people that both mark and create what it means to "state the obvious."[1] Insofar as it bothers to attend to what is right there to be seen—to bother, that is, to note things so obvious that they might have been overlooked—the novel associates its talk with a certain economy of self-evidence and, in so doing, generates a strangely self-abnegating authority. What is said is so clearly true it need not have been said; narrative authority becomes unquestionable in the very same measure as it is redundant. Novelistic speech and the foibles and manners and family heirlooms that are the objects of its scrutiny thus produce one another as local and ordinary, and the world of the novel stands with a presence as solid and immovable as the novel's own presence in the actual world is tenuous.

If the ordinary speech of ordinary people functions within the novel not

---

1. For an excellent account of the relation between gossip and the free indirect discourse characteristic of the nineteenth-century English novel, see Casey Finch and Peter Bowen, "'The Tittle-Tattle of Highbury': Gossip and Free Indirect Style in *Emma*," *Representations* 31 (summer 1990): 1–18.

merely as a sign of the existence of a concrete local world but also as a mode of knowing that world, then what happens when the spoken language represented within a given novel does not exist in the world of the novel's author or readers? What happens, in other words, when the language used by and within the novel to represent a certain kind of ordinariness is itself anything but ordinary?

In chapter 1 I examined the way George Eliot understood a sense of unmarked continuity between the language a novel is written in and the language its characters speak to be crucial to the English novel's creation of a particularly English universalist liberalism. By implicitly representing a given geographical space as both prior to and independent of the people who inhabit it at the same time as the language of the fictional representation is itself associated with a specific national identity, the novel renders the ideological contradictions of a notion of English liberalism noncontradictory. Thanks to the realist novel's characteristic quality of fictional plausibility—the novel is understood by its readers to be simultaneously not-true (fictional) and believable—the concrete geographical space represented within its pages can appear at once to be universally and objectively apprehensible as "real" and particularly English (because the language in which this "real" is represented is English *and* transparent). Of course, as the Frankfurt scene of *Daniel Deronda* makes clear, the political payoff of labeling such a space "English" is realizable only insofar as that space is inhabited, yet it is this peopling of the represented space with speakers that threatens to expose the contingent quality of the identification of space and nation. By asserting his Englishness in Frankfurt in language that is not positively identifiable as any specific national language yet is indistinguishable from the heretofore transparent language of the narration, the Jewish Daniel lays a claim to a place within the novelistic world implicitly identified as English that effectively disrupts the naturalness of the identification. Inasmuch as Eliot conceives of Jewish national identity as existing independent of the Jews' occupation of a shared geographical space in the form of something like a shared tradition of texts, it remains impossible for her to represent Jews plausibly within the terms that underwrite the realist novel at the same time as the Jews challenge the validity of those terms.

The Jews Eliot imagined may have made untenable the novelistic production of a geographical space that is both national and liberal by participating in a corporate identity that, in its discursive quality, resembled too closely the operation of the novel itself. But the European Jews of Eliot's era who actually contemplated producing a national literary identity around the productively contradictory form of the realist novel faced a substantially different, if not unrelated, set of obstacles. For though the ground of Jewish collective identity in the nineteenth century was, relative to the prevailing model of the European nation-state, disproportionately discursive and "immaterial,"[2] the relation between this textual tradition and contemporary Jewish linguistic practice—and the kind of national political behavior this practice entailed—was anything but straightforward. In fact the period extending from the late eighteenth century through the early years of the twentieth marked the most fundamental refiguring of the terms of Jewish identity since the end of Jewish political sovereignty in 76 C.E., a refiguring that turned on determining the proper relations among religious textuality, contemporary literary and linguistic practice, and political identity. Benjamin Harshav puts it this way:

> This society was not rooted in existential axes in a geographic area of its own—a physical *here* and *now* and a stable *we* of a normal nation. On the contrary, in their everyday awareness—as Jews—they were connected to a *universe of discourse,* a "fictional world" outside of history and geography, based on a library of texts and their interpretations (or, at least, instinctive beliefs and responses derived from that). Hence the centrality of discourse (rather than love of the land) for their self-understanding. When this universe of discourse lost its moorings (the two thousand years of "dead books" which M. Z. Fayerberg [1874–1899] denounced in *Wither*), the anchoring of a universe of discourse vis-à-vis the "real," historical world became the most important existential question for any alternative, any mode of Jewish culture, and for every individual. . . . In terms of political awareness, the break with the old universe of discourse entailed a departure from both the ahistorical perception permeating the ideology of religious Jewry and the collective nature of that ideology (with the slogan of "all Jews are responsible for each other")—and acceptance of two alternative principles essential to modern European culture: historicism and individual consciousness.[3]

Central to this crisis of textual authority—and crucial for understanding the development of the Hebrew novel in the latter half of the nineteenth century—is precisely the *textuality* of these religious texts, that is, their status as *written* language, accessible in the present only as objects of study or prayer. Although Jews traveling beyond the bounds of Yiddish-speaking Europe

2. I use this term with reservations and only provisionally, since even a cursory examination of the politics surrounding the production of Jewish national linguistic and literary identities in the nineteenth century makes obvious the inadequacy of a schema that associates the geographical and material in opposition to the discursive and immaterial. At the same time, because I believe this opposition is central to understanding not only Eliot's interest in the Jews but the Jews' symbolic function in European political discourse more generally, I employ it as a point of departure.

3. Benjamin Harshav, *Language in Time of Revolution* (Berkeley: University of California Press, 1993), 20–21, 24.

sometimes employed a rudimentary spoken Hebrew as a lingua franca, for all intents and purposes Hebrew did not exist as an active spoken language before its revival in Palestine in the early decades of the twentieth century. But although it was clear nobody was speaking Hebrew, what is more difficult to ascertain is just what constituted Hebrew literacy in the period—in what ways Jews who likely spoke Yiddish as their language of daily commerce yet nevertheless prayed three times a day in Hebrew might be said to "know" Hebrew. Though Hebrew had mostly disappeared as a vernacular by the time of Jesus, it never entirely ceased to have some active written applications.[4] Literary continuities are more easily discernible in a specifically poetic tradition, where liturgical Hebrew verse was frequently composed and used in synagogues in western Europe and the Middle East from the seventh century through the early modern era.[5] Several centuries later, a highly ornamental secular Hebrew poetry based on Arabic models developed in Andalusia and spread throughout western and northern Europe as late as the eighteenth century. Although the tradition of postvernacular prose is more spotty, Hebrew prose was variously employed for devotional tracts, chronicles, community records, legal discourse, biblical exegesis, wills, international commercial correspondence, and less ephemerally, for the medieval philosophical writings translated into Hebrew from the Judeo-Arabic original.

The extent and, indeed, the meaning of Hebrew literacy in nineteenth-century eastern Europe that spawned the pre-Revival novelists cannot be determined with anything close to certainty, in part because the standard historical method for measuring literacy—measuring a population's capacity to *write*—is unreliable in a context in which speaking the language cannot be presumed to accompany literacy.[6] With the arrival of widespread printing in the eighteenth century, moreover, students were less likely to have to hand copy the texts they were to study, further reducing the sense of Hebrew as a language that might potentially be composed in the present. This tendency was only reinforced by the fact that as a "holy tongue," Hebrew was considered to be inappropriate for secular composition by large segments of the population. Although virtually every male in eastern European Jewish society

4. The best concise English overviews of the history of Hebrew are Harshav and Robert Alter, *The Invention of Hebrew Prose* (Seattle: University of Washington Press, 1988), esp. the introduction and chap. 1. See also, translated from the Yiddish, Israel Zinberg, *A History of Jewish Literature*, trans. Bernard Martin (Cincinnati: Hebrew Union College Press, 1978), and Yosef Klausner, *Historia shel ha-sifrut ha-hadasha* [The history of modern literature] (Jerusalem, 1953). This reference and other works published in Hebrew are given in Hebrew characters in the bibliography.

5. Alter, *Invention of Hebrew Prose*, 18.

6. See Shaul Stampfer, "What Did 'Knowing Hebrew' Mean in Eastern Europe?" in *Hebrew in Ashkenaz: A Language in Exile*, ed. Lewis Glinert (Oxford: Oxford University Press, 1993), 129–40.

studied Hebrew from the ages of four to thirteen, which ought to have guaranteed a basic level of literacy, teaching quality varied widely from one school to the next. What limited religious teaching girls received was primarily in Yiddish, including abridged Yiddish editions of the Torah, and as readers of Yiddish, which employs an orthographic system similar, though not identical, to Hebrew, they would have been able to pronounce Hebrew prayers and participate in synagogue services and private prayer without literal comprehension. Because women were most often responsible for the economic support of their families, they were more likely than their husbands to have a working knowledge of the national language of the country in which they lived. A 1901 survey of Jewish workers in Minsk revealed that about 10 percent of the male masters and a full quarter of the journeymen and apprentices could not read Hebrew or Yiddish, but these percentages are probably unrepresentatively high, since the working classes the sample was drawn from were proverbially undereducated.[7] More telling, when in 1827 Nicholas I of Russia initiated the conscription quotas drafting Jews into the czar's army for twenty-five-year periods of service as part of a broader government effort aimed at converting Russia's Jews, most boys were not able to prepare independently the single page of Talmud necessary for admission to advanced study in yeshivot—even though yeshiva study offered one of the few officially sanctioned means of exemption from army service.

In short, then, when at midcentury a handful of writers began piecing together something like realist novels—those books about talking—out of scraps and fragments of a literary-religious tradition many had already abandoned as outmoded, they were describing the "ordinary" and "obvious" activities of a community whose members could not even speak the language these novels represented them as speaking, much less read these books in which their lives were represented. Most of these writers had already published widely in Yiddish, where they not only could avail themselves of all the representational tools of a contemporary spoken language but were also virtually guaranteed a large and engaged reading public. That they chose to write novels in Hebrew *despite* the confluence of circumstances militating against such a choice is what makes their lives and work interesting objects of study. I begin with a question that may seem absurdly anomalous at least in its historical scope: What does it mean to write realist novels in a language nobody speaks? But the example afforded by the emergence of the nineteenth-century European Hebrew novel seems to me to have implications extending far beyond the limits of this particular literary tradition. By exam-

7. Ibid., 130.

ining the strange case of novels written in a language without a vernacular, I hope to demonstrate how the form of the realist novel can be understood to be producing a *speaking* subject as the paradigmatic national subject.

To the extent that the realism written in normative sociopolitical settings—in communities where literary language makes claims to be, broadly speaking, continuous with a national spoken language—is designed to exhibit not only certain kinds of social behaviors but a certain kind of capacity, that is, the capacity to speak, the novel as a form produces a knowledge at once both local and infinitely generalizable, both nationally marked and objective. To highlight the structures by which the written novel produces itself as a spectacle of spoken linguistic knowledge, I read מסעות בנימין השלישי (*The Travels of Benjamin the Third*) (1896), by Shalom Yaakov Abramovitch (Mendele Mocher Sefarim), in relation to a form that takes up the issue of linguistic knowledge as its explicit concern—the national dictionary. By comparing Samuel Johnson's 1755 preface to his *Dictionary* with the dictionary preface written by Eliezer Ben-Yehuda, the first lexicographer of modern Hebrew and a major force behind the revival of the spoken language, I will reconsider models of national authorship produced by the realist novel in light of the two dictionary writers' quite different claims to national authorship. The novel, I will argue, is a crucial instrument for establishing linguistic knowledge.

At the same time, however, we would do well to be cautious about overemphasizing the anomalousness of the relation between the Jews of eighteenth- and nineteenth-century Europe and the Hebrew language. These Jews inhabit a common world that is at once possessed of too much and too little language: they are connected to one another through a shared set of texts rather than a shared geographical space organized by civil institutions, yet they have no common language with which to conduct their day-to-day activities. The upheaval of this linguistic world that makes its peculiarity present to those within and outside the established communities of Jews thus gives witness not to the normativity of the contemporary notion of a transparent national linguistic community but to the newness and the tenuousness of such a notion. It is only when people begin to believe that being able to converse with others gives them a connection that precedes and extends beyond the moment of the linguistic transaction to become a quality of who they are that the oddness of the Jews' linguistic situation becomes discernible. Only when language came to be experienced as *in competition with* other ways of understanding people to be linked to one another, such as relations of labor and commerce or shared rituals, did the Jews' (dis)connection to language in general and to written texts in particular come to seem a condition that might be reflected on or even changed. Only then, in short, did language come to seem a matter of history.

Writing about a historically coincident but very different cultural meeting, Katie Trumpener has asserted that the emergence of an exclusively linguistic notion of cultural identity—the growth of English as the unifying force of an increasingly heterogeneous "Great Britain"—marked a scaling back of the claims of culture:

> British centralization implied not only the spread and enforced imposition but also the systematic underdevelopment of Englishness. To the degree that England becomes the center of the empire, its own internal sense of culture accordingly fails to develop. And to the degree that the English language, coercively imposed on the British peripheries, comes to serve as the means of imperial absorption, it becomes an increasingly minimal basis for identifying Englishness. The peripheries, in comparison, struggle with the contradictions of [economic and political] underdevelopment, yet they retain their distinct, national and non-English character. Their very ways of speaking and using the English language remain highly distinctive, marked by a particular cultural and political history. In contrast, the language and cultural landscape of England come to seem ever paler, even to the English themselves.[8]

Whereas Trumpener imagines culture to function additively, with cultural models of greater or lesser intensity accumulating or canceling one another out, her account assumes both that the "culture" to which individual subjects are likely to cleave most closely is the one they experience as most vibrant and intense (as opposed to "pale") and also that such intensity might be experienced and produced and gauged objectively and absolutely, independent of their interaction with one another. The example of Hebrew makes it evident that insofar as the absence of a spoken language becomes most striking as a cultural oddity when language is competing with other cultural modes as a ground of social cohesion, the transparency—or in Trumpener's terms the "paleness"—of linguistic culture ought not to be understood as inhering in the nature of lnaugage itself but needs to be seen as a consequence of the local and historically specific relations of different conceptions of sociality. Moreover, to the extent that the normativity and self-evidence of spoken language as a mode of organizing culture become most palpable and most persuasive at the moment it is in flux, I propose that we can read the literary inventions that emerge from the anomalous condition of Hebrew not simply as aspiring to the condition of linguistic transparency but as intervening in

8. Katie Trumpener, *Bardic Nationalism: The Romantic Novel and the British Empire* (Princeton: Princeton University Press, 1997), 15–16.

and transforming the ways language operates as an instrument for organizing social relations.

Neither the emergence of the secular Hebrew culture exemplified by the writings of Abramovitch and Ben-Yehuda nor the ambivalence toward their status as works of *national* culture discernible within and between the two works can be properly understood without reference to the century-long political and intellectual movement that spawned them—the Haskalah, or Jewish Enlightenment (1781–1881). The movement's conditions of possibility originated outside the confines of the Jewish communities in the form of changes in the legal status accorded to Jews in their host nations: the Haskalah began with Prussian war minister Christian Wilhelm von Dohm's publication *Über die bürgerliche Verbesserung der Juden* [On the civic improvement of the Jews] in 1781[9] and Austrian emperor Joseph II's Patent of Toleration the following year, and it collapsed exactly a century later in 1881, with the explosion of widespread anti-Jewish violence in Russia, leading liberal Jewish intellectuals finally to abandon the Haskalah's moderate policy of emancipation in favor of the more radical solutions of Zionism and socialist Bundism.

Figuring the issue of Jewish political rights as the question "if and by what means the Jews can become morally and politically better than they are now,"[10] Dohm linked rights of citizenship to a notion of the human based in moral virtue. Whereas opponents of emancipation had argued that the Jews' moral decrepitude—characterized in terms ranging from the irrational superstition of their religious practices to their propensity for usury—necessarily precluded their participation in the German state, Dohm believed the state ought to be conceived as an instrument for bringing about Jewish moral regeneration. Not only was the Jews' lamentable character a result of their civic disabilities and their juridically enforced concentration in certain trades rather than any innate national degeneracy, but the experience of citizenship—the ennobling power of freedom and equality—would be essential to any moral transformation. In asserting the Jews' absolute, natural rights as citizens, Dohm departed from gradualist opponents who argued that Jews' political rights should be granted reciprocally—on condition they proved themselves morally capable of being citizens. For Dohm, the only conditions

9. Christian Wilhelm von Dohm, *Über die bürgerliche Verbesserung der Juden* [On the civic improvement of the Jews], 2 vols. (Berlin: F. Nicolai, 1781–83). Dohm, according to David Sorkin, was "an eminent practitioner of the early science of statistics." I discuss the persistent association between "the Jewish question" and the rise of statistical analysis later in this chapter. See Sorkin, *The Transformation of German Jewry: 1780–1840* (Oxford: Oxford University Press, 1987), 24.

10. Dohm, *Über die bürgerliche Verbesserung der Juden,* quoted in Sorkin, *Transformation of German Jewry,* 24.

for admission to citizenship were secular: "Our well established states must find every citizen acceptable who observes the laws and increases the state's wealth by his industry."[11] The specific debate over Jewish emancipation thus provided Dohm with an occasion to venture a more fundamental point about the nature of political power: the state was justified in intervening in civil society in the name of social liberalization insofar as it conceived of its role as one of educator, as an instrument for fulfilling a notion of human perfectibility.

But if the possibility of reform emerged from elsewhere, the terms within which the theological, political, intellectual, and institutional transformations that constituted the Haskalah were conceived came from within a history of Jewish thought. After the failure of the religious mystical movement of the false messiah Sabbetai Tsvi (1665–80) to provide the promised radical redemption of religious life, a less mystical, though still populist, alternative emerged in the form of the *musar* (ethical) literature of the late seventeenth and eighteenth centuries.[12] Central to the *musar* ideology was the *talmud hakham* (scholar) who, by virtue of his mastery of the Jewish legal and scriptural tradition, not only possessed intellectual and perhaps theological authority but necessarily stood as a living embodiment of the law, an authentication of the religious law he studied. Within such a system, study itself became identified with all religious virtues—a kind of behavior rather than a relation to a body of knowledge—but the *musar* tradition was able to serve as a guide to popular behavior expressly because study as a form of ethics was not limited to the *talmud hakham,* who was both embodiment and exemplar.

What is absolutely crucial for understanding the plans for educational reform generated out of the Haskalah's disillusionment with *musar* is the way the material rewards associated with the establishment of an official rabbinate produced a new kind of reading. From the retrospective position of the *maskilim* (adherents of the Haskalah) who rejected it, the new kind of reading, known as *pilpul* (talmudic casuistry), was based on the assumption that the rabbinical writings that constituted the Talmud were not to be understood as a straightforward series of questions and answers regarding the proper interpretation of the Bible that was its proof text but ought to be regarded as a complex web of diverging opinions and attitudes, no single moment of which could be understood without reference to the intricate and often elusive whole. Whereas such a system might seem "to maintain the unity of the Talmud and the integrity of its spiritual world," in Sorkin's account, this type

11. Ibid., 26.
12. Sorkin, *Transformation of German Jewry,* 45.

of reading in which "no statement was taken at face value" had the effect of institutionally undermining talmudic scholarship:

> Brilliance in casuistry became a path to rabbinic office in the sixteenth and seventeenth centuries, yet it had nothing to do with the conscientious scholarship that was the basis for actual legal decision. Prominence could be attained quickly without years of painstaking study. . . . Casuistry was used to reconcile legal prescriptions with actual practice, becoming a means to introduce lenient interpretations. But in its very practical application casuistry seemed to call the normative legal tradition into question. The casuist's subtle distinctions were not based on the literal meaning of the text, and thus departed from the accepted understanding of the law.[13]

In their calls for a return to the "plain" or literal meaning of the talmudic texts, the *maskilim* defended the integrity of an already completed text against the claims of new exemplary readership, against a mode of interpretation that treats the writtenness of the various rabbinical opinions as evidence of their fundamental synchronicity. Although the Talmud, a compendium of rabbinical opinion, did bring together a variety of interpretations into a single text, the discussions found within the text were in fact created over time as a series of responses and counterresponses and maintained this dialogic format even in their written form. The anti-*pilpul maskilim* contended that the interpretive excesses associated with *pilpul* were attempts to turn a communally produced text back into a thing of private authorship, an authorship of interpretation.[14]

This multiply contradictory status of Hebrew textual authority in the seventeenth and eighteenth centuries may account for the appearance of certain ideological simplifications in the program of educational reform the Haskalah writers articulated as a response to the rejection of *pilpul*. The shift away from casuistry to the plain meaning of the Talmud made its way into curricular reforms as a deemphasis on Talmud study generally in favor of direct study

---

13. Ibid., 48.

14. The historical paradox of the writtenness of the Talmud is certainly relevant in this context, but it is much too large and contested a topic to go into here. Suffice it to say that the rabbinical decision to write down the Talmud—the "oral law" contrasted with the "written law" of the Hebrew Bible—came only after vehement debate, when it was concluded that a *written* Talmud was necessary to preserve a Jewish community no longer concentrated in a single geographical area. Those who were opposed to writing down the oral law were in large part afraid of the development that the controversy over *pilpul* bears out: that writing down the law would fix what was meant to be a continuing process of interpretation and reinterpretation.

of the Bible.[15] While the *maskilim* did advocate making secular disciplines like history and natural science a more central part of a Jewish educational program, they maintained that such an emphasis marked a return to the intellectual spirit that had produced the Talmud itself, since discerning the literal meaning of many talmudic laws required solid grounding in mathematics, astronomy, and geography. For the *maskilim,* textual literalism is linked to scientific empiricism; it is only the casuists, with their persistent disdain for the literal, who have produced a Jewish intellectual parochialism that conceives of Jewish knowledge as wholly incompatible with, rather than partly distinct from, the scientific rationalism of the communities that surround it.

Their commitment to the ultimate compatibility of secular and revealed knowledge provided the *maskilim* with the general conceptual framework within which they advocated a limited revival of the Hebrew language. While the Haskalah's expansion of the linguistic capacity of Hebrew certainly contributed to the full revival of the language in the early decades of the twentieth century, the articulated goals of the early and late movements remained importantly distinct. The differences can be traced in large part to the Haskalah's fundamental commitment to a kind of pluralism of noncontradictory knowledges. Israel Bartal has observed:

> The vision of the Eastern European *Haskalah* was aimed not at *ending* the [traditional Jewish] diglossia but at *replacing* the two component languages: the state language or a European language (most commonly, German) for Yiddish, and biblical Hebrew for *leshon ha-kodesh* [literally, "the holy tongue," referring to the Hebrew of liturgy and religious composition]. . . . The *Haskalah* movement did not strive for monolingualism as a normal feature of a distinctive Jewish identity.[16]

But even as the Berlin *maskilim* envisioned a continued Jewish bilingualism, the vast majority refused to embrace the familiar European Enlightenment division of public and private languages according to which the fully emancipatable individual was the one who spoke the language of the dominant national culture in public, while speaking whatever language he or she desired within the home or local community. For most *maskilim,* Hebrew was a tool of modernization.[17] Although these intellectuals viewed Hebrew as a classical tongue, the sign of a golden age of national culture, and as a result sought to

15. See Moshe Pelli, "Did the *Maskilim* 'Hate the Talmud'?" in *The Age of Haskalah: Studies of Hebrew Literature of the Enlightenment in Germany* (Leiden: E. J. Brill, 1979), 48–72.

16. Israel Bartal, "From Traditional Bilingualism to National Monolingualism," in *Hebrew in Ashkenaz: A Language in Exile,* ed. Lewis Glinert (Oxford: Oxford University Press, 1993), 145.

17. Yaacov Shavit, "A Duty Too Heavy to Bear: Hebrew in the Berlin *Haskalah,* 1783–1819: Between Classic, Modern and Romantic," in Glinert, *Hebrew in Ashkenaz,* 119.

purify it by cleansing it of the residue of its postbiblical—that is, talmudic—linguistic forms, they also regarded translation *into* Hebrew as the means of giving heretofore narrowly educated Jews access to the burgeoning secular knowledge of science and philosophy. In making the case for linguistic reform, the *maskilim* argued that as long as the use of Yiddish defined the boundaries of the Jewish communal encounter with the outside world, not only was any coincident use of Hebrew politically irrelevant, but the Jewish public, as a Yiddish-speaking one, was itself condemned to political irrelevance.

But the *maskilim* did not choose to claim Jews' significance as political actors at the cost of their Jewishness by simply exchanging a politically deficient, constitutively unformed Yiddish public sphere for a German-speaking one, within whose economy political significance and Jewishness would remain opposed. In insisting on the power and significance of Hebrew as an instrument for understanding an external world whose elements are, at least theoretically, equally knowable to all, the *maskilim* implicitly offered new criteria for publicness, a publicness in which the common knowability of a common natural world would replace a public sphere whose terms of inclusion had been above all political and national. In this the *maskilim* might have seemed merely to be keeping faith with the basic tenets of European Enlightenment individualism. But in designating as a possible language of universal knowledge a language (Hebrew) other than the one that was spoken (German), the ideology of the Haskalah challenged what I hope to show is a central—yet necessarily unarticulated—aspect of Enlightenment philosophy: the presumption that the *capacity to speak* stands as the paradigm of knowing.[18] Once Hebrew becomes the language by which Jews might demonstrate their fitness as national subjects, politics is no longer an activity best done face-to-face, no longer an engagement that presumes geographical proximity.

The paradigmatic status of speech for Enlightenment thought followed from its capacity to designate knowledge of a potentially infinite array of historical circumstances while being limited by, or to, none of them. But this capacity to remain disentangled from the historical specificity of the object world depends on speech's freedom from historical marking. The marginality of the novel as a genre for the Haskalah (the favored prose form throughout most of the nineteenth century was an elaborately labored journalism of biblical-style Hebrew, and the first Hebrew novel did not appear until 1853)

18. There is, of course, a huge literature on this topic, especially surrounding the work of Jürgen Habermas, for whom the Enlightenment is characterized by its elevation of direct, transparent speech into a paradigm of Enlightenment sociality. See also the extensive recent work on the notion of "Republic of Letters" in eighteenth-century France.

thus seems to me not merely the result of the perceived inadequacies of the language. If the *maskilic* position on the limits of Hebrew, insofar as it bifurcated *spoken* linguistic knowledge from the knowledge of natural science, undermined the fundamental presumptions of the normative European novel, so too did the theoretical and actual instability of the Hebrew novel challenge the Haskalah's ardent hope for a universalism that would be no less Hebrew than German. It is the *good faith* of the *maskilim*'s commitment that lends a tragic dimension to their exposure of liberalism's insufficiency to its self-appointed role as the inclusive political organization of a human condition of shared knowledge.

It may be tempting to dismiss the battle between the *maskilim* and the casuists as "talmudic" in the most small *t,* parochial sense of the term: internecine, befogged by detail, and finally irrelevant to the large intellectual and social movements engaged and brought into being by European Enlightenment thinkers and their nineteenth-century inheritors. But the specific terms in which the *maskilim* frame their denigration of casuistry demonstrate that the dispute over which texts ought to be at the center of Jewish study and how those texts ought to be read can been seen both to participate in and to help produce paradigms of cultural authority that circulate well beyond European Jewish intellectual communities. In criticizing the casuists for reading the debates contained within the Talmud not as a diachronic series of questions, answers, and counterresponses but as a vast, synchronic textual tapestry, any threads of which might be drawn together in a pattern that would justify whatever cultural or institutional practice required legal sanction, the *maskilim* imply that "right reading"—and indeed a sound communal life—turns on the proper understanding of texts in time and of textuality as a temporal engagement, a site of negotiation with historicity for reader and writer alike.

I believe we can best understand the significance of the debate over talmudic *pilpul,* as well as the pedagogic program offered as an alternative to *pilpul* and finally the viable Hebrew novel that emerges as a response to the failed promise of the Haskalah, by considering the Talmud within a generic history where it is not conventionally read—the genre of the multiauthor text. I shall address the late eighteenth- and nineteenth-century debate about how to read the Talmud, as well as the modes of Hebrew literary production that emerged as a consequence of this debate, in relation to other texts that represent themselves as anthologies, as compendia of other texts (here Samuel Johnson's *Dictionary of the English Language* and Eliezer Ben-Yehuda's *Dictionary of the Hebrew Language, Ancient and Modern*). By thinking about it this way, we can see both the *pilpul* debate and Johnson's incorporation of multiple

literary examples into the format of his *Dictionary* as part of a single movement to figure cultural authority and social coherence as a relation to existing
texts, a relation to existing uses of language. Moreover, by tracing the ways
the Hebrew novel emerged from within the context of the *pilpul* debate, as
well as the novel's deliberate revision of and deviations from a European novelistic tradition, we can understand the realist novel to be engaging the very
issues of language and cultural authority raised by the multiauthor texts. Relocated within this genealogy, the realist novel, which juxtaposes the language
used by its characters in dialogue with the sometimes markedly different,
sometimes seemingly contiguous linguistic acts of the narrator, comes to appear a kind of "multiauthor text," [19] with the play between the linguistic authority of characters and narrators working to represent and rearticulate the
limits and possibilities associated with tying social connectedness to the fact
that people use the same language.

In figuring their own authority as a relation to the authority of existing
texts, anthologies like the Talmud and Johnson's *Dictionary* become the occasion for staging the question of how it matters to people in their daily uses
of language that a record of other people's uses of language is before them.
At once constituted as relations to texts and as generative of new texts and
textual authority themselves, these multiauthor forms join theory to practice
and thus offer themselves as something like ideological switching points, sites
where the prevailing cultural forces of both an existing corpus of writing and
a sociality founded on shared linguistic habits become not merely visible and
describable but subject to deliberate manipulation. But as the brief account
of the conflict between the *maskilim* and the casuists makes evident, the status of the textual—the question of what it means to understand oneself to
be using language in explicit relation, even response, to existing writing—
becomes a question precisely because so many different sorts of authority,
figured especially as various relations to temporality, accumulate around the
idea of the text. As we shall see, writing is variously represented as dematerialized, as a purely temporal mark of the pastness of an occasion of language
use, as a mark of the historical specificity of the linguistic act and its embed-
dedness in the web of question and answer of social function, and finally as
the mode of freeing itself and those who would produce and read it from the
vagaries of historical change.

Because the two dictionaries and Abramovitch's novel present their au-

---

19. I mean this multiple authorship as a deliberate formal effect rather than as the sort of unavoidable heteroglossia of the sort described by Mikhail Bakhtin. Bakhtin's formulation assumes that novels
can emerge only from within a culture saturated with varieties of language use, a presumption belied by
the case of the Hebrew novel.

thority as existing in oblique rather than transparent relation to writing, the works operate, to very different ends, to enlist the materiality of writing in order to challenge the authority of land, of geographical place, as the self-evident material ground of social commonness. And once common geographical space has been rendered a contingent rather than a self-announcing foundation of the national likeness, other relations that undergird the political economy of English liberalism—and the representational logic of the realist novel—are disrupted as well. The category of labor no longer functions unproblematically to attach individual subjects to the common space of the nation, and language is no longer easily envisioned as just another form of labor, one whose diachronic history of production might be subsumed in the self-evident presence of place. If the decline in the authority of the landed gentry to represent the interests of the whole of England leads Johnson to assemble an "English" language comprising the fragments of existing texts that can act in its stead, the example of the Hebrew novel, in which fragments of texts do not simply assume the abstract function of the nation but indeed literally constitute its space, troubles the terms of Johnson's solution. In this context the Jews of the Haskalah period and beyond, who understand their relation to one another to depend not on common civil institutions or a shared geographical space but on a shared set of texts, work as a sociological enactment of the multiauthor text. As such, Jews become the discursive and social locus around which social authority and historicity come to be recognized as contingent and hence manipulable—as national, in short—in post-Enlightenment Europe.

Samuel Johnson and the Labor of Language

Among both scholars of Samuel Johnson and historians of lexicography, it is by now a commonplace to read his 1755 "Preface to the *Dictionary*" as a document of its author's fall into a kind of moderate pragmatism. The grand gestures of his 1747 *Plan of a Dictionary of the English Language*—to supply "new rules . . . for pronunciation [and thereby] to provide that the harmony of the moderns will be more permanent"—give way under the pressure of two very different lexicographical traumas: his confrontation with the vast and unwieldy mass of material that seemed plausibly to lay claim to being part of English usage and his break with the project's early patron, Lord Chesterfield.[20] In a well-known anecdote in Boswell's *Life of Johnson*, John-

20. Samuel Johnson, *The Plan of a Dictionary in the English Language: Addressed to the Right Honourable Philip Dormer, Earl of Chesterfield* (London: J. and P. Knapton, T. Longman, and T. Shewell,

son boasted that whereas it had taken the forty members of the Académie Française forty years to produce their *Dictionnaire,* he would single-handedly complete his own *Dictionary* in three.[21] In fact it took him closer to nine. But if Johnson was chastened by his failure to live up to his own blustering prognostications, the sheer vastness and unassimilability of his material presented him with an opportunity to assert a new kind of power, one that no longer took the orderliness of the English language to be a quality discoverable in the *words* of English. The research and composition appear to have transformed Johnson's sense of his own authority as a dictionary maker from one derived from the largesse of an external patron to one founded in his own reading and writing. We should not, however, be too quick to assume that Johnson's newfound sense of his self-generated authority as the creator of the *Dictionary* led him to extend the same power of linguistic self-authorization to the English men and women whom he imagined either as potential users of his dictionary or as writers or speakers of English.

For Johnson, not all uses—or users—of English are created equal or considered equally worthy of being codified in that "pragmatic" document to which he appended his famous "Preface to the *Dictionary.*" Not only does he deliberately—if not entirely straightforwardly—distinguish between written and spoken English in terms of the cultural authority that should accrue to each, but he also conceives of the entire field of activity organized around the use of the English language as a realm unto itself, discontinuous from the other sorts of behavior along whose lines social relations might be organized and categorized. If Johnson is reluctant to extend the authority he appropriates for himself as he plows through text after text on his way to gathering the heap of literary examples that will become the *Dictionary,* his reluctance, I maintain, is not simply the result of a desire to consolidate the prerogative of his own text, or even an attempt to constitute the category of professional writer. Rather, Johnson distinguishes between the authority of the text of the *Dictionary* and the authority of those who would make use of it (or ignore it altogether in favor of their own habits of speech) as part of his effort to install language use as the constitutive activity of the nation, the behavior that brings

---

1747); quoted in Howard D. Weinbrot, "Samuel Johnson's *Plan* and *Preface to the Dictionary:* The Growth of a Lexicographer's Mind," in *New Aspects of Lexicography: Literary Criticism, Intellectual History and Social Change,* ed. Howard D. Weinbrot (Carbondale: Southern Illinois University Press, 1972), 82. See also Allen Reddick, *The Making of Johnson's Dictionary, 1746–1773* (Cambridge: Cambridge University Press, 1990), and James H. Sledd and Gwin J. Kolb, *Dr. Johnson's Dictionary: Essays in the Biography of a Book* (Chicago: University of Chicago Press, 1955). De Witt Starnes and Gertrude E. Noyes, *The English Dictionary from Cawdrey to Johnson* (Amsterdam: John Benjamins, 1991), offers a history of the dictionary from a more technically linguistic perspective.

21. Boswell, quoted in Reddick, *Making of Johnson's Dictionary,* 15.

the social into being.[22] In identifying the fundamental social activity as the power to use language, Johnson's *Dictionary,* its "Preface" included, is able to shift the definition of "nationality" from an ongoing, temporally diffuse set of activities into a kind of identity, transporting the locus of such nationality from the social unit as a whole to the individual subjects who constitute the nation. In effecting this transformation, Johnson attempts to imagine a model of subjectivity that not only would remain free of the sorts of historical vagaries he saw as plaguing the English language before his own lexicographical intervention but would be able to absorb and subsume all sorts of non-linguistic historical events. By engineering this redefinition of sociality from activity to identity, moreover, Johnson's *Dictionary* attempts to sort out the contradictions that trouble the notion of public culture newly emerging in the eighteenth century.

As will quickly become apparent, Johnson's characterizations of both the English language he is gathering and the methods he employs to bring order to this language are rife with contradictions. In the pointedly digressive excursis that is the "Preface," Johnson details a variety of contradictory accounts of the materiality of language and its consequent relation to time: writing is both like and unlike labor; language is both produced laboriously through history and developed into effortlessly; writing ideally represents speech and is most stably material in its achievement of this transparent representation. Rather than marking the incoherence of Johnson's conception of the English language, these contradictions are just what enables the category of language to produce a sense of a common "Englishness" that landed property or abstract labor are no longer able to ground. By suspending these contradictions, language transforms Englishness from a set of ongoing and disputed social and political relations mediated by institutions into a kind of individually manifested, deinstitutionalized identity.

Johnson's effort in the "Preface" is to displace a sociality of labor by a linguistic identity. To embark on such an effort too strenuously—to allow it, in short, to appear too labored—would undo the force of the substitution. Johnson's persuasive tools are thus of necessity as much tonal as logical: whereas the 1747 *Plan,* written as Johnson was preparing to begin work on the *Dictionary,* loudly heralded its power to fix and regularize the historical accidents of the English language, the "Preface," written at the conclusion of his labors, presents the dictionary writer as a reluctant toiler. He ends his

---

22. Although she argues for the constitutive role of the Celtic fringe in defining British national identity, Katie Trumpener, in *Bardic Nationalism,* has characterized linguistic nationalism as a kind of "minimalist" grounds of cultural unity. I believe it is precisely this transparent quality of the linguistic that gives it its power to underwrite culture.

lexicographical labors not, as we might anticipate, by looking on the goodness, or at least the efficacy, of what he has done but by lamenting the necessity of the project and turning, not without a certain wistfulness, to a world
in which his labor would not even have been necessary:

> The language most likely to continue long without alteration, would be that of a
> nation raised a little, and but a little, above barbarity, secluded from strangers, and
> totally employed in procuring the conveniences of life; either *without books,* or like
> some of the Mahometan countries, with very few: men thus busied and unlearned,
> having only such words as common use requires, would perhaps long continue to
> express the same notions by the same signs. But no such constancy can be expected
> in a people polished by arts, and classed by subordination, where one part of the
> community is sustained and accommodated by the labour of the other. Those who
> have much leisure to think, will always be enlarging the stock of ideas, and every
> increase of knowledge, whether real or fancied, will produce new words, or combi-
> nations of words. When the mind is unchained from necessity, it will range after
> convenience; when it is left at large in the fields of speculation, it will shift opinions;
> as any custom is disused, the words that expressed it must perish with it; as any
> opinion grows popular, it will innovate speech in the same proportion as it alters
> practice. (25–26)

In this account, linguistic instability is the consequence—if not quite the
"product"—of a condition of leisure made possible by the labor of others.
This divided labor system ("a people . . . classed by subordination") offers
certain of its members a freedom from the necessity of laboring that paradoxically results in the *necessary* production of new ideas and the language to
represent them. If those whose "minds are unchained by necessity" boast a
certain freedom from labor, they nevertheless seem as historical actors to be
moving under some kind of compulsion. To the extent that these leisured
actors are viewed not as individual subjects but as one element within a larger
matrix of social relations, their behavior of "enlarging the stock of ideas" to
produce "new words or combinations of words" appears a great deal like
just another sort of labor, with simply an immaterial rather than a material
"stock" to point to for their efforts. Here writing seems to be a form of *labor*
when viewed from the perspective of the entire society and a form of *leisure*
when viewed from the perspective of the individual subject. (Notice how
those with the freedom to indulge in the leisure-time activity of idea production lose their status as identifiable grammatical subjects as their ideas gain
not only syntactic authority but motive power in an elaborate chain of causality.) The intellectual activity of language production thus is at once outside
the system of divided labor (the product of a "leisure" set against others'

labor) and the paradigmatic form of that labor. Leisure, "ranging after convenience," becomes both the enabling ground and the goal of intellectual production. As the distinguishing sign of a system of divided labor, writing is both accidentally and necessarily synecdochal; it announces the fact of specialization insofar as it is one profession among many, yet it also marks and brings about a certain stage of development into a condition of civilization and economic specialization. By this second account, the division of labor comes into being with the historical emergence of the professional writer.

In John Barrell's account of eighteenth-century England, the era's politics are generated out of a loss of confidence in the capacity of gentlemen landowners to act in the interest of the nation as a whole. If the mere fact of landed wealth no longer functions as self-evident proof of the gentry's long-term, and hence "public," investment in the fate of England, then such gentlemen must produce some other grounds to guarantee their capacity to represent the nation at large:

> If the gentleman is described as a man of no determinate occupation, it must seem that any degree of participation on his part in the affairs of society must compromise him, must oblige him to descend from the elevated viewpoint his status and leisure define for him. . . . But if he does nothing, he can learn nothing: his ownership of land will give him at best a potential to grasp the relations in a complex society, but one which can never be fulfilled.[23]

Barrell's account offers an illuminating context within which the paradoxes of Johnson's "Preface" become recognizable, if not altogether resolvable. Johnson describes a mode of social organization in which labor and leisure are less ontologies than epistemologies, less objective descriptions of a certain kind of behavior or activity than alternative ways of reading the relation between the experiences, values, and interests of individual subjects and those of the society as a whole. In Barrell's view, writing is directly assimilable into the analysis he offers, a form of labor like any other, with Johnson's *Dictionary* to be understood as a concerted effort to create the idea of a national language common to all English men and women by reference to a shared "custom" that in point of fact excludes spoken language as the language of the working classes. By this account the *Dictionary* does not solve the theoretical problem at issue in eighteenth-century England's new politics of the market (If the general interest is to be produced out of the interaction of the private interests of individual subjects, then what is the perspective

23. John Barrell, *English Literature in History, 1730–1780: An Equal, Wide Survey* (London: Hutchinson, 1983), 136.

202 / Chapter Three

from which such a general interest might be discerned?) so much as it cuts
through the conundrum. In constituting a dictionary of the English language
out of words collected exclusively from *writings* in the language, Johnson
does not locate a general interest but instead renders the partial interests of
those who write—the leisured—synecdochal for the interests of the whole.
Johnson need not make a case for the particular representativeness of writing
because his *Dictionary* makes other forms of language disappear or, more
aptly, slide into silence.

But if we look more closely at the elaboration of the relation between writing and labor in the "Preface," we will see that simply to treat writing as one
sort of labor among others—as a sort of labor that, like others, can be imbued with value from the perspective of the individual subject or that of the
social whole—is to overlook both the particular qualities Johnson attributes
to writing and the complexity of the *Dictionary* itself as a political intervention. The ambiguity surrounding the designation of writing as labor is closely
related to the shiftiness the "Preface" shows on the materiality of language
itself. Johnson's justification of the limits of his lexicographical project, which
occurs a few pages before the passage we have been examining, turns on just
this ambiguity:

> That many terms of art and manufacture are omitted, must be frankly acknowl-
> edged; but for this defect I may boldly allege that it was unavoidable: I could not
> visit caverns to learn the miner's language, nor take a voyage to perfect my skill in
> the dialect of navigation, nor visit the warehouses of merchants, and shops of arti-
> ficers, to gain the names of wares, tools and operations, of which no mention is
> found in books; what favourable accident, or easy enquiry brought within my
> reach, has not been neglected; but it had been a hopeless labour to glean up words,
> by courting living information, and contesting with the sullenness of one, and the
> roughness of another.[24]

Here the language of art and manufacture is omitted from the *Dictionary*
because it fails to attain the status of language, that is, because it is indistinguishable from the variety of labor that produces it. For most of the passage,
Johnson justifies his failure to include this language of commerce not strictly
in terms of language but in terms of the inaccessibility of the crafts themselves. While Johnson implies that such commercial language is inaccessible
because the activities that produce it are themselves inaccessible, the very im-
plicitness of the logic is rhetorically crucial in producing the conflation of the

---

24. Johnson, "Preface to the *Dictionary*," in *Johnson's Dictionary: A Modern Selection*, ed. E. L.
McAdam Jr. and George Milne (New York: Pantheon, 1963), 22.

language of arts and manufacture and the *labors* of miners, merchants, and artificers. And if it is the particularities of Johnson's own *language* that render the language of others so material as to be not quite language—inaccessible on the grounds of the inaccessibility of the labor with which they are associated—then it follows from the paradoxical systematic ambiguity that when Johnson does make specific reference to language ("the *names* of wares, tools and operations *of which no mention is found in books*"; emphasis added), language becomes like material labor—and hence not quite language—insofar as it remains immaterial, spoken rather than "found in books."

Johnson engineers two transformations in the movement between this passage and the last. First, the changeability of the English language—the condition Johnson claimed was motivating the dictionary project—is redescribed from being a consequence of writing to being a consequence of speech. Whereas in the previous passage the existence of "books" was the mark of an economy of divided labor and consequently of the existence of a segment of the population with leisure time to devote to the sort of intellectual pursuits that make languages change, here the ephemerality of language is attributed to *unwritten* language (those "names of wares, tools and operations of which no mention is found in books") associated with a laboring class rather than a leisured class. Second, and relatedly, *writing* itself comes to assume two very different sorts of functions. On the one hand, as in the first passage, writing functions symbolically, as a mark of a general state of civilization, part of a given society's movement from barbarism to civilization. On the other hand, writing works over time to stabilize language, to prevent the significant history and ideas of a society from diffusing into the silent air like so much artisanal ephemera. In the first sense writing becomes the *sign* of a certain relation to temporality, a stage of historical development, but is not itself related to time. In the second case writing is defined precisely in terms of its relation to time, as something that can be apprehended through time, marking time by way of its insensibility to it. Both with regard to its shifting relation to the changefulness of language characteristic of civilization at a certain stage of development and with regard to its dual relation to temporality, writing for Johnson is marked in ways that make it not entirely assimilable to the social logic articulated around labor during this period. Language is thus comparable to labor without being quite identical to it, and it is this capacity to perform the "work" of constituting society without quite itself being work that defines the terms within which language's emergence as an organizational principle comes to matter politically.

Moreover, as we shall see, the contradictions that structure Johnson's "Preface"—language is both like and not like labor, writing is both like speech and different from it—turn out to be the contradictions around which the fictionality of the realist novel is structured. Novels boast language that is written and spoken at once (dialogue) and that is like and unlike labor: it "merely" represents labor and yet, to the extent that the fictional representation is plausible and compelling, becomes identical to labor. If the incoherencies that emerge around Johnson's effort to create a dictionary of the English language are rendered tractable by the fictional logic of realism, considering the dictionary and the novel as different generic approaches to a single complex of cultural issues allows us to see the occlusions and disputable foundational principles by which the realist novel is able to achieve its particular efficacy. What in Johnson's "Preface" looks like terminological slipperiness, a kind of rhetorical sleight of hand, becomes visible in the novel as the category of fiction itself, a fact that appears to resolve the tension between the individual agency represented within the novel in the form of speech acts and the common language within which such agency is represented by refusing to choose between them.

Johnson's contention that the emergence of writing, and the linguistic instability that follows from writing, can be read as the evidence of a given society's general state of development entrenches the "Preface" firmly within the Scottish Enlightenment's four-stage model of human development, theorized by thinkers such as William Robertson, John Millar, and Dugald Stewart and receiving its most influential elaboration in books 3 and 5 of Adam Smith's *Wealth of Nations*. This evolutionary model of history, which identifies four stages of socioeconomic development through which societies inevitably pass—hunting, pasture, agriculture, and commerce—is notable for its insistence on linking a society's mode of economic subsistence with its distribution of power and forms of social interdependence. Smith's *Wealth of Nations* famously offers the example of native North Americans who, as hunters and gatherers of uncultivated fruits of the earth, not only exemplify the "lowest and rudest" stage of development but are also characterized by a high degree of personal liberty, since their lack of economic interdependence or private property makes elaborate political institutions unnecessary.[25]

The evolutionary quality of this model, Katie Trumpener asserts, effec-

25. For a good general account of the emergence and circulation of this discourse see R. H. Campbell and A. S. Skinner's introduction to Adam Smith, *An Inquiry into the Nature and Causes of the Wealth of Nations* (Oxford: Oxford University Press, 1976). See also Istvan Hont and Michael Ignatieff, eds., *Wealth and Virtue: The Shaping of Political Economy in the Scottish Enlightenment* (Cambridge: Cambridge University Press, 1983). For a reading of the appropriations of this universalist model by more explicitly nationalist writers of late eighteenth- and early nineteenth-century Ireland and Scotland, see Trumpener, *Bardic Nationalism*, 28.

tively "emphasiz[es] the inevitability with which each developmental stage, each historical culture is replaced by the next, more advanced one. What shapes, destroys and replaces cultural formations is an apparently impersonal, endlessly recurring historical process."[26] Within this discourse, clearly, the unit of historical action on which change is registered is the society—for Johnson, the unit whose advancement and economic interdependence is registered by the proliferation of writing and the linguistic instability that follows from this proliferation. Given this essential arc of development, the progress of different societies at any given moment can be measured and explained by a process of comparison. But as James Chandler has recently claimed, the very notion of "uneven development" by which the four-stage theory of development packs its analytical punch depends on a fundamental historiographical contradiction. For the condition of different societies to be registered as "uneven," a common measure must be established, and for *that* to happen, the unit of analysis by which such a comparison might be made needs to be generalized from one historical stage to all four. "The unevenness implicit in the code, one might say, depends dialectically on the evenness implicit in the analogy, and vice versa."[27] If, as the Scottish Enlightenment thinkers would have it, the sense of history is itself subject to historical change, then some historically specific version of history needs to be emphasized over others before any comparison can take place. So whereas the North American Indians Smith cites are characterized by their relatively weak ties to one another—indeed, it might legitimately be said that they do not quite constitute a "society"—that the societal, in its strong, deeply interdependent sense, is the fundamental unit of historical action and measurement across all four developmental stages implies that in the latter half of the eighteenth century the appeal to history cannot be separated from a certain vision of social interconnectedness.

In relocating the site of linguistic instability from the writing of the leisured class to the all too fleeting speech of miners, sailors, and artisans, Johnson implicitly transforms his working definition of writing. As a form of leisure writing functions symbolically, as the immediately apprehensible mark of a general stage of advanced development registered by and upon the social unit as a whole; but as a form of labor figured in contrast with the transitory speech of the working class, writing matters as it is apprehensible through time. Indeed, it is the very means by which ideas and words might be made

26. Trumpener, *Bardic Nationalism*, 29.
27. James Chandler, *England in 1819: The Politics of Literary Culture and the Case of Romantic Historicism* (Chicago: University of Chicago Press, 1998); quotation on 100.

discernible over time, might be made permanent. Writing serves both as a common denominator—a transhistorical ground of comparison—and as the thing being compared whose meaning changes over time. Writing is able to perform both these tasks at once in that it turns agency from a mode of change to one of nonchange.

If in one regard Johnson considers the dividedness of contemporary England's labor to be what renders the English language all too changeable, in another regard such dividedness presumes that its subjects have a keen sense of the temporal extendability of labor and the products of labor. In the terms of Scottish Enlightenment thinkers like Smith, individual laborers would not be willing to participate in a system of divided labor, producing much more of any single sort of wares than they could consume themselves, unless they were able to imagine those wares being convertible into commodities. That is, laborers engaged in one sort of task must understand their labor as being convertible into a form (money) that would allow them to exchange the direct products of their labor for goods (products of labor located elsewhere in this divided system) they do need.[28] To imagine one's labor as convertible, however indirectly, into the products of someone else's labor is to imagine the persistence of one's labor through time, as writing—an activity made writing—a text.

At the moment he refuses to assimilate writing to a more general model of labor, then, Samuel Johnson transforms his *Dictionary* from a project of capturing and preserving the products of Englishness to remaking the very terms of measurement. By insisting, at least sometimes, that labor is characterized by an ephemerality that pointedly distinguishes it from writing, Johnson offers a model of society alternative to the processual, diachronic one that lurks disquietingly (for him) within his description of divided labor. Working the limits of the paradoxical logic that his own divided account of divided labor helps make visible, Johnson offers a version of the sociality he would call Englishness in which the very emphemerality of individual subjects' labor turns the quality of being part of that society from an action into an identity. If labor here disappears in the instant those jabbering artisans halt their exertions, then the social need no longer be understood as brought into being in order to keep people linked to one another long enough to make one person's labor useful to someone else.

The *Dictionary* will be able to bring about this transmutation—this alchemy of varied labor into laborers, into Englishmen—only by distinguishing among *different sorts* of writing. The *Dictionary* marks good writing off from bad, finding distinctions where others would see none. By the time he writes the "Preface" Johnson has at least outwardly repudiated his earlier ambition to fix the meanings of the words he gathers into his dictionary, but he is far less sanguine about the variability of the writing itself. For Johnson, the orthography (spelling) of the words, rather than their etymology, should provide the basis for any regularizing of the language the *Dictionary* undertakes. What matters is not what a word originally meant, but how it was originally written. Johnson's discussion of orthography turns on a somewhat elusive distinction he draws between accidental and original irregularities in spelling:

> In adjusting the *orthography*, which has been to this time unsettled and fortuitous, I found it necessary to distinguish those irregularities that are inherent in our tongue, and perhaps coeval with it, from others which the ignorance or negligence of later writers has produced. . . .
>
> As language was at its beginning merely oral, all words of necessary or common use were spoken before they were written; and while they were unfixed by any visible signs, must have been spoken with great diversity. . . . When this wild and barbarous jargon was first reduced to an alphabet, every penman endeavoured to express, as he could, the sounds which he was accustomed to pronounce or to receive, and vitiated in writing such words as were already vitiated in speech.[29]

The sly, idiosyncratic skew of the binary "original" ("those irregularities inherent in our tongue and perhaps coeval with it") versus "accidental" ("others which the ignorance or negligence of later writers has produced") suggests and undoes the logic of each. Whereas irregularities of the first type seem worth preserving because their chronological precocity lends them a quality of necessity, or inherence, by the second half of the sentence it is the "ignorance and negligence" of the writers, rather than their belatedness, that appears to be the source of "the improprieties and absurdities, which it is the duty of the lexicographer to correct or proscribe." But as Johnson details a narrative of origin designed to elaborate the distinction between desirable and undesirable irregularities, the source of authoritative writing becomes less self-evident, not more so. Having begun his discussion on orthography by distinguishing between an originary and necessary orthography and an accidental sort, Johnson goes on to admit that *no* writing has an inherent, necessary, or original relation to language. "As language was at its beginning merely oral," all writing turns out to be not an instance of language but a

29. Johnson, "Preface," 4–5.

representation, the representation of speech in writing, like so much novelistic dialogue. So whereas the passage begins by privileging a chronological priority, the elaboration of the distinction apparently disrupts these terms, since the best sort of writing is the writing that is no act of language at all. Indeed, as the second paragraph continues, what becomes clear is that the writing that requires expurgation is the writing that asserts a chronological priority, that stands as a language act itself rather than merely representing speech. The irregularities produced by "ignorance or negligence" are those produced by writing that is deliberate. Accidental writing turns out to be writing that is willed by the writer.

So while Johnson begins by locating the value of writing in its persistence over time, a description that might have associated writing with a system of divided labor in which the value of an individual's labor lies in the promise of its usefulness at some other time, Johnson's turn to orthography recharacterizes writing once again. With orthography, or at least Johnson's version of it, writing matters not because it persists over time but because it occurs at no time, its essential secondariness removing it altogether from a system of divided labor and from history. Johnson rectifies the danger posed to a society pulled together around the differentiation of its labor—that it is not able to represent itself at any single moment as capable of supplying its own needs—by positing a society organized around writing that is not quite a historical event: the record of an act of speech. Johnson can thus imagine a society likewise constituted without beginning or end. By appealing to the principles of an orthography that turns writing from a temporal process into a text, into writing without a writer, as the ground of social unity, Johnson offers a vision of sociality that, because it exists in time at all, can be tied to a population, made a form of identity rather than a diachronic cluster of social practices. Paradoxically, then, it is only by detaching writing from writers and turning it into a pointedly ahistorical textuality that Johnson is able to make writing into a thing that individuals use and are defined by using. The puzzling inconsistency we began with—Johnson implies that writing is both a kind of labor and a kind of leisure—thus turns out to reflect not his inattention but his need for *both* to be true. Understood as a form of *leisure,* writing is never quite an act and thus remains outside history; understood as a form of *labor,* it becomes something individual subjects can understand as a ground of their private identities.

And if Johnson takes delineating his orthographic method as an opportunity to theorize about this redefinition of sociality, we can read his orthographic practice of creating writing without writers as the blueprint for his dictionary project as a whole. The major formal innovation of Johnson's *Dic-*

tionary is its copious use of illustrative literary quotations to supplement the descriptive definitions of words, a format he adopts from the great Italian and French national dictionaries corporately written by the Accadèmia della Crusca and the Académie Française but that was wholly unprecedented within English lexicographic history.[30] By his own account, Johnson takes on his dictionary project in part to make a case for the equivalent linguistic richness of English, as well as in answer to calls from Pope, Addison, and Swift for the establishment of an English language academy to standardize and preserve the language. In the "Preface," Johnson explains that over the course of the *Dictionary*'s production he significantly revised his notion of how the quoted literary examples ought to work. Whereas he had originally desired that "every quotation should be useful to some other end than the illustration of a word"—that each should impart some moral or scientific truth, "all that is pleasing or useful in English literature"—by the time the *Dictionary* is published the illustrative quotations have been, in large part, "reduce[d] . . . to clusters of words." Johnson works as an individual rather than as a member of a language academy, and he emphatically lifts the texts from their iterative contexts, paring them down so as to produce something resembling his ideal of writing without a writer.[31] In assuming the authority of an *editor* by generating a text that is unlike any previously existing text yet cannot quite be said to be written by him or anyone else, Johnson produces the *Dictionary* as writing written by no one and in so doing produces himself as exactly the kind of new subject, an identity without labor, he has been theorizing. In choosing to truncate rather than selectively eliminate the illustrative quotations that in early drafts conveyed a sense independent of their formal function, he turns the *Dictionary* into a text, a compendium of already existing writing, and creates a text written at leisure, erasing the authorial labor that went into all the writing quoted there.[32] What might appear to be a proprietary, even authorial pride in the efficiency of his production of the *Dictionary*

30. Reddick, *Making of Johnson's Dictionary,* 14–15. One of the most significant points of historical intersection between the dictionaries of Johnson and Eliezer Ben-Yehuda, whose work I will examine in the next section, is the common influence, explicitly acknowledged by Ben-Yehuda, of the French lexicographic tradition. See Ben-Yehuda, "Yetsirat milim hadashot b'lashonenu" [The creation of new words in our language], in *Ha-halom v'shevaro* [The dream and its fulfillment: Selected writings on language of Eliezer Ben-Yehuda], ed. Reuven Sivan (Jerusalem: Mossad Bialik, 1978), 175–85.

31. Johnson, "Preface," 17. For an interesting reading of the role of the notion of "anthology" in constituting romantic and postromantic notions of aesthetic authority see Philip Fisher, "A Museum with One Work Inside," *Keats-Shelley Journal* 33 (1984): 85–102.

32. Frederic Bogel argues that Johnson's interest in divided sorts of literary authority like biography and editorship was part of his fundamental ambivalence about authorship and authority. See Bogel, "Johnson and the Role of Authority," in *The New Eighteenth Century,* ed. Felicity Nussbaum and Laura Brown (New York: Routledge, 1987), 189–209.

thus becomes at once more and less than that: the paring away of writers and discourses into pure writing, an editorial imperiousness that is at the same time a self-erasure, a disappearance staged by Johnson for the promise of ballooning out to timelessness.

But while Johnson imagines the transformative power of his dictionary project to lie in the paradox of his editorship, the unfolding of that editorship—the history of the reception of Johnson's own text—proves less an instantaneous escape from history by the crossing and recrossing of logically contradictory models of labor and textuality than the narrative of a successive movement from one preexisting and only partly adequate model of language making to another. Speaking on "The Evolution of English Lexicography" at Oxford on 22 June 1900, James A. H. Murray, editor of the recently published *Oxford English Dictionary,* opens his lecture with an anecdote about Johnson's *Dictionary:*

> When the "Act to facilitate the provision of Allotments for the Labouring Classes" was before the House of Commons in 1887, a well-known member for a northern constituency asked the Minister who had charge of the measure for a definition of the term *allotment* which occurred so often in the bill. The Minister somewhat brusquely told his interrogator to "look in the Dictionary," at which there was, according to the newspapers, "a laugh." The member warmly protested that, being called upon to consider a measure dealing with things therein called "Allotments," a term not known to English Law, nor explained in the Bill itself, he had a right to ask for a definition. But the only answer he received was "Johnson's Dictionary! Johnson's Dictionary!" at which, according to the newspapers, the House gave "another laugh," and the interrogator subsided. The real humour of the situation, which was unfortunately lost upon the House of Commons, was, that as agricultural allotments had not been thought of in the days of Dr. Johnson, no explanation of the term in this use is to be found in Johnson's Dictionary; as however, this happened to be unknown, alike to the questioner and to the House, the former missed a chance of "scoring" brilliantly, and the House the chance of a third laugh, this time at the expense of the Minister. But the replies of the latter are typical of the notions of a large number of persons, who habitually speak of "the Dictionary," just as they do of "the Bible" or "the Prayer-book," or "the Psalms"; and who, if pressed as to the authorship of these works, would certainly say that "the Psalms" were composed by David, and "the Dictionary" by Dr. Johnson.

Murray continues:

> For, the English Dictionary, like the English Constitution, is the creation of no one man, and of no one age; it is a growth that has slowly developed itself down the

ages. Its beginnings lie far back in times almost prehistoric. And these beginnings themselves, although the English Dictionary of to-day is lineally developed from them, were neither Dictionaries, nor even English.[33]

Murray offers a version of language in which timelessness and authorlessness go hand in hand. With the juxtaposition of the evidentiary mode around the noncommittal semicolon taking the place of any causal claims, Murray describes an English whose lack of origin stands as evidence for the language's incapacity to be authored. The creation of "no one man," English becomes by Murray's grammatical sleight of hand no one's creation and consequently uncreatable. Because language is made at no time in particular, it can be made by no one and hence becomes equally everyone's.[34]

In a marked departure from Johnson's own writing about the *Dictionary,* Murray is openly scornful of the dueling partisans of the House for their failure to keep in mind that "the Dictionary" is in fact "Johnson's," and that as a consequence the English they discover, or fail to discover, within is *dated* both literally and figuratively. But though Murray might at first glance appear simply to adopt Johnson's language as his own, in fact he does so with an

33. James A. H. Murray, "The Romanes Lecture 1900: The Evolution of English Lexicography," reprinted in *International Journal of Lexicography* 6, 2 (1993): 101. Subsequent passages will be cited in parentheses within the text. For a biography of Murray, the first editor of the *Oxford English Dictionary,* see K. M. Elisabeth Murray, *Caught in the Web of Words: James Murray and the Oxford English Dictionary* (New Haven: Yale University Press, 1977). See also John Willinsky, *Empire of Words: The Reign of the OED* (Princeton: Princeton University Press, 1995).

34. Murray's articulated conclusion implies that from this anecdote about how a gathering of British MPs uses Johnson's *Dictionary* we are meant to learn that it does not matter how one chooses to use it, since the same ongoing changefulness that makes the *Dictionary* unauthorable would make any particular act of using it insignificant. But the details of the anecdote provide another story—or stories. The conclusion at which Murray arrives—that the *Dictionary,* like the Psalms, the Bible, or the Prayer Book, is "the creation of no one man"—follows from the anecdote's illustration that people speak of and use it as though it had no author. But if Murray's anecdote purports to show what the *Dictionary* means by showing how people use it, it is striking that the incident he chooses to illustrate the illuminating power of the popular use of the *Dictionary* is one in which the *Dictionary* is never in fact "used." Or to be more accurate, the use made here of the *Dictionary* constitutes an invocation of its authority that makes perusing the text not only unnecessary but counterproductive. The bluff conclusions of the passage's end thus take up, rather than diffuse, the manner of a bluff; the early part of the narration presents a situation in which the changefulness of the language, far from precluding the individual authorship of dictionaries, makes that authorship all too apparent. Whereas Johnson laid claim to creating a dictionary that presents a language without beginning or end by virtue of having been written by no one, the dictionary that Murray's MPs gesture toward, if they do not quite use, marks its status as the work of an individual author by the datedness of its language; its condition of not being quite started is announced by the (undiscovered) absence of a definition of "allotment." Because they forget that the *Dictionary* was written by Samuel Johnson, recalling his authorship only "if pressed," they are quick to assume, first, that the English language, in its excessiveness to the authorial wranglings of any individual subject, remains fundamentally unchanged by the movement of history and second, that its ongoingness allows it to function as the foundation for the more transient human activity of lawmaking.

important difference. Whereas Johnson argues that it is the authorlessness of the writing constituting his *Dictionary* that makes the English language ongoing and therefore outside history, for Murray it is the authorlessness of the writing of the *Dictionary* itself that constitutes the near lack of origin of the *dictionary form.* Whereas Johnson's call to arms identifies the constitution and *language* of England ("we have long preserved our constitution, let us make some struggles for our language"), Murray's analogy, less hortatory than descriptive, equates the English constitution and the English *dictionary.* In refusing to assume an identity between the text of the *Dictionary* and some abstract, not quite definable entity "the English language," Murray implies that if the English dictionary and the English language are finally identical to one another, it is not because of what the dictionary is but because of what it does. In tying the meaning of the dictionary not to the ongoing writerlessness of the English language but to the ongoing, writerless genealogy of the dictionary form, and by insisting in his anecdote on the separability of the authority of the *Dictionary* and the ways it is used, Murray effectively redefines the dictionary as the site of an event, a relation between text and reader. Within the terms of Murray's revision, the mere fact that no particular writer can be assigned to a text is no longer evidence of that text's removal from historical process. Writing becomes one way among many of using language rather than a self-generating, self-sustaining system for organizing and making sense of the acts of autonomous individuals.

Murray's story of the *Dictionary* called for but left unread helps illuminate the kind of social "work" the *Dictionary* is performing in its claim to be the opposite of work. In Johnson's account, it is a quality of writing *in and of itself* that has the power to sustain language over time and allow it to circulate. By representing the material qualities of writing as somehow generating the conditions that lend it social authority, Johnson lays out a version of writing that takes the place of civil and communal institutions. Insofar as writing itself is the source of its own timelessness and circularity, it takes over the functions we have come to understand as the consequences of the development of the printing press, the establishment of book fairs, copyright and censorship laws, libraries, literary salons, and the liberalizing of suffrage laws.[35] Murray's anecdote, by forcefully distinguishing the textual existence

35. The scholarship on the history of the book is extensive. See especially John Feather, *A History of British Publishing* (New York: Routledge, 1988); Martha Woodmansee and Peter Jaszi, eds., *The Construction of Authorship: Textual Appropriation in Law and Literature* (Durham, N.C.: Duke University Press, 1994); Mark Rose, *Authors and Owners: The Invention of Copyright* (Cambridge: Harvard University Press, 1993); and Lucien Febvre and Henri-Jean Martin, *The Coming of the Book* (London: Verso, 1976).

of Johnson's *Dictionary* from the various ways it might wield authority, undermines Johnson's suggestion that the *Dictionary* does away with the need for institutions and thus makes evident the *Dictionary*'s own operation as an institution.

Having established the significance of the history of the uses of Johnson's *Dictionary*, a history discernible in the distinction between dictionary author and form, Murray goes on to offer a genealogy of that form. Once we come to see the *Dictionary*, with its alphabetized entries of the multiple literary occasions of the use of individual words, not simply as text to be used but as an ongoing theory of use, we can discover the way the *Dictionary* works to turn individuals' use of language into a mode of experiencing their own historicity. In the genealogy Murray presents, the form that begins as a glossary for translating Latin has been transmuted by the first decades of the eighteenth century into what, according to him, are effectively "dictionaries of hard words" (114). As Murray describes them, the two moments are united by the persistence of a presumption that the "dictionary" is a genre of the extraordinary rather than the normal, of self-conscious exertion rather than unmarked daily acts, and implicitly of writtenness rather than speech. "No one appears . . . to have felt that Englishmen could want a dictionary to help them to the knowledge and correct use of their own language. That language was either an in-born faculty, or it was inhaled with their native air, or imbibed with their mothers' milk; how could they need a book to teach them to speak their mother tongue?" (110).

Returned to its generic genealogy, a history of the genre as a history of use that transmutes the dictionary from a text into an institution, Johnson's *Dictionary* turns out to be constituted by a paradox. The national language it claims to embody is developed into rather than labored over, yet the preservation of this effortlessly acquired language is achieved only as a result of the mighty "struggle"—the labor—that defines Johnson's "work." While the *Dictionary* defines its comprehensiveness on the model of an individual's unlabored—that is, developmental—relation to language, its claims of completeness can be upheld only insofar as they are different from any given individual's temporal movement into language yet identical to an individual user's language at any single moment. If the *Dictionary* is complete in defining a national language, it is so insofar as it includes the language people learn without exertion; but if the *Dictionary* is complete, its language is always already learned.

As Johnson abandons his early goal of making each quotation valuable in itself rather than "merely" as an illustration of the possible use of a given word, the cluster of quotations that constitutes each entry comes to resemble nothing so much as synchronic representation of the normally diachronic process of language learning, that "language imbibed with mother's milk" that until the end of the seventeenth century was considered beyond the provenance of the dictionary's own labors. The innovative feature of Johnson's *Dictionary*—its piling up of examples as a means of staging its uses, representing rather than explaining a word—is precisely the aspect that makes it formally resemble the process by which individuals come to know language through repeated, "multiauthor," and mostly accidental encounters with the word.

As the newly "national" dictionary claims comprehensiveness by virtue of its inclusion of ordinary language—language that is developed into, rather than labored over—the quotational structure's status as a formal representation of this development stands as evidence in support of this claim. On the other hand, that the individual's language learning occurs *over time* establishes that process as putatively effortless, labor free. In formally recreating that learning in synchronic terms, the *Dictionary* participates in each of the otherwise generically opposed categories of labor and development without being fully either. Since each of the illustrative examples is "written" by a different person, the inductive movement from individual examples to a generalized "meaning" is never reducible to the psychological experience of an individual subject's development into language. By inviting its readers to experience the words they look up in the *Dictionary* as a synchronized replaying of their own "laborless" childhood experience of learning language over time, the multiple examples lend the *Dictionary* the authority of the already known without identifying that condition of knowing with any particular person's knowledge.

Although a convincing case can certainly be made for reading Johnson's innovative use of multiple textual examples as a synchronic version of the dictionary users' learning process, the user nonetheless requires additional knowledge in order to negotiate his or her movement among the different entries. In the most straightforward, literal sense, the dictionary user must know the alphabet of the language of the *Dictionary*, since it is the order of the alphabet that structures the relation of the various entries to one another: the alphabet names the knowledge demanded of the dictionary users that is not entirely contained within individual entries. But if our association of the alphabet with the most basic material demands of writing implies that this unassimilable knowledge is knowledge possessed by a subject produced by *writing*, knowledge of "alphabetical order" can nevertheless be seen to figure a more general, extratextual linguistic knowledge. While dictionary users must know the order of the alphabet to locate the particular entry they may be after, even more fundamentally they must know that a word exists in order even to begin the search. One must "know" the language, a vernacular shorthand that, if we fill in its terms, we discover to be knowledge of the vernacular itself. Excessive to writing, such knowledge becomes something like, if not entirely identical to, the capacity to speak, a *representation* of speech.

In Johnson's *Dictionary* we find a form that presumes its users' knowledge of the English language even as it casts as its raison d'être its capacity to tell readers what they do not already know. But this formal tendency to present the experience of coming to know what one already knows, of experiencing one's process of knowing the world, is not limited to Johnson's ambivalent structure of examples. It is also present, though perhaps less obviously, in the *Dictionary*'s alphabetical organization. By the end of the nineteenth century when James Murray wrote his genealogy of the dictionary and published his magisterial *OED,* one excruciating letter at a time,[36] the alphabetical format had become so closely associated with dictionaries as to take the dictionary's name as its own; yet Murray's description of the advantages afforded by the format is nonetheless revealing:

> The very phrase, "Dictionary order," would in the first half of the sixteenth century have been unmeaning, for all dictionaries were not yet alphabetical. There is indeed no other connexion between a dictionary and alphabetical order, than that of a balance of convenience. Experience has shown that though an alphabetical order makes the matter of a dictionary very disjointed, scattering the terminology of a particular art, science, or subject, all over the book . . . it is yet that by which a word or heading can be found with least trouble and exercise of thought.[37]

Over the course of the seventeenth and eighteenth centuries, the linear, argumentively demonstrative organization of scientific encyclopedias gradually gave way to an alphabetical format, a change, according to Wilda Anderson, that freed the user of such works from being forced to conform to a single narrative line of thought.[38] Such freedom is of value because it makes it easy for users to pursue their own connections within the material. But while Anderson's account of this epistemological shift celebrates the intellectual freedom afforded by the new format, the new encyclopedia or dictionary user she imagines is not only free but knowing. By implicitly contrasting the already

36. See Willinsky, *Empire of Words,* chap. 3.
37. Murray, "Romanes Lecture 1900," 107.
38. Wilda C. Anderson, "What Is a Dictionary?" in *Between the Library and the Laboratory: The Language of Chemistry in Eighteenth-Century France* (Baltimore: Johns Hopkins University Press, 1984), 35–52.

organized quality of the individual entries with the "free" movement among them enabled by the alphabetical structure, the dictionary masks how far that movement from entry to entry is itself structured by the nontextual but nonetheless highly structured patterns of knowledge brought to it: for Johnson the sort of knowledge that allows one to speak, even if the language produced by such knowledge is too ephemeral ever to reach the vaunted timelessness of the textual.

To the extent that, for Johnson, the capacity of his *Dictionary* to produce national subjects lies in its power to align the developmental trajectories of individual subjects with the synchronic text, we can say that the subject produced by and productive of the *Dictionary* is fundamentally an *autobiographical* subject. Our reading of the "Preface" has thus far shown that the *Dictionary* can substitute for civil institutions only where the individual subjects' linguistic knowledge and the written text endlessly and seamlessly produce one another—that is, where writing creates and marks the existence of an individual subject whose identity (identity, rather than behavior) is defined first as the power to write. The subject whose identity is defined as power to write at the most fundamental level is, in a word, an autobiographer. The subject who writes—the laboring subject—is joined to the autobiographical object, the thing written about, whose action/labor is by force of genre necessarily in the past: the laboring subject and the subject at leisure come together in the single historical figure of the autobiographical writer.

The *Dictionary* is, by Johnson's reckoning, both a form of institution—an instrument for creating national (linguistic) subjects—and its opposite, a mere description of what need not be made at all. If this double rhetoric sets the terms within which the individual subject might be called "autobiographical"—a self both the source and the outcome of writing—it also governs the ambiguous relation among different autobiographical subjects. The editor of the *Dictionary* and the individuals who would use it are both identical with and productive of one another. The editor of the *Dictionary,* as mere arranger of texts, produces writing without writing and does nothing but describe the writing that is already used. The editor who creates the *Dictionary* as an institution, a text that becomes usable, capable of teaching individuals things they do not already know, does so by making a fundamentally new text out of the thousands of textual fragments he gathers, arranging those bits into the usable order of the alphabet. This editor, who works in the perpetually self-sustaining space of circularity between writing as text and writing as act, does everything and nothing to make the *Dictionary* and consequently stands as both the *Dictionary*'s exemplary autobiographical subject and its representative, first among equals and merely equal.

Johnson's suggestion that as editor of the *Dictionary* he is not presenting a new text but merely offering writing without a writer requires him to occlude his own organizational labors—his alphabetizing—as well as the extratextual knowledge demanded of those who would use the *Dictionary*, a knowledge I have associated with spoken language. But despite his reluctance to acknowledge the labor he expends in making his *Dictionary* take one form rather than another, Johnson does come to admit at least one failure of organization. Whereas the absence of the language of miners and artisans was, according to Johnson, attributable to the inadequacies of those languages, here the *Dictionary* itself falls short:

> My labor has likewise been much increased by a class of verbs too frequent in the English language, of which the signification is so loose and general, the use so vague and indeterminate, and the senses detorted so widely from the first idea, that it is hard to trace them through the maze of variation, to catch them on the brink of utter inanity, to circumscribe them by any limitations, or interpret them by any words of distinct and settled meaning: such are *bear, break, come, cast, full, get, give, do, put, set, go, run, make, take, turn, throw.* If of these the whole power is not accurately delivered, it must be remembered, that while our language is yet living, and variable by the caprice of every one that speaks it, these words are hourly shifting their relations, and can no more be ascertained in a dictionary, than a grove, in the agitation of a storm, can be accurately delineated from its picture in the water. (14)

Heaping metaphor upon metaphor in a futile effort to name the challenge to his classificatory efforts posed by these idiomatic verbs, Johnson nevertheless notes the existence of a category whose disruptive power can be anticipated from the *Dictionary*'s more general structural logic. He points out most straightforwardly that these words are unclassifiable because their meanings change too quickly; in this regard these idiomatic verbs resemble the mostly oral jargon of laborers. But whereas the transience of the artisanal language was a consequence of its being left unwritten, as Johnson describes it, it is the quality of the idiomatic language itself that prevents it from being fixed in writing. But if Johnson is more cryptic in accounting for the unfixability of the idiom than he was in his account of laborers' language, his slide into figurativeness here is expressive in its obfuscation. The ephemerality of the language is linked rhetorically to the difficulty of distinguishing the material world from the language used to represent it. Not only do the grove and its reflection appear identical, but the rapid movement of the storm—a temporal rather than representational relation—seems to eliminate any difference between the two, as though the wind lifts the reflective medium of the water into the trees' space at the same time as it tears leaves from the branches to float on the rippling surface of the water, simulacra of reflections.

Put another way, the language of idioms fails to be stable and ongoing exactly because it cannot be identified with any stable space. The transience of the language is here made of a piece with the transience of the space of the trees, and it is the fact that language and space come into being together, neither more ongoing than the other, that precludes the idiom expressed here from hardening into an element of an ongoing linguistic *identity* rather than remaining an isolated, contingent linguistic act. By the deep logic of Johnson's *Dictionary,* these words do not appear to be part of the body of linguistic knowledge a dictionary user is presumed to know in order to use the dictionary because they cannot name a geographical space or be easily imagined to occur within it. As will become evident, Johnson's conception of national language is founded centrally on the feasibility of rendering the capacity of a given language to describe a geographical space identical to the association of that language with that space.

The indistinguishability of the linguistic and the material figured by this description means that the idiomatic language cannot itself be fixed because it fails in its designated function of fixing the world. Paradoxically, however, the impossibility of halting in writing the idiomatic, figurative verbs—which leads to their incapacity to name and, in naming, to halt the historicity and changefulness of the material world—stems not from the indistinguishability of language and action but from their nonintersection. That is, it is because there is no moment when anyone might literally perform the actions named by the idiomatic verbs that the action cannot be named as an act of labor and, in this naming, be generalized out of history into a form of linguistic leisure. The idiom's figurativeness disrupts the complex dynamic of labor and leisure that enabled the nameability of individuals' acts to function as evidence for both the autonomy of those individuals and the reconcilability of this autonomy to the demands of the social. Nameable, Johnson's logic had it, individual acts become socially legible. Such a strategy involved redefining individual subjectivity from being a variety of behavior to being a variety of identity, from a matter of what one has done to a matter of what one *can* do. Here, by contrast, the language of the idiom, written by no one but spoken by all, insists on a sociality that occurs in time rather than by means of its stripping away.

The Dictionary as Autobiography: Eliezer Ben-Yehuda and the Revival of Hebrew

Like Samuel Johnson, Eliezer Ben-Yehuda, who completed the *Dictionary of the Hebrew Language, Ancient and Modern* in 1909, envisioned his project of dictionary making not simply as a program of linguistic reclamation but as a means of transforming the nature of the national subject. Like Johnson, Ben-Yehuda articulated his ideas about the particular role of linguistic reform within a general program to link national consciousness to civil institutions, and like Johnson he opted to present these ideas in a preface he appended to his published dictionary. But whereas Johnson imagined his *Dictionary* as a tool for creating stable national subjects out of a populace that spoke too much, Ben-Yehuda saw his dictionary project as a means of creating national subjects—if not altogether stable ones—out of a population that could not speak at all. And whereas Johnson's "Preface" laid out a model of a linguistic subject, and a dictionary maker, that might finally be construed as autobiographical in the logic of its deep structure, Ben-Yehuda's preface was overtly and unabashedly autobiographical.

It is Ben-Yehuda's penchant for self-advertisement, his willingness—many would say his eagerness—to turn the twentieth-century revival of the Hebrew language into so many incidents and consequences of his own life, that now commands the bulk of the historical attention directed toward him. Once lionized as the heroic progenitor of an unprecedented linguistic renaissance, now, more than seventy-five years after his death, Eliezer Ben-Yehuda has become a bit of an embarrassment. Under the glare of scrutiny turned on them by Israel's "new historians"[39] of the 1980s, Ben-Yehuda's claims to have single-handedly revived the Hebrew language, to have taught a nation to speak again, have withered to become the decidedly lonely, even plaintive, cries of the self-mythologizer.[40] The litany of overstatement is long and, by now, familiar: as late as 1902, more than twenty years after Ben-Yehuda initi-

---

39. The term was coined by historian Benny Morris in the self-described "liberal-progressive" United States bimonthly magazine *Tikkun*. For the historiography of the movement, see the special issue of *History and Memory* devoted to it (7, 1 [1995], ed. Gulie Ne'eman Arad).

40. The most elaborate challenges to the Ben-Yehuda myth include Shlomo Haramati, *Shlosha lifney Ben-Yehuda* [Three before Ben-Yehuda] (Jerusalem: Yad Yitzhak Ben Zvi, 1938), and Jack Fellman's *Revival of a Classical Tongue: Eliezer Ben-Yehuda and the Modern Hebrew Language* (The Hague: Mouton, 1973). Early lionizing efforts included the plethora of memoirs written by a number of Ben-Yehuda's close relatives, as well as the scholarly efforts of Israeli literary historian Yosef Klausner and the not quite so scholarly efforts of his English-language biographer Robert St. John, who wrote *Tongue of the Prophets: The Life Story of Eliezer Ben Yehuda* (Garden City, N.Y.: Doubleday, 1952), a popular biography, although he did not himself speak or read Hebrew.

ated his multipronged efforts to revive the language, only ten families in Jerusalem actually spoke Hebrew in their homes.[41] Besides his dictionary and his much-ballyhooed establishment of the first modern Hebrew-speaking household in Palestine (in which he fathered the "first Hebrew-speaking child"), Ben-Yehuda also created a series of "Hebrew-speaking societies" and language councils whose institutional histories reveal an almost parodic gap between pretension and cultural effect. The Techiyat Yisrael (Revival of Israel) society he founded in 1882 with Yechiel Pines, Jerusalem's most prominent enlightened Jew, began with an agreement among its members to speak nothing but Hebrew not only in their homes but in the streets and markets as well in order to extend the scope of the group's compact. The project ended six years later, with a grand total of six members.[42] Although his efforts at introducing Hebrew as the language of instruction in the schools of the Palestinian Yishuv (prestatehood settlements) and at creating a Hebrew newspaper in Palestine bore more fruit, Ben-Yehuda's labors at revival, however dogged, do not begin to account for the process by which a Hebrew that existed for the most part in the form of religious texts thousands of years old came to be spoken as the daily language of a community whose members all spoke other languages with greater ease.[43]

But in their zeal to disown the tradition of the heroic Ben-Yehuda as one of the more egregious manifestations of a now-defunct Zionist hagiographical historicism that would figure all acts of state making as momentous acts of will, contemporary historians may be missing the point. The ease with which they dismiss the cult of Ben-Yehuda as the symptom of something like a collective but lately transcended fantasy of the power of willing means they are likely to miss the ways autobiography bears a complicated, intense intimacy with the project of dictionary making. As literary genre rather than psychological symptom, autobiography does not simply describe the complex relations linking writing, individual and national identities, and historical change but also stands as an active, deliberate intervention into those relations. But if, as I suggested in relation to Johnson's "Preface," autobiography makes discernible the disjunction between the autobiographical writer and the subject

41. Fellman, *Revival of a Classical Tongue*, 43.

42. Ibid., 44.

43. One interesting approach to the role of individual will in the revival of Hebrew can be found in the scholarship on the history of Hebrew-language pedagogy. Shlomo Haramati makes the argument that the reading of the history of modern Hebrew that elevates Ben-Yehuda as heroic reviver is part of a more general tendency to denigrate Sephardic contributions to the history of the Yishuv. See Haramati, *Shlosha lifney Ben-Yehuda*.

represented (and between public and private language) even as it claims their identity, Ben-Yehuda's autobiographical "Preface," written in a language that is not even available as a private, spoken language in the period when most of the events narrated take place, manages to harness the theoretical instabilities of the genre as an active tool of language making. Ben-Yehuda sees his dictionary as simply one component of a comprehensive program to revitalize Hebrew as a spoken language and in that regard departs sharply from the relatively modest claims for Hebrew made by the *maskilim*. But to the extent that the authority of the autobiography hinges on the distinguishability of public and private, written and spoken languages, he is able to turn the restraint of the Haskalah position on Hebrew into an eloquent, if unwitting, articulation of the plausibility of his own much more ambitious program of revival. By claiming the rights of Hebrew not as one national language among many but as a pedagogical tool for making the natural sciences available to heretofore benighted Jews via Hebrew translation, the German-Jewish *maskilim* in their political forbearance—or at least in Ben-Yehuda's reinterpretation of this policy of forbearance—end up generating a threat to the discourse of the European Enlightenment far more profound than the mere demand for national equivalency would have been.

The peculiar representational politics of the Haskalah's linguistic program set the terms within which the ideology of a full revival of the Hebrew language was to take place, even as those advocating the transformation of the mostly textual Hebrew into an everyday spoken language articulated their programs as alternatives to the failed meliorist politics of the Haskalah generally and of Haskalah bilingualism in particular. The movement's intellectual center had migrated steadily eastward by the time the 1881 Russian pogroms put an end to the political and intellectual viability of the Haskalah's calls for liberal integration. The collapse of the Haskalah program generated two waves of migration—to western Europe and the United States and to Palestine—as well as two new political ideologies—Bundism (Jewish socialism) and Zionism.[44] As the increasing assimilation of Jews into German culture eroded the base of Hebrew readers and the consequent practical tenability of a policy of bilingualism, the movement's Hebrew "institutions," consisting

---

44. For a detailed history of the thirty-year period of anti-Jewish violence in Russia that began in 1881 and ended with the 1917 Bolshevik revolution, see John D. Klier and Shlomo Lambroza, eds., *Pogroms: Anti-Jewish Violence in Modern Russian History* (Cambridge: Cambridge University Press, 1992). An important account of the development of Zionism and Bundism in the wake of the 1881 violence is Jonathan Frankel, *Prophecy and Politics: Socialism, Nationalism and the Russian Jews, 1862–1917* (Cambridge: Cambridge University Press, 1981).

mainly of a handful of narrowly circulated and often sporadically published Hebrew newspapers[45] and even less formal literary circles of Hebrew writers, reestablished themselves. First they appeared in various cities throughout Galicia and, by 1840, in Lithuania and in the Russian "Pale of Settlement," the fifteen provinces in the western regions of European Russia to which Jewish residence had been restricted in 1835 in an attempt to protect established mercantile elements in Moscow and Smolensk.[46]

Johnson, we recall, imagined the autobiographical authority of the subjects produced by the *Dictionary* to offer a way of creating national subjects without the need for civic and educational institutions, but hardly by way of the straightforward and transparent egoism of which Ben-Yehuda's detractors would accuse the Hebrew dictionary maker a century later. Such critics imagine that Ben-Yehuda's use of an autobiographical preface is incontrovertible evidence of his belief in his power simply to will a spoken national Hebrew into being.[47] But if we remember that it was not the *willed* quality of his authority as a dictionary maker but its relation to the dictionary's *writtenness* that led Johnson to think his *Dictionary* would allow him to dispense altogether with institutions of national culture, we will see that Ben-Yehuda's adoption of the autobiographical genre reflects a far more complex relation to the concept of the institutional than might otherwise be apparent. Johnson saw the material quality of writing that supposedly enables it to take the place of institutions as resting entirely on the assumption that individual subjects' language and writing already existing in the public domain are identical—conditions patently contrary to the facts for late nineteenth-century Hebrew. Ben-Yehuda's adoption of the autobiographical form can be seen as an attempt to theorize a relation between individual subjects and institutions rather than to dismiss its significance.

For as Ben-Yehuda explains in the opening of his preface, the project of national language making emerges not out of a need to reconcile a variety of

45. On the development of Hebrew periodical literature in Europe see Klausner, *Historia shel ha-sifrut ha-hadasha*, vol. 5. and Zinberg, *History of Jewish Literature*, vol.12, esp. chaps. 1 and 2.

46. "Within these areas, the Jews were permitted to move from place to place as they desired and to acquire land and property of any sort, save estates settled with serfs (Provision no. 12). There was to be no more forced resettlement, that is, expulsions from villages. . . . Temporary sojourns outside the Pale were permitted for the acquisition of inheritance, the securing of rights at judicial venues, study at academic institutions, and some commercial affairs. First-guild merchants were permitted to travel to both capitals [Moscow and Saint Petersburg] and to seaports and to reside in Moscow for periods of up to six months at a time." Michael Stanislawski, *Tsar Nicholas I and the Jews: The Transformation of Jewish Society in Russia, 1825–1855* (Philadelphia: Jewish Publication Society of America, 1983), 36–37.

47. To be sure, there is plenty of evidence that Ben-Yehuda did feel this way at least part of the time. I discuss the megalomaniacal aspects of his work and self-making below.

socially divided and divisive linguistic uses but out of a need to bring the isolated words that an individual might or might not know from a corpus of already-written religious texts into relation to a whole set of everyday social institutions:

ושוב ראיתי, כי בזה בודאי אין הבדל בין יחיד לציבור. אם עלולה לשון, שחדלה מהיות מדוברת
ולא נשאר ממנה אלא מה שנשאר לנו מלשוננו ,לשוב להיות לשון הדיבור ליחיד בכל צרכי
החיים, אין מקום לפקפק אם יכול תוכל להיות לשון מדוברת גם לציבור.

[And again I saw that in this regard there was clearly no difference between the individual and the public. If there is a likelihood of a language that ceased to be spoken so that all that remained of it was what remains of our language returning to function as the spoken language of the individual for all necessities of life, there is no room for doubt that it will be able to be a spoken language for the public as well.] (139)[48]

The challenge of the revival of Hebrew, in other words, is not finding—or even imposing—a common linguistic denominator between the interests of individuals and those of the community but creating simultaneously individual linguistic knowledge and the social network within which such knowledge is not just possible but necessary—creating at once, that is, the existence of two elements that presuppose each other's prior existence. Benjamin Harshav describes the difficulty well:

If Hebrew had few names of flowers, the invention or recovery of such names from old texts was not enough; it took root when Botany teachers guided groups of school children in learning to know nature and distinguish between the various kinds of flowers; and vice versa: those distinctions could be made only with such names in hand. . . . And it could not be done in an isolated domain alone: teaching the names of flowers also required the establishment of Hebrew schools and youth movements, the writing of textbooks, the existence of publishers and distributors of books, a cult of nature, the establishment of Jewish villages—and all those involved further social and cultural systems. Thus the whole entangled network of social systems and subsystems had to be implemented at one and the same time, along with the revival of the language.[49]

If autobiography names a single person as both cause and effect, both a laborer and the beneficiary of someone else's labor, it stands as an articulation

---

48. Ben-Yehuda, *Ha-halom v'shevaro.* Unless otherwise noted, all translations from the Hebrew are my own.

49. Harshav, *Language in Time of Revolution,* 92.

224 / Chapter Three

not only of the promise of a self with the power to call a world into being—
the charge of a Zionist romantic subjectivism directed against Ben-Yehuda by
his critics—but also of the powerlessness of the subject to create even the
most rudimentary self without the prior existence of public institutions and
expressive forms. The problem of language revival Ben-Yehuda hints at in his
invocation of the autobiographical is in some sense the dilemma of historicism made prospective.

In his provocative study of historical method, Paul Veyne describes the
"paradox" of what he calls "decoupage": the assumption that historians can,
in the act of writing history, provide an objective account of events understood as to any degree the precondition of that historiographical act—in
short, that they can write about the events that make them able to write.[50]
James Chandler traces the genealogy of this historicist paradox back through
the late 1960s debate between Claude Lévi-Strauss and Jean-Paul Sartre
on the nature of the relation between history and anthropology to what
Chandler argues are its origins in the discourse on "the spirit of the age" in
early nineteenth-century Britain. With the emergence of this discourse, according to Chandler, we can understand historical dating as the process of
encoding two sorts of relations between events: an "ordinal" function, organizing events chronologically, in a relation of before and after, and a "cardinal"
function, which registers historical moments horizontally, measuring "chronological distances and densities," sometimes comparing the density of eventfulness in different cultures at a single moment, sometimes comparing the
intensity of eventfulness in a single place or culture at different historical moments.[51]

Whereas Johnson's strategy in the *Dictionary* was to assert the givenness
of the stabilizing qualities of writing and thus to conflate the two forms of
historicity so that each canceled the effects of the other, Ben-Yehuda presents
an autobiography that, in its most careful and subtle moments, manages to
keep both types of historical coding in play simultaneously. By evoking, with
varying explicitness, the Haskalah's pointedly *diaglossic* program of linguistic
reform, Ben-Yehuda offers a version of autobiography that continually rein-
troduces the pressure of horizontal linguistic difference—the specific division
of linguistic labor, as it were—even as it enacts the subject's unidirectional
development into writing. That is, even as the writtenness of Ben-Yehuda's
autobiographical text announces the achievement of both a sociotextual au-

---

50. Paul Veyne, *Writing History*, trans. Mina Moore-Rinvolucri (Middletown, Conn.: Wesleyan University Press, 1984), 44.
51. Chandler, *England in 1819*, 67.

thority and a facility with Hebrew, the shadow of the Haskalah's insistence on maintaining a distinction between written and spoken uses of language, as well as the formal instability of autobiography, works to keep the historical particularity of all the various moments of language use in plain view. Dilated by the continuity of its encounters with other languages, the activity of writing Hebrew is never turned entirely into the text of writing, nor does the history of the uses of the existing biblical and rabbinical writings—a history in which the text itself becomes the organizing center for an infinite variety of ceremonial readings, commentaries, and oral disputations—disappear into the transparent linguistic capacities of contemporary individual users of Hebrew.

In this light Ben-Yehuda's assertion that if "a language that ceased to be spoken . . . return[ed] to function as the spoken language . . . for all necessities of life" "there was clearly no difference between the individual and the public" ought not to be understood as a claim that one can be made to stand in for one another in a representative relation of part to whole.[52] For Ben-Yehuda, individual speaker and public institutions of language cause one another—each is necessary but not sufficient for producing the other, and thus each needs to be understood as operating within its own cluster of historical shapings and pressures. The historical condition of Hebrew seems to subvert a fundamental presumption of cultural analysis by which the *synecdochal* relation between individual cultural actors and larger-scale representational logics is read as an indication of an irreducible historical particularity. The example of the Hebrew revival that Ben-Yehuda offers intimates, by its own negative counterweight, that the analogousness of the language of individual subjects and more general cultural discourse marks not the manifestation of a kind of historical particularity but a stripping away of the experience and palpability of such particularity. As we fill in the gaps of his pronouncement, what becomes apparent is that, for Ben-Yehuda, the irreducibility of individual and public to one another testifies to the historical specificity of the moment of Hebrew revival: "If there is a likelihood of a language that ceased to be spoken so that all that remained of it was what remains of our language returning to function as the spoken language of the individual for all necessities of life, there is no room for doubt that it will be able to be a spoken language of the public as well" (139). What appears to begin as a kind of historical analysis based on the generalizability of chronological, developmental narratives ("if there is a likelihood of a language that ceased to be spoken") quickly gives way to an analytical mode in which it is the absolute and tauto-

52. Ben-Yehuda, *Ha-halom v'shevaro*, 139.

logical uniqueness of the situation ("so that all that remained of it was what remains of our language") that finally testifies to the mutual imbrication of the individual and "the public." In this way both the autobiography and the institutionality that announce the irreducibility of individual and social to one another become the sites for the emergence of a new kind of historicity.

Borrowing Veyne's terminology, we might say that, in implicitly linking the project of reviving Hebrew to the problem of writing about history, Ben-Yehuda reveals the challenge of revival to be the "paradox of *institutional* decoupage." As I have been saying, Ben-Yehuda's autobiographical preface ties the difficulty of speaking Hebrew in the early years of the twentieth century to the problem of narrating a history of the relation between individual subjects and the public. In this way, in a move whose implications I hope will become increasingly apparent, Ben-Yehuda lets us see institutions as being engaged above all in transforming individual subjects' relation to time. Johnson imagined that his *Dictionary,* as an unauthored compilation of temporally transcendent writing, might render unnecessary the sort of external social authority provided by civil and cultural institutions by aligning individuals' experiences of their own development—their experience of a chronological relation of before and after—with their encounters with a constitutively unchanging written text. By contrast, Ben-Yehuda's dictionary links the project of creating Hebrew institutions with the temporal reversibility of a destabilized autobiography; the retrospectivity of Ben-Yehuda's autobiography insists on the difference between the writing self and the past self written about and suggests that this difference produces two narratives—the individual subject's development into speech and the development of Hebrew institutions. The existence of such dual narratives implies in turn that institutions operate by shifting an individual subject's primary experience of temporality from the before and after of his or her lifetime to the momentariness of the engagement with the institution, in which the subject's connections to other subjects simultaneously engaged with the institution come to take precedence over the subject's own past and present.

If, in Harshav's words, individuals could come to speak Hebrew not simply when the Hebrew words for flowers were recovered or created but when "botany teachers guided groups of children in learning to know nature and distinguish between the various kinds of flowers," these sorts of steps are effective, and count as the work of institutions, because they allow those children to experience their knowledge of the names and shapes of flowers as following entirely from earlier events in their lives, even as they experience those earlier events as not necessary in themselves, that is, as not simply one element in an absolutely continuous chain of development from past to present. One child can rely on her friends to understand what she means when she uses a word—and can rely on her reliance—when she knows she has learned that word, or could have learned it, on a nature walk they all took together. But it is the experience of the abstractability of that moment of her life—the nature walk—from other moments that both defines it as the operation of an institution and becomes the grounds of its efficacy.

But while the picture of an institution Ben-Yehuda paints allows us to see it as characterized by its power to generate a sense of temporal detachability or reversibility—the isolatability of the date from the chronological trajectory in which it might otherwise be embedded—the terms defining his project of linguistic revival are far more specific. For Ben-Yehuda's project is not simply to describe how institutions work but to bring them into being where none existed before. Veyne's analytical "paradox of historical decoupage" can be extended to institutions, but in the context of a project of institution *building* it becomes less a descriptive paradox than a practical impasse. While Ben-Yehuda's preface may implicitly define institutions in terms of their temporal reversibility, the task before him is to bring such institutions into being—in other words, to place the condition of temporal detachability into some kind of chronological trajectory, a relation to a before and after. I propose that while he sees institutions as producing in their subjects a sense of the detachability of specific moments of their lives as a kind of abstract, ongoing condition, Ben-Yehuda understands the *creation* of institutions to require that individual subjects actively and deliberately, even violently, break off a given moment of their lives—the moment of using his dictionary of modern Hebrew—from the lives they have led until that point. The process of institution building that Ben-Yehuda attempts to describe and initiate by way of his dictionary thus manages to bring together Veyne's two aspects of historicity—the chronological and the cultural/epochal—but can make them simultaneously palpable only as a moment of deliberate and traumatic loss. One can experience the ways one has been made by the events of one's past, Ben-Yehuda avers, only by self-consciously and violently pulverizing the traces of that past upon one's subjectivity. As we shall see, it is by this paradoxical act of deliberate self-loss, a paradox enacted in the name of pragmatism, that institutions and the subjects forged by them can be created together where neither has existed before.

But even as Ben-Yehuda describes the profound psychic and social costs of such institution building, his writings exhibit an ambivalence toward the imperative that such wages must be paid. Alongside his textual accounting of the trauma of institution building, in accompanying passages and by means of what finally amounts to an allegorizing of his life, he attempts to enact in his person and in his social relations what for Johnson remained a purely textual fantasy—the fantasy of textualization. As the momentum of his analysis brings him face-to-face with the specter of the undone self made mandatory by his own project of revival (in order to be brought back to life something must first die), Ben-Yehuda shifts to a model of cultural making structured entirely around a chronological form of temporality. Positing, like Johnson, an absolute identity between subject and language, Ben-Yehuda asserts his place at the origins of a new society, himself the beginning before everything, and intimates that such temporal priority is sufficient to make him first creator of language as well.

As recalled in the memoir that also serves as the dictionary's preface "החלום ושברו" [The dream and its realization], Ben-Yehuda's early life is notable mainly for the closeness with which it conforms to the prototypical *maskilic* narrative of spiritual development. Born Eliezer Perelman in the Lithuanian village of Luzhky in 1858, Ben-Yehuda began to study Hebrew locally at age three and, as an especially promising student, at thirteen was sent for advanced study to the nearby city of Polotsk, where he came under the influence of a local *maskil*. Unable to return to his home village because of his father's resistance to his freethinking, Ben-Yehuda traveled first to Glubokia, where he was taught French, German, and Russian by Devora Yonas, the daughter of a *maskil* and the woman he would later marry, and then to Dünaberg, where he studied at the gymnasium and became involved with the Russian nationalist Narodniki movement. As Ben-Yehuda retrospectively tells it, although he had by this time largely abandoned any voluntary political or cultural identification with Jews in favor of a Narodnik-inspired embrace of the Russian peasant and Russian language, he was unable to renounce his Jewishness entirely because he could not rid himself of his lingering loyalty to the Hebrew language. This loyalty was no longer tied to a more general *maskilic* program of Enlightenment but was generated out of his reading of contemporary *maskilic* fiction and journalism. And since Ben-Yehuda rejected Haskalah before the movement's final dramatic implosion in the wake of the 1881 pogroms, he came to advocate the revival of Hebrew as a pointedly national language well before the supposedly seminal events of the collective Zionist developmental narrative: the 1896 publication of Theodor Herzl's *Die Judenstaat* and the convening of the First Zionist Congress in Basel the following year. Drawing inspiration from eastern European nationalist movements that emerged during the 1878 Russo-Turkish War and from his reading of Eliot's *Daniel Deronda*, in 1879 he traveled to Paris to study Middle Eastern culture and linguistics at the Sorbonne, where he published

a series of articles advocating a full Hebrew revival in the Hebrew journal
השחר (*HaShahar*) [The dawn].

But if the broad strokes of Ben-Yehuda's autobiography are familiar, the
details with which he fills in the lines of that trajectory display some subtle yet
important deviations from the standard narrative, and not merely because, by
going to study in Paris, he moved farther west and immersed himself more
deeply within explicitly non-Jewish cultural institutions. Ben-Yehuda describes his initial encounter with spoken Hebrew, which occurs at a café in
Paris among "הקולות העליזים של הלשון הצרפתית החיה, היפה, העשירה [cheerful
voices of the French language—living, beautiful, rich]" (139), but this movement into speech, far from separating itself from past, textually based linguistic knowledge, immediately conjures an earlier encounter with spoken Hebrew that, rendered textually, is necessarily incapable of shedding its textual
past:

. . . בימים הראשונים של "ההשכלה" שלי באחת העיירות הקטנות של ליטה, אחרי אשר
טעמתי את הטעם הראשון של הספרות החדשה, אחרי קראי בסתר את אהבת ציון ואת אשמת
שומרון, התעוררה בנפשי תשוקה גם לדבר עברית, ממש כמו אמנון ותמר ושאר הבחורים
והבתולות שפגשתי בעולם החדש ההוא, ומפעם לפעם יוצא הייתי עם אחד מחברי, שידע את
סודי ו"נחטף" גם הוא מחוץ לעיר בשדה והחבא, בגניבה, בפחד ורעדה, פן ישמעו הבריות,
סחנו בלשון הקודש.

[In the first days of my "Enlightenment" (Haskalah) in one of the small towns in
Lithuania, after I had my first taste of the new literature, after my surreptitious
reading of *The Love of Zion* (the first full-length Hebrew novel, by Abraham
Mapu) and *The Guilt of Samaria,* there awakened in my soul the desire to speak
Hebrew as well, exactly like Amnon and Tamar and the other youths and maids I
met in this new world, and from time to time I would, with one of my friends who
knew my secret and was grabbed by it as well, go out of the town to a field, and be
hidden, stealthily, with fear and trembling, lest creatures hear us conversing in the
holy tongue.] (140)

In Ben-Yehuda's account, "enlightenment" (Haskalah) has become a private process rather than an organized political, intellectual and cultural
movement. Although I will discuss the implications of Ben-Yehuda's response
to his private transformation below, for now I emphasize that his peculiarly
individualized conversion is both brought on and sustained by surreptitious
novel reading. His emphasis on the role of Hebrew novels pointedly revises
the conventional *maskilic bildung,* in which initiation is social—the result of
the tutelage of the already enlightened—and encouraged by an encounter

with some combination of Hebrew grammar books and European- and Hebrew-language philosophical and scientific texts. Moreover, Ben-Yehuda figures this new centrality of the novel as the explicit cause of his deviation from the established cultural program of the Haskalah, a program that, as we know, did not place a particular premium on speaking Hebrew.

But while the "Hebrewness" of the novels enables them to inspire, it also ensures that their inspiration is not quite "novelistic." That Amnon and Tamar speak Hebrew forecloses them as objects of novelistic identification for Ben-Yehuda. Instead, the fictional characters become potential objects of acquaintance, a relationship to be achieved at some point in the future, when he has learned the language by which he could come to know them. In this view the Hebrew realist novel is politically inspirational for Ben-Yehuda not because it is transparent but because it fails to be. As we recall, the goal of Johnson's *Dictionary* was to transform sociality from a behavior to an identity by defining it not as the relations structured by a system of divided labor but, instead, as the relations generated out of temporally transcendent, "unauthored" writing. Here, by contrast, novelistic identification—and by implication that sociality predicated on the notion of identity—is dismissed out of hand as unachievable in the moment Ben-Yehuda reads the novel. That the passage identifies a moment of reading, and by implication a moment of writing as well, forcefully marks his departure from Johnson's model of linguistic community, since for Johnson the condition of textuality was ideologically potent because it made all moments the same—brought language and those who would read, write, and speak it out of time and into ongoing identification with one another. By substituting the notion of acquaintance for that of identification (an acquaintance postponed to some undefined time in the future), Ben-Yehuda rejects the possibility of imagining social relations outside the context of the knowledge possessed at and produced by a given temporal moment.

Although Ben-Yehuda begins by using the formal instabilities of autobiography in a way that effectively challenges the ahistoricity of Johnsonian writing—writing is always the same in its power to make everything the same— the extraordinarily mobile, even vertiginous variety of the autobiographical form's significations makes it a useful tool for translating a representational instability into a kind of ontological contingency, a historicity. Moving at once forward and backward in time, sliding from subject to object, writer to speaker and back again, Ben-Yehuda's autobiography anatomizes what it pulls together. In this passage, he recounts his first public, unguarded use of Hebrew:

בימים ההם כבר עלתה השאלה לפני מה שם אקרא לספר זה, ועל אחד הדפים רשמתי:
ספר מילים או – מילון? בינתיים חליתי בגניחת דם. הוכרחתי לעזוב את למודי בבית המדרש
לחכמי הרפואה, ועל-פי מצוות הרופאים נשלחתי לעיר אלג׳יר. שם שמעתי בפעם הראשונה
מפי היהודים קריאה בלשון עברית בהברה מזרחית, ותעש עלי הברה זו רושם עז מאוד, ושם
דיברתי בפעם הראשונה עברית לא לשם הדיבור בעברית אלא מפני הצורך, מפני שלא ידעתי
לדבר בפרט עם זקנים והחכמים שלהם, שלא ידעו צרפתית, אלא בלשון הקודש, שבפי קצתם
היתה שגורה [בו?] בדיבור פה.

ויבאו לי הימים אשר שהיתי באלג׳יר ברכה כפולה. שמש אפריקה ריפא את גופי, והשיחות
שסחתי בעברית עם זקני העיר הישראלית וחכמיה השגירו את לשוני בדיבור בעברית, והיו
פעמים שכבר חשתי כי הדיבור בלשון העברית הוא דבורי הטבעי.

[In those days the question had already arisen for me: What would I call this book?
I jotted on one of the pages—"word book" or "dictionary"? In the meantime, I
had been stricken with tuberculosis. I was forced to leave my studies at the school
for the sake of my recovery and, at the advice of the doctors, I was sent to the city
of Algiers. There I heard for the first time the sound of the Hebrew language in a
Middle Eastern accent, which made a very strong impression on me, and there I
first spoke Hebrew not for the sake of speaking Hebrew, but out of necessity, since
I didn't know how to speak in particular with their elders and sages, who did not
know French but [only] the holy tongue, in which some of them were fluent.

These days in Algiers brought me a double blessing. The African sun healed my
body, and the conversations I had in Hebrew with the elders of this Israelite city
made fluent my spoken Hebrew, until there were occasions I already felt as though
the Hebrew language were my natural speech.] (142–43)

As if in anticipation of his most virulent critics, Ben-Yehuda here stages his
dictionary project in its most arbitrary, hyperbolically willful terms, then precedes to dismantle the theoretical presumptions that would underwrite the
Adamic, transcendentally world-making subject who lurks at the passage's
edge. Ben-Yehuda represents a moment of naming—not just any naming, but
the naming of his own naming project—as the choice between a neologism
("מילון") and a compilation of extant words ("ספר מילים"), or "book of
words." But even as the apparent arbitrariness of the grounds of his decision
makes the outcome somewhat beside the point, Ben-Yehuda writes the two
words down, at once evoking and refuting the Johnsonian appeal to writing
as a foundation of an authority that would extend beyond the moment and
the agent of choice at hand. That the narrative fails to report which word
Ben-Yehuda finally chooses perhaps simply reinforces the meaninglessness of
the decision, but I believe the passage is less significant as an announcement
of the arbitrariness of the relation between name and thing—and conse-

quently of the willfulness of Ben-Yehuda's project—than as a narration of the process by which the act of naming comes to be interrupted. At the moment his body is introduced into the narrative as an active force in his development as a Hebrew speaker, the tenuous retrospective link joining Ben-Yehuda the dictionary writer to Ben-Yehuda the autobiography writer begins to pull apart. As the recollection of the dilemma of inventing a name for his dictionary veers suddenly into a narrative of his Middle Eastern convalescence, the autobiography unfolds the fundamental temporal ambiguity at its center, the promise of simultaneity of linguistic and bodily identities collapsing into a serial oscillation between apparently nonequivalent subjectivities. Although Ben-Yehuda employs the characteristically novelistic "in the meantime" to suggest that his professional concerns regarding the proper structure of his dictionary are able to exist simultaneously and in harmony with the uncertain veerings of an identity born of the fact of embodiment, the narrative effect of the juxtaposition is to imply that Ben-Yehuda's embodiment—at once marked and depleted by tuberculosis—supplants the progress his professional self has undergone.

Suddenly, then, to ground the extension of his individual language-making efforts historically in the mostly accidental facts of Ben-Yehuda's individual life is in one sense to refuse to ground it at all; the body that is subject to the accident of tuberculosis likewise brings about the accident of participation in a Hebrew-speaking community, but that the same body "causes" these two logically unconnected events itself remains accidental. Ben-Yehuda might have been sent to a sanatorium in western Europe to be cured, in which case his body would have obstructed rather than advanced his more deliberate efforts at language revival; thus his body becomes a sign not of the foundational status of the material world, but of the impossibility of defining a foundation at all.

We have seen that Ben-Yehuda associates his departure from the ideological program of the Haskalah—in a word, his interest in naming Hebrew as a *spoken* language—with the particular prominence of novels and novel reading in his own intellectual and political development. The novel's capacity to represent specific moments in time that are not entirely assimilable to a detemporalized writing is vested in its description of the simultaneous activity of a variety of people. As Benedict Anderson has argued in his *Imagined Communities*,[53] the novelistic simultaneity flagged by the narrative tag "in the meantime" is able to create a notion of publicness, a sense of the existence

53. Benedict Anderson, *Imagined Communities: Reflections on the Origin and Spread of Nationalism* (London: Verso, 1983).

of a specific culture at a given moment, by signaling the connectedness of individuals who may never meet. But the plausibility of the narrative "in the meantime," its power to represent activities that a reader must read about over time as though they were happening at a single moment (which is part and parcel of its capacity to make and represent a culture), depends on the detachment of that narrative from a specific body. If elsewhere in his narrative Ben-Yehuda uses a narrative novelistic logic to disrupt the operation of the autobiographical form, here he introduces the logic of autobiography to undo the work of the novel. By staging an autobiographical moment in which the narrator's claim of simultaneity—between the dictionary's naming and his tuberculosis—is derailed by the insistence on the narrator's embodiment, Ben-Yehuda uses his autobiography to literalize, and in literalizing to undermine, the representational force of the realist novel. With this literalizing, Ben-Yehuda signals that the novel's claim to be presenting something like a homogeneous culture by its representation of "simultaneous" events turns on an understanding of that narrative voice as an individual subject, the subject's singularity providing the ground of continuity among the various simultaneous actors.

If, in the transporting of the gesture of "in the meantime" to the context of autobiography, the literal singularity of that unifying narrator prevents the events of the narrative from taking place at the same time, the narrator's embodiment also leads him into a situation in which it is the narrator's difference from a culture that allows him to communicate with its members, to speak the same language. ("There I first spoke Hebrew . . . out of necessity, since I didn't know how to speak in particular with their elders and sages, who did not know French but the holy tongue.") The "double blessing" of "those days in Algiers" announces, in point of fact, the fundamental unrelatedness of the two elements it yokes together. Ben-Yehuda identifies his own body as the organizing site of his experience of his own historicity and comes to associate the particularity of his placement in time as the connection to nothing in particular.

The dual quality of this "double blessing" marks at once a kind of radical contingency of the embodied subject without a geographical place and the transcendence of that condition into something like self-abstraction, the capacity to make a world wherever one's body lands one. This doubleness structures the odd schizophrenia of Ben-Yehuda's narrative. For while the formal instability of autobiography can be used, as we have seen thus far, as a way of insisting on the merely *accidental* quality of the link between (embodied) subjects and the language they speak, Ben-Yehuda is not entirely willing to forgo the more conventionally compensatory consolations of the form. It is at these moments, when he invokes the genre in order to assert the literal identity between the individual subject's body and language, that he comes closest to acting as the theoretically naive narcissist he is so often accused of being. If the narrative tips its hand one way or the other, it does so only by presenting the two readings as interpretations that might be chosen between, like entries in a dictionary. It is only a few short steps, less a logical progression than a subtle shift in perspective, to move from a sense of being connected to nothing in particular generated by Ben-Yehuda's experience of the power of his tubercular body—to the sort of abstraction who might simultaneously ponder the proper name for his dictionary and converse in Hebrew in the Algerian desert. And while Ben-Yehuda's Algerian interlude leads him to conclude that his disconnection and difference from those around him might enable him to speak Hebrew with them, elsewhere in his recollections he invests this sense of disconnection born of his embodiment with the power to *cause,* in itself, a community of Hebrew speakers. I noted earlier that for Ben-Yehuda institutions induce in their subjects a sense of the detachability of a particular moment of language learning from the rest of the events in their lives, from their experience of their lives as a chronology. Insofar as he reads the connection to nothing in particular that he experiences in his sojourn to Algeria as a necessary and ongoing consequence of his embodiment, Ben-Yehuda comes to conceive of the condition of embodiment as having the force of institutions.

Nowhere is this tendency more evident than in the largely truncated narrative of Ben-Yehuda's son Ben-Tsiyon,[54] "the first Hebrew-speaking child" whose rhetorical importance for elevating Ben-Yehuda's own highly specific life story to the realm of national myth led his father to prophesy the significance of the child's arrival years before his actual birth and also led him, not unrelatedly, to integrate Ben-Tsiyon/Itamar's childlike Hebrew into a dictionary designed to serve an entire, if not yet entirely present, Hebrew-speaking culture. It is in this uncomfortable lack of fit between autobiography and genealogy that we can begin not only to see the limits of autobiography as a program for linguistic revival but to account for the particular characteristics

---

54. Named Ben-Tsiyon Ben-Yehuda—literally "Son of Zion, Son of Judah"—by his father (who, like many early Zionists, Hebraicized his own birth name, Eliezer Perelman, on his arrival in Palestine), the First Hebrew Child later changed his name to Itamar Ben-AVI, the name under which he published his memoirs. Read as an acronym (as it was written), AVI refers to [E]liezer [B]en-[Y]ehuda in the Hebrew characters, making Itamar's surname "Son of Eliezer Ben-Yehuda." Read as a noun, Avi means "my father," giving Itamar a surname that is a kind of metasurname, "Son of My Father." Below I discuss Itamar's self-naming as a critique of his father's linguistic project.

of both Ben-Yehuda's Hebrew dictionary and the Hebrew novels that lay beyond the scope of his own political program.

What is perhaps most striking about Ben-Yehuda's narrative of Ben-Tsiyon/Itamar is how little space it occupies in the autobiography, given the vast theoretical and emotional weight it is imbued with by Ben-Yehuda's narrative. Ben-Yehuda's representation of his body in the context of his bout with tuberculosis effectively offered a model of politics based on the impossibility of locating final linguistic—or for that matter political—authority in any single institutional or cultural sphere. The almost thorough evacuation of his body from the narrative regarding the First Hebrew Child offers a considerably different vision of linguistic authority, one in which Ben-Yehuda is the source of a Hebrew language made communal by the formal and institutional masking of its personal origins.

We first get wind of the concept of the child who will turn out to be Itamar in the context of Ben-Yehuda's similarly brief allusion to "those first difficult days" following his arrival to Palestine with his wife, who despite having been "יעודה להיות האם העברית הראשונה [designated to be the first Hebrew mother]" (143), "עוד לא ידעה להוצא מפיה אף מילה בעברית [did not yet know to send from her mouth a single Hebrew word]." Ben-Yehuda's wife (who remains nameless throughout the entire passage) thus appears to occupy a place altogether outside present time (she is designated only for a future destiny as mother and not quite able to speak). Moreover, this temporal in-betweenness seems less the outcome of her incomplete knowledge of Hebrew, as Ben-Yehuda would have it, and more a result of a kind of "in-between" relation to language itself, rendered silent by her location at the heart of the temporal paradox of Veyne's "decoupage."

Devora's ontological in-betweenness is born of the temporally paradoxical position Ben-Yehuda assigns her, the sinister projection of his autobiographical logic. While Ben-Yehuda can at times imagine himself to be detached from any particular circumstance by occupying fully neither the moment of autobiographical writing nor the moment of being represented narratively, he turns Devora's similar temporal doubleness into a means of evacuating her of reality altogether; defined in the present by her occupation of some yet unfulfilled future perfect state of "mother of the First Hebrew Child," she is made to disappear completely. Here Ben-Yehuda's understanding of individual agency depends for its authority on eliminating all competing claims. This rhetorical evacuation of all forces potentially resistant to the creation of a spoken Hebrew—Devora Ben-Yehuda's incapacity, willed or unwilled, to allow a single Hebrew word to pass her lips, the huge grammatical and semantic gaps in the Hebrew of the nineteenth century, the absence of shared territory on which a language community might be formed—is achieved in large part by the autobiographical form itself. What seems the breathtaking willfulness of Ben-Yehuda's "designation" of his wife's "destiny"—a willfulness consistent with the scope of his more narrowly professional undertaking—becomes indistinguishable from "mere description" authorized by the retrospectiveness of autobiography. She is destined to serve this function because she turns out to do so in the future. Ben-Yehuda's role as narrator of his own life thus justifies the willfulness of his vision, with the temporal difference of autobiographical retrospectiveness standing in for the material, historical, and social otherness already eliminated by his choice of this version of autobiography as the genre within which to tell the story of the revival of Hebrew.

What the passing mention of Devora makes evident is that the double quality of the "double blessing" of Ben-Yehuda's embodiment—the oscillation between an embodiment that unravels subjectivity into a series of unconnectable accidents and a self that can create its own place—remains a choice only so long as it is understood as organizing the experience of a single subject, only so long as the doubleness of embodiment is fundamentally autobiographical. Embodiment serves as the ground of abstraction to the extent that it naturalizes the singleness of the subject. Having seized on the temporal contradictoriness of the autobiographical form to remove Devora in all her embodied particularity from the scene of cultural production, Ben-Yehuda is free to turn himself into a kind of embodied institution. The idea behind the unofficial "First Hebrew Child" plank of his plan for Hebrew revival is that by giving birth to a single Hebrew speaker, an infant without the power to speak at all, for whom learning Hebrew would be as effortless—or as effortful—as learning to speak any language, Ben-Yehuda can bring into being an entire population of Hebrew speakers. Whereas Johnson would eliminate change over time, Ben-Yehuda would eliminate everything but change over time.

Since Ben-Yehuda imagines he might bring a population of Hebrew speakers into being by propagating a line of descendants, he introduces a model of language in which there is no distinction between the particular activity of the individual and any activity or subjectivity beyond that particular. Conceived entirely chronologically, as a relation of before and after, Ben-Yehuda's fantasy is of a language that announces a relation between the particular and the abstract while bypassing the general, the social. What distinguishes the abstract from the particular is the passage of time; language is remade into a

system devoted entirely to creating the perpetuity of the individual subject—
Eliezer Ben-Yehuda himself.

But since the autobiographical form is what enables Ben-Yehuda to imagine subjects who act and are consolidated or diffused only as they move *through* time, we need to go outside his own narrative to discover both the historical moment and the culture within which his relentless narrativizing takes place. Consider Itamar Ben-AVI's best-known recollection of his childhood, bearing in its narrative neatness the suspicious marks of the fictional, but telling nonetheless. As Ben-AVI relates the story, his father isolated him from all contact outside the family lest he be contaminated by languages other than Hebrew, a situation that had the unintended effect of rendering the long-heralded First Hebrew Child mute until he was well past four years old. When Ben-Yehuda went out of town, a family friend who had betrayed a Hebrew-only pact he had made with Ben-Yehuda and was educating his own children in Yiddish urged Devora to speak to the child in another language. Ben-Yehuda returned unannounced to find Devora singing Russian lullabies to their son. The First Hebrew Child intervened in the ensuing fight with the first sentence of modern Hebrew uttered by a native speaker. A few years later, on receiving as a seventh birthday gift a Hebrew translation of *The Count of Monte Cristo* done by his father, Ben-Tsiyon/Itamar responded: "Thank you, Papa, I have already read it in French."[55]

Taken together, the two anecdotes constitute an important reminder that in the moments when Ben-Yehuda attempts to revive Hebrew by imagining language within a wholly chronological paradigm, as a system of signification that matters only through time, he is able to realize the "success" of such a paradigm only by erasing the sociality of his relations with his wife and child. In attempting to guarantee a Hebrew-speaking child by creating an environment in which Hebrew becomes the language of a "community" so radically truncated it becomes a kind of identity, Ben-Yehuda seeks to create a model of individual authority that works by masking the limitations of its extent, by creating a situation where individual intention manifests itself as social context.

If Ben-AVI's memoirs function as a specific challenge to the representative claims of his father's autobiography, we can read his own name change as a much more theoretically complicated effort to generalize a challenge that is, in a nutshell, a challenge to the legitimacy of generalization. What is perhaps most notable about the critique mounted in the particular figure of this name

---

55. Quoted in Harshav, *Language in Time of Revolution*, 107.

change is how, as a reading of the general function of the patronym, it is undertaken in the service of the much narrower questions of Jewish national and Hebrew linguistic revival. At the most general level, Ben-AVI's refusal of his father's surname highlights the way the patronym depends on its capacity to occupy a position somewhere between the literal and the figurative, the particular and the general, in order to establish its own authority to name and, in naming, to authorize a present identity in the conditions of a historical past. If normally it is the moment of transfer from father to son that both brings the patronym into being and brings it into crisis by designating it as a figurative sign of a literal biological relationship, the paradoxical adoption of new patronyms, which is one of the most visible points of intersection between Zionist political and linguistic revivals, effectively complicates the association between the linguistic and the figurative. The significance of Ben-AVI's rejection of the name Ben-Yehuda, in other words, needs to be considered not simply in relation to the general structure of the patronym but in relation to *Ben-Yehuda's* own act of self-naming and the way that act is one part of his larger political rhetoric of autobiography.

In exchanging his birth name "Perelman" for the Hebrew name "Ben-Yehuda," Ben-Yehuda simultaneously literalizes the patronym's descriptive function ("Son of Yehuda" refers to Eliezer's father, Yehuda Perelman) and disrupts the patronym's use as a sign of a social process of transfer from father to son. By choosing for himself the name "Son of Yehuda," Ben-Yehuda draws a distinction between father/son understood synchronically as a description of a particular relationship and the patronym understood diachronically and symbolically, as the sign of a social structure of inheritance. Not only does this act of self-naming rupture the conflation of literal and figurative that is crucial to the normal functioning of the patronym, but his connecting this act of rupture to the adoption of a *Hebrew* description complicates the opposition between literal and figurative that normally structures the patronym by the implicit overlaying of social context—in the form of national language—upon the particular relationship described. In adopting the name Ben-Yehuda, Eliezer makes explicit the implicitly literal aspect of the synchronic biological relation of the patronym. While this literalizing pays homage to the elder Perelman by relabeling the relation in all its particularity— by translating that label from a proper name into a description—this same literalizing gesture that might appear to honor their relationship by removing it from the socially symbolic can also be understood to render the relationship illegible. In contrast to the normal functioning of the patronym in which the significance of the biological relation is finally subsumed within the figurative purpose of the name, the embodied quality of the literal—that is to say, biological—relation between fathers and their children is revealed to be itself ahistorical, to be, in the narrow personalness of the relation marked, pursuing an identity outside history.

But for the First Hebrew Child, for whom neither the relation to Hebrew nor the relation to the Ben-Yehuda autobiography quite resembles his father's, the act of self-naming engages a different context of issue. It is these differences that help account for the strangely bifurcated quality of the name he chooses in place of the one his father offers, as well as the split, deliberately ambivalent quality of his own gesture of self-naming. The name Ben-AVI is striking both in its anomalousness and when understood as a revision of the rhetorical technique of collapsing form and content as a means of generalization that at once describes the narrative form of Ben-Yehuda's autobiography as a whole and is employed frequently within that narrative. In its two apparently appositive meanings—"son of my father" and "son of E[liezer] B[en] Y[ehuda]"—Ben-AVI evokes in an instant Ben-Yehuda's entire program of Hebrew revival, a program whose rhetorical and institutional strategy turns on making the absolutely private instance stand for the general, the social, by means of *and*—here lies the difficulty—in the service of language.

Itamar's self-naming is so blistering an indictment of Ben-Yehuda's project of revival—or at least those elements of the revival that explicitly incorporate Itamar himself—because it articulates in plain language the terms of Ben-Yehuda's strategic conflations. In the punning Ben-AVI, Itamar collapses in a single word the absolutely particular—he is the son of Eliezer Ben-Yehuda—and the entirely abstract—he is "the son of my father"—the very identification of particular and abstract that Ben-Yehuda engineers in his effort to revive a language without the participation of an existing society of speakers. Ben-Yehuda attempts to work his way out of the "paradox of institutional decoupage"—the problem of making Hebrew speakers when one needs Hebrew speakers to do so—by theorizing a kind of language use that does not depend on the preexistence of any social world, much less a society of speakers. In explicitly articulating the mechanics of the operation of the patronym in general and Ben-Yehuda's autobiography as a form of political narrative by bifurcating the absolutely local content "son of Eliezer Ben-Yehuda" and the general patronymic form "son of my father," Ben-AVI effectively turns his private refusal of his patronym into an undoing of the patronymic structure. Whereas his father's self-naming admitted the literalism that announces contingent history—he calls himself Ben-Yehuda because his father's name was Yehuda—only once, for himself, the double valence of "Ben-AVI" renders the ahistoricism of the patronym untenable once and for all, a name that describes how naming works socially in general, and in so doing renders that generalization impossible. In its place, Ben-AVI implicitly offers a historicity so uncompromising that the named subject becomes indistinguishable from the subject who names, the speaker of Hebrew whose authority begins with a gesture toward the past that must be repeated at every moment. The model of language Ben-Yehuda comes up with escapes its dependence on supporting institutions or surrounding speakers by devoting itself entirely to marking out the passage of a single subject through time. The vocabulary of this language beings and ends with "Itamar Ben-AVI."

So what are we to make of the fact that in the midst of the most ambitious and labor-intensive single project of what is arguably the most ambitious and labor-intensive social program of linguistic making in the history of modern Europe, we discover the traces of a project that is almost comic in its relative ingloriousness: an entire language, complex, endlessly involuted, without edges, brought into being to name a single man, and in so doing to imbue him with the power of persisting over time? Such breathtaking disproportion can certainly be seen to bring us back to where we began, to the "new historians" of the post–Yom Kippur War era, for whom Ben-Yehuda is the specifically *cultural* enactment of a Zionist founding mythology structured around asymmetry. Individual heroes produce civilizations, and civilizations emerge from nothing at all, both disproportions designed to naturalize the organized inhabitation of a place by people who did not always live there. By this account, and indeed in part by Ben-Yehuda's own, the heroic cultural laborer who can bring an entire language into being by mere force of will and the language brought into being and marshalled with the sole objective of naming an individual stand as the twinned devices of what is, when all is said and done, a project of dissimulation. While it certainly seems true that Ben-Yehuda's role in causing an entire population to speak Hebrew has been overstated, and that this exaggeration and others like it have frequently been employed to pernicious effect, the asymmetries between the particular and the abstract that Ben-Yehuda's narrative deploys to such striking effect reveal some significant truths about the process of Hebrew in the late nineteenth and early twentieth centuries, even as they set the stage for the subsequent telling of untruths.

If Ben-Yehuda appears sublimely egotistical in theorizing a language whose first and final purpose is to name him, we might read in his articulation of such a project evidence that he and his contemporaries experienced the speaking of Hebrew as having the power to undo the fundamental structures of the self. A quarter century of triumphant poststructuralism is likely both to have inured us to the emotional force that follows from the assertion that language structures subjectivity and to have eviscerated such a claim of any

historical particularity. Yet Ben-Yehuda's autobiographical preface to the first
dictionary of modern Hebrew makes it apparent that those men, women, and
children settled in Germany, Russia, and Palestine who considered whether
they should speak Hebrew experienced the decision to do so as having the
power to make themselves unrecognizable to themselves, to create such a gap
between their past selves and their present and future selves as to dissolve the
very subjectivity on which such a shift might be registered. If Ben-Yehuda,
frustrated by the frequent failures of his efforts to establish the sorts of institutions that might enable people to begin speaking Hebrew without giving
the matter a second thought, indulges the fantasy that he might forgo institutions altogether by becoming the First Hebrew Father, the model of language
that emerges from such a fantasy to guarantee the persistence of his own
name across time responds to the pervasively felt anxiety that speaking Hebrew might threaten the very possibility of subjectivity.

It ought to come as little surprise, then, that this anxiety about the dangers
of speaking Hebrew emerges most palpably in Ben-Yehuda's discussion—one
of the few in his preface—of the specifically formal difficulties he faces in
compiling the dictionary. The lexicographical challenge he faces in structuring his dictionary is the formal challenge offered by a language not wholly
known:

כל המילונים הרגילים שבכל הלשונות, המסודרים לפי סדר א״ב, אינם מועילים אלא למי
שיודע מלה מן המלות בלשון מין הלשונות ומבקש לדעת פירושה, דקדוקה, איך להשתמש בה,
וכדומה. אבל מי שיש לו איזה מושג, ואינו יודע המלה אליו, ואינו יודע אם יש למושג הזה
באותה לשון, מה הוא יעשה? איך הוא ימצא את מבקשו?

[All regular dictionaries in all languages ordered according to the alphabet are of
no use except to someone who knows word from word, language from language,
and wants to know the meaning, grammar, or usage, for example. But for someone
who has a concept and does not know the word and does not even know if this
concept exists in the same language, what will he do? How will he find what he
wants?] (147)

The solution Ben-Yehuda comes up with is a dictionary organized not alpha-
betically but according to subject matter, with extensive cross-references,
something like a thesaurus. Whereas for Johnson it was the alphabetical organization that prevented his *Dictionary,* with its multiple quotations, from
operating as a precise textualization of its individual users' experience of having learned language, and that consequently marked those dictionary users
as *speakers* of English, here the absence of existing speakers of Hebrew is

marked by the inadequacy of the alphabetical form. Although Ben-Yehuda, briefly, if idiosyncratically, outlines the scope of the dictionary's structure in the autobiographical preface—"every branch of research and philosophy, every figure of speech and poem" (148)—the dictionary form's imbrication in the process by which it is to be used means that it can be fully described only by means of narrative example. Here is Ben-Yehuda, writing in 1895 in *HaZvi* [The glory], the Hebrew weekly he published:

> I know that if you touch your friend lightly on his body this . . . causes a little laugh. You don't know if there exists a term in our language for this . . . nor what the term is. Now, go my friend, look in every thick dictionary you have and turn over its pages; maybe you will find what you are seeking! You will certainly wear yourself out and not find the word. Not so with my book. What you are looking for, dear reader, is the word "tickle." So you go to the word "touch," which you know, and find what you want. And, if you say, I don't know the word "touch," don't be afraid, this too has a solution in my book. Go ahead, dear friend, to the word "hand," and you'll find there the word "touch." And if you don't know the word "hand," go to the word "body" and you'll find there "hand." And if you don't know either of these words, this is not my responsibility, dear reader. . . . I have planned [my dictionary] for people who know the basics of our language.[56]

Ben-Yehuda purports, by means of this hypothetical address to an unspecified reader, to show how this reader might use the dictionary to discover the word for a concept whose very existence in Hebrew is uncertain. But in examining the logical structure of the passage, we will notice that the narrative is organized around a series of failures, concluding with an announcement of the limits of reader ignorance beyond which even the dictionary is unequipped to help. That the passage begins with the "answer" that was supposed to have been abandoned as a starting premise and is organized thereafter as a "narrative of failure" speaks less to a disingenuousness on Ben-Yehuda's part than to the structural impossibility of distinguishing between failed and successful use of a form organized around the presumption of its reader's incomplete knowledge of the language. At the same time, the problem of beginning that, as we have seen, represents the theoretical and historical specter that haunts Ben-Yehuda's writings on the Hebrew revival here manifests itself in the passage's odd, counterclockwise circlings. Once again we are beginning with the answer to the supposedly unnecessary premise that arrives at an acknowledgment of the impossibility of beginning. But here this dynamic is not simply used as a vague articulation of the condition of contemporary

---

56. *Ha-Zvi* 7 (1895): 23–24, quoted in Fellman, *Revival of a Classical Tongue*, 105.

Hebrew but instead becomes a theorizing of the role of history in the concept of the Hebrew-speaking subject.

Equally striking, and intimately connected with the conflation of "failed" and "successful" uses of the dictionary, is the fate of the body. In this passage, addressed to a hypothetical dictionary user, Ben-Yehuda implicitly links the thesaurus structure to his time in Algeria, with the dictionary form appearing as an effort to realize the relation between his own embodiment and his language-making efforts by way of genre. The passage operates as a genre in the strictest sense of the term, its insistence on moving by way of generalization, rather than in an oscillation between the particular and the abstract. The incident's exemplariness turns not on its representativeness but on its enactment, its particularity stubbornly resistant to abstraction. What the passage shows us about how the dictionary might be used cannot be codified into a set of rules—the structure of direct address, turning text into speech, insists further on this unabstractability—but can only be performed over and over, or generalized by way of another example, by generating another associative chain. The passage takes as its premise its readers' lack of the kind of shared linguistic knowledge that Johnson's *Dictionary* depended on; here, those who would use the dictionary do not know Hebrew well enough even to know whether the word they are searching for exists. Instead, the passage attributes to its readers shared *sensations*—the common, but not abstract, bodily experience that would lead one after another from "touch" to "hand" to "body" (or from "body" to "hand" to "touch") in search of the Hebrew word that might name the sensation they have just experienced. Not only does the dictionary organization presented here presume that a variety of different readers, none of whom necessarily has anything close to a comprehensive knowledge of Hebrew, nonetheless share the same patterns of sensation, but it also assumes that a particular reader can rely on the constancy of his or her own sensation, its resemblance to previous sensations, in moving from acting and speaking and experiencing the material world in a known language to doing so in a language he or she does not know.

But the generalizability of the sensation, and hence its capacity to serve as the dictionary's structural ground, depends on its users' maintaining the fragmentation enacted by the passage. They must be willing to refrain from organizing these sensations back into a whole body, back into a self that would associate such sense data with memories of a life in a particular language, a language other than Hebrew. In contrast with the "First Hebrew Father" model of language formation, which makes indistinguishable the embodied Ben-Yehuda, who produces other bodies, and the linguistic Ben-Yehuda, who produces a spoken language out of a collection of texts, the thesaurus form depends on the separability of bodily sensation and the language used to name that sensation. Sensations can function as the instrument for discovering whether a word exists in a particular language only insofar as they are experienced as separable from any particular language. If the passage announces itself as an example of how the dictionary would work and then goes on to present an associative train driven by the failure to discover what one is looking for, this apparent contradiction ought not to be understood as evidence of the incoherence of Ben-Yehuda's position. The dictionary works the same way whether or not "you" find what you are looking for—the same chain of associations are presented—because the patterns of sensation that create this chain are able to structure the process of dictionary use only to the extent that they are experienced as existing impersonally. These sensory links can lead "you" to discover a word you do not know exists only if these sensations can be experienced as existing prior to and independent of any "you" that would seek to know. You can learn how to talk about your sensation only as long as your sensation is not made yours.[57]

If we flesh out the profile of "you," that hypothetical user who pores over Ben-Yehuda's newspaper to learn how to make his or her way around the not yet published dictionary, probably in dire need of something like that dictionary to make sense of the article he or she is reading, we will get a better sense of what it means to learn a language only by losing oneself. Although most of those who were settled in Palestine in 1905—those who would have had access to Ben-Yehuda's newspaper *HaZvi*—were drawn from a variety of

---

57. Within the terms of this model of perpetual incompletion, not only do the notions of linguistic agency and causality change, but so do the prevailing understanding of material evidence and the way that evidence functions to produce corporate identity. We need to keep in mind that Ben-Yehuda's program was designed not merely to make Hebrew usable in the present, but to revive it as a national language of the Jews, a national language that might operate as such without the precondition of national territory. The narrativity that is implicit in the thesaurus structure means that though the dictionary itself assumes the persistence of a gap between its individual users' knowledge of Hebrew and the language as a "whole," individual users nevertheless can be known—though not assumed—to move from a condition of less to more extensive knowledge of Hebrew. Thus when Ben-Yehuda renounces any responsibility for designing a dictionary that could be used by people with no knowledge whatever of the Hebrew language, he in part acknowledges the tautological quality of single-language dictionaries (though, it should be noted, most of the entries in his dictionary include German and French equivalents of the Hebrew words introduced), but he seems more interested in locating historical criteria by which a newly revived Hebrew may be understood as actually, if not necessarily, Jewish. While anyone might theoretically know enough Hebrew to use Ben-Yehuda's dictionary, the Jews of the Diaspora who pray each day in an older version of the language are more likely than others to have sufficient knowledge. The theoretical difficulty of beginning a language from nothing is thus transformed into a way of generating—though not ensuring—the *national* character of the language, an idea of nation that is historical without being racial. The new Hebrew language, like the dictionary in which it is presented, classified, and created (and strikingly *unlike* the liberal aesthetic of European realism), is not meant for everybody.

countries across eastern Europe, the vast majority shared a common language—Yiddish—that each could speak far more easily than even the most linguistically gifted among them could speak Hebrew. To imagine a community of such settlers beginning to speak Hebrew is thus to imagine a group of people newly arrived to a desert landscape vastly different from the European cities and shtetlach from which they had come, deliberately opting to cease using a language they all knew in order to discuss politics, farming, street paving, or love in a language whose words for those activities were only just then coming into being—or not. Shlomo Lavi, a founder of Kibbutz Ein Harod, wrote of his early efforts at speaking Hebrew: "It cannot be appreciated how much it costs a man to go from speaking one language to another and especially to a language that is not yet a spoken language. How much breaking of the will it takes. And how many torments of the soul that wants to speak and has something to say—and is mute and stammering." [58]

For the aspirants of Ben-Yehuda's era, speaking Hebrew requires a massive and constant exertion of will in order to be unable to exert one's will, a decision to will oneself to be unable to speak in the name of being able to speak. Thus when such speakers fall back on the fragments of sensation in an effort to discover whether words exist to say what they want to say, the experience of sensation as the medium through which they recognize themselves becomes as much a reminder of loss, of what they can no longer say or be, as it is a discovery of some ongoing core of experience of their likeness to one another. If Ben-Yehuda's thesaurus-style dictionary traces the same associative trail whether one finds the word one is looking for or not, this is because to choose to speak Hebrew when it does not quite exist is to choose to have what one is looking for not matter.

The dictionary's temporal reversibility that follows from this willing suspension of causality, its refusal to conform to an unbroken narrative of linguistic development, turns it into a usable text—makes it, in short, into an institution. But the necessary abstraction of that moment of using the dictionary from the trajectory of its users' lives allows them to believe, like that child learning names of flowers on a nature walk, that others might be using the same words to link one sensation to another. Such a moment of abstraction produces the self that opens out to other sensing selves in the present, a complex, culturally differentiated moment, a present made comprehensive at the cost of being able to connect that present to anything that has come before. In this infinitely capacious moment, every word spoken in Hebrew is accompanied—made audible, really—by the hum and buzz of Yiddish and

58. Quoted in Harshav, *Language in Time of Revolution*, 138.

Russian and German and English and French. And in the roar of all that
sound, the subject that was not quite Hebrew or Yiddish or Russian fades
into silence.

⤚

I conclude this section by returning to where we began: with Ben-Yehuda and
a friend, in a field somewhere in Lithuania. Ben-Yehuda's friend, we recall,
stands in for other friends, the acquaintance not yet made with the fictional
Amnon and Tamar, characters who speak Hebrew in a novel that exists in a
world where Hebrew is not spoken and who thus must be put off to a time
in the undefined future:

... בימים הראשונים של ״ההשכלה״ שלי באחת העיירות הקטנות של ליטה, אחרי אשר
טעמתי את הטעם הראשון של הספרות החדשה, אחרי קראי בסתר את אהבת ציון ואת
אשמת שומרון, התעוררה בנפשי תשוקה גם לדבר עברית, ממש כמו אמנון ותמר ושאר הבחורים
והבתולות שפגשתי בעולם החדש ההוא, ומפעם לפעם הייתי יוצא עם אחד מחברי, שידע סודי
ו״נחטף״ גם הוא מחוץ לעיר בשדה והחבא, בגניבה, בפחד ורעדה, פן ישמעו הבריות, סחנו
בלשון הקודש.

[In the first days of my "Enlightenment" (Haskalah) in one of the small towns in
Lithuania, after I had my first taste of the new literature, after my surreptitious
reading of *The Love of Zion* (the first full-length Hebrew novel, by Abraham
Mapu) and *The Guilt of Samaria,* there awakened in my soul the desire to speak
Hebrew as well, exactly like Amnon and Tamar and the other youths and maids I
met in this new world, and from time to time I would, with one of my friends who
knew my secret and was grabbed by it as well, go out of the town to a field, and be
hidden, stealthily, with fear and trembling, lest creatures hear us conversing in the
holy tongue.] (140)

Ben-Yehuda and a friend head out beyond the confines of their town into a
nearby field to speak Hebrew out of earshot of their fellow creatures. Ben-
Yehuda's friend "knew [his] secret," and this shared secret enables them to
complete their adventure successfully. Once beyond the city limits, the two
do not hide themselves but, passively, are "hidden" ("החבא"), and "stealthily,
with fear and trembling" proceed to speak the holy tongue, a secrecy apparently transformed, paradoxically enough, from linguistic exchange into public performance. (The word I am translating as "stealthily" is literally parti-
cipial—"בגניבה [in stealing].") The ambiguity of modified object sustained by
the participle contributes not only to a more general sense, associated with
the secret, that the locus of speech's meaning must remain suspended some-

where between individual speaker and a listener who has some uncertain relation to a larger community, but also to the sense that such suspension, an unlocalizable "stealing," represents a fundamental threat to subjects who might be understood to "own" their meanings.)

Our first impulse might be to read Ben-Yehuda's penchant for secret keeping as a mild prefiguration of his later impulse to name himself "First Hebrew Father." Both the secret and Ben-Yehuda's linguistic parenting suppose that the institutional problems of spoken Hebrew can be circumvented by radically scaling back what counts as a Hebrew-speaking community. Since Ben-Yehuda's friend knows his "secret" before their escape into the field, it appears to be that secret that motivates their departure; by this account, Ben-Yehuda's desire to speak Hebrew, whetted by his novel reading, is the thing that must be kept secret. But however uncontroversial such a gloss might initially appear, it is quickly complicated by the fact that Ben-Yehuda's secrecy continues, in one form or another, even after he has left the confines of the city, as the two of them would "be hidden, stealthily, with fear and trembling, lest creatures hear [them] conversing in the holy tongue."

The passage's two sorts of secrecy—the secret understanding that leads the pair to slip away and the secret enacted by their fearful hiding—are structured, however ambiguously, around the shifting relation between bodies and language that organizes the entire preface. The nature of Ben-Yehuda's secrecy changes markedly after he leaves the city proper; whereas both his secret—his desire to speak Hebrew—and its revelation are linguistic while he remains within the city, as soon as he leaves his secrecy apparently becomes nonverbal, "behavioral,"[59] and hence gains a quality of publicness, even as it putatively means to escape public notice. The odd taxonomic status of Ben-Yehuda's furtive behavior (Why make a secret "public" by transforming it into a system of visible, bodily gestures if one is interested in keeping it secret?) calls into question a number of aspects of the narrative. What is the nature of the public Ben-Yehuda fears, if he is compelled to continue his behavior even after he removes himself from its midst? Even more confounding, exactly what kind of behavior constitutes his and his friend's stealth, particularly if we consider that, since a Hebrew language community does not yet exist, the two Hebrew speakers are unlikely to be "overheard" in any uncomplicated sense of the term?

What the passage leaves unclear, in short, is whether what is being kept

59. Of course, I mean neither that language use does not constitute a form of behavior nor that nonverbal behavior cannot communicate in ways that might be termed linguistic. I use terminological opposition as an admittedly crude point of departure; as we shall see, the narrative itself does much to complicate both terms.

secret in the field is a linguistic happening or a bodily happening, a thing said or a thing done. Do they understand the very fact of speaking Hebrew to constitute their behavior as threatening and hence subject to some kind of unspecified but no doubt negative scrutiny, or does the threat lie in what they might say? Do they crouch behind rocks or trees in order not to be heard (or seen) at all, and if they do so, is it because they fear being overheard by a public that understands Hebrew and will be offended by some aspect of the content of their talk? (Ben-Yehuda goes on, later in the passage, to describe the progression of their conversation from "childish" topics like the love of Amnon and Tamar to more weighty "affairs of state.") Is it because the mere sound of Hebrew (or nonhegemonic) speech is likely to cause rancor? Or is their hiddenness "metaphorical," an inevitable outcome of the fact that they are speaking a language for which there exists no public and that consequently cannot be overheard, so that they may wander freely through the open field to which they have escaped and nonetheless remain "hidden"? When Ben-Yehuda the First Hebrew Father entertains the fantasy that the difference between language and bodies could be made not to matter, he does so in response to the threat that in order to speak the Hebrew language, subjects must will themselves to become nothing but bodies, broken into sensing fragments.

In the most straightforward sense, we cannot tell whether bodies or language are being kept secret because we do not know who might be watching or listening, and therefore we cannot surmise what that audience's interests and aversions are. While the passage recalls the *Jewish Chronicle* review of *Daniel Deronda,* where the irregularity of the correspondence between geographical spaces and homogeneous national populations raised the possibility that anyone could be the author of a given text, here the uncertainties of overhearing are invoked to different effect. To the extent that it aligns us with an audience whose interests (in bodies or in words) are unknown, this passage keeps us from imagining just what Ben-Yehuda and his friend are doing in the field. And in this moment where the events of his autobiography become impossible to imagine, Ben-Yehuda lays out a new definition of fiction and thus theoretically, if not programmatically, places novelistic fiction at the center of his plan for Hebrew revival.

In looking forward to making the "acquaintance" of characters with whom he cannot identify, Ben-Yehuda forcefully historicizes the operation of fiction, insisting that fictional representations are not equally legible and comprehensible to all people at all times. But whereas this description of Mapu seems designed to limit and qualify a linguistic literalism by which fictional characters are presumed to speak some version of the language out of which they are constituted, Ben-Yehuda's narration of his escape to the fields works to convert this qualification into a new theory of fiction. If we hark back to where we began with Johnson's *Dictionary*, with its oddly contradictory characterization of writing as both labor and leisure, we will recall that the incoherence of his description was a consequence of the particular "work" for which Johnson enlists language—the work of overcoming the social fragmentation of divided labor. Johnson's double—we might even say "divided"—description of written language stems less from his sense of the particular difficulties attendant on making, using, or organizing the English language than from the power he attributes to language as a means of grounding a common sociality while circumventing the pitfalls of a society drawn together by the interdependence of its various forms of labor. Not only did the divided interdependence of the labor-based society of eighteenth-century Britain present a political problem (Who might represent the perspective from which the interests of British society as a whole might be discovered?), but it bespoke an even more fundamental crisis concerning the fundamental meaning of history: What is the moment at which such a society can be said to "be"? And if there is no single moment, then how can that society know about the past that has constituted it? Language provides an alternative ground of cohesion only insofar as it is understood to function as an identity—a quality of what one knows and consequently of who one is—rather than an activity. It is only by being an ongoing and distributable condition that language offers a commonness that neither elevates any particular perspective nor takes place at any particular time.

But while both the form of and the justification for Johnson's *Dictionary* can be understood as responses to the particular cultural demands placed on them, what Ben-Yehuda's unimaginable description of his escape into the field and the poignantly fragmenting thesaurus structure of his Hebrew dictionary imply is that common language can be made usefully "identitarian" only by being associated with a particular geographical space, and that it is the realist novel that accomplishes this association. If the novel's characteristic representation of language in the form of dialogue seems an instance in which the contradictions of Johnson's descriptions of language suddenly appear noncontradictory—dialogue is at once "spoken" and written and hence, within his taxonomy, both labor and leisure—Ben-Yehuda's quasi-novelistic escape to the fields works to expose the logic underlying the consolations of dialogue. As with Johnson's account of orthography, in dialogue language is at once the thing represented and the medium of representation and as such can be understood to occur at a particular moment of time—the moment of the represented speech act—and to persist through time. The representation of language in language thus becomes both the moment of transparency by which the novel's representational medium of language comes to seem authoritative and the place where the momentary "use" of language is made continuous with its ongoing (narrative) authority.

Insofar as the goal is not simply to establish an identity between the language of an individual novelistic character and the language employed by that novel's narrator but to establish language itself as an ongoing ground of social identity, however, what makes the novel matter is its power to make the language used by individuals in a particular speech act—a particular moment of dialogue—seem identical to the language used by other members of that society and to seem by virtue of its generality and ongoingness to be a permanent feature of both the individual speaker and the society at large. Ben-Yehuda's autobiographical counterexample makes apparent the way the novel accomplishes the labor of making the continuity of the language of individual speakers and the language of the narrator stand as evidence for the continuity between the language used by any given speaker and that used by the culture at large. The novel does so by presenting the language of a particular geographical space (the language in which the *narrator* describes the space of the novel) as identical with the language in that geographical space (the language spoken by those other speakers who inhabit that space). Believing in the fiction of the novel means believing that the momentary speech act of the narrator can produce the ongoing, permanent material world described in the novel, and it is this quality of fictional belief that transforms language from a momentary act into a kind of identity. But Ben-Yehuda's interlude in the field shows that the narrator's fictional authority becomes believable—the narrator's linguistic descriptions are understood as making imaginable a permanent, ongoing material world and language is made a plausible substitute for labor—only if we know what language the people who inhabit that geographical space speak. Thus if the realist novel becomes a crucial instrument for turning language from a behavior into an identity because it turns the local speech act of the narrator into an ongoing condition of the world, such authority rests on the social assumption that people who speak the same language not only inhabit the same geographical space but speak the same language as a consequence of inhabiting the same place.

But by rejecting the fundamental assumption underwriting the operation of the realist novel's fictional authority, Ben-Yehuda does not merely challenge the ongoingness of the world brought into being by the narrator's language acts. By exposing the theoretical underpinnings of the novel's authority, his autobiography lays out an alternative definition of fiction and thus invests the novel as a genre with the power to transform the meaning and operation of linguistic culture. Suddenly in that Lithuanian field—this is a linguistic situation, after all, where subjects experience their connection to their bodies as especially tenuous—it is the *impossibility* of knowing what language an audience speaks that constitutes the fictionality of the text they engage. Bodies seem to be made up out of words precisely when the language used to represent them is uncertain, when one language as well as any other could be the one out of which those bodies are forged. Whereas George Eliot understood a novel's fictionality as working to naturalize the novel's language of composition by making it neutral, the language of the world, for Ben-Yehuda fiction operates by making all languages seem as though they could potentially be the language of the fictional space. Here we can discern the hauntings of Johnson's undefinable idioms, like the figure of the tree made not only ontologically but temporally indistinguishable from its representations. Such idiomatic language, we recall, is communal by virtue of its failure to refer to the world. If Johnson's *Dictionary* expels the idiomatic for fear that, in its refusal to be attributable either to an individual linguistic subject or to a particular geographical space, it will tear English national culture from its connections to the ever more permeable and expansive boundaries of the space of Great Britain, Ben-Yehuda generalizes the figural logic implicit in the idiom into the critical force of his new conception of fictionality. It is this new fictional locale that S. Y. Abramovitch takes up in his own novel, a novel that, as we shall see, uses its fictionality not simply to challenge the association between national language and national space but also to turn the self-evidence of being in a place, and the meaningfulness of such self-evidence, into a figure of speech. Like Ben-Yehuda and the Hebrew speakers of Algeria, whose linguistic community emerges as a consequence of the difference in the languages each would speak without effort, the community constituted by the reading of fiction is a community constituted out of the very possibility of their linguistic differences.

This model of fictionality makes a compelling case for the particular efficacy of the novel as an institution of linguistic revival. Both of Ben-Yehuda's "autobiographical" attempts to create embodied Hebrew speakers were hamstrung by what I called the "paradox of institutional decoupage"—by the difficulty of creating institutions to bring Hebrew speakers into being without the prior existence of the Hebrew speakers necessary to create and maintain such institutions. Ben-Yehuda's autobiographical "institutions" attempted to get outside the paradox by privileging one term over the other. Ben-Yehuda the First Hebrew Father was constituted out of a version of Hebrew whose

252 / Chapter Three

sole purpose was to name Ben-Yehuda so as to preserve his identity *through time*. The dictionary users who could learn Hebrew only by willing the experience of themselves as prelinguistic bundles of sensation were able to experience the complexity and multiplicity of the culture(s) of the present only by acceding to the loss of their past selves. In Ben-Yehuda's version of the fictional, by contrast, it is the very multiplicity of cultures at a single moment—fictional bodies come into being with the prospect that they could be made out of any language—that produces the fictional narrative as an ongoing, pointedly diachronic narrative. In Ben-Yehuda's concept of fiction, then, it is the variousness of the single moment that stands as evidence of the significance of the past.

Talking in One Place: S. Y. Abramovitch and the Irony of *Melitza*

Although the geographical placelessness and the odd nonutility of Hebrew make the Jews particularly well suited as figures around which nineteenth-century British novelists might explore the limits of their own representational practices, the anomalousness of the Jews as a nation was not exhausted by these aberrations. Not only had the language that was accorded "national" prestige ceased to be usable by Jews in nineteenth-century Europe, but the language spoken by virtually all European Jews—Yiddish—was considered unfit for the rigors of higher cultural production. And if, as Ben-Yehuda's autobiographical preface makes evident, the simultaneous presence of a variety of national languages is both the condition out of which Hebrew revival needed to take place and the morass into which those who would speak that not quite extant language threatened to disappear, Yiddish stood not simply as the most immediate instance of linguistic multiplicity likely to be experienced by European Jews but as an *enactment* of the condition. Yiddish is not simply one dot like others on the map of European languages, but without a specific spot to call its own. It was conceived to be a language patched together out of so many other languages that many people, including those who spoke and wrote it, thought it failed to be a language at all.

So in articulating the terms of the relation between an emergent Hebrew and the Yiddish most European Jews used in their daily lives, those late-century writers and political activists who advocated the return to a spoken Hebrew found in Yiddish a site for the expression of all the ambivalences surrounding the potentials and limits of an emerging European multiculturalism. Dan Miron writes:

Throughout the nineteenth century, young men with literary aspirations would not resort "naturally" to Yiddish. That they switched to Yiddish may indicate that they found it hard or even impossible to activate their talents, or to pursue their cultural and social goals in other languages; that they did not begin with it, however, indicates that Yiddish was not a part of their notion of literature and that they had to overcome certain inhibitions in order to conceive of it as such.

. . . For a writer, the decision to choose Yiddish as his medium was much harder than the decision to employ the stiffened and unresponsive holy tongue. While the latter decision would at least secure for him a membership in an intellectual community of sorts and connect him with a literary tradition that began with the Bible itself, the former would isolate him, place him outside any recognized literary framework, sever him from all the national poetic traditions he cared to associate himself with, and drive him into what seemed to be an intellectual wasteland.[60]

Even to those writers who ultimately adopted it as the language of their literary exploits, Yiddish was an ungrammatical linguistic hodgepodge that, as a kind of deformed German, signified Jews' incapacity to share a civilization with their neighbors. At the same time, in the view of prominent nineteenth-century German-Jewish historian Heinrich Graetz, it threatened to pervert the Hebrew from which it drew not only its alphabet but about 20 percent of its vocabulary.[61]

Even Shalom Aleichem (born Shalom Rabinovitch), who eventually not only became Yiddish literature's most widely known author but also labored assiduously to create a Yiddish literary history and canon out of what had been a tradition of literary isolation and disavowal, was quick to denigrate the literary potential of Yiddish early in his career, denying the language's capacity to function within nonsatirical literary forms. Writing in 1884, he complained that Yiddish was inherently crippled as a literary language by its exclusively oral, conversational condition. This oral-centered quality not only was marked by the absence of a written tradition from which new writings might draw authority and inspiration but meant, its detractors complained,

---

60. Dan Miron, *A Traveler Disguised: A Study in the Rise of Modern Yiddish Fiction in the Nineteenth Century* (New York: Schocken Books, 1973), 11, 39. While Miron's male gendering of Jewish writers choosing between Hebrew and Yiddish might seem merely the residue of an earlier critical era, that the education in Hebrew offered Jewish girls was far more rudimentary even than that afforded Jewish boys meant that the dilemma of deciding between the two languages was for the most part limited to men. The important and obvious exception to this generalization is the nineteenth-century Hebrew prose writer Devorah Baron, whose rabbi father educated her at home in the classical religious texts. For an interesting and persuasive account of the ways the gendering of the two languages affected the terms of the nineteenth-century Hebrew-Yiddish language debates, see Naomi Seidman, *A Marriage Made in Heaven: The Sexual Politics of Hebrew and Yiddish* (Berkeley: University of California Press, 1997).

61. Miron, *Traveler Disguised*, 277.

that Yiddish was viable only as a public, communal language, inadequate for exploring and expressing individual states of consciousness. In literature, Yiddish must be treated as a given, external reality rather than as a presence within the writer to be activated; it offers those who employ it the capacity for imitation, not expression. In Shalom Aleichem's view, Yiddish writers could justify their harnessing the folksy appeal of a familiar, if necessarily buffoonish language, strictly in pedagogical terms. Only by appealing to readers in a language they can read and understand without effort could Yiddish writers hope to rescue the common Jews from the state of linguistic and political parasitism into which they had so unfortunately descended. Even as it came into being, then, the Yiddish literary tradition was supposed to be moving toward its own supersession. The language's advocates and detractors agreed that as a hybrid language without any internally consistent grammatical structure, Yiddish was structurally barred from achieving perfection and, as such, ought to be taken up only instrumentally, as a means to an end.[62]

Although a more complete account of the relation of Yiddish to Hebrew during the emergence of the Hebrew novel is beyond the scope of this book,[63] the Hebrew-Yiddish debate—and, more generally, the linguistic bifurcation of written and spoken Jewish "national" languages—set the terms within which authors of the Hebrew novel, many of whom began their careers as writers of Yiddish, understood their projects. One of the most idiosyncratic, yet influential and finally illuminating, contributions to these debates is that of Micah Yosef Berdichevski, a Zionist fiction writer, critic, and political essayist whose writings in both Hebrew and Yiddish set forth remarkably sophisticated and inventive accounts of the role of a specifically *aesthetic* culture in the establishment of an autonomous Jewish state in Palestine. Whereas Ben-Yehuda seemed to back into his advocacy of novelistic fiction as a tool for reviving Hebrew, adopting it almost by accident, a strategy intuited rather than understood, Berdichevski's elevation of the literary was part of a much more systematic and long-standing engagement with the question of the relation between politics and aesthetics. This engagement included, most famously, a fervent defense of the uses of the literary against the influential Zionist Ahad Ha-Am's railings against "the belletristic."[64] For Berdichevski in a deliberate way, as it had been for Ben-Yehuda almost in passing, the

62. Ibid., 135.

63. For a good sociological and literary overview of Yiddish, see Benjamin Harshaw, *The Meaning of Yiddish* (Berkeley: University of California Press, 1990).

64. Ahad Ha-Am's early contribution to the debate has been reprinted, in English, as "The Law of the Heart," in *The Zionist Idea: A Historical Analysis and Reader,* ed. Arthur Hertzberg (New York: Atheneum, 1986), 251–55. It was originally published in *Pardes* (Odessa) 2 (1894): 1–8. Berdichevski's contributions can be found in *Kol ma'amarci Micah Yosef Ben-Gurion* [The complete essays of Micah Joseph Ben-Gurion (Berdichevski)] (Tel Aviv: Am Ovad, 1952). For an analysis of the dispute, see

fictional becomes the way of making the existence of a variety of linguistic cultures apprehensible at once.

In "טשטוש הגבולין" ("Tishtush ha-gvulin" [A blurring of the boundaries/limits]), Berdichevski shifts the terms of the discussion from an enumeration of the relative merits of Hebrew versus Yiddish to the cultural and political purposes of the Hebrew-Yiddish debate itself. The interesting question, Berdichevski claims, is not whether writers ought to be using Hebrew or Yiddish (he uses the relatively uncommon "Yehudit"—the Hebrew word for "Jewish," to refer to Yiddish instead of the more pejorative "Zhargon," or "jargon") but whether a distinction between the two languages can even be maintained any longer.[65] Whereas in Ben-Yehuda's description of the fragmenting power of the thesaurus form of the Hebrew dictionary the uncertainty of the relation of individual speaker to a particular language was considered mainly in psychological terms, in Berdichevski's view such linguistic undecidability can be conceived most profitably as a condition of the languages themselves.[66] Can we really say, he wonders, that we possess Hebrew and Yiddish?

קוראים אנו היום דברים עבריים, ואנו חושבים לרגע כי לנו הם: ולמחרת – שוב אנו קוראים
אותם הדברים ממש יהודית.

[We read today Hebrew words, and we think for a moment that they are ours; and tomorrow, we read the same words and they are actually Yiddish] (141).

In an instant, or more precisely, in the movement from one instant to the next, the hard-fought ideological battles over national language and, by implication, over the form a Jewish national "character" ought to dissolve into a process of reading. In this view, versions of individual subjectivity no longer

Arnold J. Band, "The Ahad Ha-Am and Berdyczewski Polarity," in *At the Crossroads: Essays on Ahad Ha-Am*, ed. Jacques Kornberg (Albany: State University of New York Press, 1983), 49–59.

65. Micah Yosef Ben-Gurion [Berdichevski], "Tishtush ha-gvulin" [A blurring of the boundaries], in *Kol ma'amarei Micah Yosef Ben-Gurion* [The complete essays of Micah Yosef Ben-Gurion (Berdichevski)], 191–93.

66. Berdichevski's place within the genealogy I have been mapping out is not the consequence merely of his interest in Abramovitch's work. As Zipora Kagan has recently put it, "No figure in modern Hebrew Literature has been more closely identified with the anthological enterprise than Micha Joseph Berdyczewski.... Berdyczewski ... compiled five multivolume anthologies, and seems to have discovered in the anthological form a fitting embodiment of what he considered the nature of modern Jewish existence. Indeed, so central and fundamental a role did the compilation of anthologies play in his life that it would be no exaggeration to call Berdyczewski *homo anthologicus*."

Of the five published anthologies, three were written in Hebrew and two were written in German, while all bespoke Berdichevski's interest in undermining any clear distinction between the roles of editor and creative writer, as well as between traditional literature (*aggadah*) and new Hebrew writing. For him this blurring of distinctions of genre and authority was in translating Jewish religious tradition into a mode of apprehending history. See Zipora Kagan, "*Homo Anthologicus*: Micha Joseph Berdyczewski and the Anthological Genre," *Prooftexts* 19 (1999): 41–57.

follow automatically from the communal adoption of a given national language. Rather, the individual Jewish national linguistic subject encounters the languages of his or her community over and over again in time and in so doing not only does away with any kind of singular linguistic identity but likewise undermines the notion of a stable, communally prior national language. While hardly idiosyncratic, in Berdichevski's hands the wording of the passage enacts this shift away from a stable linguistic identity in the reversal of the order from the first instance of "we read" to the second. In Berdichevski's description of the initial encounter with the text in question, the verb precedes the subject ("korim anu"/"קוראים אנו"), a construction that, in the moments of our own reading before we reach the object of the sentence, leads us to understand the verb as a noun. (Instead of "we read," the phrase might be translated "readers are we.") So whereas the word order suggests, for a flash, that "reader" might stand as an identity that would precede and transcend specific acts of reading, our own experience of our reading process as temporal—our experience, that is, of the transformation of "korim"/"קוראים" from noun to verb as we arrive at the direct object—subverts the assertion of such an identity, the performative enactment manifested in our reading producing the phrase's semantic shift. Berdichevski thus seems to invoke Johnson's fantasy of turning language from a practice into an identity—"reading" into "readers"—only to immediately mark that fantasy's passing. When we encounter the phrase again in the second clause of the sentence ("tomorrow, we read the same words and they are actually Yiddish"), it has become "anu korim"/"אנו קוראים" the *korim* now unambiguously verbal and hence contingent, following from the subject/agent. With the first-person plural linking those who read within and outside the text, the experience of reading as a historically contingent process at once enables and is reflected in Berdichevski's polyvalent and temporally disjunct "we," who read Yiddish in the very same words (a slightly different) "we" earlier understood to be Hebrew."

Moreover, the striking literariness of his argumentation in this passage implies that Berdichevski is not merely interested in injecting a sense of the instability of national linguistic identity into the Hebrew-Yiddish debate. In his pointed demonstration of the flexibility of Hebrew word order, he seems to be making the familiar case that the revival of Hebrew depends on the willingness of Hebrew writers and readers to depart from the set phrasings of classical texts. But whereas for Ben-Yehuda the achievement of such flexibility is manifested as a movement from a primarily written notion of language to a primarily oral one, Berdichevski here offers a notion of linguistic contingency predicated on markedly literary modes of achieving ambiguity. This literariness of Berdichevski's model is not limited to the fact that his linguistic subjects are here not speakers but readers; the *korim anu* that arrests our attention and initiates our particularly aesthetic experience of its circlings and semantic reversals does so not by achieving the transparency of spoken word order but by refusing it. Berdichevski goes on several paragraphs later to lament the efforts of contemporary writers to erase the distinction between writings appearing in their original languages and in translations. Only by maintaining a sense of translatedness, rather than by striving for a necessarily elusive transparency, can writers establish a sense both of the equivalence of different languages and of their consequent adequacy and comprehensiveness as languages. Here the category of the aesthetic, or more specifically the poetic, is crucial, since in Berdichevski's view it is poetry that permanently maintains the marks of its translation, demonstrating the inseparability of form and content that renders all acts of expression and all linguistic identities historically contingent and transient. Only with poetry, he asserts, are readers constantly made aware of their status as readers.

For Berdichevski, then, not simply writtenness but the highly concentrated version of writtenness implied by the category of the literary stands both as the theoretical foundation and as an element of a practical political program for establishing something resembling a Jewish national language.[67] In contrast to Johnson, for whom writing was unifying by virtue of its supposed power to keep language from changing, for Berdichevski writing can unify because it incorporates the marks of a changing language. But while he explicitly rejects the hierarchizing conventionally associated with the Hebrew-Yiddish debate, Berdichevski's primary interest nonetheless remains Hebrew. Hebrew may no longer be easily distinguishable from Yiddish, but by the essay's midpoint the relevant categories—as blurred as the boundaries at once coupling and dividing them may be—are no longer Hebrew and Yiddish but "Hebrew" and "not-Hebrew." And though Berdichevski, by locating historical contingency in a "Hebrew" reader's experience of an always linguistically marked literary form, apparently avoids the too personal biographicalism of Ben-Yehuda's First Hebrew Father model, that such literary forms are created, if not read, in the absence of a broader community of linguistic users means that Berdichevski's vision of a politics of aesthetic form is haunted by

67. See also Berdichevski's famous debate with Ahad Ha-Am, Micah Yosef Ben-Gurion, "Tsorech v'yecholet" [Necessity and capacity] (1897), in *Kol ma'amarei Micah Yosef Ben-Gurion* [The complete essays of Micah Yosef Ben-Gurion (Berdichevski)], 153–85. (Tel Aviv: Am Oved, 1952). Writing in response to Ahad Ha-Am's antibelletristic manifesto in the inaugural issue of the Hebrew journal *Ha-Shiloach*, Berdichevski argues against the position that Hebrew writers ought not produce imaginative literature until after other cultural institutions have been established. Indeed, for Berdichevski, the fictionality of Hebrew literature becomes a crucial strategy for creating political sovereignty. The essay is reprinted in Berdichevski's collected essays.

a threat of private language similar to the one that dogged the dictionary maker.

Berdichevski's emphasis on the experience of a Hebrew reader as opposed to a Hebrew author, as well as his attempt to understand linguistic usage as a relation to a necessarily public genre rather than as a process aimed at achieving apparently transparent individual speech, implicitly posits a Hebrew that is always already public, in that any present usage must be read in relation to past texts. But because this "always already" of Hebrew is historical rather than structural, Berdichevski's model gets around the problem of individual Hebrew authorship in the present by essentially ignoring it. Insofar as the Hebrew "public" he identifies is constituted across time and pointedly *not* at a single moment, the individual "style" that Berdichevski imagines will ensure that the particularity of a national language remains present to its users at any given moment of usage threatens to become the mark of a too idiosyncratic private language.

It is within the context of this theoretical conundrum that we can begin to understand just why Berdichevski invokes the literary career of S. Y. Abramovitch in constructing a politics of Jewish literary history. The sheer scope and variety of Abramovitch's oeuvre makes him central to virtually any account of Jewish writing in the nineteenth century, the particularities of its theoretical underpinnings notwithstanding. Indeed, the uneven trajectory of his career reads like a summary of the shifting trends of Jewish cultural poetics of the era. Having spent his formative years of intellectual development within the milieu of the Odessa Haskalah, in the 1860s Abramovitch undertook as his first major project the writing of a massive Hebrew *Toldot ha-teva* [Natural history], a project he abandoned at the end of the decade with only the first (zoological) cycle complete, having lost faith in the value of the natural order as the supreme paradigm of intellectual and moral truth.[68] In 1862, the same year the first volume of *Toldot ha-teva* appeared, Abramovitch published his first work of Hebrew fiction, *Limdu hetev* [Learn to do well], a virtually incomprehensible didactic romance in which characters are wont suddenly to interrupt their romantic pursuits and offer detailed programs of *maskilic* reform. Conceived as it was wholly within the terms of an Enlightenment faith in natural science as the foundation of political equality, Abramovitch's interest in writing Hebrew fiction did not survive his disenchantment with the Haskalah's elevation of the natural order, and by the end

68. Dan Miron and Anita Norich, *The Politics of Benjamin III: Intellectual Significance and Its Formal Correlatives in Sh. Y. Abramovitsh's "Maseos Benyomin Haslishi,"* Field of Yiddish: Studies in Language, Folklore and Literature, fourth collection, ed. Marvin Herzog et al. (Philadelphia: Institute for the Study of Human Issues, 1980), 4.

of the decade he abandoned Hebrew literature for Yiddish. (He did continue to publish regular essays in Hebrew on culture and national identity in a variety of Hebrew journals throughout the decade and a half in which his literary work was exclusively Yiddish.) In 1886 Abramovitch, having established himself as the foremost purveyor of "highbrow" Yiddish literature, turned again to writing fiction in Hebrew, translating many of his stories and novels from Yiddish into Hebrew by means of a complex process of self-translation that produced the most significant shift in Hebrew linguistic development prior to the establishment of permanent Hebrew-speaking communities in Palestine.

In the discontinuities and self-reflexivity of Abramovitch's literary corpus, then, Berdichevski finds not simply a model—an example of a solution—but a kind of extended meditation on the quality of exemplarity within a Jewish literary history. In "Tishtush ha-gvulin," Berdichevski identifies four distinct "Mendeles" (the name of Abramovitch's first-person narrator, Mendele Mocher Sefarim [Mendele the Book Peddler], by which Abramovitch himself, at least in his incarnation as a writer of fiction, was popularly known): Mendele in Yiddish; Mendele in Hebrew, having copied from himself (i.e., from his Yiddish works); Mendele in Hebrew copied by others; and Mendele in Hebrew, "by himself" (i.e., writing Hebrew originals). As was the case with Ben-Yehuda's body, this fourfold distinction offers in a single figure the intersecting elements of a larger cultural network in which modern Hebrew is located. But whereas Ben-Yehuda, having envisioned the transparency of individual speech within the context of classical Hebrew writings, figures his own Hebrew usage as an instance to be generalized outward, Berdichevski radically transforms the strategic and theoretical meaning of the exemplary user of modern Hebrew at the moment he considers the revival of the language within the frame of the *tishtush,* the blurring, of Jewish languages. In a sense we can summarize the movement from Ben-Yehuda to Berdichevski/Mendele as the movement from autobiography to self-translation. Once Hebrew and Yiddish are understood as not stably distinguishable or culturally autonomous, the problem of a too-personal Hebrew that, in its idiosyncrasy, threatens to become not Hebrew at all but something altogether private can be solved by translating the relation of Hebrew and Yiddish to the personal realm as a kind of self-difference. To the extent that, as with Abramovitch, the use of Hebrew stands as merely one of a range of linguistic and literary positions an individual is capable of occupying, its idiosyncrasy is transformed into mere style. Its particularity paradoxically becomes the sign of a certain imagining, the imagining of the existence of an unmarked public standard against which the tics of personal literary style are read.

Berdichevski's user of Hebrew is still first of all a reader, but instead of reading the wholly past texts of classical Hebrew, "Mendele" reads his own Yiddish texts—and other Hebrew users read Mendele. (That "Mendele" is itself a literary construction standing in some pointedly undefined relation to the historical Abramovitch—who is also Abramovitch the prose essayist— only reinforces the sense that aesthetic use has replaced the historical user as the basic unit of a yet-to-be-made Hebrew world.) Finally, in serving as an occasion for the shifting relation of Hebrew and Yiddish to be conflated with the self-difference of individual literary strategies, Berdichevski's "Mendele" makes linguistic knowledge and linguistic use the same. The irreducibility of the literary object, read, becomes the particularity of narrative—and authorial—voice. It is this quality of "voicedness" rather than transparency that stands, for Abramovitch as for Berdichevski, at once as the condition of disempowerment of a Jewish national language and as its possibility.

~

Abramovitch's Hebrew novella מסעות בנימין השלישי [*The Travels of Benjamin the Third*] (1896) is the most widely known of all his writings, fictional and nonfictional. In fact the story was one of the few works to circulate in its time beyond the overlapping communities of Yiddish and Hebrew readers when in 1885 an earlier Yiddish version was translated into Polish as *The Jewish Don Quixote*. In choosing to adapt the Don Quixote story in his own narrative of a pair of shtetl Jews whose comically errant pilgrimage to the Holy Land is finally halted for good a few versts from their point of origin when they are tricked into being conscripted for the Russian army, Abramovitch clearly makes a claim, however ironic, for his work's foundational status within the terms set out by a European novelistic tradition. But if he sees a secular Hebrew national literature as consigned to a general belatedness in relation to European literary culture, for Abramovitch this belatedness gains a positive aesthetic—and hence historical, linguistic, and political—content in its encounter with the particular conditions of nineteenth-century Hebrew textuality.

Abramovitch's return to Hebrew literature in 1886, one year after the publication of the original Yiddish version of *Benjamin the Third*, marked the first manifestation of his new conception of Hebrew literature as the outcome of a process of self-translation. As such, the novel was immediately notable for the radical and unprecedented character of its prose.[69] Although I have

69. For a fairly technical linguistic analysis of the changes in Abramovitch's usage registered in his 1886 return to Hebrew, see Lewis H. Glinert, "Did Pre-Revival Hebrew Literature Have Its Own

discussed at length the theoretical and ideological implications of a Hebrew whose communal existence was almost exclusively in the form of past texts, I have given little if any indication of the practical effects of such a linguistic situation on the prose of early Hebrew novels. In the absence of a community with an active knowledge of spoken Hebrew, Hebrew prose writers of the Haskalah strung together set phrases drawn from biblical sources in a technique known as *melitza* (high-flown figures of speech).[70] While a biblical allusiveness had long been a part of the Hebrew literary tradition, what is notable about the allusions encountered in the narrative fiction of the Haskalah is how *little* allusive work they actually do: the phrases for the most part function strictly as semantic units. When the contexts offered by the phrases' source texts are invoked, they rarely do more than add a generalized grandeur—at times used to elevate, at times satirically. By way of illustration, I quote from Alter's translation and gloss of Abramovitch's early, pre-Yiddish Hebrew work *Limdu Hetev:*

> After a few minutes one could hear from Shimon's room voices talking, *the voice of Efraim and the voice of Shimon.* And in the cookhouse *a voice from the heights was heard, Sarah rebuking the people of her house,* and servants *rushing off, hastened and pressed,* and the cry of roosters and fattened geese rose to the heavens.[71]

Langue? Quotation and Improvisation in Mendele Mokher Sefarim," *Bulletin of the School of Oriental and African Studies* 53, 3 (1988): 413–27.

70. Dan Miron defines *melitza* as follows: "a system of linguistic connective practices, which seeks to convey a certain expressive meaning by combining linguistic units—perceived as pre-constructed and as possessing a linguistic-aesthetic value of their own—without there being a link between these units and the one-off meaning which they effect. Thus the controlling power of meaning in the linguistic organization of the utterance is rather limited, sometimes being reduced to the selection of units that appear to be roughly appropriate and to stringing these units syntactically together. In no case may the meaning blur the independence of these units or melt them down to the point of destroying the autonomous wholeness which they had already acquired, as it were, before the creation of the contextual and syntactic bond between the unit and the whole. This wholeness has its coarse meaning in those familiar literary sources from which the units derive." Miron, quoted in Moshe Pelli, "On the Role of *Melitzah* in the Literature of Hebrew Enlightenment," in Glinert, *Hebrew in Ashkenaz,* 99–110, quotation on 101.

71. Alter, *Invention of Hebrew Prose:* "The phrases . . . emphasized are all drawn from familiar classical Hebrew sources; it is immediately apparent that about half the words in the passage are assemblages of such prefabricated units, a fairly typical proportion for *Haskalah* prose. There is only one nonbiblical allusion: 'rushing off' (*yechafezun*). Though only a single word in the Hebrew, this would have been recognized by readers because of its unusual grammatical form as a term from the solemn *unetaneh tokef* prayer from the High Holiday liturgy, in which angels rush off as the dread Day of Judgment approaches. Let me spell out the biblical allusions. A simple indication of two men talking, 'the voice of Ephraim and the voice of Shimon,' echoes a repeated refrain in Jeremiah (e.g. 7:34), 'the voice of gladness and the voice of joy.' The link is reinforced by an intertextual rhyme, *Shimon* and *sason* [gladness]. Whether or not the cookhouse . . . is supposed to sit on a second story, or whether the lady is standing on a bench, 'a voice from the heights was heard, Sarah rebuking the people of her house,' so that the narrator can introduce a joking citation of Jeremiah 31:15: 'a voice from the heights was heard,

In contrast, Abramovitch is able to dispense at least partially with these prefabricated phrases in the "new," more supple Hebrew he produces in the years following 1886 because of his willingness to replace the prestigious biblical Hebrew favored by the writers of the Haskalah with the more semantically and syntactically flexible, if culturally denigrated, rabbinical Hebrew. Whereas biblical Hebrew has only two verb tenses, a limited vocabulary, and a largely paratactic syntax, the language derived from the writings of the rabbinical period designated past, present, and future tenses, along with a habitual past, and used a variety of subordinating grammatical structures to indicate specific causal relations among the different elements of a sentence. Furthermore, because the Diasporic rabbinical Hebrew was used by people who came in contact with other languages, its relatively large vocabulary includes words from non-Hebrew sources adequate to both the Midrash's familiar anecdotal style and the Mishnah's legal discourse of minutiae.[72] For Chaim Nachman Bialik, the most influential Hebrew poet of the first half of the twentieth century (and coincidentally the first Hebrew translator of Cervantes' *Don Quixote*), the revolution produced by Abramovitch's movement away from *melitza* in favor of a more synthetic Hebrew was not merely linguistic but was aesthetic and even epistemological:

> [The early Haskalah prose writers] had forever been scratching around on the surface of the shell, but their pen never seemed to get inside . . . for portraying nature, it was again a case of two or three well-worn coinages lifted from the Bible. . . . Until Mendele what we had were linguistic tricks and games, linguistic capers, linguistic shreds and patches; Mendele handed us one language that was a whole. . . . He was virtually the first in our modern literature to stop imitating the Book—he imitated nature and life.[73]

Such testimony would attribute to Abramovitch the same achievement of having single-handedly turned Hebrew into a transparent, transmissible, easily adaptable modern language—what Bialik labeled *nusakh*[74]—that Ben-Yehuda claimed for himself. I contend, however, that the Hebrew of his second (post-1886) phase is not transparent, nor does it aspire to be. The

---

lamentation and bitter weeping; Rachel weeping for her children,' with the last phrase being a reversal rather than a citation of the biblical source, 'rebuking' substituted for 'weeping.' Even the scurrying about of the servants, 'hastened and pressed,' invokes a biblical formula, the urgent haste of Ahasuerus's messengers in Esther 8:14" (25–26).

72. Alter, *Invention of Hebrew Prose*, 21.

73. Bialik, quoted in Pelli, "On the Role of *Melitzah*," 100.

74. The term *nusakh*, which means literally "version" or "manner," refers to a system of cantilation by which established melodic patterns are applied to a potentially infinite number of texts.

language of Abramovitch's later work clearly undergoes a marked shift away from the stiff, formulaic, pastiche-like quality of his early fiction toward a more fluid and naturalistic conception of representation. Yet Abramovitch nonetheless remains faithful to a Berdichevskian notion that the specificity of Hebrew expressive forms, not their naturalization or putative erasure, forms the foundation of both their national cultural significance and their political efficacy.

Moreover, as I hope will become clear, Abramovitch does not figure his linguistic and formal innovations simply in relation to Hebrew—or even Jewish—linguistic and literary traditions. It is a critical commonplace to read the consistently ironic quality of his late writings as a consequence of both their Yiddish sources—Yiddish fiction is almost exclusively satirical—and the lingering influence of *melitza*'s gross tonal divisions. What finally distinguishes the irony of Abramovitch's early fiction from that of his later works is not the distinction between the linguistic and the thematic or between the unintended and the intended—between, that is, an irony that results from the inadequacy of the language of the Hebrew Bible to the task of representing a contemporary world of Jews and a situational irony designed to show, say, the futility of an individual Jew's effort to escape the physical, economic, and spiritual confines of a Russian shtetl. Rather, it is the distance between irony viewed as a mark of a condition of inadequacy and Abramovitch's relatively late-developing sense that the irony that is at once linguistic *and* thematic forms the prerequisite for European Jews' critical engagement with both the tradition of the European novel and the political and social arrangements that novelistic tradition at once explains and helps make possible.

For Abramovitch, whose own authorial identity became so thoroughly bound up with the ironizing, first-person narrator Mendele the Book Peddler (Mendele Mocher Sefarim) who frames virtually all of his mature fiction that he is most often identified by the name of the character he created,[75] irony becomes the stylistic enactment of the nontransparent, horizontally differentiated fictionality that Ben-Yehuda introduced by way of the unimaginable scene in the field. In place of a language that aspires to transparency, a fictionality by which description within a particular language is understood to indicate the linguistic hegemony within the space being described, Abramovitch's irony is structured around a "fictionality" that represents a relation between the state of the narrow Jewish world and other cultures that are tempo-

---

75. For a detailed, persuasive account of the development of the Mendele narrator and its relation to Abramovitch's authorial representation and self-representation, see Miron, *A Traveler Disguised*, esp. chap. 4, "On Native Ground," and chap. 5, "The Mendele Maze: The Pseudonym Fallacy."

rally coincident, if geographically remote. But if Abramovitch's early and persistent intellectual debts to the teachings of the Haskalah made western European liberalism an obvious ideological context from which to imagine Jewish political subjecthood, the "nature and life" that provide the more immediate context and object for his writings—the absolutist regimes of Nicholas I and Alexander II—were hardly liberal. The English liberalism that locates political right in the individual and nevertheless understands England to be English by virtue of its inhabitants' status as *liberal* subjects could suspend such a contradiction as long as its terms remained implicit. This suspension was produced and manifested by the operation of the category of the fictional within the realist novel—and disrupted, as we have seen, by the novelistically unrepresentable Jews. Insofar as Russian political ideology made explicit its linking of nationality, political right, and occupying a particular geographical space, there was no need for its ideologues—or its critics—to be thinking two things at once. The notion of a world that is not but might plausibly be that is characteristic of English realist fictionality becomes the thoroughly temporal—historical and mundanely political—disjunction between one's own power and the power of those one encounters by accident, between where one is and where one wants to be, between where one is and where other Jews reading Hebrew are, between the way the world is and the way one would like it to be, and finally between what one means to say and the words at one's disposal. In short, the world of Abramovitch's imaginings is a world that is linguistic, literary, and apparently self-contained without being quite fictional.

What Abramovitch attempts to do, in short, is to create a novel in which the history of a language is elevated to a prominence equivalent to that of the narrative presented *in* that language—equivalent, that is, to the plot of the novel. If the realist novel as it developed in England over the eighteenth and nineteenth centuries is essentially "Johnsonian" in its formal presumption that the use of a word, an act of reference, erases the record of that word's past uses, Abramovitch's Hebrew novel refutes that presumption not by illustrating the likeness of the two narratives—the plot of the novel and the history of the language in which it is written—but by insisting on their unassimilability. Structured around the logic of the ironic and the idiomatic instead of the referential or representational, *The Travels of Benjamin the Third* creates a text in which bodies and language are meaningful by virtue of their extension through time, in which textuality marks not a condition of permanence, but one of difference—the difference between how things and words once were and how they are now, between how they are and how they might be at some point in the future.

And if Abramovitch's work does not simply illuminate or unravel the formal paradoxes that structure the realist novel and lend it much of its ideological punch but seems committed to presenting another generic beast entirely, the strangeness of the novel is as much the consequence of its Russianness as of its Hebrewness. Whereas in England, as we saw in *Daniel Deronda*, Jews made evident the contradictions of a liberal economy in which subjects are defined both by their location within the geographical space of England and by their mobility through that space, the political economy of late nineteenth-century czarist Russia was such that Jews were not simply considered to be tenuously or contingently placed within the land of Russia but were seen as absolutely, constitutively opposed to Russian space. And if the absoluteness of their exclusion from the Russian landscape makes the Jews subject to political violence and oppression of an intensity not experienced in England, it also enables them to read in their own positions a logic that lets them generate new political and aesthetic forms.

The exhaustiveness of Abramovitch's efforts to remake the terms of novelistic fiction first become apparent, paradoxically enough, in that aspect of *Benjamin the Third* that seems least fictional. In Ben-Yehuda's recollection of his reading of Mapu's Hebrew novel, the novel's Hebrewness and its fictionality were one and the same: that Amnon and Tamar spoke Hebrew and the Ben-Yehuda who read about them did not meant that the novel's representational medium was the guarantee of its distance from the real. For Ben-Yehuda, the fictionality of the Hebrew novel took on a thoroughly temporalized, even utopian cast as his aspiration to "make the acquaintance" of those Hebrew-speaking characters at some point in the future world effectively sought to convert fictionality into teleology.

In choosing a traveler as his novel's protagonist, Abramovitch pointedly undoes the regular, if inverse, relation between what goes on in the novel and the language in which those goings-on are represented. Since before the full-scale Revival traveling was the only context outside Palestine in which Jews spoke Hebrew to one another as a matter or course—witness Ben-Yehuda's "travels" in Algiers—Abramovitch selects for himself the only narrative in which the very fact of being represented in Hebrew does not announce its fictionality. But Abramovitch does not write about the adventures of two hapless pilgrims in order to render transparent the Hebrew in which he writes; in any case the insistent literary echoes of *Don Quixote* would foreclose anything approaching transparency. More to the point, if the decision to write about a traveler does not have the effect of absorbing the history of Hebrew into the self-evidence of its reference, this is in large part because the ways *The Travels of Benjamin the Third* is "about" travel extend well beyond the

activity and identity of the erstwhile hero. As I hope to show, it is because
the novel does not merely conceive "travel" as a thing characters do but instead adopts it as a kind of generic deep structure that the story of Hebrew
can be told even as the language is utilized as a medium for telling stories.

What is striking about Abramovitch's novel is the way it converts what
Daniel Deronda revealed as the necessarily unarticulated ideological principle of the realist novel—that people are the way they are, and resemble
one another, because of the geographical space they occupy—into an explicit
representational precept. Whereas we might understand "traveling" (an undertaking that concerns itself above all with the relation between an individual and the landscape occupied at any given moment) to "theorize" such a
principle, in Abramovitch's novel the boundary distinguishing the qualities
that define people from the qualities that define places becomes blurry. Nowhere is this more evident than in the novel's initial description of Batalon
(Idlerstown), the fictional shtetl that is Benjamin's place of birth and point
of departure:

בטלון היא עיר קטנה באחד המקומות הנשכחים מרגל אדם, ודבר אין לה כמעט עם הישוב,
וכשיזדמן לשם פעמים אחד מעוברי-דרך, משגיחים לו מן החלונות ... [ו]משתוממים ומשתאים:
מי הוא זה ומאין זה, מה לו פה ומי לו פה, ולמה נתכון בביאתו? מפני שבאיה בעלמא
בלא כלום אי אפשר, וכי לחנם אדם את רגליו והולך ובא על לא דבר!

[Batalon is a small town in one of the forgotten places of human pilgrimage, and
there is almost nothing to it but its inhabitants. On the rare occasions when a
passer-by should happen to arrive there, they will observe him from the windows
in wonder and astonishment: Who is this person and where does he come from?
What and who is there for him here, and what is the meaning of his arrival? Because coming without reason and for nothing is impossible, and a man does not in
vain on his own legs walk and come for nothing!][76]

If Benjamin can be assured that he will remain a "Bataloni"—a resident of
Batalon and an idler—no matter how far away from his birthplace his adventures take him, this stability of identity seems as much a consequence of the
power of his identity to define the place where he is as the reverse. But the
absoluteness of the mutually constitutive relation between Batalon and its
inhabitants effectively empties the relation of its significance. That inhabitant

76. S. Y. Abramovitch, *Masa'ot Benyamin ha-Shlishi* [The travels of Benjamin the Third], in *Kol kitvei Mendele Mocher Sefarim* [The complete works of Mendele Mocher Sefarim] (one-volume edition) (Tel Aviv: Dvir, 1947), 58. Though English translations of the novel do exist, all that I have been able to find are translations from the Yiddish version. Unless otherwise indicated, all translations are my own. Subsequent pages will be cited parenthetically within the text.

and place of habitation have the power to determine each other evacuates both of any foundational authority; the identity of people and place becomes nothing more—though nothing less—than a play on words, the accident of having been born an idler in a town called "Batalon."[77]

But if "Batalonim" like Benjamin are tied to Batalon simply by the contingent accident of linguistic history that named their town, the passage suggests that the structuring force of this sort of linguistic power extends well beyond the already blurred borders of Batalon. Having rendered people and place absolutely interchangeable, Abramovitch is able to effect a reversal of the conventionally novelistic relations of place and significance that immediately exposes the contradictions at the heart of European liberal understanding of the nation-state. The passage gestures toward the generally accepted understanding of Jews' placedness as merely contingent, an accident of historical realization that does not fundamentally alter their status as a nation defined by its lack of a determinate place. But by putting this condition of contingency at the center of the description as its organizing principle—Batalon is the place of the Jews whose presence there is accidental rather than of the passers-by whose presence is in itself meaningful—Abramovitch teases apart the dual aspects of the conventional liberal subject.

When, as in *Daniel Deronda,* Jews appeared only contingently located in a particular geographical place, both the contradictions of liberalism and the novel's strenuous endeavors to stabilize those contradictions become apparent. When, as in Czar Nicholas's Russia, Jews are figured in principle as actively opposed to placedness, the very novelistic relations that conventionally work to associate free, potentially mobile liberal subjects with specific locations begin to fall apart. Only moments after we have been introduced to Batalon, whose very existence is the outcome of its inhabitants' lack of will, we are presented with another sort of landscape entirely:

ומעשה באדם מישראל, שהבא למקומנו תמר, ויהי לפלא, והיו כל בני העיר, למקטנם ועד לגדולם, רצים לראותו. נטלו את החומש והראו בו באצבע, שהתמר, תמר זה, כתוב בתורה! אטו מילתא זוטרתא היא, זה התמר הרי והוא מארץ-ישראל!... הביטו לו – וארץ ישראל נצנצה במחזה לנגד פניהם: הנה עוברים את הירדן! הנה מערת המכפלה! הנה קבר רחל אמנו! הנה כותל-מערבי! הנה טובלים ושולקין ביצים בחמי-טבריה! הנה עולים על הרי-הזיתים, אוכלים חרובים ותמרים עד בלי די, ונותנים לתוך הכלים מלא חפנים מעפר הארץ!... אוי, אוי היו נאנחים, ועיניהם מקור דמעה.

[And once there was a man from Israel who brought to our place a date, and what a wonder it was: all the people of the town, from the smallest to the largest, ran to

77. Compare with the relation of fictionality to place and institutionality in the opening of Anthony Trollope's *The Warden* (Oxford: Oxford University Press, 1998).

see it. They took down the Pentateuch and pointed with a finger: this date, it is written in the Torah! This shriveled word (thing), it is the date we see and it is from the Land of Israel! They looked at it, and a spectacular view sparkled before them: Here crossing the Jordan River! Here the Cave of Machpelah! Here the grave of our mother Rachel! Here the Western Wall! Here bathing and poaching eggs in the hot springs of Tiberias! And climbing the Mount of Olives, eating carobs and dates endlessly, and filling their buckets with dust from the Land! Oy, oy, they sigh, and their eyes are a source of tears.] (58–59)

Here, instead of providing a stabilizing backdrop for the deliberate circulations of novelistic characters, the space of the novel—or, more accurately, the concrete details that conventionally signal space—has come loose from its own place and, pried free by its resemblance to an extant textual reference, has begun to circulate itself. If we consider this passage as a kind of commentary on and complication of the relations of placedness and meaning presented in the previous description, then it becomes clear that the stabilizing capacity of conventional representations of geographical space not only depends on an erasure of the history of its inhabitants, the process by which they came to be where they are, but also depends on an erasure of the history of the space itself. Seen within the context of this passage, the claim that space acts as both context and object—that it marks the passage of time by the sign of its own persistence—becomes manifestly false. The details of geographical space can no longer be assumed to mark a history of changelessness but instead appear to depend on the cancellation of history in favor of a merely momentary description of a place.

This transformation of the concrete detail—a piece of fruit—from the mark of a stable place to the bearer of the narrative of its own movement announces Abramovitch's renunciation of a familiar form of fictional authority, as well as of the kind of ideological work accomplished by this authority. Whereas Ben-Yehuda's autobiographical—and nonfictional—description represents a historically specific moment of cultural illegibility, Abramovitch here generalizes the terms of the crisis to suggest the ways this momentary unimaginability reveals realism's dependence on and role in producing the sort of correspondence of language and space that would render the history of a language entirely imperceptible. In the work of Ben-Yehuda we could not envision the events that occurred in the field because we did not know the language spoken by those who would look at or overhear the two friends. In this passage the seeing performed by the audience internal to the text and the imagining of the scene that we would normally attribute to a narrator (standing in for an author) are collapsed into one another, made temporally

coincident, a single action. As the "spectacular view" rises before those Batalonim (who, like us, are bent over a text), we as readers external to the whole
scene cease to be invited to observe an already existing fictional scene—a
world imagined into being by the author at some point prior to and more
ongoing than the moment inhabited by the characters. Instead, we join those
characters, those Jews of Batalon who are the accidental inhabitants of their
town, to do the work of imagining a world into being. For Abramovitch's
eastern European readers, whose familiarity with Hebrew religious texts is
not accompanied by any effortless spoken knowledge of the language, his
novel offers a narrative in which the necessity of referring back to the text of
the Bible to understand the meaning—and meaningfulness—of the object
being represented does not remove them from the plot of the novel but ties
them all the more firmly within it.

The description is so expunged of temporality that it is virtually without
verbs, the movement between the repeated diexic mark of presence and the
series of place-names producing a curious evacuation of the novelistic
world.[78] We as readers become conscious of the labor of our imagining in
precisely the same degree that that imagining becomes the only activity—and
hence the only temporal movement—occurring in relation to the material
world gestured toward. The pointed absence of the kind of spatial, material
persistence normally signaled by its juxtaposition with the movement as/
within the foreground collapses the distance between real and fictional
worlds, leaving us with the sense that the visual images associated with the
place-names the passage points to are what we make of them. If we do experience movement in our apprehension of the "scene" presented, it is the movement of our own reading process, the experience of our imaginings as ordered
and constricted by the placement of one name before the next that relocates
temporality with the shriveled word/thing on the page from which it originally emerged.

Moreover, this collapse of the imagined into the real under the pressure of
temporal immediacy is registered in the framing sections of the passage, as
the figures who begin to move across the field of place-names, ascending the

78. The rhetoric of the passage turns on a grammatical effect not available in English, by which
present plural verbs can be read equally plausibly as implying first person- and third-person (impersonal)
pronominal subjects. The passage moves from a description of the Batalonim's reading process through
a description of a series of tombs and monuments in which there are no verbs whatever, and culminates
with this syntactic undecidability that makes it impossible to determine whether the readers are continuing to imagine human figures in a tableau about which they are reading or have entered the tableau
themselves. I have attempted to render the crucial ambiguity by translating the present plural verbs as
gerunds. Thanks to Amit Yahav-Brown for a helpful conversation about both the reading and the translation of this passage.

Mount of Olives and eating their fill of carobs and dates, turn out to be syntactically indistinguishable from the inhabitants of Batalon whose impulse to confirm the itinerary of the "Holy Land" date by referring to the Bible generated the entire set of imaginings in the first place. (In fact, the verbs that occur toward the end of the "scenic" section are presented in the impersonal third-person plural without any articulated pronouns; the third-person pronoun is offered as a separate grammatical unit only at the moment of return to the "frame.") As the date breaks off from some hypothetical place of origin and circulates to Batalon, eliminating the distinction between foreground and background, we as audience members join the characters to follow the date back and forth between the always already and the happening. In eliminating the distinction between what was imagined in the past and what is seen in the present, this passage makes the process of imagining contingent on the context within which it takes place. Just as our inability to presume a given language keeps us from "seeing" what is happening to Ben-Yehuda in the field, we cannot "see" the Cave of Machpelah or the Western Wall as though they are textual givens, already imagined. Both contingent, changeable processes, our seeing and our imagining must go on together.

Abramovitch's transplanting of novelistic space from background to foreground, and in particular the peculiar "meaninglessness" of Jewish habitation by which he accomplishes this transformation of the meaning of space, is likely have been inspired by a sweeping set of legal reforms imposed by the government of Czar Nicholas I concerning the placedness of Russian Jews. These reforms, which began in 1844 with the official abolition of the system of separate Jewish communal government, took their most radical—and from the perspective of the Jewish communities, their most destructive—turn in February 1853, when Nicholas decreed that the conscription of Jews into the Russian army was no longer to be organized solely through local Jewish communities. While conscription quotas were still to be assigned according to locality and administered by Jewish communal leaders (who were now officially considered employees of the Russian government), Jewish communities falling short of their quotas were now permitted to arrest Jews traveling without passports and to substitute them for local Jews eligible for the draft.[79]

Although Jews were drafted at the same rates as the general population until the last three years of Nicholas's reign (1853–55), the most notable—and onerous—departure from the norm concerned the age of the recruits. Whereas the standard draft age of Russians was set between twenty and

---

79. Stanislawski, *Tsar Nicholas I and the Jews,* 184; subsequent page citations are given parenthetically in text.

thirty-five, the 1827 "Statute on the Recruitment of Jews" established the draftable age for Jews as between twelve and twenty-five. Recruits over eighteen were enrolled in the regular forces for the standard term of twenty-five years, while younger Jews served in special "cantonist battalions" until they reached eighteen, at which time they began their full terms of service in the standard battalions. The special regulations were motivated, according to Stanislawski, by a desire to use army service as an instrument for converting the Jews; an anonymous memo issued by the Third Section of the Imperial Chancellery—the secret police—offered a proposal (never adopted) to conscript only young Jews, at double the usual quota, noting the unparalleled missionary opportunities provided by a military culture that made absolutely no special provisions for its Jewish members (15). Of the seventy thousand Jews conscripted into the Russian army between 1827 and 1854, approximately fifty thousand were minors (25). And particularly among the young, the discipline of army life—helped along by various methods of physical torture—produced the desired outcome: Stanislawski estimates that "at least half of the Jewish Cantonists and a substantial number of adult Jewish soldiers were baptized during their service" (25).

With the likelihood so remote that a Jewish boy recruited into the Russian army at age twelve would return to his community on his release thirty years later, competition to avoid the draft within the Jewish community was often ruthless. Although during the early period of conscription recruits tended to be drawn disproportionately from among the poor and unemployed, it was the final period of the conscription era—the period when local recruitment was opened up to supplementation by unlucky passers-by—that not only produced the most horrifying incidents of intracommunal betrayal but that also finally and fatally undermined the authority of the local Jewish government (the *kahal*). Because the choice of conscripts was left to local Jewish lay leaders, they were forced to decide who was to be sacrificed for the benefit of the community at large. With parents willing to go to almost any lengths to protect their children from the draft, the *kahal* leaders hired special deputies—called *khappers* (from the Yiddish word *khapn*, "to catch")—to kidnap children, search out fugitives, and locate Jewish travelers without adequate papers in order to fulfill the conscription quotas. It is these *khappers* who, meeting Benjamin and his Sancho Panza–like traveling companion Senderl on the outskirts of a village not far from their home town of Batalon, lure the two travelers into an army recruitment office with the promise of being received and honored by the local Jews. Though Nicholas relented slightly just before his death, granting a series of concessions in the terms of the Jewish conscription, the damage to the Russian Jewish communal structure had already been wrought: "The previous psychological and institutional solidarity of Jewish society in Eastern Europe was shattered, the authority of the communal leaders was subverted—never, it seems, to be regained" (186).

From the perspective of the Russian government, for whom the devastation of Jewish communal leadership structures produced by the change in conscription regulations was neither a particular goal nor a matter of particular interest when it did occur, the new laws resulted in greater compliance and, consequently, a more efficient conversion of the Jewish population. But what Stanislawski's emphasis on the most obviously coercive aspects of the relationship between the Russian government and local Jewish populations during this period is likely to obscure is the way the new conscription laws fundamentally altered the terms of Jewish national identity in Russia and, in so doing, transformed the category of Russianness as well. If a recurrent challenge facing ideologues of nationalism, both liberal and otherwise, involves producing a national history by which the present association of a given nation and a specific geographical space is more than merely accidental, then the 1853 revision of the conscription laws, in not only separating Jewish national identity and the occupation of specific land but pointedly opposing them, can be seen to produce, by contrast, a notion of Russianness inextricable from the territory called Russia. Whereas Abramovitch's opening description of Batalon suggests that Jewish identity was routinely figured throughout Europe as only incidentally occurring at a certain place, the 1853 laws make quite a different case. In not merely relegating local Jewish identities to the realm of the incidental but arguing for the subsumption of such contingent local identities within a juridically (Russian) national category of Jewishness, the new regulations posit a Jewish identity that not only lacks the right to any particular geographical space but is without the right to geographical space understood *categorically*. The general idea of occupying land thus comes to stand in explicit opposition to Jewish national identity in Russia.

It is virtually a commonplace of criticism of *Benjamin the Third* to note that for all of Benjamin's wanderings, the series of Jewish towns to which he travels are virtually indistinguishable. While this sameness is usually taken as Abramovitch's critique of the stasis and parochialism of local Jewish communal life, a parochialism he associates in many of his Yiddish stories and in his nonfiction articles[80] with the corruptions and self-interest of *kahal* leadership, that the novel's climax turns on this change in conscription laws intimates that the shtetlach at which Benjamin arrives are marked by a certain sameness

---

80. I am thinking in particular of Abramovitch's three-part article "Ma na'aseh?" [What is to be done?], *Ha-Melitz* [The advocate], nos. 1, 2, 3 (1878).

because the new regulations have rendered them juridically the same. I will discuss the relation of the ending to Abramovitch's conception of a Jewish national politics later. For now, what is even more interesting to me than the novel's explicit representation of the effects of the new conscription laws is the way he understands the historical emergence of this opposition between Jewish identity and the occupation of land to disrupt the mutually constitutive connection between conventional notions of realist *authorship* and the novelistic production of stable national space.

In their power to turn the variety of linguistic usage into a stable, ahistorical linguistic entity, the realist novel's acts of reference resemble the multiple examples of Johnson's *Dictionary,* where the textuality of the different linguistic instances of use lifts both the language and the language user out of time. By erasing any clear distinction between novelistic foreground and background, the Batalon date not only pointedly disrupts the conventional novelistic authority and the apparent linguistic stability that is such authority's consequence, it installs an entirely different sort of textual authority in fiction's stead. Here the textual authority is pointedly *not* representational, since the text makes the errant date meaningful not by taking its place but by coexisting alongside it. The pun "דבר" sublimates a "thing" into a "word," and in taking it away, shriveling it down to nothing, invests the word with a certain substantiality: "this date, it is written in the Torah." In contrast to realism, where words would pass themselves off as things even as they relieved those things of the historicity of their own materiality, here the date matters *because* it is named rather than subsumed in the text. What makes the date matter is that it has moved; it has come from the Holy Land. Textuality stands, in short, as the history of movement, both spatial and linguistic; it matters in the present *because* it is past, marking the difference of the condition of the present from that of the past rather than the persistence of one state. Whereas the liberal valuation of mobility as the mark of freedom conceives of movement as a kind of potential, presence moving into the future, the mobility marked by the Pentateuch matters because it has already occurred.

Whereas Ben-Yehuda the First Hebrew Father sought to make the Hebrew of written texts usable in the present by collapsing language and bodies into one another, Abramovitch, a generation older than Ben-Yehuda and bound by greater loyalty to the general intellectual framework of the Haskalah, envisions a model for using Hebrew in the present that involves not so much a break with past practices as a reinterpretation of them. To the extent that the conception of textual authority Abramovitch presents in the circulating date refuses the compensations of representation in order to insist on its own temporality, its own power to mark the differences between the conditions of the

past and those of the present, he is able to invoke the authority of the Hebrew
texts from which he draws his language to authorize new uses of those texts.

Accordingly, instead of working to create new institutions that would help
generate new ways of using Hebrew, Abramovitch's novel works to discover
the logic of institutions as it emerges from within his reading of the meaning
of Hebrew textuality. Consider the novel's opening lines:

אמר מנדלי מוכר ספרים:

יתברך הבורא וישתבח היוצר, שהוא מנהיג את הגלגלים בעולמות העליונים ואת ברייותיו
התחתון ומבין לכל הליכותיהם. אין לך עשב שאין לו מלאך, שמכהו ואומר לו: "גדל!" ואם
עשב כך, קל וחומר בן-אדם בו-בנו של קל וחומר אדם מישראל.

[Mendele the Book Peddler said: "Blessed is the Creator and praised is the Maker,
who establishes the destiny of the heavenly spheres and of all his creatures below
and understands all their movements. There is no grass that will sprout without an
angel to command it: 'Grow!' And if the grass is this way, how much more so
in the case of humans and if for them, how much more so for the person from
Israel."] (57)

This opening appears at first glance to circumvent altogether the relation
between language making and institutional power, since the passage's location implicitly aligns Abramovitch's fiction making with God's power to call
a world into being by a simple, formidable, speech act. But the language of
the passage qualifies such an alignment even as it is brought into being: both
the opening tag, "Mendele the Book Peddler said," which recalls the format
of the rabbinical—postbiblical—writing of the Talmud, and the body of the
passage, which alludes to the Kaddish prayer, relocate the imagery of Creation with its markedly noninstitutional notion of linguistic authority within
the interpretive framework of Jewish reading practices, of ritual.

Moreover, in invoking the Kaddish, Abramovitch does not merely connect
his own fictional authority with a central prayer of the daily Hebrew liturgy
but chooses what is essentially a metaprayer, a reflection on the rhetorically
paradoxical quality of the act of prayer. The second stanza of the Kaddish,
from which the language here is drawn, concludes with the (Aramaic) words:
[He whose לעלא מן כל ברכתא ושירתא תשבחתא ונחמתא דאמירן בעלמא. ואמרו אמן."
glory exceeds is beyond all blessings, songs, and praises that we might render
unto him: And let us say, Amen]." Although the Kaddish concerns itself with
the foundation of human authority to pray, what is striking about its language is that no reference is made to the human worshipers until the very end
of the prayer. The verbs Abramovitch stresses by adopting in his rewriting,

yitbarach ("blessed") and *yishtabach* ("praised") follow reflexive (*hitpa'el*) form, and that quality of reflexivity is further emphasized in the Kaddish by the absence of separate subject or object (literally, something like "he who blesses [or praises] himself"). The Kaddish thus articulates a notion of human rhetorical authority born of its necessary inadequacy: in essence, prayer as irony. We pray—and are defined as believers—in virtue of our recognition that our prayers can effect no meaning without God's will. But if the ironic quality of the prayer structure normally remains tacit, and if this tacitness is what ensures that the irony is wholly directed toward the ineffectual (and hence pious) supplicants, insofar as the Kaddish makes explicit the terms, it at once suggests and enacts a redirection of that always unstable irony.

But once again the autonomy of divine authority, an autonomy that manifests itself in the circularity—the nonreferentiality—of God's language, turns out to depend entirely on the willingness of those who recognize that authority to accede to its force. If it is this condition of self-reflexivity (the description, in a word, of a God wholly adequate unto himself) that consigns the humans who utter such a prayer to a position absolutely without authority, the act of articulating such reflexivity, as Abramovitch does when he adds the subjects/objects "הבורא" and "היוצר" ("Creator" and "Maker") to the reflexive verbs of the Kaddish, reflects in the redundancy of referentiality an authority that is absolute because it is language, not because its language is irrelevant. The God who, in blessing and praising himself, renders those who would speak of such self-adequacy ironically beside the point suddenly appears to have been brought into being by this heretofore unmeaning speech act (and the heretofore irrelevant speakers), the circularity of God's authority providing the very conditions of the speakers' power. Insofar as the passage defines irony as a kind of repetition with a difference, it narrates the movement from repetition to difference: whereas the Kaddish itself suggests that the endless repetition of prayer testifies finally to its ineffectuality, Abramovitch's ironic reworking of the prayer—his repetition *with a difference*—turns the circularity of God's self-authorization into the condition of its historicity. The self-enclosed, nonreferential quality of God's language—his capacity to create the world is his capacity to authorize himself—creates a version of authority that can be understood equally well as entirely ahistorical and as entirely contingent, brought into being at the behest of those who would repeat the language of power.

The circulation of the date—from novelistic background to foreground, from Palestine to Batalon—introduces the formal conventions of the realist novel in order to lay bare the possibility of seeing existing Hebrew texts as deriving their authority from their power not to stand outside time but to

mark its passing. Having thus used the novel to draw out the diachronicity
latent in Hebrew textuality—the difference within the repetition—Abramovitch turns the authority of the Hebrew texts back against the institutional
authority that would secure the writing of Europe. He begins with the Hebrew texts' most narrowly drawn battle for authority and then moves outward.

Taking a cue from Berdichevski, Abramovitch's Mendele looks first toward
the Hebrew-Yiddish debate as the historical ground from which the travels
that follow might appropriately be narrated. But finally—if paradoxically—
he grounds his authority in the undecidability of historical change, and in so
doing he qualitatively transforms the model of authorship presented by the
Yiddish version of the novel. The Yiddish-speaking Mendele of the early version figures his authorship as a stopgap measure that conforms closely to the
terms of the Hebrew-Yiddish debate: "Before the writers of Hebrew—whose
fingers are broader than my loins—before they wake up to the task of rendering the narrative of Benjamin's travels into the holy tongue, let my try to give
an abbreviated account of it in plain, everyday Yiddish."[81] Although this early
version certainly continues to resonate in the Hebrew account, the variations
are significant: here Benjamin awaits the awakening of Hebrew writers who
would "copy" ("להעתיק") "all the stories of Benjamin's travels" and "publish
them throughout all of Israel"; in the interim, he will publish a shortened account.

What is notable about the shift is the new emphasis on textuality: the
source from which any Hebrew version might emerge is already discursive
("all the *stories* of Benjamin's travels"); stories must be published and not
merely written. Moreover, the difference between a comprehensive version
and the "shortened" account placed before us accentuates the futility of
transparency as a representational goal. Authorship in this view thus becomes
a kind of editorship; but whereas Johnson imagined that an authorship
grounded in the power to arrange existing texts enabled subjects to escape
history, for Abramovitch editorship operates by virtue of its power to make
present, everyday linguistic practices no more relevant than any others. Left
crucially unarticulated is just what is missing from Mendele's rendition of
Benjamin's stories. Because we are similarly kept in the dark about the original language in which Benjamin's adventures and his accounts of those adventures take place, the state of the Hebrew language—its capacity to represent
the contemporary world of the shtetl, including the conversations of its inhab-

81. English translation of the Yiddish by Moshe Spiegel, *The Travels of Benjamin the Third* (New
York: Schocken, 1949), 11.

itants—thus becomes absolutely inextricable from the history marked by the text's referentiality, the point of intersection between the two versions of unknowability, the novel's Hebrew dialogue. Editorship—this copying—becomes repetition with a difference, but rather than proposing the need for an entirely new language to represent a modern world, it makes a case for the power of Hebrew texts to authorize their own reuse. Hebrew is capable of functioning as the language within which Benjamin's adventures will be related not because of its demonstrated capacity to represent the concrete details of nineteenth-century shtetl life, but because it is able to reveal the impulse to represent such a life as continuous with established practices of reading Hebrew.

For Abramovitch, the ability of existing Hebrew texts to tell stories of contemporary Jewish life lies not in their power to represent the streets and carts and battered fences of the Pale of Settlement, but in their constitutive eschewal of the goal of referentiality: the novel of Jewish life is to be found in the history of the Hebrew language, in Hebrew language as history. By contrast, that writing that would claim to ground its authority in the accuracy of its reportage, in its capacity to refer comprehensively and seamlessly to the material world, is not impressed by the contingency of material evidence but in fact exists entirely independent of that evidence:

כל כתבי העתים בלשונות בריתניה ואשכנז היו מרבים לספר בשנה שעברה את החדושים
והנוראות שנתגלו על ידי בנימין, יהודי פולני, בדרך נסיעתו הנפלאה למדינות המזרח. תמה,
תמה! קראו, הנהיה כדבר הזה או הנשמע כמוהו – אחד היהודים, בריה קלה זו, שאין בידו כלום,
לא כלי-זין ולא מכונות וכלי אומנות אלא טליתו ותפליו ותרמילו על שכמו בלבד, יכזה
לעלות ברגל לאותם המקומות, שאפילו תיירים הבריטניים מהגדולים והמפורסמים שבהם
לא הגיעו לשם מימיהם.

[All the British and German-language newspapers were crowded in the past year with the news and wonders discovered by Benjamin, a Polish Jew, in the course of his remarkable journey to the East. Wonder, wonder! Who has read or heard a thing such as this—that a single Jew, with nothing in his hand—no weapons, no means of transportation, or tools of art—nothing but his tallis (prayer shawl) and tefillin (phylacteries) and a pack on one shoulder managed to arrive by foot at places even the greatest and most celebrated British travelers were unable to reach?] (57)

With the details of his journey as yet unreported by the narrator Mendele, the wondrousness of his adventure is testified to solely by virtue of its having been reported in western European newspapers, an appearance made all the more remarkable by the fact of his Jewishness, since, we are meant to surmise, the doings of Jews rarely make their way into such publications. But while the discursive sweep of these newspapers is supposed to attest to the significance of Benjamin's adventures, Mendele suggests that such authority is not wholly accidental; the adventures of British explorers stand in themselves as standards of significance and, in so doing, lend their own authority to the journalistic organs that record them.

Although the narrator's enthusiastic ingenuousness here seems to carry an edge of irony, with the passage's elaboration of the circularity of national journalistic authority as much exposing its constructedness as offering its justification, the fact remains that when we finally arrive at the narration of Benjamin's adventures, what establishes the novel's fictionality is how far Benjamin's bumblings fall short of journalistic "significance." Just as Benjamin's position outside—indeed, in excess of—the mutually authorizing circle of British newspapers and British adventurers serves as the means of transforming authority into truth, the novel's capacity to present his adventures ironically depends on its implicit acceptance of the British newspapers' authority to judge, not simply confer, significance. In order to understand Benjamin as hapless, self-deluded, or at the very least ineffectual, we need to believe that the newspaper accounts Mendele refers to are actually fictional, not that they got it wrong. Because Benjamin's noteworthiness is represented as being somehow in fundamental opposition to the universe of significance to which the British newspapers subscribe, both cannot be ironized in the same gesture. The newspapers cannot be wrong if Benjamin is of little interest to them.

Inasmuch as it is understood as the authority to create fictions, Abramovitch's narrative authority seems to presume, and in presuming, to reinforce, not only the rightness of British and German institutions of journalism but their rightness *as* institutions. The newspapers' "error" becomes a sign of their status as fictions (within Abramovitch's text) as a result of the transcendent, or at least institutional, quality of their rightness; it is a rightness that is prior to any given journalistic examination and evaluation of evidence. But if the fictionality associated with British journalistic institutionality governs the most general relation of the reader to Abramovitch's text, it is a condition undermined from within by the ironizing presence of the internal, first-person narrator Mendele. That this subversion of authority occurs within the larger frame of the fiction does not necessarily mark its subordination, since, as we shall see, Abramovitch targets the formal claims of both institutionality and fiction. Represented in marked contrast to the British and German organs, the Jewish newspapers from which Mendele takes his charge to "copy the story of Benjamin's travels in the holy tongue" demonstrate a parochialism that is the obverse of the British and German newspapers' institutionalism.

Whereas the British papers are right before they have reported anything, for the Jewish papers, their institutional gaze trained unblinkingly inward, Benjamin is worthy of note not quite before he has done anything, but because he is a Jew, by virtue of a corporate identity that is wholly prior to any particular act.

While the British explorers and newspapers produce one another in a closed circuit of mutually reinforcing significance, Benjamin is able to break into this circuit because he has "managed to arrive by foot at places even the greatest and most celebrated British travelers were unable to reach": because, that is, there is no material evidence of his travels to be had. Because the Jewish newspapers' authority is figured as coincident with, rather than opposed to, Benjamin's own narration, it is subject to the irony directed toward Benjamin, irony from which the western European journals had been spared. But if the marked divergence of universes traced out by "a single Polish Jew" and the British press had the effect of translating what might have otherwise been seen as an unfortunate—and ironizable—miscalculation into a sign of the novel's fictionality, that the British and Jewish newspapers arrive at the same verdict regarding Benjamin's heroism means that the irony to which Benjamin and the Jewish newspapers are subject is made indirectly to apply to the British newspapers as well. We might be tempted to understand the necessity of indirection as an indication of the British papers' invulnerability because such indirection turns on establishing the comparability of the British and Jewish newspapers. But that the British papers are *directly* unassailable by virtue of their institutionality has the paradoxical effect of shifting the ironic assault from the British papers to institutionality generally. Abramovitch captures such undecidability within the formal wholeness of his imaginative representation as a means of establishing it firmly as the condition of Hebrew writing generally. By aligning the notion of an unspecifiable abridgment—the free indirect discourse that stands equally as a mark of the incapacity of the Hebrew language to represent dialogue and our inaccessibility to the knowledge of the language of Benjamin's own text—with the formally indeterminate authorial point of view associated with narrative irony, Abramovitch creates a model of a constitutively aesthetic linguistic use that remains historical as long as it refuses to settle itself in any one place.

In *Benjamin the Third,* the truth-telling reportorial authority of western European journalism that might appear at first glance to be subverted by the ironizing parochialism of the Jewish newspapers turns out to be constituted by the juxtaposition. It is by presenting only part of the world in their pages, limiting their coverage to the exploits of British adventurers, that the British newspapers gain the authority to tell a sort of truth, based not only, or even

primarily, on an evaluation of empirical evidence, in which newspapers come
to invest people and their exploits with significance by including them in
those pages. That British newspapers cover Britons almost exclusively makes
it an honor to appear in them; that the Jew Benjamin, armed with only tallis,
tefillin, and pack, makes the papers reconfigures their authority to invest
value into simply a matter of reference. The very power of these western European newspapers to constitute (imagined) national communities thus turns
on their power to invoke in their pages not one but two national groups simultaneously—the one they represent as a matter of course and the one they
do not. Benjamin is able to fulfill the function of turning British journalism
from a manifestation of British political power into a straightforwardly empirical operation, reference without history, not simply because he is not British and not simply because, as an explorer reaching heretofore unexplored
locations, the evidence of his travel needs to be taken on faith. Rather, since
he is a Jew, Benjamin's adventuring to places beyond empirical corroboration,
his place beyond the evidence of place, becomes a condition of identity. Since
he is at once placeless and lacking a journalistic apparatus backed by the
power of the state to track him, Benjamin's escape from the burdens of evidence is part and parcel of his Jewishness, and as such it becomes empirically
discernible *on the evidence* of that Jewishness.

Whereas Abramovitch begins his novel by using this conflation of Jews
and what they do to anatomize western European journalistic institutions, as
the novel elaborates on the dynamics of this conflation it becomes clear that
the social logic by which Jews come to be evidence for the impossibility of
evidence is distinctly Russian. By their own account, the same Jews who inhabit the otherwise forgotten Batalon thanks to a long-standing and hence
uninterpretable accident manage to do so while expending virtually no effort
to sustain themselves:

בעצמם בני העיר בטלון רובם ככלם אביונים גדולים וקבצנים נוראים, לא עליכם, אבל הכל
מודים שהם אביונים שמחים, קבצנים טובי-לב, ובעלי-בטחון משונים. כשאתה שואל את
הבטלוני: רבי יהודי, במה אתה עוסק ומה אתה ניזון? הוא עומד מבולל ואינו יודע מה להשיב.
ולאחר שנתיישבה דעתו עליו הוא משיב לך בגמגום כהאי לישנא:

‏—ניזון, ממה אני ניזון, למשל? הבל הבלים! יש אלהים, אומר אני לך, למשל, היושב וזן את
בריותיו בטובו הגדול. מזון לא חסר ואל יחסר לנו, אני אומר לך, למשל.

‏—אף על פי כן עסקך במה? איזו אומנות או פרנסה מן הפרנסות בידיך?

‏—יהי שם ה' מבורך. אני, כשם שאני לפניך בקומתי וצביוני, מתנה טובה יש לי
מאת השם יברך: פרקי נאה וקולי נעים! והריני עובר לפני התבה ומתפלל מוספים בימים
נוראים באחת העירות בסביבה זו. מוהל אומן אני ונוקד מצות, שאין דוגמתי בעולם, ופעמים
מזווג זווגים מזווג אני, גם אחוות-עולם לי – כמו שאתה רואה אותי, למשל – מקום לשבתי

בבית-הכנסת. אגב, יש עמי בביתי – יהא נא הדבר כמוס עמנו – מעט משקה למשל, יי"ש למכירה,
שממשיך לי שפע פורתא ... וחוץ לזה, אני אומר לך, למשל, הבורא יתברך שמו הוא אב הרחמים
וישראל רחמנים בני רחמנים, אומר אני לך, ומה יתאונן אדם חי?

[In themselves most of the people of Batalon are beggars and paupers, but all are
thankful that they are happy beggars, good-hearted paupers, odd optimists. When
you ask a Bataloni, Reb Jew, what is your business and how do you support your-
self? he stands confused and does not know what to answer. But a while after,
having settled on an opinion, he answers you with a stutter:

—Support myself, so how do I support myself? Nonsense! There is a God, I say
to you, who cares for and nourishes his creatures quite abundantly. I don't lack for
anything, and will go on not lacking, I tell you.

—Yes with all that, but what do you do for a living? What is your craft, or
perhaps you have a business?

—Praised be the Blessed Name! As sure as I stand before you in my nature, God
has blessed me with the gift of a lovely voice. So with the extra prayers during the
High Holy Days, I sing in the other towns in the area. I perform circumcisions, and
as matzo perforators go there's none like me in all the world. Occasionally I work
arranging marriages. As sure as you see me, I have a seat in the synagogue. Then,
too, in my house I have—and this should remain a secret between us—a bit of
liquor, moonshine for sale, that yields a little. . . . Besides this, I say to you, the
Creator, Blessed be his name, he is a merciful father, all Israel is merciful and the
children of Israel are merciful also, I tell you, so what does a living person have to
complain about?] (58)

If this representative man of Batalon seems puzzlingly busy for someone who
by his own admission need do nothing to support himself, his disingenuousness might be understood to have received a variety of official sanctions
throughout the decades of the 1840s and 1850s as the Russian government
debated the establishment and implementation of its policy of *razbor,* the
reclassification of the estate allegiance of the Jews. In 1844, one week after
the publication of the law officially abolishing the *kahal,* P. D. Kisilev, chair
of Nicholas I's Committee for the Transformation of the Jews, proposed that
Russia follow Prussia by distinguishing between "useful" Jews (guild merchants, licensed artisans, farmers, and true townspeople with permanent
urban residences) and "nonuseful" Jews: everyone else, especially those involved in the liquor trade. Until this time, most Jews had been classified as
"townspeople," though large numbers of them neither lived in towns nor engaged in the occupations traditionally associated with the category. Responding to a series of government studies that blamed Jewish economic enterprise for the financial woes of the Russian peasantry, Kisilev proposed the

new classification system as a means of restricting Jewish entry into the "townspeople" estate to Jews already owning substantial property and forcing other Jews to take up "useful" occupations like artisanship and farming. Jews deemed nonuseful would be given five years to leave their rural homes and join other estates, and those who failed to meet the deadline would be subject to serious punishment, including extraordinary conscription duties.[82] The announcement of this reclassification program inspired at least one Yiddish folk song: "Run to Romanovsky / Say you are a water-carrier / Say you are a wood-cutter / Say, say, whoever you are / Only don't remain an 'idler.'"[83]

Kisilev's *razbor* proposal met with the objections of the more liberal members of the Czarist government, who maintained that the punitive aspects of the reclassification policy were misguided unless they could be assured it would have the effect of directing large numbers of Jews toward more productive occupations. Since most Jews lacked the skills or the capital to acquire a house or enter the merchant guilds, these ministers pointed out, the policy would do little more than flood cities with Jews displaced from their rural villages because they could not bring themselves into compliance with the new regulations. The official *razbor* policy, announced in 1846 after nearly two years of government infighting, did in fact largely abandon—or more accurately, avoid specifying—the punitive measures that would be levied against those who did not comply, though the language of the legislation held the Jews responsible for their failure to assimilate to Russian national culture, a failure the law explicitly associated with the Jews' economic practices:

> [The Jews] have had at their disposal all possible means to turn to useful activities and to establish for themselves a secure prosperity.
>
> Unfortunately, however, they have not been willing to avail themselves of the opportunities presented to them, and have persisted in avoiding any amalgamation with the society under whose protection they live, existing, as before, for the most part, off the work of the rest of the population, which justifiably continually complains of this. . . .
>
> Since the Government has provided all the means for the moral and material well-being of the Jews, it is justified in hoping that the Jews will finally abandon any undertaking that endangers the interests of the rest of the population, and will

---

82. Stanislawski, *Tsar Nicholas I and the Jews*, 156.

83. S. Ginsberg and P. Marek, *Jewish Folk Songs in Russia* (St. Petersburg, 1901), quoted in ibid., 155. The song, though in Yiddish, employs the official Russian term *prazdnoshataiushchiisia* for "idler," language at once echoed and transformed by Abramovitch's use of the Yiddish Tunedavke and Hebrew Batalon ("Idlerstown") as the names of his fictional towns. The "Bataloni" thus turns out to be an "idler" by the very fact of his place of residence—"Bataloni" means both "inhabitant of Batalon" and "idler"—a conflation whose political significance I hope will become clear in a moment.

choose for themselves, like their compatriots, more sound modes of living. It is absolutely correct that the refractory and disobedient be punished as idlers who are a burden to the society of which they are part.[84]

The announcement of the *razbor* policy resulted in wide-scale panic among the Jews of the Pale of Settlement, though apparently most did in fact lack the resources necessary to reclassify themselves in response to the new edict. Faced with the virtually insurmountable task of enforcing compliance with the law, the government allowed the 1850 deadline pass without action and later reannounced the edict, extending the term for registration by first one year, then another. The last official mention of the reclassification plan came on 30 May 1852, when the deadline for compliance was extended another six months. With the Crimean War on the horizon, the bureaucratic exertion necessary for enforcing the law turned out to be beyond the capabilities of the Russian government.

That the decade-long *razbor* debate finally produced no tangible legal effects does not mean it was an insignificant incident within the historical narrative of nineteenth-century Russian-Jewish political and social relations. Indeed, that the policy remained at a discursive level might well imply that what was at stake for the Russian government was less a transformation of material relations than finding new ways of understanding the relations of economic production, geographical placedness, and individual and national identities. What is arguably the most striking aspect of the *razbor* legislation is the way it sought not to regulate certain forms of economic *behavior*—the "second-degree" economic activity such as petty trading, wholesaling, and money-lending classically labeled "nonproductive"—but to categorize and regulate those *people* who might be expected to engage in certain economic practices. As with Benjamin and the British newspapers, economic practice is effectively subsumed within a kind of identity, an association that not only enables such behaviors to be linked to otherwise unrelated social facts such as place of residence and national history but also renders them free of the contingency of historical change and limitation.

In a certain sense, the distinction between productive and nonproductive *labor* can be understood to invoke an epistemological distinction that rests on a spatial distinguishability of knowledge.[85] Productive labor can be thought of as labor whose products have value that is immediately perceptible—perceptible in the same place where the labor itself occurs—whereas the products

---

84. Quoted in Stanislawski, *Tsar Nicholas I and the Jews,* 159.

85. For the origins of the distinction between productive and nonproductive labor, see Smith, *Wealth of Nations,* bk. 2, chap. 3.

of nonproductive labor must be circulated, must move from their places of origin, for their value to come into being. The distinction thus presumes that its terms are legible in the products of the labor itself, but at the same time those products' meanings depend on their capacity to carry the contexts of their production in themselves. The products of productive labor are such because their contexts are wholly perceptible in themselves, since the objects can be presumed not to have moved at all, not to have a context that is not spatially present. To the extent that the distinction between productive and unproductive labor relies on the same terms of difference that distinguish novelistic foreground and background, terms evoked and undone by the date that makes its way to Batalon, the products of productive labor seem to be those objects that constitute background—a date on a palm tree rather than a date sold by one merchant to another. But to the extent that such an object appears as background, the self-evidence of its status as the product of labor is made tenuous. The circularity of such a formulation is evident, made apparent by the destabilizing movement of the date: the objects valued for their capacity to carry the marks of their productive contexts are those in which context and object are indistinguishable; they carry their context in their quality of their objecthood because they have no context beyond their objecthood. This quality of circularity helps account for the paradigmatic status afforded agricultural production as a form of productive labor, since, in that land can be said to be both source of production and place, it renders empirical and hence stabilizes a system of knowledge whose truth value is otherwise founded on the uncertain logical ground of tautology.

But as Abramovitch's counterrealist narrative of the Batalon date implied, the privileging of a knowledge of space and of objects present in/as space depends not so much on a reading of any inherent quality of those objects as on the cancellation of the history of those objects. An object fixed in a given place is able to act as a metonym for that place because its meaning happens not to be conceived of separately from its meaning *in that place,* not because the object itself carries the meaning of its context in itself from place to place. The very fact that a date that at one moment seems part of a landscape and hence a sign of productive labor can at the next moment (by means of the historicizing authority of the sacred text) stand as evidence of circulation shows that the distinction between productive and unproductive labor cannot easily be established as a quality of legibility in the objects of labor themselves. The revelation of the contingent quality of legibility is important in part, of course, because it shows that the evidence gleaned from examining the objects cannot necessarily be trusted, but this contingency is also important because, as we have seen, the quality of legibility in itself stands as the source of the moral value associated with productive labor.

Given the persistent difficulty of keeping the objects of productive and unproductive labor distinguishable from one another, the Russian government's move to classify the people who perform labor rather than the products of labor can be seen to have a pragmatic as well as a deliberate ideological motivation. As we have seen, the 1827 revision of Jewish conscription regulations redefined the category of Jewishness in Russia so that it not only did not include occupation of a given geographical space as a contingent element of its definition but was defined in categorical opposition to the occupation of such space. While this redefinition effectively aligned Russian national identity with the space called Russia by default—that is, by excluding other national identities from even an ideologically incidental relationship to the land—the conscription reforms were not in themselves sufficient to make the land eternally and necessarily Russian. In Liah Greenfeld's account of Russian nationalism, this tenuous quality of the "Russianness" of the geographical space presided over by the czars produces the peculiarities of Russian national development. Unlike the parallel strata in other European societies, the Russian nobility was not primarily a landed elite, and consequently its status was only weakly determined by lineage. Large portions of the nobility had gained their positions as a result of their service to the czar's court as opposed to their ownership of land (or geographical origins). In 1649 the legal enserfment of the peasantry, which gave both the service and the hereditary nobility alike the right to use serf labor, was introduced as a means of obliterating the distinctions between the two groups of nobles and of redefining the nobility as a landowning elite. Although laws passed in 1845 and 1856 sought to restrict the ranks of the nobility by raising the level of decorations that carried noble status and by reserving spaces in the universities sufficient to guarantee the nobles' numerical predominance there, the 1861 emancipation of the serfs offset these alleviating measures, "leaving the nobility a privileged order only in name, and thereby causing a sudden exacerbation of its chronic crisis."[86]

In this context, the bureaucratic reclassification of the Jews might be understood as an attempt to restabilize the category of Russianness. With the introduction in 1847 of the legal distinction between useful and nonuseful Jews, the association of Russian national identity and the geographical space

86. Liah Greenfeld, *Nationalism: Five Roads to Modernity* (Cambridge: Harvard University Press, 1992), 204–6, 220. I want to argue as well that the reclassification of the Jews in 1847 created a category of Russian land sufficiently stable to take over the ideological function that had been provided by the legal enserfment of the peasants and to enable their emancipation in 1861.

of Russia is abruptly changed. Insofar as such a classification reverses the relation between agents and objects, the changeability of the landscape emblematized by the circulation of the Batalon date and the consequent instability of national claims to that landscape are stabilized not simply by relocating the evidence of possession from the marks of labor located in the objects of the landscape to the prior identities of the laborers themselves, but by relocating it to laborers who, by virtue of their Jewishness, are necessarily unconnected to the land. Whereas neither the reversal of the relations of object and agent by the designation of useful producers nor the absolute bifurcation of Jewishness and the occupation of land established by the change in conscription laws is adequate in itself to establish Russian land as transcendently, eternally Russian, taken together the double estrangement of the Jews from the geographical space of Russia establishes, by opposition, this category of an eternal, spatialized Russianness.

Exactly how does this double estrangement work? I argued that the circulating date revealed the inadequacy of the elements comprising a geographical space as evidence of that space's persistence, stability, and (national) possessability, and also that the designation of useful and nonuseful laborers as an identity that exists before any given acts of labor might stabilize the relation between place and possession in that the labor that would normally— that is, within a liberal notion of property—bring about such possession becomes a quality of laborers' identity rather than a specific (historical) behavior. But whereas, if applied to Russian laborers, the useful/nonuseful opposition would simply relocate the evidence of possession from the objects in the world to the laborers without rendering the relation between the two necessary or absolute, that the Jewishness in relation to which the categories of laborers are established has itself been defined as standing in *absolute opposition* to the land means that this mediating role of a juridically produced, historically transcendent Jewish identity renders the Russian nation's association with the space of Russia beyond the reach of history. It is only by being figured in opposition to a Jewish identity whose historically specific acts of labor upon a presumably historically contingent geographical space are subsumed within an always already established identity that itself can have no relation to land that the apparently contingent space and the Russian identity associated with that space can be rendered noncontingent.

Moreover, in Abramovitch's own gloss of the distinction between productive and unproductive laborers, the Bataloni's "uselessness" has as much to do with the fact that most of his labor takes place within the confines of the Jewish community—his work as a cantor, as a ritual circumciser, as a matzo perforator—as it does with his statutorily nonproductive work as a moon-

shiner. The immediate visibility of value that is at least rhetorically constitutive of productive work and that is naturalized as part of the landscape itself
by the elevation of agricultural work as the ideal form of this labor thus turns
out to depend on a kind of selective looking. Abramovitch's Bataloni, who
with the same shrug of his shoulder dismisses as nonlabor his legally pro-
scribed moonshining and the Jewish ritual work that occurs beyond—or beneath—the gaze of the Russian government, thus implicitly makes the case
for understanding the geographical space that is the ground and object of
productive labor as itself a kind of instantiation of point of view, the establishment of Russian national hegemony not only within but *by means of* a
concept of landscape. Abramovitch presents a Jewish ritual labor that is
"nonuseful" because, in a sense, it is *too* local, because it does not circulate
enough, while making it clear that the terms of the useful/nonuseful distinction are generated by Russian legislative context according to which a Jew's
being designated "nonuseful" would result in his eviction from the rural areas
of the Pale of Settlement—would result, that is, in his being made to circulate
along the paths of the liquor he tenders.

With this reconfiguration we come full circle: whereas Johnson posited a
linguistic identity as a means of forging a transcendently coherent social order, one that would escape the instability and political and institutional diffusion of a society drawn together by a system of divided labor, in Abramovitch's fictional anatomization of Russian labor and residency laws it is the
transformation of labor into a form of *identity*—useful and nonuseful laborers—that announces the impossibility of distinguishing the value of labor
from the value and the valuing—the culture—of the society in which that
labor takes place. The complex of regulations that together absolutely oppose
Jewishness and space, and in so doing ensure juridically that Jews can neither
change nor be changed by the geographical space they inhabit, have the unintended consequence of undermining the foundational claims of both labor
and language by revealing both to be only contingently linked to the sort of
ongoing, persistent material world that Johnson imagined might lift sociality
out of history. In redescribing the distinction between useful and nonuseful
labor not in terms of whether the products of that labor move or stay in place
but in terms of whether that labor is valued and used by people of one national identity or another, Abramovitch's fiction not only puts forth an alternative conception of labor but turns the transparency and self-evidence of
geographical placedness into a figure of speech. The distinction between the
mobility or immobility of the products of labor is thus revealed to be of secondary importance to the language in which such labor and the space where
it takes place are described. Whereas Johnson's *Dictionary* assumed that the

process of using a language to refer to the material world would cancel the history of the language even as this same process of reference idealized and rendered permanent the material world, Ben-Yehuda's narration of the interlude in the field revealed the ways the power of national language and national space to constitute one another as transhistorical grounds of culture depended on a cultural logic borrowed from and promulgated by the realist novel. Abramovitch fundamentally redefines the logic and operation of fictional representation. In *Benjamin the Third,* as was the case for Ben-Yehuda, an object of fictional reference becomes imaginable—produces bodies—only so far as it is experienced as having been representable in any language. Within this analytical framework of a newly defined novelistic fictionality, then, the fact of linguistic reference does not render the language in which such reference takes place either necessary or inevitable but instead makes each moment of linguistic reference stand as a rearticulation of the history of the process by which the particular language came to name its object.

The Travels of Benjamin the Third closes with an unexpected flurry of events: unexpected because until now the novel has proceeded at an often maddeningly leisurely pace, and unexpected because Benjamin and Senderl's adventures up to this point have been remarkably of a piece with one another, the pair wandering haplessly among villages that seem increasingly large, yet equally parochial, versions of one another, encountering Jews indistinguishable from the Jews they have left behind in Batalon. Although the pair are met with reactions ranging from indifference to hostility, the episodic, even repetitious quality of the narrative goes a long way toward supporting my contention that Abramovitch's primary concern in the novel is exploring the processes by which limited (linguistic) knowledge may be used to gain a more comprehensive account of knowledge already accessible to a culture generally. Virtually the *only* thing distinguishing these encounters from one another is the language in which they are written. As the novel rambles toward its close, however, both the pace and the character of events change significantly. Benjamin and Senderl are greeted enthusiastically by a pair of distinguished-looking men who identify themselves as representatives of the local Jewish community and who, having gotten wind of the travelers' heroic pilgrimage, wish to organize a fete in their honor. As the group heads "to the bathhouse" to prepare for the festivities, they find themselves not in the town baths but in the local army recruitment offices. The "local representatives" turn out to have been *khappers*. In a rapid-fire succession of events, Benjamin and Senderl escape from the barracks they have been assigned to, only to find themselves court-martialed. At the court-martial, Benjamin delivers an eloquent, impassioned—and strikingly un-Benjamin-like—speech on the injustice of being forced to fight a war in which they have no interest. The presiding officers, labeling the pair of Jews mad, release them, and the novel closes.

It would be a mistake to assume, however, that the series of almost implausibly quick shifts of plot with which *Benjamin the Third* ends signal a turn away from the emphasis on language making and questions of linguistic authority that has characterized the novel until now. In engineering a narrative in which Jews who think they are going to the bathhouse end up being drafted into the Russian army, Abramovitch grafts onto a plot about the systematic legal disempowerment of the Jews a cautionary reflection on one strategy by which such legal disabilities might be removed. If Benjamin and Senderl are caught unawares, their surprise results from their having fallen prey to the seductions of the realist plot, having taken as natural the transparency of national language and geographical space. In their failure to attend sufficiently to the language in which their lives take place, the two travelers overlook that, in "being taken to the bathhouse"—in Yiddish, *firm emetsn in bod arayn*—they are, in the Yiddish idiom, being duped.[87]

In this literalizing in Hebrew of a common Yiddish idiom—a rhetorical trick to which he frequently returns throughout his literary corpus—Abramovitch establishes *Benjamin the Third* as a kind of chronicle of contemporary Hebrew usage, a movement from prayer to the mixed genre of *melitza* to a symbol, if not the realization, of a transparent spoken Hebrew. If we recall for a moment the particular taxonomic—and indeed theoretical and political—conundrum that idiomatic language posed for Johnson in composing his *Dictionary*, the critical stakes of Abramovitch's act of literalizing ought to become more apparent. Because idioms were neither created by individuals nor clearly referential, they directly challenged the mostly unarticulated narrative strategy of the "exemplary" dictionary structure Johnson developed. Within this narrative, the individual dictionary user experienced the resolution of a variety of uses of a given word into the referentiality signaled by definition, a resolution that likewise marked that dictionary user's own ascension into linguistic knowledge, an ascension that followed the trajectory from (written) language understood as use or behavior to a linguistic knowledge that, in its marked transcendence of particular context, was implicitly spoken. In literalizing "being taken to the bathhouse," Abramovitch adopts the necessarily implicit narrative of Johnson's dictionary structure as his own explicit compositional procedure: the idiom is transformed from an instance of lin-

---

87. Both Miron and Norich and Menakhem Perry identify this pun. See Perry, "Thematic and Structural Shift in Autotranslation by Bilingual Hebrew-Yiddish Writers: The Case of Mendele Mokher Sforim," *Poetics Today* 2, 4 (1981): 181–92. Forms of the idiom exist in English as well: consider the expressions "being taken to the cleaners" and "taking a bath" on something.

guistic behavior whose meaning can be understood only in relation to a historically local context of other people's past and present usages into language whose meaning is derived from its references to the actual world.

Literalizing thus becomes the sign, if not the enactment, of a transparent linguistic knowledge, a language whose status *as knowledge* is the manifestation of its having been detached from any particular community or historical moment of usage. The repetitious, ritualistic quality of the prayer form with which *Benjamin the Third* began presumed a notion of language as performative and then introduced moments of referentiality in order to associate the particular content of the linguistic performance, and not simply the general fact of performance, with the historical specificity of a contemporary Jewish world. The movement into referentiality associated with the literalizing of the Yiddish idiom, however, is meant to figure an ideal in which the historicity of language is subsumed by a relation between an individual's knowledge of the language and the objects of the world to which that language might be transparently attached. But the novel's outcome suggests that to read literally is to read badly, is to forget the historicity and partiality of any given use in favor of the paradoxically transcendent referentiality of an ideal of linguistic knowledge associated with both national language and the transparent fictionality of realism. And as Mendele himself might have said (though he did not), bad readers make good citizens.

Bibliography

Abramovitch, S. Y. *Masa'ot Benyamin ha-Shlishi* [The travels of Benjamin the Third]. In *Kol kitvei Mendele Mocher Sefarim* [The complete works of Mendele Mocher Sefarim]. One-volume edition. Tel Aviv: Dvir, 1947.

אבראמוביץ, מסעות בנימין השלישי. מתוך כל כתבי מנדלי מוכר ספרים. (הוצאת ״דביר״ תל־אביב (1947

———. *The Travels of Benjamin the Third*. Trans. from Yiddish by Moshe Spiegel. New York: Schocken, 1949.

———. "Ma na'aseh?" [What is to be done?]. *Ha-Melitz* [The advocate], nos. 1, 2, 3 (1878).

——— ״מה נעשה?״ המליץ 1,2,3 (1878)

Alderman, Geoffrey. "English Jews or Jews of the English Persuasion? Reflections on the Emancipation of Anglo-Jewry." In *Paths of Emancipation: Jews, States, and Citizenship*, ed. Pierre Birnbaum and Ira Katznelson, 128–56. Princeton: Princeton University Press, 1995.

Alter, Robert. *The Invention of Hebrew Prose*. Seattle: University of Washington Press, 1988.

Altmann, Alexander. "Introduction" and "Commentary." In *Jerusalem,* by Moses Mendelssohn, 3–29, 143–240. Hanover, N.H.: University Press of New England for Brandeis University Press, 1983.

Anderson, Amanda. "George Eliot and the Jewish Question." *Yale Journal of Criticism* 10, 1 (1997): 39–61.

Anderson, Benedict. *Imagined Communities: Reflections on the Origin and Spread of Nationalism*. London: Verso, 1983.

Anderson, Wilda C. "What Is a Dictionary?" In *Between the Library and the Laboratory: The Language of Chemistry in Eighteenth-Century France,* 35–52. Baltimore: Johns Hopkins University Press, 1984.

Appleby, Joyce. "Locke, Liberalism and the Natural Law of Money." In *Liberalism and Republicanism in the Historical Imagination*. Cambridge: Harvard University Press, 1996.

Arendt, Hannah. *On Revolution*. New York: Penguin, 1965.

———. *The Origins of Totalitarianism*. Part 2. New York: Harcourt Brace Jovanovich, 1950.

Aristotle. *On Poetry and Style*. Trans. G. M. A. Grube. Indianapolis: Bobbs-Merrill, 1958.

Armstrong, Isobel. *Victorian Poetry: Poetry, Poetics and Politics*. London: Routledge, 1993.

Armstrong, Nancy. *Desire and Domestic Fiction*. Oxford: Oxford University Press, 1987.

Armstrong, Nancy, and Leonard Tennenhouse. *The Imaginary Puritan*. Berkeley: University of California Press, 1992.

Aronson, I. Michael. "The Anti-Jewish Pogroms in Russia in 1881." In *Pogroms: Anti-Jewish Violence in Modern Russian History,* ed. John D. Klier and Shlomo Lambroza, 44–61. Cambridge: Cambridge University Press, 1992.

Atiyah, P. S. *Promises, Morals and Law*. Oxford: Clarendon Press, 1981.

———. *The Rise and Fall of Freedom of Contract*. Oxford: Oxford University Press, 1979.

Ayers, Michael. *Locke: Epistemology and Ontology*. London: Routledge, 1991.

Bailey, Richard W. *Nineteenth Century English*. Ann Arbor: University of Michigan Press, 1996.

Balibar, Etienne, and Immanuel Wallerstein. *Race, Nation, Class: Ambiguous Identities*. London: Verso, 1991.

Band, Arnold J. "The Ahad Ha-Am and Berdyczewski Polarity." In *At the Crossroads: Essays on Ahad Ha-Am,* 49–59. Albany: State University of New York Press, 1983.

Barrell, John. "The Language Properly So-Called: The Authority of Common Usage." In *English Literature in History: An Equal, Wide Survey*. London: Hutchinson, 1983.

Bartal, Israel. "From Traditional Bilingualism to National Monolingualism." In *Hebrew in Ashkenaz: A Language in Exile,* ed. Lewis Glinert, 141–50. Oxford: Oxford University Press, 1993.

Barthes, Roland. "The Reality Effect." In *French Literary Theory Today,* ed. Tzvetan Todorov, 11–17. Cambridge: Cambridge University Press, 1982.

Baucom, Ian. *Out of Place: Englishness, Empire, and the Locations of Identity*. Princeton: Princeton University Press, 1999.

Ben-Gurion, Micah Yosef [Berdichevski]. "Tishtush ha-gvulin" [A blurring of the boundaries]. 1913. In *Kol ma'amarei Micah Yosef Ben-Gurion* [The complete essays of Micah Yosef Ben-Gurion (Berdichevski)]. Tel Aviv: Am Oved, 1952.

מיכה יוסף בן-גוריון (ברדיצ׳בסקי) "טשטוש הגבולין" כל מאמרי מיכה יוסף בן גוריון. הוצאת "עם עובד" תל-אביב–1913

———. "Tsorech v'yecholet" [Necessity and capacity]. 1897. In *Kol ma'amarei Micah Yosef Ben-Gurion* [The complete essays of Micah Yosef Ben-Gurion (Berdichevski)]. Tel Aviv: Am Oved, 1952.

———"צורך ויכולת" כל מאמרי מיכה יוסף בן-גוריון. הוצאת "עם עובד" תל אביב 1952) 153–5

Ben-Yehuda, Eliezer. "Yetsirat milim hadashot b'lashonenu" [The creation of new words in our language]. In *Ha-halom v'shevaro* [The dream and its realization: Selected writings on language of Eliezer Ben-Yehuda], ed. Reuven Sivan, 175–85. Jerusalem: Mossad Bialik, 1978.

בן-יהודה, אליעזר. "יצירת מילים חדשות בלשוננו" החלום ושברו. ראובן סיבן (מוסד ביאליק: ירושלים 1978)

Berdichevski. *See* Ben-Gurion, Micah Yosef.

Biale, David. *Power and Powerlessness in Jewish History.* New York: Schocken, 1986.

Blair, Sara. "Documenting America: Racial Theater in the American Scene." *Henry James Review* 16 (1996): 264–72.

———. *Henry James and the Writing of Race and Nation.* Cambridge: Cambridge University Press, 1996.

———. Response: Writing Culture and Henry James." *Henry James Review* 16 (1995); 278–81.

Bogel, Frederic. "Johnson and the Role of Authority." In *The New Eighteenth Century,* ed. Felicity Nussbaum and Laura Brown, 189–209. New York: Routledge, 1987.

Bourdieu, Pierre. *Outline of a Theory of Practice.* Cambridge: Cambridge University Press, 1989.

Boyarin, Daniel, and Jonathan Boyarin. "Diaspora: Generation and the Ground of Jewish Identity." *Critical Inquiry* 19, 4 (1993): 693–725.

Boyarin, Jonathan. *Storm from Paradise: The Politics of Jewish Memory.* Minneapolis: University of Minnesota Press, 1992.

Brantlinger, Patrick. "Nations and Novels: Disraeli, George Eliot and Orientalism." *Victorian Studies* 35, 3 (1992): 255–75.

Brent, Richard. *Liberal Anglican Politics: Whiggery, Religion, and Reform, 1830–1841.* Oxford: Clarendon Press, 1987.

Browning, Robert. *The Poems.* New York: Penguin, 1981.

Burrow, J. W. *A Liberal Descent: Victorian Historians and the English Past.* Cambridge: Cambridge University Press, 1981.

Cameron, Sharon. *Thinking in Henry James.* Chicago: University of Chicago Press, 1989.

Chandler, James. *England in 1819: The Politics of Literary Culture and the Case of Romantic Historicism.* Chicago: University of Chicago Press, 1998.

Chase, Cynthia. "The Decomposition of the Elephants: Double- Reading *Daniel Deronda,*" *PMLA* 93 (1978): 215–27.

Cheyette, Bryan. *Constructions of "the Jew" in English Literature and Society: Racial Representations, 1875–1945.* Cambridge: Cambridge University Press, 1993.

Cohen, Murray. *Sensible Words: Linguistic Practice in England, 1640–1785.* Baltimore: Johns Hopkins University Press, 1977.

Collins, Wilkie. *The Woman in White.* 1860. New York: Penguin, 1985.

Unsigned review of *Daniel Deronda. Jewish Chronicle,* 8 September 1876.

Daston, Lorraine. *Classical Probability in the Enlightenment*. Princeton: Princeton University Press, 1988.

Dohm, Christian Wilhelm von. *Über die bürgeliche Verbesserun der Juden*. 2 vols. Berlin, 1781–83.

Douglas, Ann. *Terrible Honesty: Mongrel Manhattan in the 1920s*. New York: Farrar, Straus and Giroux, 1995.

Dowling, Linda. *Language and Decadence in the Victorian Fin de Siècle*. Princeton: Princeton University Press, 1986.

Edel, Leon. *Henry James: A Life*. New York: Harper and Row, 1985.

Eisenberg, Melvin Aron. "The Responsive Model of Contract Law." *Stanford Law Review* 36 (May 1984): 1107–67.

Eliot, George. *Daniel Deronda*. 1876. Ed. Terence Cave. New York: Penguin, 1995.

———. *The Lifted Veil*. 1879. New York: Penguin Books, Virago, 1985.

———. "Looking Inward." In *Miscellaneous Essays*. Boston: Estes and Lauriat, 1883.

———. "The Natural History of German Life: Riehl." . In *Complete Works of George Eliot*, 6:188–236. London: Blackwood, 1883.

———. Personal Correspondence to Harriet Beecher Stowe. In *George Eliot: The Critical Heritage*, ed. David Carroll, 405–6. London: Routledge and Kegan Paul, 1971.

Ermarth, Elizabeth Deeds. *Realism and Consensus in the English Novel*. Princeton: Princeton University Press, 1983.

Feather, John. *A History of British Publishing*. New York: Routledge, 1988.

Febvre, Lucien, and Henri-Jean Martin. *The Coming of the Book*. London: Verso, 1976.

Feldman, David. *Englishmen and Jews: Social Relations and Political Culture, 1840–1914*. New Haven: Yale University Press, 1994.

Fellman, Jack. *Revival of a Classical Tongue: Eliezer Ben-Yehuda and the Modern Hebrew Language*. The Hague: Mouton, 1973.

Finch, Casey, and Peter Bowen. "'The Tittle-Tattle of Highbury': Gossip and Free Indirect Style in *Emma*." *Representations* 31 (summer 1990): 1–18.

Finestein, Israel. "Anglo-Jewish Opinion during the Struggle for Emancipation, 1828–58." *Transactions of the Jewish Historical Society of England* 20 (1964): 113–43.

———. *Jewish Society in Victorian England*. London: Vallentine Mitchell, 1993.

Fisher, Philip. "A Museum with One Work Inside." *Keats-Shelley Journal* 33 (1984): 85–102.

Frankel, Jonathan. *Prophecy and Politics: Socialism, Nationalism and the Russian Jews, 1862–1917*. Cambridge: Cambridge University Press, 1981.

Freedman, Jonathan. "The Jew in the Museum." In *The Temple of Culture: Assimilation and Anti-Semitism in Literary Anglo-America*. Oxford: Oxford University Press, forthcoming.

Fried, Charles. *Contract as Promise*. Cambridge: Harvard University Press, 1981.

Friedman, Lawrence. *A History of American Law*. 2d ed. New York: Simon and Schuster, 1985.

Gallagher, Catherine. "George Eliot and *Daniel Deronda:* The Prostitute and the Jewish Question." In *Sex, Politics and Science in the Nineteenth Century Novel,* ed. Ruth Bernard Yeazell, 39–62. Baltimore: Johns Hopkins University Press, 1986.

———. *Nobody's Story: The Vanishing Acts of Women Writers in the Marketplace, 1670–1820.* Berkeley: University of California Press, 1994.

Gilmore, Grant. *The Death of Contract.* Columbus: Ohio State University Press, 1974.

Ginsberg, Asher. *See* Ha-Am, Ahad.

Givton, Minna, Aviva Gottlieb, and Shmuel Werses. "The Jewish Reception of *Daniel Deronda*." In *"Daniel Deronda": A Centenary Symposium,* ed. Alice Shalvi, 11–43. Jerusalem: Jerusalem Academic Press, 1976.

Glinert, Lewis H. "Did Pre-Revival Hebrew Literature Have Its Own *Langue*? Quotation and Improvisation in Mendele Mokher Sefarim." *Bulletin of the School of Oriental and African Studies* 53, 3 (1988): 413–27.

Graver, Suzanne. *George Eliot and Community.* Berkeley: University of California Press, 1984.

Green, T. H. "Lecture on 'Liberal Legislation and Freedom of Contract.'" In *Lectures on the Principles of Political Obligation and Other Writings,* ed. Paul Harris and John Morrow, 194–212. Cambridge: Cambridge University Press, 1986.

Greenfeld, Liah. *Nationalism: Five Roads to Modernity.* Cambridge: Harvard University Press, 1992.

Ha-Am, Ahad [Asher Ginsberg]. "The Law of the Heart." In *The Zionist Idea: A Historical Analysis and Reader,* ed. Arthur Hertzberg, 251–55. New York: Atheneum, 1986.

Hacking, Ian. *The Emergence of Probability.* Cambridge: Cambridge University Press, 1975.

———. *The Logic of Statistical Inference.* Cambridge: Cambridge University Press, 1965.

———. *The Taming of Chance.* Cambridge: Cambridge University Press, 1990.

Haramati, Shlomo. *Shlosha she'kadmo Ben-Yehuda* [Three before Ben-Yehuda]. Jerusalem: Yad Yitzhak Ben Zvi, 1938.

שלמה הראמתי, *שלושה שקדמו לבן-יהודה* הוצאת יד יצחק בן-צבית ירושלים תשל"ח ראשית
התינוך העברי בארץ ותר ומתו רהחיישת הלשון הוצאת ראובן מס, ירושלים, תשל"ט

Hardy, Thomas. *The Selected Writings of Thomas Hardy: Stories, Poems and Essays.* Ed. Irving Howe. Greenwich, Conn.: Fawcett, 1966.

Harshav, Benjamin. *Language in Time of Revolution.* Berkeley: University of California Press, 1993.

———. *The Meaning of Yiddish.* Berkeley: University of California Press, 1990.

Haviland, Beverly. "'Psychic Mulattos': The Ambiguity of Race." *Common Knowledge* 3 (winter 1994): 127–43.

Hedrick, Elizabeth. "Locke's Theory of Language and Johnson's *Dictionary*." *Eighteenth-Century Studies* 20 (1987): 422–44.

Henriques, H. S. Q. *The Jews and the English Law.* London: J. Jacobs, 1908.

Henriques, U. R. Q. "Bastardy and the New Poor Law." *Past and Present* 37 (July 1967): 103–29.

History and Memory 7, 1 (1995). Special issue, ed. Gulie Ne'eman Arad.

His Majesty's Commisioners Report for Inquiring into the Administration and Practical Operation of the Poor Laws. London, 1834.

Holmes, Oliver Wendell, Jr. *Collected Legal Papers.* New York: Harcourt, Brace, and Howe, 1920; Peter Smith, 1952.

———. *The Common Law,* 1881. Ed. Sheldon M. Novick. New York: Dover, 1991.

Hont, Istvan, and Michael Ignatieff, eds. *Wealth and Virtue: The Shaping of Political Economy in the Scottish Enlightenment.* Cambridge: Cambridge University Press, 1983.

Horwitz, Morton J. *The Transformation of American Law, 1780–1860.* Cambridge: Harvard University Press, 1977.

Hughes, Linda K., and Michael Lund. *The Victorian Serial.* Charlottsville: University Press of Virginia, 1991.

Hunter, Paul J. *Before Novels: The Cultural Contexts of Eighteenth-Century English Fiction.* New York: W. W. Norton, 1990.

Irwin, Jane, ed. *George Eliot's "Daniel Deronda" Notebooks.* Cambridge: Cambridge University Press, 1996.

James, Henry. *The Complete Notebooks of Henry James.* Ed. Leon Edel. Oxford: Oxford University Press, 1987.

———. *"Daniel Deronda:* A Conversation." *Atlantic Monthly,* December 1876, 684–94. Reprinted in *George Eliot: The Critical Heritage,* ed. David Carroll. London: Routledge and Kegan Paul, 1971.

———. "The Pupil." In *Complete Stories, 1884–1891.* New York: Library of America, 1996. *What Maisie Knew.* 1897. New York: Penguin, 1987.

———. *William Wetmore Story and His Friends.* Boston: Houghton Mifflin, 1903.

The Jewish Chronicle, 1841–1941: A Century of Newspaper History. London: Jewish Chronicle, 1949.

Johnson, Samuel. *The Plan of a Dictionary in the English Language: Addressed to the Right Honourable Philip Dormer, Earl of Chesterfield.* London: J. and P. Knapton, T. Longman, and T. Shewell, 1747..

———. "Preface to the *Dictionary.*" In *Johnson's Dictionary: A Modern Selection,* ed. E. L. McAdam Jr. and George Milne, 1–29. New York: Pantheon, 1963.

Kagan, Zipora. "Homo Anthologicus: Micha Joseph Berdyczewski and the Anthological Genre." *Prooftexts* 19 (1999): 41–57.

Kaplan, Amy. *The Social Constructions of American Realism.* Chicago: University of Chicago Press, 1988.

Katz, David. *Jews in the History of England.* Oxford: Clarendon Press, 1994.

———. *Philo-Semitism and the Readmission of the Jews to England, 1603–1655.* Oxford: Clarendon Press, 1982.

Katz, Jacob, ed. *Toward Modernity: The European Jewish Model.* New Brunswick, N.J.: Transaction Books, 1987.

Kaufmann, David. *George Eliot and Judaism: An Attempt to Appreciate "Daniel Deronda."* 1876 (German); 1877 (English). Reprinted New York: Haskell House, 1970.

Klausner, Yosef. *Historia shel ha-sifrut ha-hadasha* [The history of modern litera-
ture]. Jerusalem, 1953.

קלוזנר, יוסף. *הסטוריה של הסיפרות החדשה* (ירושלים, 1953)

Klier, John D., and Shlomo Lambroza, eds. *Pogroms: Anti-Jewish Violence in Modern Russian History.* Cambridge: Cambridge University Press, 1992.

Langan, Celeste. *Romantic Vagrancy: Wordsworth and the Simulation of Freedom.*
Cambridge: Cambridge University Press, 1995.

Leavis, F. R. *The Great Tradition.* New York: Anchor, 1954.

Lederhendler, Eli. *The Road to Modern Jewish Politics: Political Tradition and Political Reconstruction in the Jewish Community of Tsarist Russia.* New York: Oxford University Press, 1989.

Liu, Alan. "Local Transcendence: Cultural Criticism, Postmodernism, and the Romanticism of Detail." *Representations* 32 (fall 1990): 75–113.

Lloyd, David. "Race under Representation." *Oxford Literary Review* 13 (1991):
62–94.

Locke, John. *An Essay concerning Human Understanding.* 1690. Vol. 2. Ed. Alexander Campbell Fraser. New York: Dover, 1959.

———. *A Letter concerning Toleration.* 1689. Ed. James H. Tully. Indianapolis:
Hackett, 1983.

———. *Two Treatises of Government.* 1690. Ed. Peter Laslett. Cambridge: Cambridge University Press, 1991.

Lukács, Georg. *The Historical Novel.* Trans. Hannah and Stanley Mitchell. Lincoln:
University of Nebraska Press, 1983.

Macaulay, Thomas Babington. "Civil Disabilities of the Jews." In *Essay and Speech
on Jewish Disabilities,* ed. Israel Abrahams and S. Levy, 19–41. Edinburgh: Ballantyne, Hanson, 1910.

MacCormick, D. N. "Voluntary Obligations and Normative Powers": Part 1. *Proceedings of the Aristotelian Society,*suppl. 46 (1972): 59–78.

Maine, Henry. *Ancient Law.* New York: J. M. Dent, [1861].

McClure, Kirstie. *Judging Rights: Lockean Politics and the Limits of Consent.*
Ithaca: Cornell University Press, 1996.

McKeon, Michael. *The Origins of the English Novel, 1700–1840.* Baltimore: Johns
Hopkins University Press, 1987.

Mendelssohn, Moses. *Jerusalem, or On Religious Power and Judaism.* 1783. Trans.
Allan Arkush. Hanover, N.H.: University Press of New England for Brandeis University Press, 1983.

Meyer, Susan. "'Safely to Their Own Borders': Proto-Zionism, Feminism and Nationalism in *Daniel Deronda*." *ELH* 60 (1993): 733–58.

Michaels, Walter Benn. "Jim Crow Henry James?" *Henry James Review* 16 (1995):
286–91.

Mill, John Stuart. *On Liberty.* 1859. In *"On Liberty" and Other Essays.* Oxford:
Oxford University Press, 1991.

———. "What Is Poetry?" In *Essays on Poetry by John Stuart Mill,* ed. F. Parvin
Sharpless, 3–22. Columbia: University of South Carolina Press, 1976.

Miller, D. A. *Narrative and Its Discontents: Problems of Closure in the Traditional Novel*. Princeton: Princeton University Press, 1981.

———. *The Novel and the Police*. Berkeley: University of California Press, 1988.

Miron, Dan. *A Traveler Disguised*. New York: Schocken, 1973.

Miron, Dan, and Anita Norich. *The Politics of Benjamin III: Intellectual Significance and Its Formal Correlatives in Sh. Y. Abramovitsh's "Maseos Benyomin Haslishi."* Field of Yiddish: Studies in Language, Folklore and Literature, fourth collection, ed. Marvin Herzog et al. Philadelphia: Institute for the Study of Human Issues, 1980.

Morrison, Toni. *Playing in the Dark: Whiteness and the Literary Imagination*. Cambridge: Harvard University Press, 1992.

Murray, James A. H. "The Romanes Lecture 1900: The Evolution of English Lexicography." Reprinted in *International Journal of Lexicography* 6, 2 (1993): 100–122.

Murray, K. M. Elisabeth. *Caught in the Web of Words: James Murray and the Oxford English Dictionary*. New Haven: Yale University Press, 1977.

Newsom, Robert. *A Likely Story: Probability and Play in Fiction*. New Brunswick, N.J.: Rutgers University Press, 1988.

Nicholson, Peter P. *The Political Philosophy of the British Idealists*. Cambridge: Cambridge University Press, 1990.

Novack, Sheldon M. *Henry James: The Young Master*. New York: Random House, 1996.

Parry, J. P. *Democracy and Religion: Gladstone and the Liberal Party, 1867–1875*. Cambridge: Cambridge University Press, 1986.

Pateman, Carole. *The Sexual Contract*. Stanford: Stanford University Press, 1988.

Patey, Douglas Lane. *Probability and Literary Form: Philosophic Theory and Literary Practice in the Augustan Age*. Cambridge: Cambridge University Press, 1984.

Pelli, Moshe. "Did the *Maskilim* 'Hate the Talmud'?" In *The Age of Haskalah: Studies of Hebrew Literature of the Enlightenment in Germany*, 48–72. Leiden: E. J. Brill, 1979.

———. "On the Role of *Melitzah* in the Literature of Hebrew Enlightenment." In *Hebrew in Ashkenaz: A Language in Exile*, ed. Lewis H. Glinert, 99–110. Oxford: Oxford University Press, 1993.

Perry, Menakhem. "Thematic and Structural Shift in Autotranslation by Bilingual Hebrew-Yiddish Writers: The Case of Mendele Mokher Sforim." *Poetics Today* 2, 4 (1981): 181–92.

Poovey, Mary. "The Anathematized Race: The Governess and *Jane Eyre*." In *Uneven Developments: The Ideological Work of Gender in Mid-Victorian England*, 126–63. Chicago: University of Chicago Press, 1988.

———. *Making a Social Body*. Chicago: University of Chicago Press, 1995.

Posnock, Ross. "Henry James and the Limits of Historicism." *Henry James Review* 16 (1995): 273–77.

Ragussis, Michael. *Figures of Conversion: "The Jewish Question" and English Identity*. Durham, N.C.: Duke University Press, 1995.

Reddick, Allen. *The Making of Johnson's Dictionary, 1746–1773.* Cambridge: Cambridge University Press, 1990.

Rose, Mark. *Authors and Owners.* Cambridge: Harvard University Press, 1993.

Rosenberg, Daniel. "'A New sort of Logick and Critick': Etymological Interpretation in Horne Tooke's *The Diversions of Purley.*" In *Language, Self and Society: A Social History of Language,* ed. Peter Burke and Roy Porter, 300–329. Cambridge: Polity Press, 1991.

Rossetti, Christina. "Goblin Market." In *Norton Anthology of English Literature,* ed. M. H. Abrams et al., 5th ed., 2:1508–20. New York: W. W. Norton, 1986.

Rowe, John Carlos. *The Other Henry James.* Durham, N.C.: Duke University Press, 1998.

Salbstein, M. C. N. *The Emancipation of the Jews in Britain: The Question of the Admission of the Jews to Parliament, 1828–1860.* Rutherford, N.J.: Farleigh Dickinson University Press, 1982.

Scheppele, Kim Lane. "Facing Facts in Legal Interpretation." *Representations* 30 (spring 1990): 42–77. Special Issue: "Law and the Order of Culture," ed. Robert Post.

Seidman, Naomi. *A Marriage Made in Heaven: The Sexual Politics of Hebrew and Yiddish.* Berkeley: University of California Press, 1997.

Semmel, Bernard. *George Eliot and the Politics of National Inheritance.* Oxford: Oxford University Press, 1994.

Shalvi, Alice. *"Daniel Deronda": A Centenary Symposium.* Jerusalem: Jerusalem Academic Press, 1976.

Shapiro, Barbara J. *Probability and Certainty in Seventeenth-Century England: A Study of the Relationships between Natural Science, Religion, History, Law and Literature.* Princeton: Princeton University Press, 1983.

Shavit, Yaacov. "A Duty Too Heavy to Bear: Hebrew in the Berlin *Haskalah,* 1783–1819: Between Classic, Modern and Romantic." In *Hebrew in Ashkenaz: A Language in Exile,* ed. Lewis Glinert, 111–28. Oxford: Oxford University Press, 1993.

Simpson, A. W. Brian. "The Beauty of Obscurity: *Raffles v. Wichelhaus and Busch* (1864)." In *Leading Cases in the Common Law,* 135–62. Oxford: Clarendon Press, 1995.

Simpson, Christopher. *The Splendid Blond Beast: Money, Law and Genocide in the Twentieth Century.* New York: Grove Press, 1993.

Sledd, James H., and Gwin J. Kolb. *Dr. Johnson's Dictionary: Essays in the Biography of a Book.* Chicago: University of Chicago Press, 1955.

Smith, Adam. "Considerations concerning the First Formation of Languages and the Different Genius of Original and Compounded Languages." 1761. In *Lectures on Rhetoric and Belle Lettres,* ed. J. C. Bryce, 201–31. Oxford: Oxford University Press, 1983.

———. *An Inquiry into the Nature and Causes of the Wealth of Nations.* 1776. Oxford: Oxford University Press, 1976.

Sorkin, David. *The Transformation of German Jewry, 1780–1840.* New York: Oxford University Press, 1987.

Stampfer, Shaul. "What Did 'Knowing Hebrew' Mean in Eastern Europe?" In *Hebrew in Ashkenaz: A Language in Exile,* ed. Lewis Glinert, 129–40. Oxford: Oxford University Press, 1993.

Stanislawski, Michael. *Tsar Nicholas I and the Jews: The Transformation of Jewish Society in Russia, 1825–1855.* Philadelphia: Jewish Publication Society of America, 1983.

Starnes, De Witt, and Gertrude E. Noyes. *The English Dictionary from Cawdrey to Johnson.* Amsterdam: John Benjamins, 1991.

St. John, Robert. *Tongue of the Prophets: The Life Story of Eliezer Ben Yehuda.* Garden City, N.Y.: Doubleday, 1952.

Stocking, George. *Victorian Anthropology.* New York: Free Press, 1987.

Taylor, Dennis. *Hardy's Literary Language and Victorian Philology.* Oxford: Oxford University Press, 1993.

Temple, Kathryn. "Johnson and Macpherson: Cultural Authority and the Construction of Literary Property." *Yale Journal of Law and the Humanities* 5 (1993): 355–87.

Thomas, Brook. *American Literary Realism and the Failed Promise of Contract.* Berkeley: University of California Press, 1997.

Trollope, Anthony. *The Warden.* 1855. Oxford: Oxford Univesity Press, 1998.

Trumpener, Katie. *Bardic Nationalism: The Romantic Novel and the British Empire.* Princeton: Princeton University Press, 1997.

Tucker, Irene. "Writing Home: *Evelina,* the Epistolary Novel and the Paradox of Property." *ELH* 60, 2 (1993): 419–39.

Vetter, Jan. "The Evolution of Holmes: Holmes and Evolution." In *Holmes and "The Common Law": A Century Later,* ed. Benjamin Kaplan, Patrick Atiyah, and Jan Vetter. Holmes Lectures, Occasional Pamphlet 10.Cambridge: Harvard Law School, 1983.

Vining, Joseph. "Generalization in Interpretive Theory." *Representations* 30 (spring 1990): 1–12. Special Issue: "Law and the Order of Culture," ed. Robert Post.

Waldron, Jeremy. *Liberal Rights: Collected Papers, 1981–1991.* Cambridge: Cambridge University Press, 1993.

Warren, Kenneth. *Black and White Strangers.* Chicago: University of Chicago Press, 1993.

———. "Still Reading James?" *Henry James Review* 16 (1995): 282–85.

Watt, Ian. *The Rise of the Novel.* Berkeley: University of California Press, 1957.

Weinbrot, Howard D. "Samuel Johnson's *Plan* and *Preface to the Dictionary:* The Growth of a Lexicographer's Mind." In *New Aspects of Lexicography: Literary Criticism, Intellectual History and Social Change,* ed. Howard D. Weinbrot, 73–94. Carbondale: Southern Illinois University Press, 1972.

Welsh, Alexander. *George Eliot and Blackmail.* Cambridge: Harvard University Press, 1985.

———. *Strong Representations: Narrative and Circumstantial Evidence in England.* Baltimore: Johns Hopkins University Press, 1992.

White, G. Edward. *Justice Oliver Wendell Holmes: Law and the Inner Self.* Oxford: Oxford University Press, 1993.

Willinsky, John. *Empire of Words: The Reign of the OED.* Princeton: Princeton University Press, 1995.

Wolin, Sheldon. *Politics and Vision: Continuity and Innovation in Western Political Thought.* Boston: Little, Brown, 1960.

Woodmansee, Martha, and Peter Jaszi, eds. *The Construction of Authorship: Textual Appropriation in Law and Literature.* Durham, N.C.: Duke University Press, 1994.

Zinberg, Israel. *A History of Jewish Literature.* Trans. Bernard Martin. Cincinnati: Hebrew Union College Press, 1978.

Index

Abramovitch, Shalom Yaakov (Mendele Mocher Sefarim), 188, 251
  in Berdichevski, 258–60
  "Ma Na'aseh?" (1878), 272n. 80
  Masaot Benyamin HaShlishi [*The Travels of Benjamin the Third*] (1896), 2–4, 6, 9, 32, 187, 259, 264–90; contingency in, 265–90; geographical space in, 265–90; idiom in, 288–90; labor in, 266, 267–90; Polish translation of, 260; Yiddish version of, 258–60, 276–77
agency, 10, 16, 22, 25, 30
  elimination of, 79, 89, 151–52, 245–46
  interpretation as, 154–55
  Jews in Russia, 267–68
  and narrative, 131–33, 151–55, 266–67
  types of evidence for, 124–31, 149–52, 153–55, 157–59
Alderman, Geoffrey, 58n. 16
Aleichem, Shalom (Shalom Rabinovitch), 253–55
Alter, Robert, 186nn. 4, 5, 261nn. 71, 72
Altmann, Alexander, 4n. 8
analogy
  as argument for belief, 52–53
  as mode of belief, 52–53, 98
  as relation to geographical space, 44
  See also belief
Anderson, Amanda, 54n. 12
Anderson, Benedict, 4–5, 232n. 53
Anderson, Wilda, 215–16
anonymity
  and biography, 56, 62, 65–68, 80–81

"George Eliot," 54–57, 61–69
  as guarantee of material freedom, 54–57, 61–69
  as means of creating audience, 76
  and print culture, 67–69
  pseudonymity, 54–57, 62, 65; as means of combatting antisemitism, 53–54, 57, 61–69; as mode of fictionality, 31; offering access to antisemitism, 63–69; and reputation, 35, 54, 56
  See also Jewish Chronicle reviewer
anthology
  dictionary as, 196–97, 209–10, 213–18
  Hebrew novel as, 196–97, 260–71
  realist novel as, 196, 273
  Talmud as, 195–96
Appleby, Joyce, 36n. 2
Arendt, Hannah, 19–20
Armstrong, Isobel, 64n. 25
Armstrong, Nancy, 7, 10–12, 23–25
Armstrong, Nancy, and Leonard Tennenhouse, 7n. 7
Aronson, I. Michael, 1n. 3
Atiyah, P. S., 123n. 1, 130n. 7, 134–36
autobiography
  dictionary as, 219–21
  embodiment in, 231–37, 246–52
  simultaneity in, 232–34
  as substitute for institutions, 220–28

Bailey, Richard, 33n. 1
Bakhtin, Mikhail, 196n. 19

306 / Index